Also by Caroline Alexander

One Dry Season

THE WAY TO XANADU

THE WAY TO XANADU

by Caroline Alexander

Alfred A. Knopf

New York

1994

THIS IS A BORZOI BOOK
PUBLISHED BY ALFRED A. KNOPF, INC.

Copyright © 1993 by Caroline Alexander
All rights reserved under International and Pan-American Copyright
Conventions. Published in the United States by Alfred A. Knopf, Inc.,
New York. Distributed by Random House, Inc., New York. Originally
published in Great Britain in 1993 by Weidenfeld & Nicolson, London.

Library of Congress Cataloging-in-Publication Data
Alexander, Caroline, [date]
The way to Xanadu / by Caroline Alexander. — 1st American ed.
p. cm.
Includes bibliographical references.
ISBN 0-679-41900-4
1. Coleridge, Samuel Taylor, 1772–1834. Kubla Khan.
2. Coleridge, Samuel Taylor, 1772–1834—Knowledge—Geography.
3. Alexander, Caroline, [date]—Journeys. 4. Exoticism—In literature.
5. Geography—In literature. 6. Voyages and travels.
I. Title.
PR4480.K83A44   1994
821'.7—dc20   93-38353
CIP

Manufactured in the United States of America

First American Edition

To George, who let me lead the way

ACKNOWLEDGMENTS

I owe many debts to many people for this book.
In addition to those named in the text,
I would like to thank the following:
my sister, Joanna, George Andreou, Diane Cleaver,
Professor C. T. Hsia, my mother, Elizabeth Kirby,
Dr. Richard Lynn, Dr. John Olsen,
Sonny Mehta, Jan Mitchell, William Rayner,
Dr. Morris Rossabi, and Anthony Sheil.
Special debts of gratitude are owed—as always—
to Laura Slatkin, and above all to Robert Gottlieb,
who sent me on the way.

CONTENTS

Faust: *Wohin der Weg?*

Mephistopheles: *Kein Weg!*

KUBLA KHAN

or a vision in a dream. A fragment

In Xanadu did Kubla Khan
A stately pleasure-dome decree:
Where Alph, the sacred river, ran
Through caverns measureless to man
    Down to a sunless sea.
So twice five miles of fertile ground
With walls and towers were girdled round:
And there were gardens bright with sinuous rills,
Where blossomed many an incense-bearing tree;
And here were forests ancient as the hills,
Enfolding sunny spots of greenery.

But oh! that deep romantic chasm which slanted
Down the green hill athwart a cedarn cover!
A savage place! as holy and enchanted
As e'er beneath a waning moon was haunted
By woman wailing for her demon-lover!
And from this chasm, with ceaseless turmoil seething,
As if this earth in fast thick pants were breathing,
A mighty fountain momently was forced:
Amid whose swift half-intermitted burst

Huge fragments vaulted like rebounding hail,
Or chaffy grain beneath the thresher's flail:
And 'mid these dancing rocks at once and ever
It flung up momently the sacred river.
Five miles meandering with a mazy motion
Through wood and dale the sacred river ran,
Then reached the caverns measureless to man,
And sank in tumult to a lifeless ocean:
And 'mid this tumult Kubla heard from far
Ancestral voices prophesying war!

    The shadow of the dome of pleasure
    Floated midway on the waves;
    Where was heard the mingled measure
    From the fountain and the caves.
It was a miracle of rare device,
A sunny pleasure-dome with caves of ice!

    A damsel with a dulcimer
    In a vision once I saw:
    It was an Abyssinian maid,
    And on her dulcimer she played,
    Singing of Mount Abora.
    Could I revive within me
    Her symphony and song,
    To such a deep delight 'twould win me,
That with music loud and long,
I would build that dome in air,
That sunny dome! those caves of ice!
And all who heard should see them there,
And all should cry, Beware! Beware!
His flashing eyes, his floating hair!
Weave a circle round him thrice,
And close your eyes with holy dread,
For he on honey-dew hath fed,
And drunk the milk of Paradise.

PREFACE

By the time I encountered Coleridge's "Kubla Khan," at age eleven, I had already traveled to many distant kingdoms. We had no television set in our family, and we rarely went to movies, so books were the medium of transportation—books of fairy tales, *Arabian Nights,* and, later, the early explorers' books of travel and adventure: worlds conjured by words in the intimacy of one's own imagination.

Like many people who first encounter "Kubla Khan" as children, I did not completely comprehend the poem, but was left with a visceral conviction of its greatness. "Kubla Khan" seemed to me to be more like a fairy tale than anything else—a vision of a distant, domed kingdom glittering under an alien sky; but, as in a fairy tale, undercut by something dark and ominous. The final stanzas made the poem most mysterious, for they implied that unlike a fairy tale, Xanadu was inaccessible, even to the imagination.

Years later, I found out that most grown-ups too were uncertain of the poem's meaning, and I came to accept the proposition that "Kubla Khan" is not really *about* anything. After all, there is no overt action, for example, only shifting scenes and a hint of events to come ("And 'mid this tumult Kubla heard from far / Ancestral voices prophesying war!"). Like Yahweh in Genesis, the Great Khan effects events by will or decree, himself remaining an awe-ful shadow presence behind the scenes, omnipotent, but at the moment passive.

Nonetheless, like a fairy tale, the poem resonates with possibilities, touching on humankind's most basic desires—those of power, wealth, sex, death, and the creative impulse. Mysteriously, these primal compulsions are not stirred by a human actor or agent; indeed, the poem does not describe Kubla Khan, or any other person—it describes only land.

With the exception of the poem's final stanza, virtually every line is descriptive of landscape—and landscape that, although exotic, is not fanciful. The realm of Xanadu may strike one as being an utterly romantic fabrication, but its individual features are not unfamiliar—walled gardens and forests, scented trees, rivers and chasms, and spectacular displays of water—we have all seen some of these. The great achievement of "Kubla Khan," I came to realize, is that it transports one to a realm of the imagination by means of images that are altogether of this world; and in so doing, it offers the reminder that the natural world of experience can be similarly transporting.

The circumstances of "Kubla Khan"'s creation have led many scholars to regard it as the supreme feat of pure literary imagination. Coleridge's own account of the act of composition is almost as famous as the poem itself, and more often than not is published with it as a preface:

> In the summer of 1797 the Author, then in ill-health, had retired to a lonely farm-house between Porlock and Linton, on the Exmoor confines of Somerset and Devonshire. In consequence of a slight indisposition, an anodyne had been prescribed, from the effect of which he fell asleep in his chair at the moment he was reading the following sentence, or words

of the same substance, in "Purchas's Pilgrimage": "Here the Khan Kubla commanded a palace to be built, and a stately garden thereunto: and thus ten miles of fertile ground were inclosed with a wall."

According to Coleridge, the poem was composed in the profound opium sleep that followed, "if that indeed can be called composition in which all the images rose up before him as *things.*" On awakening, he began at once to recall the dream poem on paper, finishing some fifty-five lines before he "was unfortunately called out by a person on business from Porlock." This visit lasted an hour, and when Coleridge finally freed himself to return to his poem, he found the as yet unwritten lines beyond recollection: "with the exception of some eight or ten scattered lines and images, all the rest had passed away like the images on the surface of a stream into which a stone has been cast."

Supreme among those images he did retain was that of Xanadu, whose dream origins and romantic character led me to assume for a long while that it was fictive. But eventually my long fascination with the poem goaded me into undertaking some research into its Mongol namesake, and I discovered that while it did not appear in any modern atlas, Xanadu—or Shangdu, as it is more properly called—was a real place and lay in what is now the Zhenglan Banner of the Autonomous Region of Inner Mongolia, in northeast China.

As an adult, I came to read travel literature for some of the same reasons that I read fairy tales as a child—to be transported to those distant, often glittering, realms, where alien, even magic, laws prevail and undreamed-of things are possible. Now, the prospect of going to Xanadu offered the opportunity of a real journey to a kingdom that had intrigued me since my childhood. And although I knew I would not be traveling through the exotic landscape of Coleridge's vision, still, the possibility of crossing the physical threshold of this legendary site was beyond my power to resist. Whatever I might find, going to Xanadu would be like traveling to the back of the North East Wind, or to the Snow Queen's Kingdom; it would be, I believed, the single most romantic journey of a lifetime.

THE WALLS AND TOWERS

The Imperial Pavilion of Great Peace
    thrusts upward to great heights,
And gorgeous gate towers pierce the sky
    endowing Shangdu with magnificence.
Rainbows encircle embankments,
    bright ripples fine;
Dragons writhe on whitewashed parapets,
    emerald hills flat.
All luminaries salute our Pole Star,
    for here is greatness equal to Heaven and Earth;
The myriad states make obeisance to the Yuan,
    for It shines with the brightness of sun and moon.
From detached jade halls,
    pure as clear water,
Music of the ancient Sage-King Shun is sometime heard—
    phoenixes in song.
—Jia Lu, Commander of the Imperial Forces (1297–1353)

These gate towers of Heaven reach into the great void,
Yet city walls are low enough to welcome distant hills.
      —Miscellaneous Songs on the Upper Capital

My inspired journey was almost blocked at the outset by the prosaic fact that the remains of Xanadu, or Shangdu, in northeast China, lie in an "army-occupied area" closed to foreigners. In the autumn of 1988, however, the year in which I first determined to attempt the trip, I received a telephone call from an old friend who was attending university out West. In answer to her question about what I was then planning to do with my life, I replied, with an edge of smugness, that I was contemplating a trip to Xanadu, if I could find a way around the daunting Chinese bureaucracy. Stella's annoyingly unexpected counter to this statement was that she was working on a degree in Mongolian and Central Asian archaeology. In fact, her adviser was an expert in this field. His name was Dr. John Olsen, and she said she would send me some articles he had written.

My memory stirred: Had Dr. Olsen once lived in Florida? I asked. Stella replied that she thought he had. As we spoke, I was standing in the kitchen of my mother's home in Tallahassee, in North Florida, looking out of the window at the white house across the road that I used to visit almost daily as a child, when I had played with my friend John Olsen. He had been my first playmate when my family had moved to this country. I had not seen or heard of him since I was twelve years old.

"Well," said the voice lazily at the other end of the line when I called the number Stella had given me. "This goes back some years." As my luck would have it, my former playmate could claim the friendship of a high-ranking official in the Bureau of Cultural Relics in Inner Mongolia, and he promised to see what he could do. The Tiananmen Square uprising, however, erupted some months later, and all plans of going to China had to be postponed. But when, two years later, I was ready to try again, Dr. Olsen happened to be posted for the year in Beijing and was thus able to act as a direct liaison between me and the Inner Mongolian authorities.

Months of silence passed, broken only by an occasional letter or fax from John, relaying or requesting information. I had resigned myself to an indefinite period of irresolution when one morning in June, I awoke to find what appeared to be an ancient Chinese scroll unfurled across the floor. It was a lengthy fax, handwritten in Chinese characters, that had come in overnight from the authorities in Hohhot, the capital of Inner Mongolia. It contained an itinerary, an estimate of expenses, and, surmounted by a facsimile seal, a visa issued for myself and my traveling companion, George, to visit Shangdu.

KHUBILAI KHAN WAS, of course, not the only Mongolian Khaghan, or Great Khan, nor had Shangdu been his only imperial residence. Khubilai was born on September 23, 1215, the fourth of four brothers and a grandson of Genghis Khan, the legendary warlord whose unified nomadic forces extended Mongol power from China to the Adriatic and made his name a byword for terror. Khubilai's father, Tolui, the youngest of Genghis's sons by his favorite wife, had been a military man, whose heavy drinking had probably led to his death at the age of forty-two. His mother, Sorghaghtani Beki, was recognized as one of the most remarkable women of her age, and her intelligence, administrative abilities, and upbringing of her sons were widely praised by contemporary writers. She was a Nestorian

Christian but was notably tolerant of other religions, a trait her son would inherit. Khubilai was brought up in the Mongol homelands, the share of Genghis's empire that had been allocated to Tolui along with northern China shortly after his father's death. A rash political move by the ruling house of Ögödei effectively passed on the Genghisid line of power to Tolui's descendants in 1250. Disputes over the legitimacy of claims to the throne were to continue throughout Khubilai's reign and after his death.

A contemporary portrait of Khubilai by the Chinese artist Liu Guandao shows a man with a smooth, round face, dark hair and beard, heavy jowls, and shrewd eyes, all composing an expression of great complacency. The image's accuracy, however, must be questioned, given its striking similarity to a portrait of Genghis Khan dating from the same era, and differing only in that in this case the generic face has been given wispy white hair and whiskers. There are other inconsistencies. According to the thirteenth-century Persian historian Rashīd al-Din, Khubilai was "swarthy"; Marco Polo, on the other hand, describes him as being "fair and ruddy like a rose." The Great Khan, he notes, was of moderate height, with "handsome black eyes" and a shapely nose "set squarely in place," evidently a noteworthy trait amidst his subject Chinese population.

In 1251, at the age of thirty-six, Khubilai was mandated civil and military authority over Mongolian China by his ruling brother, Möngke, a turn of affairs that brought him into the political limelight. Like earlier Mongol leaders, Möngke was intent upon the subjugation of China, an undertaking in which Khubilai played a decisive part by leading significant victories in the territory of the southern Sung Kingdom. This campaign was brought to a temporary and inconclusive end, however, with the death of Möngke in 1259, when Khubilai's attention was subsequently turned to the more pressing issue of succession. Word had come to him that his youngest brother, Ariqböke, who had been left to administer the Mongol homelands, was making a bid for their brother's title.

The two brothers were of very different views regarding the future orientation of the contested empire, with Ariqböke seeking to sustain the practices of traditional nomadic steppe life and Khubilai drawn towards the luxurious sedentary life manifested by the Chinese imperial court. This dispute with his brother was effectively resolved only with Ariqböke's death (reportedly of natural causes) some years later. Nonetheless on May 5, 1260, at his residence in Shangdu, Khubilai was unanimously elected the sixth Great Khan at a hastily gathered *khuriltai*, or Mongol princely assembly. His throne secured, Khubilai resumed his campaign in southern China, and the eventual dismantling of the Sung dynasty in 1279 marked the conclusive subjugation of China as a whole. It was the first time since the Tang dynasty, which had ended in the early tenth century, that China had been united.

At the time of Khubilai's reign, the empire of the Yuan dynasty—the Mongol dynasty founded in 1206 through brute military force by Genghis Khan—extended from the Qipchaq steppe and Persian Gulf to the Indus River and the East China Sea. As Great Khan, Khubilai was not only ruler of China but the supreme lord of all the individual Mongol domains, including the Persian Il-khanate, the Golden Horde of southern Russia and the Mongolian steppes; his subjects represented the largest population thus far in history to acknowledge the sovereignty of a single man. Recognizing that the traditional political framework of the Mongols, who were, after all, a nomadic people, was not in any way equipped to govern an empire, Khubilai surrounded himself with a staff of Confucian advisers and relied upon the ancient bureaucratic structure that he had inherited from the Chinese, although for reasons of security he made a practice of staffing it with foreigners (such as the Venetian merchant Marco Polo).

Khubilai's reign was characterized by clemency towards his foes in war and tolerance in times of peace towards his subjects, who were allowed to continue unmolested in the practice of their traditional religions, customs, and arts. All evidence indicates that the Great Khan was a man possessed of an enormous worldly appetite and unbounded curiosity, who greatly encouraged those enterprises that could garner him knowledge about the world beyond his vast domain. To this end, expeditions were mounted that ventured as far as Madagascar and Java, while special privileges conferred upon merchants ensured a far-reaching exchange of commodities and ideas—the extensive trade routes encompassed within his empire, it has been claimed, provided foreign trade and intercourse not matched until modern times.

Although the Mongolians, as nomads, had traditionally been tent dwellers, an imperial residence had been established as early as Genghis Khan's rule. Karakorum, in the heart of the steppes, had been a wall-enclosed complex consisting of a military garrison and markets. Initially, it had been comprised of tents, but under Genghis's successors, permanent structures were introduced. Although different seasonal residences had been maintained by at least one Mongol khan before Khubilai, he is nonetheless remembered for being the greatest builder of his dynasty. Khubilai was eventually to establish four palace cities, which were visited in turn according to the season. Of these, the two earliest would remain the most important: Shangdu ("Upper Capital," also referred to as Chandu, Sandu, Luanjing, Shangji, Keminfu, and Kaiping), his official summer residence, and the Yuan capital proper, Dadu, the site of modern-day Beijing.

Khubilai shrewdly took great pains to ensure that he be viewed as a legitimate Chinese emperor, rather than a conquering barbarian Mongol, and architecturally as well as bureaucratically his court had a distinctively Chinese cast. For all this, he was never completely absorbed by the culture of his conquered people, and Yuan historians record that he gave orders for the fragrant steppe grass to be brought to his palace in Dadu so that his descendants might not be forgetful of the land in which they had originated, nor he himself of his humble origins. In the same vein, Shangdu served not only as a retreat from the lowland heat but as a place where the Khan could practice the hunting and riding arts of his people and relax in Mongolian style.

> Out the Pass, traveling with face raised to the sun,
> Hurrying to Court, delighted to be approaching Heaven—
> Where the Detached Palace opens to its pleasure gardens,
> The Royal Thoroughfare stays free of wind and mist.
> —Liu Guan

The fourth moon of every year marked the departure of the Great Khan and his retinue from Dadu to his summer residence. Before he left, Khubilai held a feast for his officials in the Lin-gyu, or Zoological Gardens, which lay to the east of the Hill of Ten Thousand Years. As the Great Khan left his island palace in its artificial lake, the *liushouguan*, or "officer who stays behind to guard," cut the bridges, to prohibit passage until he should return.

According to Marco Polo, the retinue accompanying Khubilai on a hunting expedition from Dadu included as many as ten thousand falconers. The Great Khan himself

> always rides on the back of four elephants, in a very hand-some shelter of wood, covered inside with cloth of beaten gold and outside with lion skins. Here he always keeps twelve gerfalcons of the best he possesses and is attended by several barons to entertain him and keep him company. When he is travelling in this shelter on the elephants, and other barons who are riding in his train call out, "Sire, there are cranes passing," and he orders the roof of the shelter to be thrown open and so sees the cranes, he bids his attendants fetch such

gerfalcons as he may choose and lets them fly. And often, the gerfalcons take the cranes in full view while the Great Khan remains all the while on his couch. And this affords him great sport and recreation.

The Great Khan remained at Shangdu throughout the summer months, ending his sojourn on the same day of every year, the twenty-eighth of August. The elaborate ceremony of departure for the return trip to Dadu, as described by Marco Polo, betrayed a specifically Mongolian character: mare's milk, from the Khan's stable of over ten thousand snow white mares and stallions, was flung into the air and poured on the earth as a libation to the spirits that guarded the Khan's possessions, his "men and women, beasts, birds, crops, and everything besides."

Shangdu lay at a distance of fifty parasangs from the Great Court, or about two hundred miles due north, a journey of approximately ten days for the cumbersome procession. The rate of travel was leisurely, and there were frequent stops for hawking. Along the route, at intervals of three to four miles, stood watchtowers and post houses equipped with runners, providing military protection, convenient halting places and communications centers. According to Marco Polo, the postal system was so efficient that within ten days, news could be transmitted over the distance of a journey of a hundred days. He adds that in the fruit season, produce gathered in the morning in Dadu could be delivered by evening of the next day at Shangdu.

The specific route taken by Khubilai on this seasonal migration is described in some detail by Rashīd al-Dīn:

> There are three roads from the winter residence: one road which is reserved for hunting and along which no one may travel except couriers; another road by way of Joju [modern Joxian], to which one travels along the banks of the River Sangin, where there is [an] abundance of grapes and other fruit and near which is another small town called Sinali, the

people of which are mostly from Samarquand and have laid
out gardens in the Samarquand fashion; and there is another
road, by way of a low hill, which they call Sing-Ling, and
when one passes over that hill the steppe is all grassland and
[suitable for] summer pasturage up to the town of Kemin-Fu
[that is, Shangdu].

As the crow flies, today one could reach the ruins of Shangdu
after no more than one day's travel from modern Beijing. While
no direct road exists from one place to the other, a Chinese traveler may make the journey in a roundabout way by local buses.
But the official itinerary laid out for George, my companion, and
me described a tortuously triangular route: First, we were to fly
from Beijing to Hohhot, the capital of the Inner Mongolian Autonomous Region, some two hundred miles northwest of Beijing; then from Hohhot to Xilinhot, some three hundred miles
northeast; thence, an indeterminate distance to a village to the
south, from where at last we would be in striking distance of the
ruins of Xanadu.

Nei Menggu, or Inner Mongolia, is one of five autonomous
regions of the People's Republic of China. At an average elevation of approximately three thousand feet, it is essentially an upland plateau ringed by mountains, which in the northwest slopes
away towards the Gobi Desert. It encompasses an area of nearly
164,000 square miles, sharing an 800-mile borderline with northern China. To the west, south, and east, it is bounded by other
Chinese provinces, and to the north by the Mongolian People's
Republic, or Outer Mongolia. The distinction between Inner
and Outer Mongolia was made as early as the seventeenth century, although in modern times it has generally indicated the territories' alliances with the People's Republic of China and, until
its collapse, the Soviet Union, respectively.

The Mongol population has been reduced even in relatively
recent years by disease: In the last century, bubonic plague was

endemic, and as late as the late 1940s, an estimated 60 percent of the adult population was infected with syphilis. In Chinese Mongolia, immigrant Han Chinese now outnumber Mongolians by a ratio of over eight to one; as much as 84 percent of the region's total population of nearly 20 million is Chinese, while only 10 percent is Mongol, with various minority groups—including Manchus, Koreans, Dahurs, and Ewenkis—accounting for the remaining some 6 percent.

The historically well-established mix of Chinese agrarian and Mongolian pastoral cultures is retained today, although the extreme harshness of the winter prohibits extensive agricultural exploitation of this rich land. The majority of the population are found just north of the Chinese–Nei Menggu border, indicating the line of encroachment of the incoming, and ongoing, flow of Chinese immigrants. A map of Inner Mongolia typically shows a vast brown expanse, representing its miles upon miles of windy grassland, scratched by a few tenuous red lines that denote roads. The farther north one goes, away from the settlements and a handful of really big cities, the more in touch one feels with the "real" Mongolia, the steppeland of herdsmen and horsemen. This view falters when comparison is made with Outer Mongolia, however, whose population of just 2 million luxuriates in an area of undeveloped grasslands well over three times the size of Nei Menggu.

Hohhot (a less merciful spelling is Huhehaote) was established as the region's capital in 1954. The perpetual briskness of the air that blows in from the steppes, together with the city's slight elevation, give the atmosphere a chilling blue-tinged clarity: Even bright sunlight appears wan and cold, and the town's monumental Soviet-style architecture—broad, barren thoroughfares and the calculated space of its "people's squares"—seems to have been etched against a panoramic backdrop of rarefied space. This physical and spiritual coldness is mitigated here and there by odd touches of color, such as the surprising number of flowers in pots and shade trees that edge the roads, or the whimsical events staged in the People's Park—a predawn fox-trotting dance club, for example, or dromedary rides. Temples and vestiges of the old town, which dates from the sixteenth century, can be found in the jumbled streets that lie safe miles from the high-rise concrete of the "new city."

The resurgent nationalism that has marked the recent history of the Mongolian Republic has no parallel in Chinese Mongolia. The potentially dangerous cult of Genghis Khan that has resurfaced in Outer Mongolia to great political effect has been cannily preempted by the Chinese authorities controlling Nei Menggu: One of the two most visible icons, represented in plaster statuary and a variety of logo-style paintings, is of the proud Mongolian warlord, usually rendered with ambiguous Eurasian features. Appearing blatantly everywhere as he does, the subliminal message appears to be that he must be a kind of Chinese hero. (The other icon, incidentally, is the cheerful panda that is assiduously marketed as the embodiment of the new China, and which is increasingly coming to resemble Mickey Mouse.)

Further evidence of the official Chinese attitude to things Mongolian is to be found in the Museum of Inner Mongolia, which houses both Chinese and Mongolian artifacts, such as Mongolian saddles and traditional costumes. The term—*cultural relics*—used to describe these objects struck me as being an unwarrantedly cynical label for a culture that, albeit much diminished, is not yet quite extinct. Although the official reason for keeping the site of Xanadu off limits to foreigners is its proximity to militarily sensitive territory, it is also possible that the Chinese government does not relish the prospect of a trail of tourists coming to pay homage to the former imperial residence of the Great Khan—and only foreigner who held the whole of China in his thrall.

Under the terms of the visas issued to George and me, our exploration of the site had to be made in the close and abiding company of a handful of officials. Luckily for us, the extreme good nature of the chosen individuals meant that this was to be no hardship. The representative from the Bureau of Cultural Relics, who oversaw our welcome, was a handsome Mongolian man whom I judged to be in his late forties, possessed of the kind of inscrutable dignity with which Hollywood once fondly endowed its Red Indians and other noble savages—impassive, chiseled features, bolt-upright bearing. When he addressed us, he looked somewhere into the middle distance above our heads, where he would hold his gaze while his utterance was translated.

Our interpreter throughout the journey was a young Chinese woman named Na. Her delicate features wore a perpetual soft frown of concentration and mild anxiety, which I took to be the direct result of her commission to come between us and the Chinese world over the next week or so. She had a certain instinctive flair that led one to believe she had seen something of the world, yet for all her quiet style, she had, in fact, ventured only once or twice outside Hohhot, the city of her birth. She was a student of English literature, however, which, I surmised, accounted in part for her distinctive, outward-looking air.

Mr. Hada was the representative from the bureau chosen to oversee the excursion. Unlike Na, he appeared to carry the burden of his assignment very lightly on his shoulders. His face was alternatively creased in a grin or crumpled in a toothy smile. He was a young and energetic man, his movements characteristically restless and abrupt. Unmistakably, the opportunity of our upcoming trip was personally welcome to him, and he intended to enjoy its every minute.

A few words should also be added to introduce George, in essence a man who would undoubtedly have been happiest living as a gentleman in nineteenth-century England. Like his British forebears, he possesses a clear, inexorable, and utterly obsolete code of personal honor, which he naïvely believes binds his contemporary fellowmen, a blind spot that has led to many a pitfall.

He is also a genuine outdoorsman and, more unusually, the producer and director of the movie *Pumping Iron*, and so responsible in great part for bringing Arnold Schwarzenegger to the world's attention.

THE MORNING FLIGHT to Xilinhot was made in a tiny prop plane that lurched into a sky of harsh, pristine blue. Below us, the green swathes of Hohhot's parks and gardens suddenly gave way to a dull brown wash of sand and sediment, cut by oxblood-colored rivulets and dried-up streams. A scalloped line indicated the terraced foothills of the Daqing Mountains, which appeared as a bank of dramatic contours. Like a final sighting of land before setting out to sea, this range represented the last identifiable feature on the earth before we launched over the mustard-colored barrenness that is Mongolia.

One and a half hours later, the plane touched down on a field of bumpy turf. In front of the single airport building, a small crowd was already jostling in readiness to surge forward and claim places on the plane for its turnaround flight back to Hohhot. Towering conspicuously above all the other people was a tall, angular, shaven-headed figure—and the only other European we were to meet in Nei Menggu—who called out to us urgently as we passed.

"Book your flight back immediately! There are only two flights out a week. Book your flight back now!"

The fact that one arrives at Xilinhot not by way of a progression of other towns, cities, or villages but after a flight over a desolate stretch of barren grasslands indicates that Xilinhot did not arise "naturally" in the vanguard of ordinary waves of settlement but was calculatedly placed upon this spot. A booklet that I came across representing an optimistic, if unpersuasive, attempt to attract tourism proclaims Xilinhot "the Shining Pearl on the Grassland," but in the next line it offers the prosaic fact that the city is in "an area with rich underground minerals." Xilinhot is, in many respects, a last frontier; it is the most remote point to which foreigners are normally allowed to travel, and for this reason it is the best place from which to see the grasslands and remnants of Mongolian traditional life—for the present, at least, for in Xilinhot the future of Inner Mongolia as envisaged by the controlling Chinese authorities is unambiguously revealed. For all its 100,000 inhabitants, Xilinhot is merely a frontier town built in preparation for the carefully projected boom that will follow the mass exploitation of the "rich underground minerals," lovingly enumerated in the tourist booklet as "reserves of chromium, copper, iron, tin, as well as natural alkali, mirabilite, marble, refractory clay and limestone," in addition to the large reserves of oil and coal on the city outskirts.

The town itself is purposefully laid out on a no-nonsense grid of wide functional streets and unadorned buildings. The brand-new residential houses are attractive in their way, somewhat resembling solid brick cottages, and, en masse, reminiscent of a Victorian housing estate. Each is surrounded by a wall, which, we were told, is the custom of the country—perhaps for privacy, perhaps as an extra buffer between the winds and snows of Mongolian winter. While the average temperature in the summer is around seventy-seven degrees Fahrenheit, on bitter winter nights the icy winds from Siberia drive it down to lower than forty degrees below zero. A mild wind blew continuously at the time of our visit, but an occasional biting gust was a reminder that it is a factor that must always be taken seriously. Indeed, the city looks wind-scoured, as if a great dust storm had just rolled through it.

Because we were officially under the auspices of the Bureau of Cultural Relics, it had been deemed necessary that we visit Shangdu not only under escort of the Hohhot delegation but in the presence of the director of Xilinhot's Cultural Relics Station. Mr. Batu was a Mongolian of untypically lanky build and height. His face beneath his luxuriant salt-and-pepper hair was the color of copper, and his narrow eyes seemed to squint at the sun from behind his heavy glasses, a tendency that was exaggerated by his habit of turning his face up towards the sky. He was the most smartly dressed individual I encountered in the whole of China, and on meeting us he was wearing a trilby hat, a dark checked suit, and a tie pinned neatly by a minuscule portrait of Genghis Khan. Having seen us safely settled into the local hotel, he announced that he would take us to the grasslands. *Grasslands* was a word that I had heard reverently whispered since our arrival in China: "You will see the grasslands"; "You are going up north? Then you must see the grasslands."

"I am looking forward very much to seeing the grasslands," Na had said to me in Hohhot, and it was from her demurely contained excitement that I glimpsed how far away this legendary realm was to the average Chinese person.

Turning out of Xilinhot, a single narrow road curved into low hills and the grasslands proper, a mustardy gold plain of tufted grass. The annual rains of July and August briefly transform this prairie into an unbounded meadow of succulent, tender green; but we were at summer's end, and apart from scanty showers, the rain had long since evaporated under the unrelenting sunshine of the perpetually windswept skies.

Some distance out, we came upon an enormous domed tent erected on a wooden platform, which we were told was a reconstruction of Genghis Khan's palatial yurt, and a remnant of the set for a Chinese television film about his life. Although its imperial silks had been badly tattered by the wind and it wore an air of general neglect, the yurt was soon to be put to new use as the rallying point for an annual festival of traditional Mongol sports to be held a few months hence. A truck had been drawn up to one side of the platform, from which some workers were unloading an extraordinarily large supply of beer, which was to be laid down under the Great Khan's floorboards.

Small blips appearing against the mustard-colored plain resolved themselves as we drew closer into a tiny settlement of
three yurts that resembled large steamed puddings bound in
cheesecloth. A delicate Tinkertoy windmill whirred incessantly
beside them, firing the battery of a dented car parked beneath it,
next to a heavy, antiquated motorcycle. Beyond the yurts, three
sturdy shaggy ponies stood loosely tethered, one of them sad-
dled and harnessed with an elaborate high-pommeled, silver-
embossed saddle.

An old woman wearing a kerchief and the long caftan of
Mongolian traditional dress came out of the kitchen and, after
giving her welcome, invited us to step into one of the yurts. Inside, three Mongols, thoroughly modern and thoroughly drunk,
greeted the lot of us—the director, Na, Mr. Hada, George, and
me—like brothers and insisted that we join them in a drink.

"Traditional Mongolian hospitality," whispered Na, who
had clearly read all about this ethnic trait. A refined-looking
woman sat discreetly to one side, both observer and participant
in the ongoing, inescapable camaraderie. Many toasts of vodka
were now drunk, interspersed with bowls of evil salty tea and
soft cheeses that tasted like crème brûlée. Eating and drinking
seemed to be the principal activities of the yurtsmen, judging by
the heaps of used cups and bowls and watermelon rinds that
bedecked the hut. Milk products of one kind or another and
mutton are the staples of the Mongolian diet. Other delicacies
of the Xilinhot area show marked Chinese influence—hot can-
died camel hump, for example, or camel paws braised in brown
sauce and bull's penis liquor.

Mongolian hospitality continued apace for some time, with
the oldest of our hosts becoming aggressive in his refusal to accept my disinclination to drink more vodka.

"The director is a typical Mongol," whispered Na worriedly.
It was true that Mr. Batu was manifestly loath to leave the
springs of his native hospitality, and, as we were all in his hands,

we remained, like him, cross-legged in the yurt. The yurts themselves are essentially cozy domed tents of woolen felt stretched
over a frame, which, as befits a nomadic people, is easily collapsible, and in this case was gaily painted red and blue. Brightly patterned rugs and cushions had been spread on the floor, and a low
table placed in the middle of the room. A small shrine to Genghis Khan faced the entrance.

The sky had dimmed considerably by the time we were allowed to stumble outside. The little windmill was whirring
more frenetically than ever and a soft *whoosh* of wind filled the
barren space. In the distance, a herdsman was parading his long
file of black-and-brown cattle. For the moment, raising livestock
still ranks as Nei Menggu's primary economic activity, and
Mongols therefore contribute significantly to the region's economy by practicing their traditional way of life—as herdsmen
and as tourist attractions. But in less than five years' time, Xilinhot is scheduled to have an international airport, with direct
connections to Beijing, Ulaan Baatar, and points in what was
formerly the Soviet Union. A tarmac runway is to be built on
the grass strip on which our prop plane landed, and other
reaches of the famous grasslands will, no doubt, be mined or
under concrete. The Mongolians have been assiduously written
into Chinese history up until this point, but it will be interesting
to see how many of their traditional traits they will be encouraged to retain once this dream of industrial development is
realized.

IN THE MIDDLE of the night before our departure for Shangdu,
I awoke with the certainty that I was going to be ill in some
as-yet-unspecified way and sensed with sleepy indeterminacy
that I was in a brief interlude between health and real trouble. In
the morning, I discovered that I did not want to leave my bed.
For nearly two weeks beforehand, it was true, I had suffered
from a racking cough that was the aftermath of a bad cold I

picked up on travels George and I had made before coming to China. I felt this was now, suddenly, much worse, and I had, moreover, a dull pain in my lower back.

"We can stay, and leave tomorrow, Carolina," said Na in her worried way, contemplating me while I still lay in bed.

"I think we should go as planned, and you can rest in the car; you will probably be better by the time we arrive at the site," said George, ever the optimist. I agreed with him, as I was wary of the least change in schedule and continuously braced against an impending announcement that our special permits were no longer valid.

The director, spruce and dapper in a new suit and jaunty hat, awaited us in the hotel driveway, where our official van had been parked. The weather had changed dramatically from the days before and a windy rain lashed out upon us from dirty skies. All of Xilinhot's color, I was now made to realize, had come from the sun, or had been the mere illusion of a blue heaven, and the reality abiding behind this bright veneer was a hard world of grayness and cold. The director took his place in the front seat beside the driver, who was, like him, Mongolian, and who had brought along his own supply of music—a single tape of "Moscow Nights" sung in Chinese. George and Na took the row behind him, with Mr. Hada in the jump seat beside them, and I went in the back. I had planned to sit up and quietly observe the land we were to pass through, and so be thoroughly rested and recovered by the time we actually drew close to Shangdu. But to my surprise, I found that I was unable to sit up at all and that it made me dizzy to look out the window. The road ran before us, firm and undeviating, straight to the horizon, and yet for all the uncompromising confidence of its line, it seemed somehow senseless and random, as there was nothing, in whatever direction one might turn one's head, that could count as a "destination"—not a hut, yurt, tree, or hill marred the bleak contours of the grasslands.

"How are you feeling?" George asked every now and then,

turning to where I lay stretched out on the backseat, and I replied, in all honesty, that I was all right. I did not feel ill, after all, just incapacitated. It was true that at certain moments I had begun to shiver uncontrollably, but I had ascertained, by a silent inward scrutiny, that this was the result of spasms of pain from my lower back. The fact that this was explicable made it seem reasonable, even in order.

From time to time over the next four hours, I lifted my head to get a bearing, and in this disconnected way I saw the grasslands give way to an expanse of less wild terrain; then to bleached dunes of sand sprouting little tufts of foliage; and then, as the day slowly brightened, again to a land of inviolate golden grass. The sky became once more irrevocably blue, studded with big cheery mounds of clouds that cast massive swift-moving shadows. It did not seem to me that we were driving into a landscape of hills and mountains, valleys or geophysical features, but, rather, into rolling, ponderous shadows that in their constant movement continually recontoured the land. My head began to spin and I lay back down.

"Oh, you must see this!" George exclaimed, looking out of the window somewhat later, and I struggled up to see what had transfixed him. We seemed to have plunged into a scene from a Brueghel painting, or, alternatively, from a Chinese propaganda poster. The landscape that had showed few signs of a human presence, let alone habitation, for so many miles was now peopled by sturdy, bronzed, red-cheeked peasants dressed in blue Mao-style work uniforms and industriously tending a blooming, fertile land. Harvesters wielded long, sweeping scythes and quick sickles; hay wains, piled with golden grass, rocked and swayed behind the pulling oxen; haystacks stood like plump cairns in the gleaned fields—not a modern farming implement intruded on this almost medieval panorama. This scene of busy, improbably cheerful industry was permeated by an extraordinary golden light that seemed to shine out of the tawny fields. Only occasionally did one spot a pleasant brick-and-tile hamlet, and it was not evident from where this bustling populace had come.

In the early afternoon, we came to a small town, where, the director informed us, we would stop for a late lunch and rest. We drove into the rough courtyard of a guest house, which was built motel-fashion, with its rooms forming one long wing. The thought of food of any kind nauseated me, and I was taken to one of the bedrooms—apparently, we were the only guests. It struck me, as I crossed the yard, that the town must be very new, so new that it did not yet seem to sit securely under the vast sky, which threatened to overwhelm it. The proprietor was a friendly Mongol woman with hectic red cheeks and a long braid of black hair. My room was spartan, but I appreciated its modest virtues: its cleanliness, its restful green-and-white walls, its well-boiled sheets, its quiet. Before she left for the dining room, Na looked in and outlined the remaining program.

"We will rest here for a few hours. We will then drive to an historic site nearby, which is called Yenshan-tu and is of the time that you are interested; then we will go to Duolun."

Duolun was Dolonnur, the town that all past travelers to Xanadu had used as their point of reference: Whenever I had written to the authorities in Hohhot about arranging a permit, I would describe Xanadu as "Shangdu, the remains of Khubilai Khan's summer residence near Dolonnur."

"And from Duolun we will go to Shangdu?" I now asked Na.

"Yes," said Na, with her worried, gentle face looking down at me where I lay on the bed. "It is not far from here, Carolina."

A few hours later, we were back in the van. I had convinced myself that I felt better after the rest, and I planned to sit up for this last, short leg of the trip; but as soon as we were on the road, I had second thoughts and once again lay down.

A range of hills seemed to be rising ahead of us. The van veered to the left. The director turned to shout something over "Moscow Nights," which Na translated to mean that we were near the first site. I began to wish that we had postponed this mysterious "historical site" for the return trip: I did not feel that I had energy for more than one place.

The van began to bump up and down, then turned right and drew to a sudden halt. The doors were flung back and the director poked his head inside to say something. I started, feebly, to get out.

"If I were you, I'd stay inside," said George, who had been looking for birds through his binoculars en route. "If I see anything really interesting, I'll tell you."

"We do not have to be long, Carolina," said Na.

With relief, I lay back down. I had no curiosity about this particular site—what it was, whose it was, how it might relate to Khubilai Khan. Some forty-five minutes later, the group returned. George's face was beaming.

"It's pretty terrific there. I'd love to come back, if we get a chance. There's even loose pottery lying around."

I had a brief vision of myself wandering over an overgrown plowed field, slipping between old furrows and twisting my ankles in hidden rabbit holes, and I shuddered. Then, as the van got under way again, I recalled that we were now headed towards the place on earth I had planned and connived to get to for two years; I pulled myself together, and sat up. The day was glorious, the sky blue without flaw—blue without prettiness or vapidity, but profound and weighty, capable of filling the vast, otherwise-unimpressionable land with somber, heavy shadows. The dark range of hills towards which we were driving appeared to stretch across our path and block the way, but a cleft appeared between them, and through this the road could be seen spiraling up the peaty hills: It was the first stretch of road we had encountered so far that was not absolutely ruler-straight. I tried hard to take note of every detail, to commit the entire journey to memory— frowning hills; now cultivated fields; the outskirts of a bustling town, the roads made narrow by wayside fruit vendors and rolling, jostling wagons. Expecting that we would drive straight through the town and continue on through countryside like that which lay behind us, I was startled when we pulled off the road into the compound of a large and vaguely official-looking building. The driver turned off the engine.

Mr. Batu, as was his way, had his door open and had briskly swung himself outside almost before the van had stopped. He lit a cigarette and, with his back to us, contemplated the buildings in front of him.

Feeling suddenly, frighteningly alert, I asked Na whether we were going on to the next site as planned.

"We stay the night here," she said, suddenly evasive.

My blood began to pound harder. "I thought we were going to Shangdu."

"Shangdu is in an army-occupied area, closed to foreigners," said Na. Then added, "I myself thought we were going. I did not know it was an army-occupied area."

"Now the important thing is to stay cool," said George pleasantly as I turned to him with a look of burning outrage. "We have come a long way," he said to Na, then launched into a speech about the deep friendship between us, the lone travelers from America, and them, our hospitable and charming guides.

"What were our special visas for, if not access to a forbidden area?" I demanded, following a more direct line of questioning. Na and Mr. Hada exchanged anxious looks. The driver had walked off towards the buildings, while Mr. Batu sat insouciantly on the curb, smoking a cigarette.

"We know you have come a long way," said Na, faltering. "We know it has costed you much moneys. I myself, until this moment, did not know that past Duolun was an army-occupied area. And we thought you wanted to see Duolun," she finished lamely. "It is a very old, historical town."

"*This* is where we want to go," I said angrily, and with a dramatic flourish I took from George's hands a map we had brought with us, which I had found in an old archaeological journal.

Na and Mr. Hada bent their heads over it, tracing various lines with their fingers. Suddenly, Mr. Hada began talking excitedly and looked up at us, smiling.

"But this map is of Yenshang-tu, where we just came from. Remember, I pointed out the stream?"

Slowly, fact by fact was marshaled forth, and my mind, by necessity now more or less functioning and in focus, was forced to recognize that I had declined to get out of the van at the very place I had traveled so far to see.

"Shangdu means 'head place, high place,'" said Na. "Yuan means 'of the Yuan dynasty.' Yuan Shangdu means 'the capital of the Yuan dynasty.'"

So all was settled in tears and laughter. It was determined that we would not spend the night in Duolun as had been planned but would race back to Shangdu.

"We must hurry," said George, his photographer's eye ever on the sky. "The light will be gone."

Once in the van, the driver called out something over his shoulder and then hunkered down over the wheel.

"He says," Na called back in turn, "that he will get us there before the sun goes down!"

Back through town, we raced, down along the winding road, which emptied us between the dark hills onto the valley floor. Once on level ground, we roared away until we came to the right-angle turnoff, which we took in a cloud of churning dirt and dust. A narrow stream was crossed and strange elliptical earthworks passed before we ground to a halt in the palatial compound of the inner city.

> *Saddles off west of the Shan*
> *Ended our northward trail.*
> *Along the ancient road*
> *never a farmer seen.*

But vast flat sands, fine grass, pale green,
where the Jinlian river's daily rains prevail.
—Feng Zizhen

The mandate to build Shangdu had come to Khubilai from above in 1256, from his brother Möngke, the Khaghan who preceded him. Möngke's instructions to his younger brother specifically were to found a city nine *li* (roughly three and a half miles) northwest of the site that is now Duolun, his plan being to establish a Mongol center that, like Karakorum, could function as military camp, marketplace, and palace. The location chosen for the city was charged with symbolism, being both on the fringe of China's northeast borders as well as squarely in the Mongol homelands. The establishment in this region of the official residence of a high-ranking member of the imperial Genghisid line unequivocally indicated to the world the political role to which the Mongolian dynasty aspired; it also indicated a readiness to forgo the attempt to "govern from horseback" and to assume instead the prerogatives of the sedentary life.

According to Rashīd al-Dīn, a site to the east of an existent town, Keminfu, had initially been chosen but then was abandoned after Khubilai had an ominous dream—in real life as in poetry, the inspiration for Xanadu came from beyond the realm of the senses. Scholars and engineers were consulted and a new site was eventually selected in accordance with the principles of the ancient Chinese art of geomancy, beside a *na'ur*, or pond, in a meadow north of the Luanshui River and south of the Dragon Hill. Rashīd's description of the elaborate pains subsequently taken to drain the *na'ur*, and its resulting effect on the landscape, provides a fascinating insight into how some of the more exotic features characteristically associated with Xanadu actually came into being:

> Now in that country there is a stone which they use instead of firewood [i.e., coal]; they collected a great quantity of this and also of charcoal. Then they filled the *na'ur*, and the spring

which fed it, with pebbles and broken bricks and melted a
quantity of tin and lead over it until it was firm. They raised
it up to a man's height from the ground and built a platform
on it. And since the water was imprisoned in the bowels of
the earth, it came out in the course of time in other places in
meadows some distance away, where it flowed forth as so
many springs.

The palace complex was laid out in the form of three squares,
each fitting inside the other. The largest, and all-encompassing,
delineated the Great Khan's hunting park; the second, situated
in the southeast corner of the park, contained the imperial city;
while the innermost square, set slightly north of center within
the imperial city, contained the palace enclosure. Beyond the
walls was a landscape that, according to contemporary descriptions, was as luxuriant and enticing as that within: a mountain-
encircled land covered with forests, particularly pine, that were
the haunts of a profusion of birds and animals—wolves, stag,
roebuck, and leopard. Over the centuries, human inhabitants depleted and finally eradicated altogether the forests of the area,
overgrazed their herds on the lush meadowland, and hunted the
birds and animals out of existence. The result is the barren, majestic sweep of uncontained grass that one traverses today, popu-
lated by occasional small settlements of peasants and their
livestock and rabbits.

Our van had come to a halt in a roughly square enclosure of
some eighteen hundred by two thousand feet bounded by uncertain earthen walls. Directly abutting the northern wall stood the
sole remaining structure, such as it was, a mud-brick platform
approximately thirty feet high. A line of jagged but clearly deliberate holes gaped like small caves in the platform at ground level,
giving it the appearance of an enormous brick oven. This had
been the inner palace enclosure, whose earthen walls, now diminished and covered with turf, once stood as high as sixteen

feet and had been surmounted by turrets in each corner and on either side of its entrance gate.

The mud-brick platform had been the foundation of the imperial palace, Da'an Ge, or the Pavilion of Great Harmony, which had consisted of five separate halls connected to one another by covered corridors and fashioned in the shape of an inverted U. This was the building whose splendor and beauty had been extolled by Marco Polo, who described a "huge palace of marble and other ornamental stones. . . . Its halls and chambers are all gilded and the whole building is marvellously embellished and richly adorned." Architecturally, the palace—as indeed the layout of the city complex as a whole—was Chinese. Yet behind the elaborate walls, embellished by Chinese artisans, and under the bright cobalt and green glazed roof tiles with their dragon-headed gargoyles, the interior trappings of the palace—the felt hangings, animal skins, and carpets—would have been Mongolian.

Facing the palace platform was a rectangular mound of earth that indicated the former site of another, unidentifiable structure. Apart from this, no trace of the original thirty-odd imperial buildings remains, although two stone column bases, almost lost to the grass and weeds that have overgrown them, stand like stumps a short distance beyond the platform, and what appears to have been a cistern can be made out to one side. A child-sized statue depicting a man holding a cup, made of gray stone so badly weathered as to be almost unidentifiable, greets one near the entrance, but this is an interloper of sorts; predating Shangdu by hundreds of years, it was transported to the site in the last century by Lamaists, who established a monastery within easy access of the bricks and stones and other useful building materials furnished by Xanadu's crumbling walls and towers.

Remains of the original thirteenth-century timber that had once reinforced the brickwork of the palace platform were pointed out to me by our driver, who, with nimble, irreverent fingers, pried out sizable chips for closer inspection. The jagged holes at ground level, said Na, had been made by local peasants, who used them as cellars in which to store their potatoes.

Bricks and turf crumbled beneath my feet as I scrambled to the top of the platform; but no one stopped me, and I was shortly joined by the Director of Cultural Relics himself, who was nonchalantly gathering shards of pottery and occasional chunks of glazed tile. From this vantage point, I looked down upon a conglomeration of small ashen mud-brick huts abutting the wall outside the palace city. These were not, as I first imagined, storerooms or similar outlying chambers contemporary with the palace but, rather, the domicile of the aged peasant couple who had built them, and who came out later to share a watermelon with us. It is their potatoes, presumably, that are safely stored in the Great Khan's cellar.

Taking advantage of the platform's height, I gained my first overview of the walls of the second city in the distance, great earthen ramparts spanning 4,500 feet on each of its four sides. The sun was low now and the walls were clearly etched against the grassland by their own shadows. Away on the heights of the guardian mountains to the north, the remains of the Khan's beacon-crowned watch posts showed as smooth nipple-shaped silhouettes. A strong wind had been blowing all day, but so evenly and consistently as to have assumed an abiding place in the landscape—one would no more wish for the wind to stop than for the grass to turn blue or the sky to lower.

> Rafter upon rafter, the storeyed pavilion
> reaches the azure sky,
> A picture painted in gold
> floating atop seven precious pillars.
> —Zhou Boqi

The few travel accounts that describe this site had led me to expect that something of the inner city would be intact but not much more. I had not foreseen that I would be awarded this overview of the city's entire perimeter, discernible and unbroken, the blueprint, as it were, of its foundations; nor had I anticipated the surviving sense of containment, of a place marked off, foursquare from the surrounding wilderness. Yet here below me was the palace enclosure; and there, darkening all the while, the walls of the imperial city; and farther yet, only barely visible on the horizon, the distant walls of the hunting grounds, once reserved for the exclusive use of Khubilai Khan. The initial scare that we would not get here, the wind, the extraordinary light, the vision of Xanadu at my feet—all this had set my adrenaline racing, and I forgot that I was ill. Indeed, I felt keen, alert, almost on fire.

We left the royal compound just as the sun was going down, intending to get back to our former guest house before dark, but a staggering sunset stopped us in our tracks, and we halted again outside the imperial city's western wall. The ground still showed signs here and there of being marshy—perhaps the Great Khan's drainage program is only now giving way. A flock of cranes rose in clattering flight from a bed of reeds and, taking up their stalwart, timeless flight formation, vanished somewhere towards the sun: Marco Polo, too, had remarked upon the cranes of Xanadu.

"The Khan must have chosen this spot for its light," said George. The sky was like beaten gold, and no other color or feature of the landscape was now a factor in the scene before us. What mattered was light—light caught and reflected off the individual blades of grass, light gleaming from the loaded hay wain that trundled past us on a dirt track running through the city, light casting shadows on the earthworks. The walls of Xanadu were now dark ridges in the grassy plain, the sky the fiery gold of heat reflected from a furnace. Moments later, there appeared above this radiance a horizontal rainbow in perfect tiers of color—red, orange, green, blue, and indigo, and then up to the roof of heaven, deep violet. Away to the north, the sky remained a benign blue, the hills and the bumps of the Great Khan's watchtowers dark against it. A line of geese in earnest, long-necked silhouette passed overhead, rising suddenly from the western horizon, from the light, and as we exclaimed and pointed, more and then more, as if their arrow-straight lines were being shot from a bow positioned under the edge of the world, sending them hurtling through space, veering off over our heads.

Long after dark, we arrived back at our guest house in what we had now learned was the village of Lengqi. I was suddenly tired again. Although I knew I should eat, I could not, and while the others went to have dinner, I went to bed. Now the pain of whatever it was I was suffering from took over and I began to shake so violently that my teeth chattered. My cough, which had become incessant, seemed to cause my brains to hit the roof of my skull. When George came back from dinner, we decided to see how I felt the next morning before determining whether we should go back to Xilinhot or stay on here, as our visas permitted us several days on the site. There was only a modest clinic and no telephones, we had learned, in Lengqi.

The next morning, however, the ailment, whatever it had been, was apparently gone, although I still did not wish to eat and felt better sitting up in bed than getting dressed and walking around. The driver and Mr. Hada had set out to find petrol, so a morning visit to the site was, in any case, out of the question.

In the midafternoon, however, we returned to Shangdu. The day was as clear and blue as it had been the day before, but warm and, shockingly, without wind—the architecture of the houses behind their little protective walls, the treeless, barren landscape, and the hectic red cheeks of the people, I had taken as hard evidence that the wind blew every day the sun came up in Inner Mongolia.

Marketplace so narrow, you can't gallop a horse;
With mud that deep, it's easy to get a cart stuck.

Frozen flies gather to fight over the sunlight,
While newly arrived swallows slant to catch the wind.
Evening water-drawing brings hubbub to sandy wells;
Morning cook fires cause the breakup of wooden rafts.
Among local inhabitants it's butter tea for everyone—
Customs are simple and not all that extravagant yet.

While clouds cover the Main Street sun,
Winds blow clear the North Gate sky.
A thousand gutters turn white snow to ice,
And ten thousand cook stoves raise blue smoke.
Middays have been so sultry that I carry a fan,
Though mornings are cold enough to wear a padded gown.
That empty strip through the pines is the boundary,
Trees cut and culled no one knows how many years ago.
                    —Miscellaneous Songs on the Upper Capital

Bypassing the palace enclosure, we determined to devote the afternoon to the outer walls. Whereas there was an air of something tired and mean in the decay of the inner city, the decline of the outer walls had produced majestic hulks, which, now that we were faced with the prospect of traversing them on foot, seemed immense. While the palace city had been reserved expressly for the use of the Great Khan and his imperial retinue, the function of the inner *huangcheng*, or imperial city, was administrative and had accommodated as many as 100,000 inhabitants in mud and board dwellings. According to legend, over a hundred Buddhist and Taoist temples and Muslim mosques had also been included in this compound, reflecting the Great Khan's tolerance of diverse faiths. Its walls may have formerly been as high as eighteen feet, and between eighteen and twenty-four feet in thickness, a breadth that has more or less been retained. The ancient Chinese "rammed earth" technique was used in their construction, and for aesthetic reasons they were faced with brick and marble.

Today the cambered, overgrown ridges that rise from dimpled turf resemble barrows on a meadow more than the walls of an imperial city. Striding along the heights of these grassy battlements, one looks down into what would appear to be grazing land, and which was indeed being enjoyed by a flock of sheep that had either wandered in through gaps in the crumbled walls or used one of the city's six gates. Each gateway had formerly been flanked by granite-faced wings decorated with carved lions and dragons. The granite facing has disappeared, but the underlying earthworks have survived and still retain an air of importance, conveying as they do that the lapses in the barrows are deliberate and not an accident of erosion. The extensions of the southern gate in particular are greatly impressive: Its wings project outside the city in a swooping V, like extended arms, and cry out for a processional host to embrace. Beyond the gate, the southern walls slope away, almost to ground level, and the marshy ground of the enclosure itself has given way here and there to form stagnant ponds. From out of the eastern wall, where the slender oblong brickwork underlying the turf is exposed and well preserved, a twisted tree grew, providing mottled shade.

Some distance to the east, beyond the imperial city, there arose a small conical and apparently man-made hill, which promised to be a good lookout point. As I made my way towards it across the dry grass, I felt a sudden jolt inside me: The vague malaise that had returned after I'd left Lengqi was now sharp and gripping and had perceptibly shifted from my back to my chest. With the clarity that illness can bestow, I now knew that the problem lay in my lungs.

At the top of the hill, I sat down to rest on parched grass that hummed and cracked with locusts. From here, the palace enclosure and its resilient mud-brick platform, backed by the peasants' huts, was seen to sit humbly within the ponderous earthworks of the imperial city, like a cattle shed within its kraal. Several lines of flattened grass indicated wagon paths, leading

casually through Xanadu to somewhere else. A view of the outermost walls that contained the hunting park, which we had yet
to visit, now manifested the scale of the city complex as a whole.
To the north and south, one could see that the walls were essentially grander versions of the grassy barrows that we had already
traversed; dimly, some miles away on the horizon, one could discern the outermost western wall. To someone arriving cold
upon the scene, with no knowledge of Khubilai Khan (or Coleridge's poem), a military encampment might have come to
mind—certainly something associated with power. During
Khubilai's reign, the complex must have astonished arriving envoys, this Chinese court in a wilderness of barren space, overlooked by beacon-flaming hills. On the opposite side, close to
my lookout hill and beyond the eastern outer wall, lay a number
of elliptical, caterpillar-shaped mounds. These, like the several
moats that have been cut at various points around the city complex, had been built as channels in case of flood; the hills to the
north of Shangdu form a watershed in the rainy season and, ad-
ditionally, the little trickle that is now the Shangdu Gol had in
earlier times been a river of sufficient size to enable rafts and
flat-bottomed grain junks to ascend to this point from the sea.

Also visible from this vantage point, in the not-distant-
enough distance to the west, a clutter of smoke-spewing chimneys betrayed a sprawling village with walls and towers of its
own. Some of the chimneys, I was later informed, belonged to
the ubiquitous brick kilns that appear to stand in the vanguard
of all industrial advancement in Inner Mongolia. I had already
heard rumors that the ancient grounds of Shangdu had been
scheduled for development into wheat fields, but the presence of
the kiln smoke suggests that their fate could be less picturesque.

On coming down the hill, I met up with the rest of the group
at our van, which the driver had parked under the lone tree on
the eastern wall. My skin seemed suddenly paper-fine, stretched
tightly over my bones, as if it suffered from too much sun. I

found myself moving carefully, and I was glad that we were driving to the outer walls of the hunting park.

> *Several green elms*
> *extend east of the pavilion,*
> *With its cloud windows and rosy sunset doors*
> *decorated so exquisitely.*
> *The patterned deer in the Upper Park,*
> *taller than horses,*
> *From time to time lead gray-brown fawns,*
> *there in the jade-green grass.*
>
> —Zhou Boqi

As the inner two enclosures sit in the extreme southeastern corner of the park, the hunting grounds wrap around them to the north and west like a carpenter's square, running one and a half miles long on each side. Although small hunting parks were features of the imperial grounds of a few Chinese dynasties, the inspiration in this case appears to be native Mongolian, rather than a Chinese precedent. According to Marco Polo, the only entrance into the park, whose walls were as high as twenty feet, was by way of the palace. His description of the Great Khan's pleasure grounds is justly famous:

> [A] wall, running out from the city wall in the direction opposite to the palace, encloses and encircles fully sixteen miles of park-land well watered with springs and streams and diversified with lawns. . . . Here the Great Khan keeps game animals of all sorts, such as hart, stag, and roebuck, to provide food for the gerfalcons and other falcons which he has here in mew. The gerfalcons alone amount to 200. Once a week he comes in person to inspect them in the mew. Often, too, he enters the park with a leopard on the crupper of his horse. . . .

The imperial gardens were called Ruilin, meaning "Felicitous Forest." No buildings are mentioned by Polo, apart from a collapsible "palace" constructed of cane, which appears to have been a kind of richly decorated bamboo yurt.

As we trundled along the perimeter of the walls in the van, the enclosure seemed immense, and even without the enticement of springs and fountains, running brooks and shaded groves, one could well imagine sauntering on horseback across this naked space. In spite of Marco Polo's assertion that entrance to the park could be made only by way of the palace, there were, as in the walls of the imperial city, a number of distinct entranceways; but these could conceivably have been made at a later date. From time to time, we stopped the van so we could get out and survey the walls. The sun had begun to sink, and I was finding it increasingly difficult to clamber up the grassy slopes of each embankment.

Finally, on the summit of the northwest corner of the outer wall, when we had nearly completed our circuit of the park, I felt my chest constrict more tightly, and I knew that my time here was up. I gazed into the park one last time and then slithered down the wall, returned to the van, and stretched out on the backseat. We made one final stop before leaving the site: On the edge of the western wall, the cranes of Xanadu once again put in an appearance, although I did not see them this time, but had to imagine their silhouettes fluttering darkly against the low sun as they rose clattering from the reeds before assuming the taut line of flight that took them to wherever they disappeared each evening.

Back in Lengqi, we drove straight to the clinic, a modest stone building that was largely in darkness, as it was officially closed. The yellow bulbs that were clicked on as we passed from room to room left little pools of murky light in the empty halls. I was taken to an examination room and placed on a mattress of straw stuffed in a white slipcover, while Na, Mr. Hada, and the director gathered around my feet and George took up a position by my head. The doctor came in wearing a blue Mao jacket and the close-lipped, inscrutable expression of a grassroots Party boss or union chief—used to giving directives, used to having them obeyed, unused to being questioned. My temperature was taken while a blood sample was drawn from my earlobe.

"It is thirty-nine point nine degrees, Carolina," said Na. "You have a fever."

"What is that in Fahrenheit?" I asked George. "I don't know what that means," I said, turning to Na.

"Thirty-seven degrees is normal temperature," said Na. "You don't know what that means, but *we* know it is high."

A nurse in a white robe entered the room and said something, and Na told me I must follow her. I was working out my temperature—degrees Celsius times nine equals nearly 360—divided by 5, say 71, 72—plus 32 equals nearly 104 degrees. I was relieved: So I really was ill, and I was right to have come here—I had been right to leave Xanadu.

THE NURSE LEADS me into a tiny, dim room, empty save for a hulking X-ray machine resembling those depicted in books about early medicine. My shirt is removed but not my bra, with the result that the developed X-ray shows the two arcs of the underwire. The doctor taps the negative and nods.

"Pneumonia," Na translates. I am told that I will be given an injection.

"Is this an antibiotic?" George asks. "Is this penicillin?"

"It is for her fever," Na replies, translating the doctor's answer. The injection is given by the nurse, who holds the needle in her fist, draws back so as to gain momentum, and pounds it into my upper thigh with such force that there is a resounding thud as it hits. George laughs with disbelief.

"I am thirsty," I tell him, and he goes to the van to get the boiled water we have cooled. Na intervenes.

"The doctor says that you must drink hot waters only for your infection. You must wrap yourself in many blankets to make you sweats." All the faces in the room are turned to me, their expressions exaggerated as though seen through a fish-eye lens.

"You must sweats," Na repeats. Her face appears to be doing all the things an Oriental woman's is supposed to—floating like a flower in the night, shining white in the darkness, with dark slashes for eyes. The faces behind hers, I realize, are all miming *sweat* in languages I do not understand, running their hands over their brows, shaking imaginary droplets from their fingers.

"You must sweat, sweat, sweat." Bewildered, I feel the blood rush to my face and am aware that my temperature is rising— does the injection raise it before making it come down? I am drinking the hot water when George returns.

"You must wrap her in many blankets," Na reiterates. I am confused, for I have a vivid memory of an earlier fever, in Africa. Should I not be lying bare to the air, with strips of cloth dipped in cold water applied to my forehead, my chest, my wrists?

"You must sweats," Na repeats. "This injection will make you sweats."

We return to the Lengqi guest house, where I am placed on the big bed I have found so comforting, and Na ensures that I am wrapped in two thick blankets and a quilt. I lie stock-still throughout the evening, dozing off on occasion but mostly staying awake, dutifully sitting up to drink water, dutifully imagining myself awakening from a deep slumber bathed in perspiration.

"It is strange you are not sweating," George says cautiously, and I know he is worried. I begin to shake again and can hear my bones rattle, my teeth chatter. My cough returns and I discover I have become too weak to contain it—it threatens to detonate my skull, to shatter my frame. I end up on my hands and knees, half-barking, half-gagging.

"You must summon everything you have for this night," says George. He has been outside, I will discover later, pleading with our entourage to let us return directly to Beijing—to drive through the night and be there by morning.

It is an army-occupied area, he is told. Our visas are good only as far as Duolun. To return to Beijing, we must drive back to Xilinhot and wait two days for the next flight out to Hohhot. From Hohhot, we can fly to Beijing. Without a telephone, few advance arrangements can be made.

In the morning, my temperature has fallen one-half a degree Fahrenheit and the promised sweat has not come. Back at the clinic, I receive another injection in the same distinctive manner as before and am also given a number of medications, one of which is cough syrup.

We buy a blanket from a local shop and I am wrapped in this and put in the back of the van. The long return drive on the dirt road is bumpy, but I don't care, as I am half in a trance.

In Xilinhot, we first check in with the local hospital, where the diagnosis of the doctor at Lengqi and his prescriptions are confirmed. We then return to the White Horse Hotel, where we had stayed upon arrival. Last time, we had reached the hotel by turning off the road and driving across a patch of dirt where the grass had been worn away. But the construction of the apartment buildings opposite has proceeded at such a pace that a new way into the hotel has had to be devised; we circle the area on a makeshift driveway, spiraling inwards.

Our new room looks directly onto a factory, whose towering narrow chimneys belch black smoke that seeps in through the windows. The room is too filthy to allow one's mind to settle on any single object—not on the worn lace curtains through which the light struggles; not on the overstuffed plush red velvet chairs and the matching television cover; not on the sheets, with their unfamiliar stray black hairs, or on the dingy pillows; not on the stained, burred carpet; certainly on no object in the bathroom— the nicotine brown tub, the broken tiles that show the swirls of dirt and hair from the last cleaning rag, the nonfunctioning toilet, the one dim bulb.

Apart from twice-daily visits to the hospital for an injection, I spend the next two days in bed, with the sheets pulled up cautiously over my nose and mouth so as to filter out as much as possible the chimney smoke and the vaguely fishy odor that permeates the air—this, I discover later, is the smell of the Xilinhot brand of disinfectant. The light in the bedroom is broken, but this does not concern me, as there is nothing that I care to see.

I get out of bed once and feebly tidy up the room; my ploy is that a pretense of neatness may, by familiar association, convey an impression of cleanliness. Mostly, I lie flat on my back, under carefully arranged covers, and do not move. I think dutifully, carefully, of food; I awake and plan a taste that I can stomach— yogurt and apples, boiled potatoes with lots of salt. But when the food materializes, it never tastes as I had imagined, and I have to give up after a few mouthfuls. Our entourage is unfailingly kind and sympathetic, Na in particular going beyond the call of duty in her quest to find food that I might want to eat.

My mind refuses to take in my surroundings and I slip deeper into my half trance. To remind myself of why I am here, I conjure up in my mind's eye the walls and lost towers of Xanadu. In the night, I have a vision: I am in Xanadu at sunset. There is a glory of light, the flood of gold light reflected from a field of wheat, shining to the ether. Black geese in crisp black silhouette wing their way in an unending frieze across the heavens; in all the cosmos, there is only black earth and gold, heavenly—above all, purifying—fire.

On the third night, I awake in alarm. The thin mattress is soaked through, all the way from top to bottom. I touch myself and discover with amazement that I am the cause. I am in a cold sweat that will soak through two additional pairs of sheets, but the fever has broken.

Our flight to Hohhot is the next day. While lying in this room, I have missed a number of events. The director has held a great feast and there has been a local dance at the White Horse

Hotel. I am sorry not to have taken advantage of this hospitality;
but now the moment of departure has arrived, I at last admit to
myself that I loathe the place and am ready to flee.

On the morning of departure, I have a final injection and then
we drive to the airport. Our good-byes are warm and the director gives us each a blue prayer shawl and bestows on George his
Genghis Khan tiepin.

We board the plane, and for the first time in my life, I regard
the prospect of flying with no apprehension—if I was meant to
have been finished off on this trip, it would surely have happened by now. For weeks afterwards, I will have motion sickness
as a side effect of one of the prescribed drugs: I have been taking,
unawares, three separate massive courses of antibiotics, one of
which is used for treatment of bone-marrow infections.

The plane trundles out for takeoff on Chinese time, which is
to say exactly on schedule. The propellers spin; the plane shakes
and rattles, then pulls away, slipping on the grassy runway.
Clouds of locusts whir out of the brittle gold grass as we advance, and then, strangely, the clouds follow the plane, perhaps
attracted by its heat. We slowly rise, and through the window
beside me, I watch the wheels pull up; and we have left the grass
and locusts behind.

THE REIGN OF the Great Khan Khubilai represented the height
of Mongol power, indeed, a landmark of world civilization.
Among the distinctive achievements of his rule was the expan-
sion of the imperial communications network, which, by the end
of his reign, had established fourteen hundred postal stations in
China. Khubilai paved roads and renovated the Great Canal,
which runs eleven hundred miles from Hangchou to Beijing.
Traditional Chinese literature as well as fine arts benefited from
his patronage, resulting most notably in the resurgence of the
theater and the development of the novel. Similarly, the study of

medicine and science flourished under his farsighted regard: Two branches of imperial hospitals, staffed primarily with Muslim doctors, were established in Shangdu and north China; Persian astronomers were invited to his court and in 1271 the Institute of Muslim Astronomy was founded in Dadu.

But Khubilai's reign was characterized by weaknesses, as well as strengths. His own health, for example, had never been particularly good—it is recorded, for instance, that in 1269 Khubilai sent to Korea for special fish-skin shoes to relieve his gouty feet—but from 1279 onwards, it began to worsen, exacerbated no doubt by the heavy drinking in which it seems all of the Khans indulged. His various ailments not only took a personal toll on the aging Khan but were to have disastrous repercussions on the management of his empire. A number of his officials, most notably his finance minister, were convicted of crimes involving graft and exploitation of the Khan's Chinese subjects. With affairs at home threatening to get out of control, Khubilai lost some of his characteristic tolerance and issued anti-Muslim edicts, perhaps partly in reaction to the dominance by Western Muslim states over Mongol allies, and perhaps also because many of the ministers who had betrayed his trust were Muslim.

In 1281, Khubilai's favorite wife, Chabi, died, and in 1286 he was struck yet another blow with the death of his son Chenchin, whom he had carefully groomed to be his successor. His biographer, Morris Rossabi (from whose book most of the details of Khubilai's personal life have been taken), suggests that these personal tragedies marked the beginning of the Great Khan's end. His court became increasingly lavish, possibly owing to the fact that Chabi, whose name had been a byword for frugality, was no longer around to exert her influence. Increasingly, he turned to heavy bouts of eating and drinking and, to quote Rossabi, "grew obese and suffered from ailments associated with alcoholism."

The weaknesses of his reign were disastrously evident abroad,

as well as at home. An attempt to invade Japan in 1281 (to avenge
the failure of an earlier invasion) ended dismally with the loss of
an estimated 130,000 allied and enemy lives. Campaigns in South
Asia resulted in similar, if less spectacular, losses. By the 1280s
and early 1290s, rebellions in Tibet and Manchuria, outlying regions of the empire, indicated that the Great Khan was losing his
grip.

Chinese sources state that by 1294, Khubilai was dangerously
obese, exhausted, and depressed. The *Yuanshih,* or official history
of the Yuan dynasty, notes that an old comrade-in-arms arrived
in court with the hope of raising his spirits but did not succeed.
Finally, on February 18, 1294, in his eightieth year, the Great
Khan died in the Zitan, or Hall of Purple Sandalwood, of his
Dadu palace. His body was buried somewhere in the Hentiyn
Mountains east of Karakorum, although exactly where and in
what manner has never been determined. Posthumously, he was
awarded by his officials the title *Shizu,* or founder of a dynasty; to
the Mongols, he was always Setzan Khan—the Wise Khan.
Khubilai's grandson Temür, by his favorite, lost son, Chen-chin,
was his immediate successor. The Yuan emperors were to hold
sway over China until 1370 and, in all, ten successors of Khubilai's house would sit upon his imperial throne in Dadu.

While Shangdu continued to be used as a summer residence
by the Yuan emperors who followed Khubilai, it appears that it
eventually lost the cachet of a capital city, although the fact that
it continued to serve as the enthronement site of several later
emperors indicates some vestige of its original importance. Its
official status lost, the former Upper Capital was apparently
transformed into a private pleasure area. Certainly successive
Khans enjoyed it primarily as a hunting ground. Other summer
palaces were also built in the same area later in the Yuan dynasty—clearly the proximity of the site to the great grasslands of
the steppes continued to attract the Mongol emperors.

Glimpses may be caught of the later history of the summer

palace in *Zezhi tongjian houbian* (*Supplement to Comprehensive Mirror to Aid Government*), which includes a chronicle of events of this region over the thirteenth and fourteenth centuries. We read, for instance, that one night in 1301, the northwestern portion of the city was flooded by heavy rains; that 1321 was a year of ambitious building—a *dian*, or hall, was erected in honor of a certain lama, a golden tower was constructed for the holy remains of a Buddhist monk, and the city wall was improved and strengthened. Two years later, strangely, all gold- and silverwork ceased in Shangdu. In 1354, an imperial order was given to lay a stone road from Dadu, leading north to Shangdu. And in 1358, in a war of rebellion, Shangdu was invaded by the Hongjin, or red-capped bandit forces of Guan Duo, who occupied the city for seven days, set the palace aflame, and then moved on. Shangdu continued to be inhabited for several more decades, but it was no longer frequented by the Khans.

The Yuan empire had been critically weakened by the domestic and military crises of Khubilai's later years. None of the subsequent Khaghans proved as able a statesman as the Great Khan, and the internal decay that began under his reign progressively worsened after his death. Mongol authority was further eroded by factional infighting, and real power ended up in the hands of individual warlords. In addition, the demoralized empire had to contend with a wave of natural disasters in the 1330s and, later, in the 1350s. From the time they assumed power, the Mongols had excluded themselves from taxation and had essentially lived off the Chinese peasantry, thus creating an economic and social imbalance that had long been resented. Now, in the 1340s, small- and large-scale rebellions, especially in the south, which had always been less than securely held, haphazardly broke out among the disgruntled Chinese peasants. When finally, in 1368, an organized assault was led by one of the peasant leaders, the Mongol forces had neither strength nor wits enough to stave them off.

The last Khan, Toghon Temür, who had assumed the impe-

rial throne at the age of thirteen, fled Dadu in 1368 and made for
the steppes and Shangdu, where he held out briefly before being
decisively defeated the following year. The Chinese troops entered the summer palace, took prisoner the children of the city's
important officials, and set fire to the city a second time. In
Dadu, power was assumed by the bandit rebel Zhu Yuanzhang,
who had led the successful rebellion and who then installed himself as the first of the Ming emperors. Thus was the Yuan the
shortest-lived of China's major dynasties.

From 1370, Shangdu served essentially as a border post
manned by Chinese forces, from where an eye could be kept on
the movements of the Mongols to the north, who continued to
conduct a campaign of unabated, if futile and disorganized,
harassment. Toghon Temür died of an illness the same year in
Karakorum, the site of the first official Mongolian palace, to
which he had continued his flight for sanctuary. Sanang Setzen,
the poetical historian of the Mongols, commemorated the loss
of the last of the Yuan emperors by putting into his mouth the
following lament:

> My vast and noble Capital, my Dadu, my
>   splendidly adorned.
> And Thou, my cool and delicious Summer
>   seat, my Shangdu . . .
> Ye also, yellow plains of Shangdu, Delight
>   of my godlike Sires.
> I suffered myself to drop into dreams—
>   and lo! My Empire was gone.

In 1430, five years into the reign of the fifth Ming emperor, the
northern frontier of Inner Mongolia was contracted to the line
of the Great Wall, and the garrison that had been posted at
Shangdu was moved south to Dushikou. With its removal,
Shangdu ceased to exist as a vital center and became one of a
number of deserted ruins on the outskirts of the Chinese empire.

Over the centuries, the abandoned site saw only a handful of travelers who left reports. In 1691, a French Jesuit, Jean François Gerbillon, paid a short visit to Shangdu in the course of accompanying the Chinese emperor on a hunting trip. Gerbillon offers no description of the site, other than remarking that the ruins of Shangdu lay in a plain by a little river; but the account is interesting for the evidence it provides that the area was still enjoyed by imperial hunting parties and that it maintained, at this date at least, a vestige of its formerly abundant game: Gerbillon states that stags, leopard, tigers, roebuck, mountain goats, fox, hares, and boar were encountered by his party.

In 1872, Reverend Stephen Wootton Bushell of the British Legation in Peking, en route from Peking north to Dolonnur, made a day trip to the site, which was by this time locally known as Chzhun'-nayman-sume, or the City of One Hundred and Eight Temples, a nod to the former glory of the Great Khan's legacy. He found the walls of the city, "built of earth, faced with unhewn stones and brick," still standing, but in a dilapidated state. Over the entrance gate to the palace enclosure, however, there rose "a perfect arch 20 feet high, 12 feet wide." The platform, which centuries before had served as the foundation of the Great Khan's palace, described by Bushell as a "bare square earth fort, faced with brick," had been decorated with "the usual ragged streamers of silk and cotton tied to sticks"; these Bushell took as evidence of the "superstitious regard" in which the Mongols continued to hold the site, but they may, in fact, have indicated its use by Buddhist lamas as a temple. The foundations of some of the other buildings that had formerly stood in the palace enclosure could still be traced in the overgrown grass. The ground was strewn with blocks of marble and "broken lions, dragons, and the remains of other carved monuments" lay scattered haphazardly in the tangled overgrowth. The best preserved artifact was a broken memorial tablet "in an ancient form of the Chinese character, surrounded by a border of dragons boldly carved in deep relief." Bushell's account dwells upon the sense of desolation that pervaded the abandoned scene, and on the brooding landscape of volcanic hills and rolling prairie, the "rank weeds," the foxes, owls, prairie rats, and partridges that had inherited the site.

A more extensive, but no less bleak, description was given by a Russian traveler, Andreev Pozdneev, who passed through in 1898—Pozdneev was no casual visitor, for he had been the chief archaeologist at the site of the earliest Mongolian palace in Karakorum. Arriving near dark at the end of a rainy day, he endured a miserable night in a wet tent before venturing out at daybreak the following drizzling morning. Unlike Bushell, whose exploration seems to have been confined to the palace enclosure, Pozdneev doggedly paced the sodden outer walls, which he found generally well preserved, and commented that "in some places they stand so sturdily and are so undamaged that it is difficult to believe that these ruins have survived five centuries." He, too, discovered a quantity of glazed tiles as well as decorations carved in granite; the Chinese inscription described by Bushell was still intact, and even "beautifully polished." In the northeast corner of the second, imperial city, he came upon significant ruins of a fallen round watchtower; in the other city corners, only the vertical beams of the towers remained.

Within the palace enclosure, Pozdneev found a mishmash of foundation lines and rubble. More clear-eyed than Bushell, he sums up his observations by declaring that "it is absolutely pointless to set forth my conclusions about the functions of all these buildings and their parts, or the various sections of the city ... without a doubt, not a single hill here looks the way it would have in the Yüan capital; because on all these ruined buildings, already more than once, new structures were built, of which are now preserved only ruins and disordered mounds of refuse." He goes on to cite the intermediate superstructures, such as the Chinese garrison, the sheds built by transient Chinese merchants for trade, the fences and walls erected by nomads, who used the remaining stones as pens for their sheep and camels. Perhaps more telling than the neglect and mistreatment of the physical ruins is the ignorance of his Mongolian companions regarding the former palace of one of their greatest countrymen, an ignorance that Pozdneev bitterly mocks:

> The local Mongolians, according to legends, know that Chzhun'-nayman-sume was the capital of Kublah, they even show the place where his palace stood; but, skipping over the most important periods of changes in Chzhun'-nayman-sume, i.e. the Ming dynasty, they go on to tell in great detail about how here lived a regiment of Chinese soldiers in the time of the Khans and with naive surprise will assure the listener of the great artistic capabilities of these soldiers, who had built enormous barracks inside the city wall, using its bricks.

Only four years later, in 1902, another Englishman made his way to the ruins. Charles William Campbell, the British consul at Wuzhou, published his brief comments in an official report he sent to the Foreign Office regarding a journey he had taken through Mongolia. Campbell had read Bushell's account (but evidently not Pozdneev's, which was published only in Russian) and professed that he had "nothing of importance to add to Dr. Bushell's description." He added offhandedly, however, the striking fact that since Bushell's visit "some vandal lamas have collected most of the interesting marbles and stone work and made an *obo* of them." At this time, the enduring arch of the great southern entrance, "under which Khubilai himself must have passed frequently," still stood, as Bushell described, but showed "signs that the ruins were being drawn upon for building materials." The final line of his report may prove prescient: "As soon as the line of Chinese immigration invades this part of the Shangtu Valley, the disappearance of these interesting ruins will be a matter of a very few years."

The reports so far mentioned were the result of fleeting visits, but in 1925, Lawrence Impey, an American diplomat in Peking, spent an entire month in the remains of the palace complex. His thorough and methodical measurements of the walls and earthworks resulted in a twenty-one-page article, complete with a map of the ancient city and cross sections of the remaining walls, in the American *Geographical Review*. Impey's journey from Peking took him along the ancient route used by the khans, and he remarks that "all the way up, from the Nankow pass above Peking to the last miles of marshland that bring one into the ruins of Shangtu, one finds watchtowers that guarded the trail." In essence, his detailed description reveals that little had changed since the visit of the last traveler. He notes, however, that "the arch of the southern gate has now collapsed," although its remains are clearly defined. He observed a great quantity of blue and green glazed tiles in the wall, evidence that "the Great Khan had his kilns on the site and that the throwouts not used for roofing were dumped into the wall work." These colorful tiles were doubtless particularly attractive to later scavengers. Impey found a mass of tiles, pottery, and stonework, which he carefully cataloged according to where each piece was discovered, and concluded his article with the plea that, especially in view of the recent discoveries by Russian excavators in Karakorum, "it would be well worth the while of some museum to take up the quest at the point where the author was forced from want of time and money to relinquish it."

Impey's plea was answered, in part, in July of 1937, when a team of six Japanese archaeologists representing "the Archaeological Seminar in the Faculty of Letters of Tokyo Imperial University" arrived at the site. The party set up camp near an abandoned Lamaist temple "of recent construction," which had been erected upon the rectangular mound that now blankly faces the palace platform within the inner city. From here, guarded by eleven Mongolian soldiers, they conducted a week-long investigation. The result of their sojourn is a weighty publication, in

Japanese, with extensive photographs of the site and of the artifacts haphazardly referred to by the other reports—the milky blue and green pottery, the stonework embossed with rosettes, lotus blossoms, and floral scrolls, the grinning-lion jambs, the florid turquoise-and-gold dragon's heads, the chips of gold-leaf lacquer, the inscribed steles, the cobalt, green, yellow, and rich brown glazed tiles, the roof *shibis,* the monumental carved tortoise used as a base to support imperial inscriptions, the stone lion.

The Japanese archaeologists' map of the ruined city does not differ significantly from that drawn by Impey, whom they cite, noting that his survey and report were "tolerably correct." Instead of retreading old ground, therefore, they devoted themselves to other tasks. No actual spadework was implemented by this archaeological team; rather, they contented themselves with gathering up "whatever tiles, bricks, pottery and stone objects we could find on the surface of the ground"—in short, everything that wasn't nailed down—and the considerable fruits of their labor were then shipped to the Tokyo Imperial University, where, presumably, the treasures of Shangdu still survive. Thus, when in 1988 a British traveler, William Dalrymple, managed to obtain an all-too-brief glimpse of the inner palace enclosure, through dusk and driving rain, while in the process of being deported from the forbidden area by Mongolian authorities, there were, for him as shortly afterwards for us, no artifacts of note remaining to be seen.

A MELANCHOLY TONE pervades the descriptions left by the British and American travelers to Shangdu. All of them had been led to the site by "Kubla Khan," and all refer to the poem in their reports. Like me, they must have known in advance that the fallen walls of this Chinese military garrison in the wasteland of the Mongolian steppes would bear little resemblance to the

Xanadu of poetic legend. Yet, apparently, the disparity between
the poetic vision and the archaeological reality took them all
unawares.

For my part, I had come to see that the Great Khan and his
summer place of pleasure possessed a certain romantic magnet-
ism of their own, without benefit of Coleridge's poem. The sight
of Shangdu rising from the shadows of its ruins as the light subsided had exposed the surviving grandeur of this barren land,
denuded as it was of its walls and towers, gardens, ancient forests and rills. Nonetheless, this was not the landscape that had
first inspired me. And now, at journey's end, I too was struck
with a yearning for a glimpse of the poetic vision.

Where did the Xanadu of Coleridge's imagination, and
subsequently of ours, arise? The ostensible source, and that cited
by Coleridge, is Purchas's *Pilgrimage*, an early seventeenth-century
compendium of famous travel stories and histories. It was a special favorite of Coleridge, who was a voracious reader of literature of this genre. The relevant passage, which is essentially a
crib from Marco Polo's account, reads as follows:

> In *Xamdu* did *Cublai Can* build a stately Palace, encompassing
> sixteene miles of plaine ground with a wall, wherein are fer-
> tile Meddowes, pleasant springs, delightfull Streames, and
> all sorts of beasts of chase and game, and in the middest
> thereof a sumptuous house of pleasure, which may be re-
> moved from place to place. Here he doth abide in the months
> of June, July, and August, and on the eighth and twentieth
> day whereof, he departeth thence to another place to do
> sacrifice. . . .

This excerpt clearly reveals the inspiration for the pleasure
palace, the walls, the fertile ground, and the rills and streams of
"Kubla Khan." On the other hand, some of the poem's most
memorable imagery is strikingly absent—there is no mention of
a sacred river, for example, or of incense-bearing trees, a cedarn

cover, a mighty fountain, or a cave of ice. Looking no further than Purchas, one would have to conclude that the Xanadu of the poem was indeed largely a place of the imagination.

In 1927, John Livingston Lowes, an eminent scholar of English literature, published a critical examination of Coleridge's poetic methods entitled *The Road to Xanadu*. In this landmark book, Lowes demonstrated that the imagery of "Kubla Khan" was derived from a variety of literary sources in addition to that specifically mentioned by Coleridge. Throughout his life, it had been Coleridge's habit to keep a running Notebook in which he jotted down his preoccupations of the moment, whether domestic occurrences, unpaid bills, his daily schedule, or books that he was reading. It is the latter entries that are of most interest, for they contain a record of the works that had fed Coleridge's imagination prior to the composition of his poetic masterpiece. Coleridge could be very precise in his literary notations, entering not merely book titles or authors' names but specific pages, often copying out passages that had caught his fancy. It is in these pages, as Lowes notes, that one may "catch glimpses of the strange and fantastic shapes which haunted the hinterland of Coleridge's brain . . . what the teeming chaos of the Note Book gives us is the charged and electrical atmospheric background of a poet's mind."

The list of books that contributed imagery, diction, or resonance to "Kubla Khan" is impressively diverse, ranging from Pausanias to Milton and from mythological to scientific treatises. This rich variety notwithstanding, Lowes demonstrates definitively that the poem's most dominant imagery can be attributed to a small nucleus of books of travel and discovery. In many cases, the familiar images that shimmer tantalizingly from these specific works, by virtue of their striking similarity, overlapped—or, to use Lowes's terminology, formed hooks and eyes—in Coleridge's mind and melded in a single poetic vision. Thus the mystical landscape of Xanadu, improbably but incontrovertibly, was shaped by descriptions of four distinct geographical regions of the earth.

Lowes's research, then, hinted at an exciting possibility. If it was true that behind each dream image there lay a real place that had been visited and described by a traveler of another age, then this magnificent poem was less a tribute to the Mongol Khan, or to the powers of poetic imagination, than it was to the inspirational splendors of the earth. And although it was not possible to travel to the Xanadu of "Kubla Khan," one might be able to traverse its landscape.

My illness in Nei Menggu had taught me that romantic quests can run up against hard realities. This quest, however, seemed to me to be already under way, past the point of turning back. Simply put, the landscape of Xanadu had haunted me since childhood, and if I was to behold it, there were not one, but four, journeys to be made.

THE MIGHTY FOUNTAIN

*I*n 1932, the first of the Weissmuller *Tarzan* films was released and created a public sensation. Based on Edgar Rice Burroughs's well-known story about the lost son of an English aristocrat who grows up to be lord of the African jungle, this remake was greatly inspired by the success of *Trader Horn*, which two years earlier had been nominated for an Academy Award for Best Picture. The most compelling aspect of *Trader Horn* had been its spectacular and unprecedented wildlife footage, shot over three years in five different African countries. The excitement and curiosity aroused by these startling new images were what the *Tarzan* filmmakers hoped to exploit—indeed, footage left over from the earlier movie was incorporated into the *Tarzan* films.

Although the *Tarzan* films are today regarded more as high camp than authentic African adventure, they are not without their captivating images. The sight of Weissmuller, then the greatest swimmer in the world, plowing through the black jungle water is itself worth the price of admission; and the underwater sequence in *Tarzan and His Mate* (with Maureen O'Sullivan nude in the original uncut version) is a haunting vision of contrasts— two white bodies gleaming surreally in filtered sunlight against the inky darkness of the water, like holograms free-floating in space.

The filming of these sequences was, as one might expect, ar-

duous. Largely unprotected by clothing, the stars had to clamber
and frolic through rough bush, swim in water infested with giant
reptiles, and literally put themselves out on a limb for the benefit
of the cameras. The crew, too, suffered—from the muggy heat,
the insects, and the difficulty of moving around in the dense
undergrowth.

The films reveal little of these inconveniences, as the handsome stars appear always well groomed and unscathed, and the
bush is shown to such advantage as to appear almost pastoral.
The water of the rivers and lagoons, dark as it is in the black-
and-white film, is always clear as a crystal spring; cozy nests are
easily assembled among the branches of majestic vine-hung
trees, and the sunlight on the epiphytes that cloak the forest
gives the trees themselves a pleasant wooliness. These epiphytes
are sometimes fluttering ragged leaves and sometimes, if one
looks closely, Spanish moss—for the *Tarzan* films were made
not in Africa but in North Florida.

This same exotic and luxuriant landscape that evoked the vision of a jungle paradise also provided "Kubla Khan" with some
of its most powerful imagery. Coleridge's attention was drawn
to this part of the world by the work of William Bartram, an
American naturalist and writer who traveled extensively in the
southeastern states in the mid- to late eighteenth century. Born
in 1739, in Pennsylvania, Bartram was the son of John Bartram,
called by Linnaeus "the greatest natural botanist in the world,"
and often considered to be the father of American botany. The
botanical garden of the senior Bartram, outside Philadelphia,
was world-famous and no doubt contributed to his son's passion for the more exotic examples of what he termed "the vege-
table world." John Bartram had made expeditionary trips for
botanical purposes into the Allegheny Mountains, North and
South Carolina, and the Ontario wilderness, and in 1765–66, accompanied by his son, he ventured into Florida. This excursion
with his father was the incentive for William's later solitary

journey throughout the American South, made between 1773 and 1777. His account of his travels, published in 1791, six years before the composition of "Kubla Khan," made him famous; it was entitled *Travels through North & South Carolina, Georgia, East & West Florida, the Cherokee Country, the Extensive Territories of the Muscogulges, or Creek Confederacy, and the Country of the Chactaws.*

Coleridge was not the only writer captivated by Bartram's account of the South's luxuriant landscape. The *Travels* was a singular inspiration for other Romantics, and its images were insinuated, in various degrees, into the works of Wordsworth, Southey, Shelley, Thomas Campbell, Tennyson, and Emerson. While part of the charm of the *Travels* can be ascribed to the Southeast's extraordinarily exotic landscape, much credit must go to Bartram's inimitably exuberant presentation of this enchanting world. The heat, the insects, the potentially hostile Seminoles, the encounters with rampaging alligators—none of these dismay William Bartram or detract from his rapturous survey of this corner of the Almighty's globe.

"How glorious the powerful sun, minister of the Most High, in the rule and government of this earth, leaves our hemisphere, retiring from our sight beyond the western forests!" exclaims Bartram on an evening in this Florida June of 1774, when the temperature would have raged somewhere in the muggy nineties. "I behold with gratitude his departing smiles, tinging the fleecy roseate clouds, now riding far away on the Eastern horizon."

Bartram has been called the first interpreter of the American landscape, and the attribute is significant. It was the uncritical, almost willful naïveté of Bartram's poetic vision that made his narrative so congenial to the Romantics. Bartram embellishes neither his exploits nor mishaps for the sake of narrative drama; his self-prescribed role is that of a humble observer of Nature's bounty, not its heroic conqueror, and as a consequence the land over which he rhapsodizes appears in a largely neutral light. In its presentation of Nature stripped of the savagery—and even discomfort—of the wilderness, the *Travels* is not unlike the idyllic tropical jungles of the *Tarzan* films. Both the book and the films seduce their audiences into dreaming of a lost Eden, of a fresh and sparkling world still innocent and untrammeled by humanity yet hospitable to it.

The North Florida connection with "Kubla Khan" was a matter of more than passing interest to me, having spent the first twenty years of my life less than half an hour's drive from Wakulla Springs, one of the two sites chosen to represent Africa in the *Tarzan* films. When my parents first emigrated from England to this part of the world in the early fifties, they had, I think, imagined perhaps not a Utopia but a land somewhat similar to the *Tarzan*/Bartram Eden—an exotic wilderness not entirely savage, and admissible of human habitation. They knew that the part of Florida to which they were moving would not be like Miami, the only place in Florida about which much was known in England, and they expected a frontier.

They had lived first in Gainesville, some sixty miles northwest of the site that had provided for Coleridge, by way of Bartram, the imagery for the "incense-bearing trees," the "mighty fountain," and the river "meandering with a mazy motion" of "Kubla Khan." Arriving in August of 1955, my mother had traveled south from New York by air-conditioned train, which had not prepared her for the heat that met her like a furnace blast when the doors opened at the Gainesville railway station. Her first impression of Florida was that she had arrived in the midst of an accident—that a terrible fire was raging somewhere around the station.

Shortly afterwards, my parents moved to Tallahassee and settled in following the traditional protocol of all good colonialists. I was registered at birth with the British consulate, as I would have been had I been born in, say, Timbuktu. We subscribed to the London *Times* in the special airmail edition printed on tissue-thin paper and at night we listened to the BBC

"World News" on our shortwave wireless. Not until I was in junior high school and faced with a social science project that entailed reading about local civic affairs did I discover that the *Tallahassee Democrat* was the newspaper of choice of my fellow townsfolk.

This illusion of colonial self-containment could have been perpetuated in very few other places in the United States. The frontiers of the West, for example, have their own, deeply American mythologies. But we were in the tropics, or the subtropics, and were surrounded at every turn by phenomena that were recognizable to us only from the travel accounts and popular lore regarding Africa, the Indies, Malaya, India—all the great outposts of the Empire. Our windows were screened against mosquitoes, as they had been in Jamaica (where we had lived briefly), as they would have been in Africa—and for the same reason; the last case of malaria in Florida occurred as late as 1948. Enormous cockroaches walked boldly about the houses, as they had done in Jamaica, as one believed they would do in Malaya or Borneo. In the rainy summers, grass grew so quickly that our garden could be overgrown in a week; in the springtime, it was ablaze with pink azaleas, wisteria, dogwood, and magnolia. The distinctiveness of our surroundings was continually reinforced by my parents' bemused, incredulous, or awed reactions to domestic concerns, such as the lack of real tea and bread, or the disconcerting confidence and savoir faire of even the youngest natives—at every turn the gulf between the normative world represented by England and this new "posting" was driven home.

My sister and I were told our entire childhood to be careful: The coarse grass ("not a real lawn") harbored snakes. Rabies was—and is—endemic, and every raccoon, possum, stray dog, and squirrel was regarded by us, if not by our more acclimatized neighbors, with great circumspection. In the summer, un-air-conditioned houses—and there were many then—fell prey to mildew, which speckled the walls and woodwork. These considerations, compounded by the heat and—above all—the humidity, of which there was no bare conception back in England, were crosses borne by all of us who found ourselves stationed, in whatever part of the globe, in remote tropical outposts.

Wakulla Springs lies fifteen miles south of downtown Tallahassee and is the centerpiece of what is now a 2,900-acre state park. The spring itself is one of the largest in the world, emitting 600,000 gallons of water a minute into a basin that is 250 feet at its deepest point and four and a half acres in area. One of the reasons Wakulla was chosen for location shooting of *Tarzan* (and other less well-known films) was that, in addition to looking more like Africa than Africa, its water is some of the clearest in the world, and therefore ideal for underwater photography.

Throughout my childhood, a trip to Wakulla was never a casual outing, but more akin to an expedition. Inevitably, one arrived at the spring through the Wakulla Lodge, a mildly upmarket hotel set in grounds abounding with live oak, magnolia, and pine, which roll down an incline to the chain-link fence that marks off the swimming area and the spring. But even with these inescapable elements of domestication at one's back, one looked through the fence to confront the wilderness.

The spring basin was ringed with forest, its true shoreline never entirely discernible behind the vanguard of bleached cypress trees and broken knees that rose starkly from the water, which was itself always dark and colored by the weather—forest green on sunny mornings, deep blue when the sun was high, and almost black when it was overcast. Birds of prey called from the trees, and above them black buzzards drifted in endless languid circles, causing one always to wonder what they had spotted hidden in the forest reaches.

To one's right, the spring narrowed to form the six-mile-long outflowing Wakulla River, which wends its way between jungle-covered banks to the Gulf of Mexico. To one's left was the great deep basin of the spring and, reached by a decaying catwalk, a wicked-looking thirty-foot diving tower of gaunt and corroding steel. The triumph of diving Tarzan-like into primeval depths provoked a very special kind of joy, but it was also true that people had drowned in the unfathomable underwater caves beneath the tower and that our neighbor (the father of my Mongolian contact, John Olsen) had mastodon bones that he had gathered from these deeper recesses of the springs.

Adjacent to the chain-link fence, a thin strip of sand served as a beach, while a stone's cast away alligators sunned themselves on the opposite shore. Generally, these creatures live peaceably with the visitors, but there have been mishaps, and as recently as 1987, the tourist jungle boat, on one of its regular cruises up the river, glided past something that was taken at first to be the carcass of a deer but which closer inspection revealed to be a very different kind of animal: Thus it was discovered that fifteen miles from the center of a state capital, in the most industrialized nation on earth, a human being had been devoured alive by an alligator.

"I am getting Sick and tired of F[lorid]a," wrote a farmer to his friend in 1852, the day after a severe storm. "This is the worst Country that I Ever Lived in and it seems if I Make anything on this Plantation it is distroyed of Late years by the heavy Rains and Storms. . . . I have understood that Tallahassee is tetotialy Ruined."

While the gentler aspects of the landscape—the soft air, the extravagance of flowers—were obviously the most seductive, I also took a kind of perverse comfort in its harsher elements. The greatest threat to any environment, after all, is man, against whom the power of Nature presents a welcome counterforce. Thus, when vast tracts of forest were needlessly plowed up to make way for yet one more gimcrack apartment block, or for a new shopping mall when old ones lay empty, it was a solace of sorts to know that these, too, would in time be worn down by the elements and reclaimed by the uncontainable land. The lightning and thunder that rattled our house, the storms that whipped the Spanish moss around the oak limbs, the hurricanes and tornadoes, the pounding torrents of the rainy season—all of these reinforced my romantic belief that I lived in an enduring wilderness.

My own sensibilities to this land were thus admittedly extreme, shaped, after all, less by the common pride that everyone possesses for his surroundings than by the awe of the resident outsider: a colonialist's appreciation of living in a part of the world that other people—like Coleridge—would only ever read about. From the diving platform at Wakulla Springs, past the dark inlet into which Weissmuller dived from the shaggy, vine-entangled tree, overlooking the cruise-boat pier and swimming buoys, I used to look down a river that, for me, led to Africa, or somewhere like Africa about which I had yet to learn, and it may well be that my predisposition to travel derived in great part from my belief that I was already "out there."

> And there were gardens bright with sinuous rills,
> Where blossomed many an incense-bearing tree;
> And here were forests ancient as the hills,
> Enfolding sunny spots of greenery.

In our garden in the late afternoon, sunlight fell fuzzily through the Spanish moss that draped the canopy of great oak boughs overhead. From our house, it is still possible to look around the neighborhood and see the remnants of Bartram's world looming behind the other houses on our street. I was still in high school when I first learned that the landscape of North Florida had inspired Xanadu, and I nodded to myself at the discovery. Walking home on a spring evening when the scent of honeysuckle and gardenias hung heavy in the humid air; or gingerly crossing our coarse lawn, harsh and blinding green in the sun; or diving into Wakulla's forest-encircled depths—the uninitiated might be surprised at the connection, but I well understand how Florida furnished Xanadu with its incense-bearing trees, its sunny spots of greenery, its underwater caverns measureless to man. Previously, I had felt no interest in the specific places Coleridge read about in Bartram—my own vision had no need of them. But faithful to my quest, I was now prepared to seek them out.

FOR COLERIDGE, Bartram's *Travels* was not a casual find, but a work that he read on and off throughout his life, a book that traveled with him to his various residences and that he read from and recommended to friends. References to the *Travels* in Coleridge's Notebooks and correspondence are scattered over many years, and it is not possible to determine exactly when he first discovered the work, but in all probability it was sometime between the years 1793 and the beginning of 1795, a period when Coleridge was reading avidly about America. He and a handful of close and idealistic friends (which included the future poet laureate Robert Southey) were fixated upon the idea of immigrating to the New World and there forming, in Coleridgean terminology, a "pantisocratic" (or "all-governing," i.e., "governed by all") society, in which they would live a life of communal harmony, passing the days in mild farmwork ("two to three hours a day"), reading, writing, and engaging in stimulating conversation; this dream of a Utopian garden world of creativity is strongly echoed in "Kubla Khan." Although the plan ultimately proved short-lived and ill-fated, Coleridge, true to character, had pursued it with great earnestness and had even gone so far as to make an improvident marriage, on the premise that spouses would be required by all pantisocrats to ensure the domestic stability of the commune.

The pantisocrats eventually determined that the Susquehanna territory of Pennsylvania was the most suitable for their purposes, but it is difficult to believe that Coleridge, who character-

istically cast a wide net when researching a new subject, would
not have come across Bartram's well-known book at this time;
and if he did, how could his restless imagination, in this Utopian
quest, not have fallen prey to the spell and possibilities of this
southern Eden?

Coleridge's Notebook for 1797, the year of "Kubla Khan,"
contains two lengthy passages about alligators from Bartram's
Travels, an entry describing the tears of his son Hartley after a
fall, and the following enigmatic lines:

> —some wilderness-plot, green and fountainous and unvi-
> olated by Man.

The first of the two long passages from Bartram describes an
"old Champion" alligator; the second is a page-long account of
Florida's exotic flora and fauna—the "milkwhite fragrant blossoms" of the *Gordonia lasianthus*, which grows by ponds and rivers,
and the "Snake-bird" with its long, slender neck and glossy
feathers. Several entries later, there is another, final reference to
Bartram, in this case to his fanciful description of the "Life of
the Siminole" as being one of never-ending sport and play. The
sources of these disjointed references are to be found between
pages 127 and 221 of the *Travels*, and thus suggest the known
parameters of Coleridge's reading at this time.

The enigmatic reference to the "wilderness-plot, green and
fountainous" recurs in a letter Coleridge wrote to his brother
not long afterwards in the following interesting context:

> Laudanam gave me repose, not sleep; but you, I believe, know
> how divine that repose is, what a spot of enchantment, a
> green spot of fountain and flowers and trees in the very heart
> of a waste of sands!

Now, on page 157 of the *Travels*, flanked, as Lowes reminds us,
"by our old friends the crocodiles and snake-birds," is this enticing passage, in which is echoed the common language of Coleridge's letter and the "wilderness-plot" Notebook entry:

I was however induced to . . . touch at the inchanting little Isle of Palms. This delightful spot, planted by nature, is almost an entire grove of Palms . . . blessed unviolated spot of earth! rising from the limpid waters of the lake; its fragrant groves and blooming lawns invested and protected by encircling ranks of the Yucca gloriosa; a fascinating atmosphere surrounds this blissful garden; the balmy Lantana, ambrosial Citra, perfumed Crinum, perspiring their mingled odours, wafted through Zanthoxilon groves. I at last broke away from the enchanting spot. . . .

The fact that Coleridge associated images of fountains and flowers with laudanum—as we know from his letter—makes it all the more likely that as he slipped into the historic laudanum dream that presaged "Kubla Khan," his mind had already drifted into Bartram's landscape. For it is here on the little Isle of Palms that one finds the chief inspiration for Xanadu's encircled gardens, blossoming with many an incense-bearing tree, and with its forests enfolding sunny spots of greenery.

Bartram's second contribution is yet more central to the poem. On pages 230–31 of the *Travels*, there occurs a singularly lyrical and captivating description of "the admirable Manate Spring." Although it lies outside the parameters of Coleridge's reading of Bartram as documented by the Notebook, it does so by only nine pages. The text, however, which affords a taste of Bartram's narrative at its most inimitably lush, is too suggestive to mistake:

We now ascended the chrystal stream; the current swift: we entered the grand fountain, the expansive circular bason, the source of which arises from under the bases of the high woodland hills, near half encircling it; the ebullition is astonishing, and continual, though its greatest force or fury intermits, regularly, for the space of thirty seconds of time; the waters appear of a lucid sea green colour, in some measure owing to the reflection of the leaves above; the ebullition is perpendicular upwards, from a vast ragged orifice through a bed of rocks, a great depth below the common surface of the bason, throwing up small particles or pieces of white shells, which subside with the waters, at the moment of intermission, gently settling down round about the orifice, forming a vast funnel. . . .

In addition to "Manate Spring," Bartram offers another candidate for the "mighty fountain" of "Kubla Khan." On page 165, just beyond the *Gordonia lasianthus* that Coleridge mentioned in his Notebook, Bartram writes:

I seated myself upon a swelling green knoll, at the head of the chrystal bason . . . in front, just under my feet was the inchanting and amazing chrystal fountain, which incessantly threw up, from dark, rocky caverns below, tons of water every minute, forming a bason . . . a creek of four or five feet depth of water, and near twenty yards over, which meanders six miles through green meadows, pouring its limpid waters into the great Lake George. . . . About twenty yards from the upper edge of the bason . . . is a continual and amazing ebullition, where the waters are thrown up in such abundance and amazing force, as to jet and swell up two or three feet above the common surface: white sand and small particles of shells are thrown up with the waters. . . .

It does not take much imagination to see how the graphic lines of these two passages were combined into the dream cadence of "Kubla Khan":

> . . . *And from this chasm, with ceaseless turmoil seething,*
> *As if this earth in fast thick pants were breathing,*
> *A mighty fountain momently was forced:*
> *Amid whose swift half-intermitted burst*
> *Huge fragments vaulted like rebounding hail,*

Or chaffy grain beneath the thresher's flail:
And 'mid these dancing rocks at once and ever
It flung up momently the sacred river.
Five miles meandering with a mazy motion
Through wood and dale the sacred river ran,
Then reached the caverns measureless to man,
And sank in tumult to a lifeless ocean . . .

From Bartram's itinerary, we know that the little Isle of Palms and the mighty fountain were to be found in the same corner of the Florida landscape: The mighty fountain is both Manatee Spring, some twenty miles west of Gainesville, and Salt Springs, set squarely in the Ocala National Forest; the Isle of Palms lies off Rocky Point on the northwest shore of Lake George and the meandering sacred river is Salt Springs Run, which winds five miles from the springs down to the great sea of Lake George.

THE POPULAR PERCEPTION of Florida as a place of beaches and holiday sites does not, generally speaking, accommodate the wilder Africanesque features highlighted by Bartram's writings and the *Tarzan* films. But if the stereotype doesn't apply, it is because the north of Florida is little visited and little known, and is historically, demographically, and climatically, as well as scenically, a world apart from the popular central and southern regions. The fact that over 80 percent of the total population resides in the central and southern two-thirds is in itself telling. While all of Florida is extremely low-lying (on average less than a hundred feet above sea level), what hills exist are in the north. Northern Florida is subtropical (on the same latitude as Egypt), with an average annual temperature of 68 degrees Fahrenheit, compared with 77 degrees in the far south, which means that in addition to the ubiquitous pines, palms, and cypresses, the northern forests harbor magnolia, tulip, sweet gum, and hickory trees. The north is mostly rural, and its mores are more akin to those of the Old South than to anything found in the aggressively developed urban central and southern areas, which foster the hot spots of artificial culture for which Florida is best known, such as Disney World and Miami Beach.

When telling people about Tallahassee, I have often described the city and its outskirts as seen from an airplane—rolling hills and dense forests, then, closer to the airport, the thin rivers and dark lakes that alone break through the trees; and always when peering out of the plane window myself, on the verge of return, I am somewhat taken aback to see that the land appears exactly as it is elsewhere in Florida—board-flat. From the air, the tree cover appears extensive but seems to be composed mostly of new pines; it does not really warrant the term *forest.*

The weather was dull throughout this particular trip in search of the landmarks of Xanadu, which may have accounted for the lackluster appearance of the greenery and the muddy streams that wound through it as my plane approached for landing. In the few cleared plots, one could see where the grass had been worn away to reveal an insubstantial sandy substratum. A few of these clearings were for trailer parks, which I did not remember having seen before.

I had chosen my mother as guide for the journey, the sites in question lying just outside Gainesville, and thus in territory that she knew from her pioneering days. We left Tallahassee on another dull June day, taking Florida Route 27 south to Gainesville through drab roadside scenery of monotonous pine plantations and low scrubland, tenuously settled by solitary shacks and small ramshackle communities. Intriguing dirt trails lead off from the main road into forest, but as few people have cause to follow them, the overwhelmingly common impression must be of roughly cleared land and hastily built convenience stores and houses. Occasionally, these are built ranch-style in harsh red brick, but more usually in sloping, weathered wood.

Sometimes a handsome wooden house set picturesquely under live oaks of inordinate size and age will indicate a family place of several generations, but ordinarily the buildings one passes give the appearance of having been constructed from the necessity or inspiration of the moment, and never intended to do more than serve their present occupants.

Manatee Spring lies off the east bank of the Suwannee River, some 200 miles down its 250-mile course from the Okefenokee Swamp to the Gulf of Mexico. Like most of Florida's springs of greater magnitude, it is now enshrined within the confines of a state park, and while situated in dense forest, its southern bank has been converted to a discreet picnic area, set in kempt grounds and adorned with neat pine trees. The north shore of the spring basin, which measures some one hundred feet in diameter, recedes between cypress knees that rise from the water like the knuckles of a giant hand, behind which a scanty beach retreats into an unmolested ash and gum-tree forest. The opposite bank, by contrast, is reinforced by a retaining wall to which a ladder is affixed, providing easy access to the water. In a similar gesture of thoughtfulness, an elaborate wooden boardwalk directs the visitor around the southern shore, which is also overlooked by a boathouse and refreshment stand, built of "natural" wood and thus intended to be unobtrusive. Close to the spring itself, a plaque attached to the wooden railing of the boardwalk is engraved with Bartram's captivating description of the "astonishing and continual" ebullition—a reminder to the modern tourist that he is following in the footsteps of an earlier traveler who, not so very long ago, was able to contemplate the scene in its former sparkling glory.

By way of the strategic ladder, I lowered myself into the chill water, which like that of all of Florida's springs hovers somewhere between 68 and 72 degrees Fahrenheit. While Bartram had suggested that the "sea green" color of the spring was a reflection of the overhanging greenery, the clear dark water that I entered seemed to be colored by the spring's depths. The trees were, in any case, changing color: The tips of the feathery cypress leaves were now, as if it was autumn, a blur of gold, yellowy green, and red. Under the water close to the eastern shore, a clump of trees had apparently fallen headlong and now lay like moss-covered monuments to be dredged up at a later date— cannons from a sunken ship. Below them, a deep ledge of jutting rock marked the entrance to an underwater channel leading to an adjacent pool. A few small fish wound peaceably around the long grass tendrils that stretched towards the exit channel to the south, rooted in a long swathe of displaced sand. This movement, I soon discovered, was caused by the spring boil, the specific point whence the underwater stream breaks with hidden force into the pool. Swimming towards it underwater, I was suddenly punched backwards into a small and murky cloud of fine sand that had been flung up by the boil from the basin floor. This was the mighty fountain, whose force over two hundred years ago had shown itself to Bartram above the surface of the spring; but the groundwater pressure that once produced the fountain had dwindled over the centuries as land was drained and developed.

Two divers had just emerged from a journey through the narrow underwater channel linking the spring with the pool that lay a hundred yards or so beyond, a seemingly perfect round hole of impenetrable and sinister darkness set incongruously in the placid picnic grounds behind us. A fine covering of duckweed had absorbed the outer edges of its absolutely opaque water as though to form a kind of fantastic abstract painting. According to the divers, the underwater channel passes through an extensive two-thousand-foot-long system of caves, the most renowned of which was dubbed Catfish Hotel. A permanent rope guides the way through the central passage, and the side channels and attendant caves thus tend to go unexplored. The water had been murky on this run, I was told, but these underwater caverns are said to be very beautiful, being an unexpected red-dish brown. Florida's porous limestone substructure is riddled with such subterranean waterways, which break out into open ground to yield the sinkholes, springs, and basins that pock the forests: Twenty-seven of the nation's nearly eighty major springs are in Florida. The enduring temptation to explore these caverns measureless to man is great, and each year exacts its fatalities: Two divers had drowned in the Manatee Spring channel the preceding August.

One of the present divers reentered the water to retrieve the motorized, lamp-lit underwater scooter on which he had trun-dled around in the darkness of the black pool's bottom. His un-derwater progress could be marked by the intermittent line of slow-breaking bubbles that temporarily disturbed the duckweed. Above him in the picnic grounds, a group of female prisoners on an outing from the local jail had disembarked from their bus and were sullenly taking their places on the wooden picnic benches, while their guards stood and chatted with one of the park officials.

The outflowing of the spring was channeled down a corridor of trees about a quarter of a mile long into the Suwannee River, which from this vantage point appeared dark and placid. This vista at least, one could happily imagine, had changed very little since Bartram's time. Behind me, two families, out-of-state tour-ists, judging from their accents and comments, approached the springs with their myriad children. The little boys stood warily in a line along the spring edge, commenting on the weeds and fish and depth of the water. Their careful reverence was a re-minder of what I felt myself to be lacking—namely, a sensibility capable of elevating the scene above the merely picturesque to something worthy of its romantic pedigree.

In a passage that could well serve as a definition of the Ro-mantic point of view, Coleridge praised Wordsworth for his gift "of spreading the tone, the *atmosphere* . . . of the ideal world around forms, incidents, and situations of which, for the common view, custom had bedimmed all the luster, had dried up the sparkle and the dewdrops." The landscape of "Kubla Khan" (like that of Bartram's *Travels*) is privileged space, and the sense the poem gives of uncommon access to an unaccustomed realm is part of its powerful attraction. Here in the state park, however, little meaningful distinction could be drawn between common and poetic views of this landmark of Xanadu; a visitor could not but be aware of the countless beholdings of this same scene by others, of the manifold layers of perceptions that had been laid upon it. As Bartram and Coleridge had proved, landscape is less memorably described than it is interpreted; and if one can romanticize a raw setting by point of view alone, one can, surely, likewise domesticate it.

THROUGHOUT THE AGES, geography and poetry have been powerfully intertwined. "Many geographical myths have a poetical tradition before becoming a generally accepted belief promoting voyages and discoveries." The author of these words was not referring to the legend of Xanadu but to that of the Fountain of Youth, which had been one of the primary lures (the other being gold) that led Ponce de León, the "discoverer" of Florida, to the peninsula in the first place. The legend derived from fanciful accounts of an Earthly Paradise somewhere "extra Gangem," in which the Fountain was said to lie. According to medieval traditions, the Fountain of Youth burst forth in a forest of evergreen trees set in a blooming landscape that was fanned by breezes bearing the sweet perfume of flowers. In the face of compelling scientific evidence to the contrary, faith in these poetic legends was great enough to convince explorer after explorer, from Columbus onwards, that in the tropical landscape of the New World they had found the fabled land beyond the Ganges—testimony, as one historian has written, "to the influence of legendary geography over actual experience."

The early explorers apart, Florida has historically attracted people on romantic quests. Beginning in the 1820s, when the introduction of steam riverboats made the waterways accessible to travelers, invalids made their way down south, dreaming of finding health in Florida's legendary sunshine. A century later, there began the land-speculation boom in the wake of the mass migration of resort seekers and retirees from the cold northern and midwestern states, the first of multitudes to fall prey to the Utopian dream of a haven of rest, and perhaps, too, of some miracle of rejuvenation akin to the Fountain of Youth. On first entering Florida during his tramp across the country, John Muir, the patriarch of American wilderness preservation, wrote in his diary that

> in visiting Florida in dreams, of either day or night, I always came suddenly on a close forest of trees, every one in flower, and bent down and entangled to network by luxuriant, bright-blooming vines, and over all a flood of bright sunlight.

The organized marketing of this apparently perennial dream of youth, sun, health, and flowers constitutes Florida's modern tourist industry, which caters to 30 million people a year. Nearly half of Florida's 58,500-square-mile area is consigned to beaches, forests, and federal and state parks, the latter managed, according to a tourist brochure I came across, "to appear as they did when the first Europeans arrived . . . Florida's state parks fulfill an important purpose as representative examples of 'Original Natural Florida.' "

"Original Natural Florida" was, in fact, inhabited, before the coming of the Europeans, by Indians, who are believed to have migrated down into the state as early as ten thousand years ago. The first inhabitants were primarily hunters, gatherers, and fishers and, from around 500 B.C., farmers. By the mid-eighteenth century, these Florida peoples had been driven into virtual extinction by the Europeans and the Creek, whose arrival brought alien diseases, wars, slave raids, and religious persecutions.

In 1565, the Spanish established the mission of St. Augustine on the northeastern coast of Florida, the first permanent European settlement in the New World. Fever, the hostility of the local inhabitants, and the wildness of the land and weather, however, prohibited development, apart from a few other doomed mission and military stations along the coast and coastal rivers. In 1763, England exchanged Havana with Spain for Florida, and the next twenty years saw a period of emigration from England to the new possession; it was during this brief period of British occupation that Bartram made his travels. In 1779, Spain declared war against Britain, and West Florida was subsequently captured by the Spanish governor of New Orleans. Four years later, under the terms of the Treaty of Paris, Florida was formally handed back to Spain. West Florida first came under U.S. jurisdiction in 1803, on the ground that it had been included in the land sold to the United States under the terms of the Louisiana Purchase. But only in 1819, after many vicissitudes of possession and fortune, were East and West Florida jointly ceded by Spain to the United States.

In 1817, the first of what would be three Seminole Wars broke out, ostensibly over the government's concern to recapture runaway slaves who had settled among the Seminoles. Although most Floridians regard the Seminoles as "our" original natural inhabitants, this tribe—whose name, Seminole, is believed to have derived from the Spanish *cimarrón*, meaning "wild"—did not, in fact, appear in Florida until the late eighteenth century, some two hundred years after the arrival of the Europeans. Descended from the Muskogean-speaking Creek tribes, the Seminoles were migrants who broke away from the Georgia Creeks and were later joined by runaway black and Indian slaves; Florida had become a haven for fugitive slaves from 1699 under Spanish rule, when a royal decree promised protection to all slaves who reached Florida and converted to Catholicism.

That land was the real issue behind the Seminole conflicts

became unambiguously apparent in the course of the next two wars, which were fought on and off until 1858. In contention was the territory north of Lake Okeechobee, which had been designated a Seminole reserve but had come to be coveted by white settlers whose fundamental aim was the complete removal of the Seminoles from Florida. Their attempts were almost successful. In 1842, at the end of the second war and shortly before Florida was awarded statehood, most of the tribe was transported to the Creek reservation in what is now Oklahoma. Only a handful remained in Florida, and while in Bartram's time the Seminoles possessed "a vast territory: all East Florida and the greatest part of West Florida," the present population is estimated at only one thousand. Virtually no vestiges of their once-pervasive presence remain, apart from the euphonious names with which they endowed their villages, lakes, and rivers.

At the time when civil government was imposed in 1822, the Florida territory constituted a vast expanse of unexplored wilderness and a twelve-hundred-mile coastline that had never been properly surveyed. A few years later, only a modest stretch of road had been built and only sixty-three miles of rail laid. Until the establishment of rail networks in the late nineteenth century, transportation depended upon the extensive waterways of this wild and difficult land. In northern Florida, few rivers offered more intriguing possibilities than the one the Indians called Welaka, later to be renamed the St. Johns. Although the primary route of William Bartram's famous travels, its source and entire course were not known at the time of his journey. A prospectus written by the explorer Le Conte in 1821, nearly fifty years after Bartram, for an expedition up the river eloquently conveys the challenge of discovery. In language reminiscent of the earliest explorers of other unknown continents, it cites as its main goal the desire "to explore the St. John's river to its source, through a country utterly unknown, and it is believed as yet untrodden by the foot of a European."

Welaka in Seminole means "river of lakes," a name indicating that the precursors of the Europeans had understood the essential nature of the uncharted river, which in its three-hundred-mile course from the St. Johns Marsh in southeast Florida to the Atlantic opens out periodically, forming a chain of lakes. The beauty of this river, even in eyes less forgiving than Bartram's, was legendary. An army soldier traveling in the course of duty during the early years of the Second Seminole War—a man whose official duties, surely, precluded Bartram's naïve ebullience—eulogized the river in a manner entirely befitting his effusive predecessor: "Never shall I forget my sensations at that rare and beauteous sight!" he exclaims, recalling his entry to the river.

> A succession of glorious scenery was constantly presented to the sight, as we rapidly stemmed the St. Johns; whose banks, now receding, now approximating so as merely to admit our boat between them, were bright in loveliness on either side with every species of tree and shrub. From orange groves, whose golden fruit and snowy blossom stood in beautiful contrast to their dark foliage, we'd pass on to long rows of tall and slim palmettoes; their graceful trunks shooting up along the river banks for miles. Then a change would come over the beauty of the scenery; and in place of orange and palm trees, would appear the spreading oak, the bay, the beautiful cedar, and stately magnolia; their pendant branches casting mysterious shadows on the St. Johns. . . .

Salt Springs lies off the western shore of Lake George, which, at eleven miles in length, is the largest of the chain of lakes opening off the St. Johns River. The history of the springs site reflects much of the history of Florida as a whole. In the early seventeenth century, rights to it and to the outflowing Salt Springs Run were granted by the king of Spain to the Hernandez family, local Portuguese settlers with whom the sovereign was on friendly terms. The land remained, undeveloped, in their possession until the late 1800s, when an entrepreneur from Georgia laid claim to the more or less forgotten grant, seeing especially in the run a possibility for an inland shipping route to the Jacksonville depots. In 1908, the scrub forest surrounding the springs was made a National Forest, although, being in the backwoods, the spring remained undiscovered by tourists. In the 1920s, the Hernandez land grant was sold by the Georgian entrepreneur to a family in the area, who in turn sold the bulk of it outright to the federal government in 1979 for $12 million. The story of this lengthy and complicated transaction is part of local lore, and it seemed that every resident of the area contests the legality of one detail or another. No one in this tiny self-contained settlement, however, accepts the fact that the springs in which they grew up swimming and fishing now belongs to the U.S. government.

BASS'N, ETC. FISHING GUIDE SERVICE, located on the edge of Highway 19 in the Salt Springs township, was, I had been told, the best place from which to hire a boat. Although I had been given specific and accurate directions, the town came and went so quickly that we had passed through it before we started to look for landmarks. Backtracking, we soon found it among the few roadside buildings, a small red-and-white wooden lean-to selling fishing gear and tackle and otherwise catering to the limited needs of its community.

Layman Lane, our guide-to-be, was a good ol' boy of sorts, although tamed to some extent by his love for his wife, Glenda, a diminutive, fiery woman and one of the descendants of the legendary Portuguese Hernandez family. We were, we were made to understand, on her family's property.

Hitching his boat expertly to his truck, Layman led the way off the main road and down towards the water, driving along a sandy lane overshadowed by moss-draped oaks. Here, well hidden behind the drab scrubland and the make-do buildings, lay, largely undisturbed, the land that Bartram had rhapsodized over and the inspiration of poets. The basin of the spring proper was ringed with massive oaks to the left, while the boat pier and the adjacent boathouse faced directly on the run. An aloof egret rooted in the screen of reeds watched our departure in the boat. The spring was empty and the lone caretaker of the boathouse appeared to be the only other person around.

The day, which had begun dull, had not brightened and the water was gray and clear and, according to Layman, waving a hand at a band of parasite bulrushes by way of evidence, not doing well, although in this case the culprit was unexpectedly not man but nature. A constant easterly wind impedes the outflow of the run's waters, thus allowing the waves of Lake George's brackish tannin-tinged water to surge in. Layman Lane could remember when the bulrushes had not been there and when the water had been truly pristine. He had come here from the Blue Ridge Mountains of Tennessee in 1956, looking for work. In season, he is a fishing guide; off-season, he fishes for himself in the run, which teems with bass and mullet, and in favorite cypress swamps nearby.

The crowns of small palm clusters showed their heads above the forest of the run's narrow shores and the foliage was brightened here and there by cascading clumps of white water violets. Cranes and egrets stood immovable in the reeds, an unutterable weight of silence contained in their unbudging silhouettes. The steady, vandal easterly flickered up the pale undersides of the leaves of the higher trees but made little dent in the massive luxuriance of the lower foliage. On the left shore, a shell midden stood out against the greenery, a casual token of the generations of Indians who once inhabited this land.

At the entrance to Lake George, two important landmarks came into view: a rocky point on the left bank, mentioned by

Bartram, and the great shaggy wedge of Drayton Island, now privately owned. Between these two, a low-water warning marker was the only feature to break the tea-colored water, and on cautious approach, one could see the V of a low-water current catching the sand. This marker arises from the water in the exact spot where one would expect to find the little Isle of Palms, that blessed, unviolated spot of earth with its incense-bearing trees. Perhaps accumulated river silt has incorporated it into the river delta, or perhaps two hundred years of storm and erosion have washed it away, down into the dark brown sun-defying sea of Lake George.

With a diameter of six miles at this point, the lake's own shores are distant and indistinct, offering little to view apart from a rough low line on the horizon. From the vantage point of the run's mouth, the near shore, too, was unremarkable, a high sandbar covered with saw grass and palmettos. But on nearby Drayton Island, one could glean some idea of what the little Isle of Palms might have looked like. The island is covered with two thousand acres of forest, which from the tossing boat appeared unviolated, although Layman reported that there had been a great fire here some years ago. Close to the water's edge, benefiting from its warm currents, a striking grove of palms claims the shoreline, their shafts and crowns the only features for miles around to make any impression between the dark water and the dull sky. The flora on the island, as everywhere in the area, however, has sadly been diminished since Bartram's time: A severe freeze that descended in February of 1835 killed off the fabled centuries-old orange groves whose scent wafting over the river had been admired even by toughened conquistadores.

Just beyond the delta of the river mouth, heading back into the run, we passed an old man contentedly fishing in a moored boat.

"He's a retired fisherman," Layman informed us approvingly. It was by now early evening and the shore vegetation had begun to blur into a featureless bank of shadows. Two wildcats spat and thrashed from somewhere in the forest, and an osprey, perhaps disturbed by their antics, shot out of the treetops. The same somber sand-mound crane stood at stiff attention on an overhead branch framed with Spanish moss, and back at the entrance to the springs, the same spotless egret gleamed out from the dark reeds he was guarding.

The small boathouse was being closed up as we disembarked, but there was time enough to visit the shop and to read the literature taped to its walls, odds and ends relating to the history of the springs. A newspaper cutting detailing an alligator attack some years back was displayed with, one sensed, some pride and as a kind of warning to the northern sun bunnies who make their way here during winter and spring vacations that this is a place to be taken seriously. Tourism did not come to Salt Springs until the 1960s, when Highway S-19 opened up the Ocala National Forest. The lack of motels and tourist conveniences bespeaks the fact that visitors are only grudgingly received, and most have to make do with campsites. One has to have lived here a long time to count as more than a newcomer.

A stone's throw from the boathouse, beyond the egret's reeds, lay the spring itself, a circular basin measuring some one hundred feet in diameter, set in a grove of ancient twisted-rooted oaks. The spring takes its name from the mild salty flavor of the water, resulting from trace minerals and saline residues in the limestone through which it filters and retained from an era when this place was under the sea. As far back as Indian times, medicinal value was attributed to the water, which even today is used for "healing." It is claimed by some that Salt Springs, with its preservative salts and minerals, is the Fountain of Youth sought by Ponce de León—but of what spring in Florida is this not said?

Five boils barely rippled the surface of the basin, but when the groundwater has been raised by a period of sustained rain, these jets have been seen to spurt as high as four inches above the water. In Bartram's time, the boils had formed a spectacular fountain, flumes of water erupting from the basin floor with force enough to carry along fragments of sand and shell. Now, only a cloud of sand, seen through the crystal water, betrayed hidden boils.

Glenda Lane, dispossessed inheritor of the spring, had come over to show us around while her husband cranked the boat back onto its trailer. It was dark by now, and the concrete retaining walls and guardrails—a benefit of national park status—could happily be overlooked. Mrs. Lane was not concerned whether the park was officially open or closed.

"The U.S. federal government will charge you one dollar and fifty cents for the privilege of crossing this strip of grass," she said with unconcealed contempt. No one at the ticket booth had attempted to extract an admission fee from us, but then we were with Glenda Lane.

"The U.S. federal government owns only the grass," she informed us. "If you swim in from the run, there is nothing they can do." Glenda Lane was among the many local people who repeatedly came out at night to tear down the wire fence the U.S. government had attempted to erect around the area shortly after it had acquired the property. While not necessarily romantically inclined, the people of Salt Springs, Florida, had matter-of-factly recognized the beauty of this site, and it was only with bitterness and resistance that they surrendered their blessed, unviolated spot of earth.

"THE IMAGINATION," COLERIDGE wrote, "I hold to be the living power and prime agent of all human perception." Certainly, it was imagination that had forged my own early romantic perception of Florida. The trick is somehow to maintain, as Coleridge admonished, "the fine balance of truth in observing with the imaginative faculty in modifying the objects observed."

However, the elusive images of Xanadu could not, on this particular journey, be apprehended by truthful observation of the places that inspired them—the vanished little Isle of Palms and the exhausted, domesticated fountains. The one place where they might reside, I did not visit, being unwilling to risk disturbing remembered images by an actual journey to Wakulla. Truthful observation might prove me wrong, but I believe it was there, years ago, that I saw the "wilderness-plot, green and fountainous," of Coleridge's imagination.

In some sense, then, this particular journey was one I had no need to make—like Coleridge, I could have conjured what I sought without straying far from home. But the other objects of my quest lay far afield and on unfamiliar territory.

THE CAVE OF ICE

One of Coleridge's most endlessly projected works was a collection of six poems to be entitled *Hymns to the Sun, the Moon, and the Elements.* This would-be masterpiece was outlined, discussed among friends, researched extensively—but never begun. Nevertheless, his incessant quest after material for his opus led him down many an interesting byway, nor was it to prove entirely fruitless—the results of his research contributed substantially to "The Rime of the Ancient Mariner."

Two pages after the long passages copied from Bartram's *Travels,* the following consecutive entries appear in the 1797 Notebook:

> Hymns Moon
> In a cave in the mountains of Cashmere an Image of Ice, which makes its appearance thus—two days before the new *moon* there appears a bubble of Ice which increases in size every day till the 15th day, at which it is an ell or more in height: then as the moon decreases, the Image does also till it vanishes.
> Read the whole 107th page of Maurice's Indostan.
>
> Sun
> Hymns—Remember to look at Quintius Curtius
> —lib. 3. Cap. 3 and 4.
> Major Rennell

The first passage quoted is from a work entitled *The History of Hindostan*, written by the Reverend Thomas Maurice and published in 1795. This is an ambitious two-volume undertaking that not only expounds on the arts, sciences and, above all, religions of India but relates them to "The History of the Other Great Empires of Asia, During the Most Ancient Periods of the World." Crammed as it is with arcane mythology and history, it was a work after Coleridge's own heart. The excerpted passage in full reads thus:

> In a cave of the same mountainous subah a very singular phaenomenon is said, in the Ayeen Akbery, at certain periods to make its appearance. Though to the last degree absurd and incredible, the relation will yet illustrate the present subject, and what will hereafter occur concerning their computation of time by the bright and dark appearance of the moon's orb. In this cave, says Abul Fazil, is sometimes to be seen an image of ice, called AMERNAUT, which is holden in great veneration. This image makes its appearance after the following manner:

There follows the passage noted by Coleridge.

On the page preceding this, Maurice cites the Roman historian Quintus Curtius, giving a book and chapter reference that Coleridge had simply jotted down (misspelling his name) to confirm firsthand, as was his habit, at a later date. The abbreviated reference to Maj. James Rennell's work, *Memoir of a Map of Hindoostan or the Mogul Empire*, however, is more intriguing. Maurice, in the "Preliminary Chapter" to his history, directs his "reader's attention to the intelligent Memoir, and very accurate map of Hindostan, presented to the world by Major Rennell." In the section on "Cashmere," the region wherein was said to lie the cave of ice that had clearly captured Coleridge's imagination, Major Rennell breaks momentarily away from his characteristic dry tone and offers the following memorable tribute:

The valley or country of Cashmere, is celebrated throughout upper Asia for its romantic beauties, for the fertility of its soil, and for the temperature of its atmosphere. . . . It is an elevated and extensive valley, surrounded by steep mountains, that tower above the regions of snow. . . . The author of the Ayin Acbaree dwells with rapture on the beauties of Cashmere . . . [the] emperors of Hindoostan visited it also, and seemed to forget the cares of government, during their residence in *the happy valley*. . . . Only light showers fall there: these, however, are in abundance enough to feed some thousands of cascades, which are precipitated into the valley, from every part of the stupendous and romantic bulwark that encircles it. . . . In a word, the whole scenery is beautifully picturesque. . . . All Cashmere is holy land; and miraculous fountains abound.

A final literary reference needs to be mentioned, although Coleridge does not name it in his Notebook. In the first paragraph of his dissertation on "Cashmere," Major Rennell cites François Bernier, a French physician who in the seventeenth century had traveled extensively in the valley while in the service of the Mogul king, and was, according to Rennell, "the most instructive of all Indian travellers." It is difficult to believe that Coleridge, who was clearly hot on the Kashmiri trail, would have overlooked this compelling citation. That he did in fact follow up this reference appears more likely when one considers what Bernier has to say in his chapter entitled "Journey to Kachemire":

The most beautiful of all these gardens is one belonging to the King, called *Chah-limar*. The entrance from the lake is through a spacious canal. . . . It leads to a large summer-house placed in the middle of the garden. A second canal, still finer than the first, then conducts you to another summer-house, at the end of the garden. . . . In the middle is a long row of

fountains, fifteen paces asunder. . . . The summer-houses are
placed in the midst of the canal, consequently surrounded by
water. . . . They are built in the form of a dome. . . .

Returning from *Send-brary*, I turned a little from the high
road for the sake of visiting *Achiavel*, a house formerly of the
Kings of *Kachemire*, and now of the *Great Mogol.* What principally constitutes the beauty of this place is a fountain. . . .
The spring gushes out of the earth with violence, as if it issued from the bottom of some well, and the water is so abundant that it ought rather to be called a river than a fountain.
. . . The garden is very handsome, laid out in regular walks,
and full of fruit trees—apple, pear, plum, apricot, and cherry.

We know, to quote Lowes, "beyond peradventure" that
Coleridge had read Maurice; we know he intended to read
Major Rennell, and more likely than not did so; he may well
have read Bernier as well. In the collected writings of these authors, one may discern the romantic chasm, the holy place, the
dome, echoes of the mighty fountain and—found in no other
source—the cave of ice of Xanadu. The Notebook, therefore,
shaped the itinerary for my third journey around three places in
Kashmir: the Shalimar Gardens outside modern Srinagar; the
Achabal Gardens lying just off the main road to the hill station
of Pahalgam; and the Amarnath Cave situated at some thirteen
thousand feet in the foothills of the Himalayas.

TWO DAYS BEFORE my departure, I went to the Indian consulate to pick up visas.

"You must step upstairs, into the main embassy, I'm afraid,"
said the pleasantly smiling woman behind the counter grille.
"They must just want to talk to you," she added when with mild
alarm I queried why I alone of the queuing crowd had been thus
singled out.

Upstairs, I was shown into the office of a somber-looking man, who sat regarding me in silence for a few minutes before clasping his hands and leaning forward to address me.

"You cannot go to Kashmir. You know we are having troubles there." I knew very well. It was the summer of 1991 and Kashmir was—as it still is—embroiled in a radical secessionist movement; several hundred thousand Indian government troops—or security forces, as they are officially called—had been sent to the region to fight the guerrillas and to guard India's border with Pakistan. Only a few months beforehand, rebels had kidnapped some Israeli tourists who had been staying on a houseboat on one of the lakes. The captives had been marched out into the darkness at gunpoint—where they had eventually overpowered their guards and escaped. I was, therefore, circumspect about traveling to Kashmir—but also determined to do everything within reason to get there. My plan was to reach Delhi at least, from where I felt the situation could be assessed more reliably. So great had been my concern to be "sensible" about embarking on this enterprise that in a spirit of complete responsibility I had, perhaps foolishly—certainly needlessly—entered Kashmir on my visa application, which requested a list of the places in India that I intended to visit.

"You cannot go to Kashmir." This statement was repeated intermittently throughout the interview by the gentleman whose specific title I never learned. When it emerged that I wanted to go hiking in the mountains—the Amarnath Cave being several days' journey by foot away from the nearest hill station—I was gently but firmly instructed to take my walk elsewhere. Downstairs again, I collected our passports with their visas and was also handed a packet of leaflets expounding the rugged beauty of Himachal Pradesh.

George, my traveling companion in Mongolia, and I arrived in Delhi in early August, towards the end of what should have been the relatively cooler rainy season. The monsoon had not come, however, and the city was encased in a wadding of stolid, begrimed air. As both of us were dual nationals, we had two important embassy visits to make.

"I cannot emphasize strongly enough that officially I have to warn you not to go to Kashmir," said the British consul. "The principal danger is of being caught in cross fire. We cannot be responsible for you."

"He said *officially* he had to warn us," I said to George afterwards. "*Privately,* he may have thought very differently." To our distress, the terse directive we received from the American embassy conveyed the same message: "Due to recent terrorist activity in the Kashmir portion of the state of Jammu and Kashmir, Americans should defer travel to the valley of Kashmir until further notice."

Although we both agreed that the State Department characteristically tended to be overcautious, my spirits had by now been somewhat dampened. There was, however, one way to reconcile my desire to be sensible with my determination to see the cave of ice. In the years before the recent political troubles, as many as thirty thousand devout Hindus went annually to the mountains of Kashmir to view the image of Amarnath, which, as Coleridge had read, was "holden in great veneration" and is to this day still very much an object of religious reverence. As in Coleridge's time, it is believed that the "image" in the cave of ice waxes and wanes in size in accordance with the phases of the moon and that the most propitious time to approach the holy site is during the full moon of the Hindu month of Shravan, which corresponds with July or August of the Gregorian calendar. Because of the troubles, the pilgrimage had been suspended for the two previous years—an unprecedented break in a centuries-old tradition. But, according to the Kashmir Tourist Office in Delhi, the pilgrimage, or *yatra*, was to be reinstated this year under heavy armed guard. Clearly, the safest—not to mention the most auspicious—way to see the cave of ice was to become *yatris* of Lord Shiva.

. . .

POLITICALLY SPEAKING, KASHMIR denotes the northern region of the northernmost Indian state of Jammu and Kashmir, which lies between the Punjab plains and the Himalayas. Popularly speaking, it tends to refer specifically to the Vale of Kashmir, a lush and abundant valley in the northwest of the state, contained by the spurs of two great chains of the Himalayas. Measuring some eighty-five by twenty miles in length and breadth, the valley is the basin of an ancient lake, rimmed by mountainous boundaries that stand as high as sixteen thousand feet.

The troubled political history of the state is reflected by its three borders: That to the north and east is shared with China, which since 1962 has illegally occupied a segment of Ladakh, a region of Jammu and Kashmir; that to the northwest is shared with Pakistan, which maintains a territorial claim on Kashmir; and that to the south is shared with two Indian states, one of which, Punjab, is embroiled in a secessionist movement of its own.

Prior to 1947, the year in which the departing British raj divided the subcontinent into India and Pakistan, Kashmir had been an independent princely state, enjoying virtual autonomy from the rest of India under the government of the Kashmiri maharajah. The establishment of the two newly independent nations, however, pressured the maharajah to pledge allegiance to one or the other. Before he had come to a decision, a rebellion of his predominantly Muslim subjects, who were in favor of a union with Pakistan, abetted by an invasion of Pathan tribesmen, prompted the intervention of Indian forces. It was India's rescue of the beleaguered maharajah that determined the fate of the principality as an Indian possession, a status still contested by Islamabad. Border skirmishes have plagued Kashmir since its annexation and on two occasions, in 1965 and 1971, have escalated into wars, both of which eventually ended to India's advantage. A United Nations mandate issued in 1949, calling for a plebiscite to determine the state's allegiance with either India or Pakistan, has never been honored. The ongoing antagonism is not purely territorial: Kashmir is a principally Muslim state within a principally Hindu nation.

Since 1990, the situation in Kashmir has progressively worsened, and it continues to hover somewhere between what can euphemistically be termed "political unrest" and outright civil war. According to local authorities, as many as 120 different guerrilla factions are involved in the ongoing insurrection, ranging from those who seek Kashmir's complete liberation and restored independence to those who seek its formal annexation to Pakistan and establishment as a fundamentalist Muslim state. The Indian government, for its part, contends that the situation has assumed such dangerous proportions because the guerrillas are trained and sponsored by an enemy nation—a charge that is substantiated in part by reliable outside sources who confirm that the Pakistani army's intelligence unit runs training camps for fundamentalist guerrillas. This fact notwithstanding, a number of human-rights organizations have reported abusive treatment of Kashmiri civilians by the Indian military and, especially, paramilitary forces—which tends to indicate that the government's hostility is not aimed exclusively at Pakistan. As many as 300,000 paramilitary and military troops are now estimated to be more or less permanently stationed in Kashmir.

India clearly fears that the secession of Kashmir would precipitate the fragmentation of its multiethnic nation by fueling further separatist rebellions, such as those currently under way in Punjab and Assam. And beyond the political considerations is a simple economic fact: the Vale of Kashmir has since time immemorial enjoyed the reputation of being one of the most beautiful places on earth, and up until the last three years, it has been India's most lucrative tourist hub.

Traditionally, the Amarnath pilgrimage has begun with a ven-

eration of the holy trident in Srinagar, the capital of Jammu and
Kashmir. This year, however, so as to skirt the most troubled
areas, the pilgrimage formally commenced in the city of Jammu
and then proceeded directly to Pahalgam, the first official camp
of the five-day trek to the cave. The unorthodox starting point
had led many pilgrims to head for Pahalgam on their own and to
wait there for the main processional body, or, like us, to follow
the traditional, if perilous, course and start out from Srinagar.

At Srinagar airport, soldiers encircled our plane and greeted
the disembarking passengers with pointed rifles. Ours was the
only commercial plane on the tarmac, all others belonging to the
Indian air force. Inside the terminal building, as obvious foreigners, we were requested to fill out elaborate forms explaining our
purpose in coming to Kashmir. The statement that we had come
to participate in the pilgrimage raised no eyebrows; doubtless
there has been a well-established history of Western enthusiasts
partaking of this experience.

In days of peace, Srinagar was a fairy-tale town, a small gem
of almost Central Asian architecture wound around two lakes of
surpassing loveliness, and threaded with cobbled alleys and wil-
low-lined canals. The present city dates back to the first century
A.D. and has for centuries been a center of learning: Its name in
Sanskrit means "city of knowledge." Rising nearly six thousand
feet above the lowland plains, it has been enjoyed as a summer
retreat at least since Mogul times.

The city has managed to retain its charm in spite of its disconcerting transformation into a garrison. Sandbagged sentry
posts were stationed every hundred yards or so along the airport
road and the main streets of the city. With its narrow alleys and
passageways, gable-roofed balconies, its deep, dusky shops overstuffed with piles of fruit, hookahs, and carpets, Srinagar strikes
one as being designed explicitly for intrigue, and its policing
must be a logistical nightmare. The population is over 800,000,
and the pervading atmosphere seemed to be a mixture of

business-as-usual bravado and sullenness. To a traveler arriving directly from Delhi, the people are strikingly un-Indian in appearance. One sees the rather heavy-featured, handsome faces of a mountain people, and their clothing, like their architecture, is more Central Asian than Indian—the women were dressed in baggy pants and chadors, the men in pants and short caftans.

We were advised to stay in a houseboat on one of the lakes immediately to the north of town, rather than in Srinagar itself—in actual fact, few visitors would ever choose to stay anywhere else. The season had been dry, and the sentry-lined streets were dusty, the roadside herbage sparse, and riverbeds brown and silted. Lake Nagin, when we reached it, was low, its former waterline showing brownly on its rushes. Whereas the Mogul occupiers of Kashmir left exquisite gardens, the houseboats are the peculiar legacy of the British raj and were the means by which the British circumvented the Kashmiri maharajah's prohibition against their acquiring land in his kingdom, as they did elsewhere in India.

Ineffably romantic in theory, the houseboats are in reality bizarre manifestations of British ideas about what constitutes the exotic—miniature fluvial Xanadus from the nation that invented follies and doilies. The houseboat we eventually acquired was a craft whose every visible surface was so intricately and floridly carved as to be nearly porous. Inside, six good-sized bedrooms were ranked along one long corridor, which opened up towards the bow into a dining room, living room, and, at the tip of the bow, a canopied porch. The interior, too, was relentlessly embellished with wood carvings and filled with heavy furniture and other decorations in keeping with this mercifully unique melding of British and Indian 1930s suburban taste.

From the small porch, one could look down the long line of houseboats moored along the shore like ours, with their sterns to land, their bows facing out into the water. We had arrived at the lake in the late afternoon and dusk approached with eerie quiet. The summer nightlife on the lakes of Kashmir had once been famous, and at this time of evening there should have been lights, music, and voices reflecting off the darkening water. But there was no sign of any other people at all, and I later learned with some astonishment that we were two of only five houseboat occupants. Lake Nagin alone harbors two hundred houseboats, each of which is equipped to accommodate at least half a dozen people—and each of which, just two years earlier, would have been booked to capacity. In the 1980s, more than a million Indian and foreign tourists a year provided Kashmir with its most reliable source of income, and virtually all tourists coming to the vale would spend at least one night in Srinagar.

Looking more closely at the lake scenery, I saw that its abandonment was taking a heavy toll. Many of the boats lay at awkward angles in the water or with their sterns sunk a little too deeply in the shoreline rushes. In some places, empty mooring posts rose senselessly from the water. The surface of the water itself was dimpled by thick weeds that choked the lake and spread like lichen just below its surface. I was to learn the next day that it had been two years since the government had bothered with the usual annual weed cutting—there was little justification now for this expense. The opposite, western shore of the lake had already disappeared, its margin blurred with a mass of weed and high grass. To the right of our boat, the shore was lost in a more picturesque manner amid stiff, waxy pink-tipped lotus blossoms and their enormous circular leaves. The occasional flopping of a fish indicated that the lake was not yet entirely dead.

At sunset, Lake Nagin momentarily regained its legendary beauty, its mossy waters reflecting the orb of the sun in brief perfection. The distant mountains that form the background of all scenes in Kashmir gained color and presence as dusk approached and claimed the foreground. To the southwest, the remains of Akbar's hill fortress were reduced to an arrogant silhouette. A variety of birds suddenly put in an appearance; fish eagles, kingfishers, and swallows swept past the porch, perched on abandoned mooring posts or on the sagging power line that stood shakily in the water, or hovered overhead, on the lookout for prey, with a flagrant confidence that dismissed the threat of human presence.

As the sun began to disappear, there flashed across the western sky white streaks of gunfire, accompanied by the stammer of automatic rifles, reduced at this distance to mere firework pops. The reflection of the sun continued to spread across the water, and the birds continued to swoop and sing. At six-thirty, the mullah's call to the faithful echoed and resonated around the lake in stereophonic sound, issuing as it did from loudspeakers in a number of different mosques. This surreal cacophony—the deep thrum of the mullah's ancient call punctuated by the rattle of gunfire and the fearless chatter of the birds—eventually passed, and an unnerving quiet settled in with the night. Until the mullah's morning call, there was nothing at all to be heard throughout this floating ghost town except the soft, insidious lap of water against the boat.

KASHMIR WAS RULED by Hindu kings from the eighth century until the end of the thirteenth, when the assassination of the reigning monarch by his Muslim vizier marked a change of order. The fortunes of Hindu as well as the less numerous Buddhist subjects over the next century were essentially determined by the temperament of the dictator at the time, reaching an unhappy nadir at the close of the fourteenth century under the notorious Sikander, "breaker of idols." Elsewhere in India, an old acquaintance, the Mongols, had appeared on the scene, under the command of Timur Khan, better known as Tamerlane, to whom Sikander submitted and paid tribute. Mongol invasions continued into the sixteenth century, escalating from border skirmishes to the outright conquest of Delhi in 1525. In 1588,

Mogul rule was brought to Kashmir by Akbar the Great, and it remained in effective power until the mid-eighteenth century, at which time the valley fell to the hands of the Pathans, the notorious and cruel Afghan lords; thus it was they who held sway at the time Coleridge was reading about the beauties of Kashmir. The Pathans lost the valley in 1819 to the Sikh monarchy of the neighboring Punjab, who retained their prize until 1846, when it was lost in turn to British forces in the Sikh Wars. Initially, under the terms of the Treaty of Lahore, it had been stipulated that tribute should be paid for the state to the British government, but this demand was later waived as a personal favor to Gulab Singh, Sikh General and also maharajah of the neighboring principality of Jammu, whose neutrality during the wars and important role in the subsequent peacemaking process was rewarded with a grant of independent sovereignty over Kashmir.

Within this sequence of foreign rules, that of the Moguls proved to be one of the most beneficent—*Mogul* being the term used to refer to the Mongol empire in India. The Mogul emperors were descendants of the Chaghataid khans of Central Asia, who had adopted the Muslim religion. They brought to India in general and to Kashmir in particular their religion, military might, administrative skill, and exquisite aesthetic taste, which in Kashmir was most strikingly apparent in their gardens.

Our word *paradise* is borrowed from the Persian *paradesh*, the walled gardens that surrounded a palace. The Mogul gardens represent one of the world's great landscape traditions, which should be no surprise when one considers the painstakingly wrought floral patterns and motifs that abound in all forms of Persian art—its manuscripts, carpets, and architecture. This love is also, if less expectedly, revealed in the written memoirs of the Kashmiri Moguls: There is a kind of stunning incongruity in reading of the garden-making and botanical passion of men who also record that they were capable of watching their enemies being flayed alive.

"Kashmir is a garden of eternal spring," wrote Jahangir,

Akbar's youngest son, in his autobiography. "Its pleasant meads and enchanting cascades are beyond all description. There are running streams and fountains beyond count. Wherever the eye reaches, there are verdure and running water. The red rose, the violet, and the narcissus grow of themselves."

In addition to such natural gifts, the acquisition of India and Kashmir exposed the Moguls to the informal exuberance of the more ancient Hindu temple gardens. Flowers were, and are, an integral part of Hindu worship; flowers and masses of rose petals are brought to temples as offerings, and floral designs are used in religious decorative carvings.

Shalimar Gardens, the first of the two gardens described by Bernier, were only a *shikara* ride away from our houseboat. Laid out in the early seventeenth century, the gardens were shaped by two men, Jahangir and his son Shah Jahan, who also gave the world the Taj Mahal. (Surely, one of the most formidable dynastic lines in history is that of Genghis Khan and his descendants, which included Khubilai Khan, Tamerlane, Akbar, and Shah Jahan.)

A small, brightly canopied punt, or *shikara*, a kind of Kashmiri gondola, appeared in the morning off the stern of our houseboat to take us to Shalimar. The air was cool at this hour, the water dark with the crinkled tendrils of the runaway moss. Drifting past the deserted houseboats and the reedy shore, we entered a long channel at the northern end of Lake Nagin that was overhung with willow trees and that took us into the far larger Lake Dal. Burnt-brick and wooden-shuttered houses lay in the willow shade, and the close air underneath the channel trees was briefly and intriguingly fragrant. At the broad waters of Lake Dal, we passed under a clattering bridge, which was heavily sandbagged at each of its sentry-guarded ends, its traffic moving ponderously through the checkpoints. Drifting between a smoking construction site on the left shore and floating islands of vegetation, we began to cross to the far side of the lake by way of an avenue of lotus lilies that rose, crisp and waxy, to shoulder height and were silver-beaded with water. In open water again, we came upon moored punts, from which men and women were harvesting the rich lake sludge for use as fertilizer in their fields. Crouched in the extreme bow end of her shallow craft, as if weighing anchor, a woman was vigorously uprooting choice lily leaves, which would be used as fodder for her cattle.

The buildings of Srinagar came into sight on our left, with the white dome of a riverside mosque gleaming conspicuously. We approached an island on our right, breaking into its mirror-perfect reflection. A broken column, jagged and charred, rose among landscaped trees; it was, we were told by the *shikara* punter, all that remained of a once lovely and popular teahouse: It had been burned as a "political act," whether by militants or army, no one knew. The water and sky were the same teal color by the time we had plowed through a last meadow of lotus lilies and reached the shore.

Once upon a time, one entered the gardens directly from the lake, by way of a canal edged with green turf and shaded by poplars, but a road that is being constructed around Lake Dal prohibits this entrance. The dry canal channel is blocked by construction and piles of sand, and the last mile or so must be traveled by road.

From the moment of entering the wall-enclosed garden, one is compulsively drawn towards the long, shallow canal that forms a central aqueous avenue and that is fed by a spring arising beyond the far wall. The canal is shaded by majestic and dense chenars, a kind of Oriental plane tree, which, together with towering poplars, also dot the lawns that spread away on either side. Flanking the walkways are beds of flowers that, like the poplars which were brought from Italy, are oddly familiar—roses, bougainvillea, gladioli, roses of Sharon, magnolia, crepe myrtle: Somehow, one does not expect to come upon marigolds and sweet william in the pleasure gardens of the Mogul kings. While contemporary accounts, including the memoir of Jahangir, make it possible to identify the kinds of trees and flowers used by the Moguls in other gardens, nothing is known about the specific layout of those at Shalimar.

The greatest achievement of the garden does not in any case lie in these natural phenomena. Its distinctive serenity derives mostly from its man-made features—its proportions, the long ornamental canals, the large rectangular pools, the fountain jets, and Bernier's summerhouses, to which all the canals proceed. While the love of the powerful and often cruel Mogul emperors for their gardens might strike one as paradoxical, this is to overlook an essential feature of the gardens: that of absolute and utter control of all key elements—water, earth, and even light. The serenity of Shalimar does not lie in its prettiness. Rather, it is the assured tranquillity born of power—regal, majestic, and unassailable; as with "Kubla Khan," one sensed a mighty shadow presence behind the scene. The garden's encompassing stone wall is low, in part so as not to obscure completely the view of the distant snow-peaked mountains, but also, one feels, because the peace contained within is so secure as to make a defensive wall unnecessary.

Flowing into the smallest of the rectangular pools is an artificial cascade that is presided over by the first of the summerhouses and a black marble slab that served as the emperor's throne. Behind the throne room, the pool narrows, then opens again into an even larger pool. Here, set in a broad square of water, is the garden's centerpiece, an imposing pavilion of black marble. A three-tiered gabled roof surmounts each building, although originally they had been domed.

It was the vista from the black pavilion that had so captivated Bernier when he described "the most admirable of all these Gardens," with its painted pleasure houses and its jetting fountains of water. The decorated ceilings, architraves, and columns that one sees today were painted, somewhat heavy-handedly, in the mid-nineteenth century; the pools and canals are filled with water but also with dead leaves, which, downstream, a woman was vainly trying to whisk away with a bracken broom. A sentimental travelogue written in the early 1920s describes the "terraced pools separated by the lace of falling waters and embroidered with the pearls which constantly drop from the fountain spray"; but today the cumbersome equipment of a defunct sound-and-light show rusts beside the corroded fountain jets, which appear to have dried up for all time: Whether they had been turned off because of the "troubles" and the lack of tourists or because they were old and a nuisance to maintain, I did not learn.

The use of black marble for the main pleasure house was a stroke of genius. Inside, its dark walls seem remote from the brightness of the exterior world and impervious to heat; outside, the building, formidable though it is, blends unobtrusively with the heavy chenar shadows. Centuries earlier, of course, the shadow of this dome of pleasure would have floated on the waters of the ornamental pools. As it is, ripples of light reflected from the water bounce around the roof eaves, where, mingled with the flowery decorations of the painted ceiling, a famous Persian quotation is inscribed: "If there be a Paradise on earth, it is here, it is here, it is here."

PART OF THE tradition of renting a houseboat is that one is taken under the wing of the owner and his family, who provide meals and advice and act as guides on any excursion. Mr. Guru had been recommended to us by the Jammu and Kashmir Tourist Board in Delhi as being knowledgeable about the Amarnath pilgrimage route in particular. He was a plump and prosperous-looking merchant, with the bustling air of a man who had not enough hours in the day for the conduct of his successful business. He admitted with feeling that, with the tourists gone, these were terrible times for Kashmir, and yet he left us with the impression that he spoke for other, less capable people—he himself, we had no question, had been resourceful enough to turn his hand elsewhere. Something of his consummate entrepreneurial skill was displayed in the adept and lightning-quick manner in which he "sold" us a guide, a cook, and two pack ponies to conduct us on our trek. He had made the Amarnath pilgrimage twice, although he was a Muslim. Somewhat unexpectedly, I witnessed no evidence of antagonism on the part of the Muslim residents of the valley towards the Hindu pilgrims, or vice versa. Every underling in Mr. Guru's establishment, it soon transpired, was his son or daughter, and, in marked contrast to their father, all were lean and wiry, dark and intense. Of these, Ahmed had been chosen as our cicerone, because of his knowledge of the Amarnath route and the history and traditions associated with the pilgrimage; Samson was to be the cook. We were advised that meat was prohibited on the pilgrimage in deference to the Hindus—again, the matter-of-fact tolerance of, even empathy with, the particular practices of the different faiths was striking.

From Srinagar to Pahalgam, the starting point of the pilgrimage, is a journey of only sixty miles, but one that takes four full hours by car, partly because of the terrain, partly because of the congested army traffic. The road follows the course of two rivers, running first to the southeast with the Jhelum, then, doubling back from the village of Anantnag, running northwest with the Lidder.

The same emotional disjunction aroused in Srinagar by the sight of beauty under siege is accentuated in the countryside, where there is an uneasy juxtaposition between the accoutrements of war and a geography not only possessed of surpassing loveliness but suggestive of paradisiacal peace. Some of the soldiers, it appeared, had fallen prey to this spell, for while they maintained their assigned posts at one-hundred-yard intervals along the road, they were often to be seen sitting or reclining comfortably under the willow trees that dipped over the road-side canals. The road, which passed through fields of terraced paddy and brilliant saffron, was clogged with slow-moving army vehicles carrying supplies and open-backed trucks piled with soldiers, their rifles pointing nonchalantly ahead of them, and inadvertently towards us. The narrowness of the road prohibited our overtaking them, and so we became unwilling participants in the trundling, exhaust-choked convoy. Dark poplar trees flanked the lanes traversing the fields and formed sentry-straight shadows against the foothills of the distant mountains. While the mountain peaks stood out cleanly and clearly in the pellucid high-altitude air, the towns, villages, and roadways of the valley floor were characteristically tinged with exhaust pollution. This pervasive smog appeared to be a deep-rooted problem caused by more than the relatively recent influx of army vehicles, for streamers of black fumes could be seen trailing behind most private cars and taxi vans, as well.

Every so often, one side of the road was blocked by small boulders, sometimes overseen by sentries, more often not; these appeared to serve more as a reminder of a potential military presence than as an actual deterrent. Sometimes the line of traffic swerved to bypass a donkey cart or a canopied autoricksha.

On the road itself, Ahmed and Samson were noticeably tense, braced always for a random checkpoint, but in the towns, they appeared to drop their guard and to relax. A town's shops stood directly on the thoroughfare, with their dwelling quarters above them. Looking down, sometimes with wistfulness, sometimes with bemusement, from the seclusion of these handsomely shuttered windows were often to be seen the households' women, half-veiled, or with veil in hand, ready to be drawn. Farther along the road and higher into the mountains, one came upon villages nestled on some choice spot beneath trees and beside some form of running water, such as a canal or a stream. The typical burnt-brick and wood architecture of the buildings, with their almost-alpine upper balconies and shuttered windows, had the appearance, on this small village scale, of gingerbread houses. The majority of Kashmir's population practices subsistence agriculture, but here in the valley the overwhelming impression was of well-ordered prosperity. The streets, the irrigation channels, and the houses themselves appeared strikingly well tended, and the shop stalls and vendor wagons were piled with fruits, vegetables, and pulses. Houses were being built; bricks were being manufactured; fields were being tended. Increasingly, I found myself thinking that the inhabitants of the Happy Valley would manage very well running their own kingdom.

SOME TWENTY MILES outside Pahalgam is Achabal, the site of the second of Bernier's gardens, designed primarily by Nur Jahan, Jahangir's beloved wife. The waters of the Achabal spring have from ancient times been considered holy and spectacular: An account written in the late sixteenth century describes it as "a fountain that shoots up to the height of a cubit."

The waters from this still-powerful spring are directed into two narrow channels and a broad central one, the latter, as in Shalimar, breaking into a series of ornamental ponds. At the head of the central channel, two small pavilions flank an impressive artificial cascade; the main pavilion forms a little island in the most extensive of the pools. None of these are the original Mogul buildings, but stolid stone structures of a recent date. It has been speculated that on some of the foundations—such as those beside the main cascade—tents or marquees would have been erected, rather than permanent buildings. The only Mogul original is set back some distance from the canals, strictly speaking outside the modern boundaries of the garden, and is picturesquely overgrown with wild roses. Inside, bats were whirring around and around in the cavity of its former dome.

The gardens are maintained by the Department of Forestry and Floriculture, and a government fish farm has now taken over part of their territory. The grounds were strikingly well kept, although somewhat marred by modern shrubbery that bespoke the influence of the British raj more than the deft touch of the Moguls. More so than at Shalimar, the gardens of Achabal seem to be a natural extension of the lush and mountainous Kashmiri landscape, in part because they are situated outside a small town as opposed to a dusty city, in part because of the specific nature of the surrounding land—the Achabal spring rises at the spur of the Achabal Thung mountain, which directly abuts the far garden wall.

Whereas the tense political situation in Srinagar discouraged casual enjoyment of the Shalimar Gardens, the atmosphere at Achabal was considerably more relaxed. Under the shade of one of the groups of chenar trees, a Hindu family was having a picnic, the two women dressed in tangerine-and-rose-colored saris, the men in white. Another man joined them, bearing an armful of orange gladioli, which he laid beside the women on the grass. The picnickers were a reminder of another lost feature of the gardens—the handsomely dressed Moguls themselves, strolling the grounds, reclining on their magnificent carpets spread out on the lawns or in their airy tents, or, as Bernier saw, lighting their candle lanterns beside the night waters.

PAHALGAM LIES AT approximately seven thousand feet at the northern end of the Lidder valley, between the junction of the Aru and the Sheshnag, two branches of the majestic Lidder River, which flow through defiles at the valley head. Perhaps the most popular of Kashmir's hill resorts, Pahalgam is well provided with cheap hotels, restaurants, and handicraft stores that once catered to backpacking tourists. Like the houseboat owners, however, most proprietors have closed down their establishments, and although the reappearance of the pilgrims after the two-year hiatus had brought out postcard vendors and caused a few hopeful shops to reopen, the town had the forsaken air of an out-of-season resort. From a selfish point of view, this was entirely desirable, for there can have been few occasions in recent history when the Lidder valley, at the most picturesque and pleasant time of year, was not overrun with trekkers and tourists. Spread along the verdant banks of its rivers, Pahalgam is overlooked by mountains capped with snow and covered with soaring deodar, or Himalayan cedar. The town is not large, and beyond its central cluster of buildings, the Lidder rolls through unsullied and spectacular alpine scenery.

The *yatra* is run not unlike a well-organized military campaign, and it was, in fact, overseen by army personnel. Registration took place at the *yatra* headquarters, a tented city of administrative centers, medical and veterinary facilities, and tents providing food and shelter. The officer presiding over the registration table told us that an estimated six thousand pilgrims would be taking part, a healthy number for any enterprise of this kind, but nothing compared with the tens of thousands who turned up in the years before the "troubles."

It was now possible to take stock of exactly what we were letting ourselves in for. The pilgrimage to Amarnath is first mentioned in the *Rājataraṅgiṇī*, the earliest extant written history of Kashmir, dating from the mid-twelfth century. Following an ancient peregrine route, the journey traditionally requires five days. Although the distance to the cave from Pahalgam is only thirty miles, the *yatra* path runs through rough, mountainous terrain that climbs to nearly fifteen thousand feet—the trail is snowbound for the greater part of the year and is open only from mid-June to mid-October. A brochure published by the Tourist Department of the Jammu and Kashmir government, under whose auspices the pilgrimage is run, stated that each pilgrim should come equipped with "sufficient woollens, raincoats,

umbrellas, waterproof boots/shoes, walking stick and torch."
Pack ponies and porters were available for hire at an officially
established rate, and it was also possible to rent tents or to make
bookings for a space in the tented camps that would stand ready
at the end of each traditional stage of the journey. This was all
welcome news, making us feel less like overburdened Westerners
with our own pack ponies and tents; in fact; by the day's end,
eight thousand *yatris* had turned up, considerably more than had
been provisioned for, and both tent space and food were to fall
short at the camps.

The pilgrims themselves formed an excited, happy crowd of
people from every imaginable walk of life—young executives
in shiny dress shoes and mohair sweaters, white-haired women
in saris and flip-flops, teenagers in jeans, wild-haired sadhus in
nothing at all except for saffron-colored loincloths. The pilgrimage is not a local affair, or a peculiarly Kashmiri celebration.
The *yatris* who had turned up at Pahalgam had come from every
part of India; many, unable to afford the air or train fare, had
made their way from as far away as Calcutta, traveling for many
weeks on local transport. Some pilgrims had made the journey
before, but most had not, and, for many, their arrival in Pahalgam this year represented the realization of a long and fervently
held dream.

It is one thing to go trekking in a foreign country, but it is a
different thing entirely to take part in the holy rite of another
people's faith, and there was, inescapably, something bogus in
our participation. In the *Amareshvara Mahatmya*, an ancient sacred
Sanskrit text, Shiva instructs his divine consort, Parvati, saying:

> One who even hears with devotion the story of the pilgrim-
> age, shall be put at par with the one who actually visited the
> shrine. A visit without full knowledge of the greatness of
> Lord Shiva would be as futile as incurring the sin of betray-
> ing the holy pilgrimage.

As one personally possessed of imperfect knowledge of Lord Shiva, I accepted this warning that my journey would be, in at least one important respect, ultimately futile; but as a teller of the pilgrimage story, I took some encouragement from Shiva's words.

HISTORICALLY, HINDUISM AROSE in India from the convergence of indigenous Dravidian religious beliefs with those imported by the Sanskrit-speaking Aryans who invaded the subcontinent in 1500 B.C. There are today well over 700 million people of this faith, or over 13 percent of the world's religious population. It is one of the most difficult of religions to characterize, for while it possesses a great many sacred texts, it has no paramount bible, no hard dogma, no founding figure, and no central overseeing authority. This lack of a measure for orthodoxy allows a generous range of beliefs and associated practices. Hinduism holds that all manifestations of the divine are to be revered, and it is therefore markedly tolerant of other faiths; indeed, a Hindu can embrace another religion and still remain a Hindu. Hinduism has been called a religious conglomerate, but this is to overlook the essential unity of its traditions: It is perhaps best regarded as a religious civilization.

The diversity of Hinduism notwithstanding, it is possible to isolate certain fundamental elements, among them the belief in an infinite and eternal, transcendent and all-encompassing impersonal principle, called Brahma, the creator, generator, and preserver of all things, the sole reality and both the source and goal of all existences. This is the Absolute, Being-in-itself, which, although a principle and not an entity, may be conceived of as a personal god, such as Vishnu, the protector, or Shiva, the destroyer. There is also a universal belief in the authority of the Veda, or ancient Hindu scriptures, and in the Brahmin clans, who are the scholars of the Veda; a respect for all life, of which vegetarianism is a manifestation; and the belief that a person's karma, or the sum of his actions in one of his states of existence, determines his fate in other existences, to which the soul transmigrates. Pilgrimages in general are an important characteristic of Hindu worship, the sacred sites being typically beside rivers or in locales of exceptional wild beauty, such as that for which the Himalayas are renowned.

One of Hinduism's most important specific forms, although more a local folk phenomenon than an orthodox religion, is Shaivism, in which Shiva—as opposed to Vishnu—is regarded as the supreme god. The Sanskrit word *shiva* means "auspicious," but the god is revered as both healer and destroyer, the storm god who lashes the land but who also brings needed rain. Despite his name, his "goodwill" cannot be relied upon, and it his uncontrollable, uncultivated, unreliable aspect that is feared— he is, in this respect, not unlike the Hellenic Apollo. This essential ambivalence is reflected in other aspects of Shiva's nature, for he is both ascetic and lover. For Shaivists, Shiva is the ultimate source and the ruler of all life. The most important attributes of Shiva are the trident, which symbolizes both his power and his ambivalent nature, and a representation of which is carried at the head of the pilgrimage procession; and the *linga*, or phallus, which together with the *yoni*, its female counterpart, is worshipped as representing the creative and generative principles. "Phallus worship," as this ritual is conveniently, if somewhat inaccurately, called, predates the association of the *linga* with Shiva and is an example of how a very ancient folk ritual came to be assimilated into a later, dynamic cult.

Shiva's consort, Parvati, is important to the Amarnath story. Parvati was born of mortal parents, the daughter of a Himalayan king, and as a child determined that she would marry no one but Shiva, who was at this time roaming the earth as a mendicant beggar and living in a cave. When she came of age, her parents attempted to marry her off to wealthy princes, but she resisted.

Finally, they invited all eligible suitors to their palace for a great
party that was to be attended by the gods. Among the guests was
Shiva, who appeared first as a prince, then as a beggar. Finally,
after Parvati's mother cried out that her daughter would never
marry a mendicant, Shiva began his *Tāṇḍava* dance; snow began
to fall as he shaped the rhythm, then a rain of silver, gold, and
diamonds. The parents relented, and Parvati and Shiva were
married. Their marriage night was celebrated in the cave of
Amarnath: This is the abode of Shiva, and it was here that he
recounted to Parvati the secret of creation.

The Amarnath Cave is a holy and enchanted place not only
because of its legendary association with Shiva's marriage but
also because of a striking natural phenomenon. Every year, at the
back of the cave, there arises a natural *linga*—a domed pillar of
ice rising up to nine feet in height. The pilgrims regard it as the
darshan, the glimpsing of god. For them, according to the *Amareshvara Mahatmya*, "every particle of earth, sand and rock, every
drop of water and every leaf of vegetation is sacred to this site."
In Shiva's own words, recorded in the same sacred text, "by seeing and touching Shiva Lingam, uttering mantra, offering flowers, one gets free of all sorts of sins," and incurs "much wealth,
long life, many children, and also fame in this world." Most im-
portantly, *darshan* of the *linga* releases the pilgrim from the cycle
of future rebirths. This is the "image of ice" of which Coleridge
had read.

WITH THE REGISTRATION completed, we set about finding a
site where we could pitch our tents. Pahalgam is renowned as a
shepherd's town—the trails that are so popular with trekkers are
in fact made and maintained by the shepherds and goatherds
who migrate from mountain pasture to pasture with their flocks.
Around Pahalgam itself, the valley's choice thick, springy turf
has the appearance of an English country green, but higher up-

stream it narrows by degrees and becomes rough with boulders; accordingly, the mountainous range that is at some distance from the town center is dramatically banked on the water's edge higher upriver. We chose a site where the turf was still tame but the mountains close enough to form a dark, precipitously sloping wall on the opposite banks. Somewhat downstream from us, Ahmed said, was the area that was traditionally marked off as a camping site for the pilgrims.

"*Thousands* of people," he said. "Many thousands—you cannot imagine. You would not be sitting here in peace. The tents would be *there* and *there*." This year, all the pilgrims seemed to be contained within the tented city at the registration compound, or to have gone on ahead to the first official camp of the pilgrimage trek proper. The disparity between what the valley had so recently been and its present appearance was a theme to which Ahmed kept continually and angrily reverting.

"People will be ruined. They have no money. Only the tourists brought money." He was insistent that there was no danger for visitors like ourselves, and when asked about the kidnapping of the Israeli tourists, he was contemptuous.

"Tourists? Six Israelis with their heads shaved because they are still in the army, carrying automatic weapons? Tourists? They were part of the team of Israeli advisers the Indian government has been using to help them occupy Kashmir—we have seen many of them around. No tourists have been troubled."

"The climate of Cashmere is admirably suited to the European," wrote Major Rennell, an observation that is echoed in the numerous travel memoirs written about the valley. Its temperature, its capacity to grow the fruits and flowers that suit European tastes, its suitability for long romantic walks are among its most frequently cataloged assets. Reliance on the tourist dollars of European visitors had, over the years, clearly shaped the economy, the sociology, and in small degrees the topography of the Happy Valley—the mossy waters of Lake Nagin, for example, have not been cleared because there are no longer people around for whom clear water is important. And yet, ironically, Kashmir itself shaped European assumptions about natural beauty. The glorification of lonely walks in sites of wild and spectacular beauty is a central topic of the British Romantics. The echo, specifically, of the fountains and disquieting mountains in "Kubla Khan" is detectable in Shelley's "Mont Blanc," to give one notable example of Romantic alpine description. The Kashmir landscape is seductive to the European not only because of its astonishing beauty but because it is part of a familiar poetic landscape that still stirs his soul. When describing our campsite in my journal that first night, I found myself fighting to resist using the terms that in fact rose most spontaneously to my mind; but how else to capture the savage beauty of the precipitous rockface, dark with cedar pine, slanting athwart the Lidder chasm and its tumultuous waters, than with the dream terms of "Kubla Khan"?

At dusk, a soldier sauntered over to our camp and, after commenting on the fineness of the evening, pointed into the cedarn shadows of the mountain, warning that there were terrorists lurking there. We had built a fire for cooking dinner, but when the darkness came, it still seemed immense, and nothing now seemed capable of penetrating the depths of the forest stronghold opposite. The presence of the military forces cast a shadow on our pleasure—the ancestral voices of each side may well be prophesying war.

THE FIRST DAY'S march is by far the easiest, being some ten miles along a gently climbing road—in fact, this stage can be made by car or jeep, an option many pilgrims took advantage of. The road to Amarnath follows the Sheshnag, or eastern Lidder defile, out of the valley. Puffs of yellow dust stirred by the unremitting parade of pilgrims rose in the air and hung above the trail, along which, at this early stage, vendors of incense, postcards, tea, rice, and other basic goods had industriously set up business. Shiva's blessings are bestowed upon all *yatris* who worship at his mountain shrine, irrespective of the manner in which they might arrive there, a provision that allows for a striking variety of modes of transportation. Many, like us, went on foot, carrying small packs; far more traveled in cars overloaded with the equipment they would have to reassemble at the end of the road at Chandanwari; many rode patient mules and pack ponies, led by a guide; and a picturesque few rode in dandies, or wooden chairs that are carried aloft Roman-style on the shoulders of four sweating bearers.

Chandanwari lies at an altitude of approximately nine and a half thousand feet, a climb of two and a half thousand feet from Pahalgam, on a road that parallels the Lidder River. With the gentle shepherds' pasturage of Pahalgam behind, the way becomes dramatically bare and rocky. The pilgrimage road hugged the more benign face of the Lidder gorge, while the opposite face veered off at a precipitous near-perpendicular slope. Although it reared several thousand feet above us, one thought not of its soaring height but of its headlong downward plunge to the Lidder River. Streaked with moraines and rock and glacial scars, cluttered with the debris of fallen shattered trees and boulders, every feature on its uncompromising surface evoked not height but giddying depths. In the relentlessly clear sunlight, the cedar pines that stood valiantly rooted against the escarpment's irresistible downward course appeared green-black, and the Lidder itself, far below them, glacial blue. At one point, what appeared to be a marble bridge was seen straddling a torrential passage of water, but was, in fact, a ridge of compacted perennial snow, a favorite landmark of the *yatra*.

The option to travel by car or by more traditional means, and the fact that many pilgrims had made their first camp at Chandanwari and not Pahalgam, rendered the first day's march a scattered, disorganized affair. The camp itself had been established in a choice meadow cut by the intersection of two rivers and contoured by mountains: It was here that Shiva once observed a strict thousand-year penance, and the meadow is his ashram. Another tented city comprised the official main camp, with army-issue canvas tents set up in orderly lines off a central roadway. Pilgrims with tents of their own, like ourselves, took to the lower meadow by the river, where the most immediately pressing task was to clear the ground, not only of stones but of the piles of human excrement that dotted this otherwise-enticing meadow like cowpats in an extremely well-frequented paddock. A late-nineteenth-century British description of Kashmir had noted that "picturesque as these pilgrimages are, they have their ghastly side as cholera-conductors," words whose import had not been as compellingly clear to me at the time of reading as they were now. As late as the 1930s, as many as five hundred pilgrims had died on one Amarnath trek.

At the main camp, the pilgrims had settled into the makeshift routines of refugees. The excess numbers, unforeseen by the *yatra* authorities, were now woefully apparent, and the sturdy tents bulged with extra camp beds and were overhung with a haze of smoke. Family groups cooked their food on stoves they had brought with them or by burning wood they had purchased at the camp, while other pilgrims frequented the small restaurant and tea sheds that had been squeezed in among the rank and file of tents. A steady stream of people strolled up and down the main thoroughfare, occasionally looking over the shops or stopping to pull back a tent flap in order to check up on a friend or relative. The clearest evidence that this gathering of eight thousand–plus people had some more than worldly purpose was furnished by the sadhus, who formed a sometimes belligerent, often provocative, and always conspicuous presence. These holy men were readily identifiable by their near nakedness and their mass of at least waist-length dreadlocks. At the vanguard of the tents, they established their own open-air and very public camp around a single fire, where they sat streaked with ashes and wreathed in wood and ganja smoke. Ganja, or *bhang*, is as much a universally recognized attribute of the sadhus as their saffron loincloths and meager cloaks. According to Ahmed, many kilos were regularly carried and traded by the sadhus on the *yatra*, but this year the "Kashmir situation" had blockaded their supply lines.

The sadhu is a Hindu ascetic whose indifference to such fleshly concerns as warmth, shelter, and food is exhibited in his lack of clothing, leathered, ash-streaked skin, and extreme thinness. If he is a devotee of Shiva, he impersonates Shiva the mendicant and may carry a small trident or miniature *linga*. The ashes, which when thickly applied give the sadhu a harrowed, deathly appearance, are smeared on both for apotropaic purposes and as a symbol of dedication to Shiva. The sadhus are central to the Amarnath pilgrimage and receive a third of the *yatri* offerings; the other two-thirds is divided between the Brahmins and the Maliks, a Muslim family with ancestral rights to the cave. The *Lal Gir Sadhu* leads the procession and, according to tradition, is meant to enter the cave first. His white yurtlike tent, bedecked with saffron banners, is set up at the head of each camp, wherein is guarded the trident of Lord Shiva.

Perhaps owing to the shortness of their ganja supply, perhaps because they well know that they exist safely beyond the pale of ordinary conduct, the sadhus seemed in unconcealed ill temper and passed the time by baiting the patrolling soldiers. One soldier withstood this treatment for some minutes before barking out a rejoinder, at which, instantly, one of the more aggressive sadhus was on his feet, scowling furiously, and, having ripped aside the strip of cotton that was his loincloth and only clothing, with dreadlocks streaming to his ankles, attacked the soldier ("Beware! Beware! / His flashing eyes, his floating hair!"). A sputtering altercation followed, ended only by the loud, derisive, and generally insincere remonstrances added by the other sadhus, following which they all seemed in better spirits.

On this first night alone, a generator had been rigged up in the general camp, and the overhanging lights enhanced the increasingly carnivalesque atmosphere. We returned to our tent by the river, picking a careful path over the intervening field. Later in the evening, while having dinner in Ahmed's cavernous field tent, we were visited by a young sadhu, who sat cross-legged by our campfire, gazing at us with disconcerting self-possession. He did not feel the cold, he said, impassively, although his most substantial clothing was an elegantly wound tangerine-colored turban, and no, he did not want dinner. Digging into the cloth satchel he carried on his shoulder, he drew out a small purse, which in turn contained various personal treasures, each of which he displayed with great reverence. Chief among these were a scrapbook of photographs of the holy sites he had visited, inscribed "Sweet Memories," and his identity pass—good for free rides on public transport; the pass showed a serious, shaven-headed young man—his mother's son. Mother, father, sister, brother—he had left them all, he said, his infinitely gentle, infinitely vacant eyes rolling upwards, betraying the ganja influence. For five years now, he had not seen anyone he knew. His parents, he reported, were "delighted." He fell into silence again, then some minutes later quietly slipped away.

The morning brought a stunning sight: thousands of pilgrims squatting in the meadow, relieving themselves before beginning the day's march. Although it was still early, a busy contingent of *yatris* was already on the road. The next camp was only seven and a half miles away, but the journey was reputed to be hard, as from Chandanwari the *yatra* route would be little more than a goat trail and would climb to twelve thousand feet.

Beyond the camp, the land opened into a rocky valley whose mountain walls were banded with forest and glacial screes and streaked with rolling water. The trail traced the escarpment edge of the river valley, then cut sharply away and upwards, zigzagging mercilessly up the steep rockface for the next hour or so. From each new tack of this back-and-forth ascent, one could look up and see tiers of toiling pilgrims on the angular spirals of the trail still above. Now every strength and weakness was displayed to the world: Plump city boys puffed and panted, old women climbed at a heroically steady pace, and, in the dainty steps their flip-flop sandals compelled, the sadhus drifted by in packs, stopping for impromptu councils and a smoke in the grassy corner of a hairpin bend. Women in saris walked with collapsible umbrellas tied to their backs, carrying plastic bags full of their possessions and, not infrequently, babies on their hips. The overburdened ponies, resigned to suffering, plodded dutifully ever upwards or were led by overly eager pony men barreling into and past the other *yatris.* There were mishaps: an overturned dandy spilled out a monstrously fat woman, entangled in the many yards of her sari; ponies went astray on false paths that eventually dead-ended, allowing them no room to turn around. The dandy carriers were hired in groups of five in order to allow one bearer to "rest" while his fellows took up their burden; but in one astonishing incident, the fifth man flogged his comrades up a particularly steep ascent.

On the lawn-fine grass of the blunt Pisu summit, tea shacks had been set up in the foreknowledge that the hordes of thirsty *yatris* would want a short siesta. Businessmen, students, schoolteachers, widows and widowers, families, the rich, the poor, from every part of India, lay star-scattered on the grass around their spread-out cloths and blankets, a scene which put one in mind, at this height and under the hard clarity of the pristine sky, of a kind of Olympian picnic, rather than a sacred procession. This exposed summit had once been the arena of a titanic fight between the gods and demons. Major Rennell's claim that "all Cashmere is holy land" is substantiated by the *yatra* map. The land is contoured by the legends attending every stream, river, glacial pool, meadow, pass, or distinguishing landmark of any type.

At over eleven thousand feet, we were now above the tree line, and after the respite of Pisu, the land became harsher, its patches of pasturage fragmented between outcrops of rock and icy streams. As though this change in the landscape correspondingly signaled some radical shift in the cosmic order, the weather shifted, too, and became suddenly harsh. Clouds loomed up, not scudding, but in immovable blocks that banked the sky and settled in. A damp cold descended, and the long line of pilgrims pulled their coats and sweaters and saris tighter about them. Farther on, the land leveled out into an open upland valley, green again, but dull now and unenticing.

Ahead of us, a crowd of pilgrims had gathered on what turned out to be, on drawing closer, the edge of an escarpment that looked down onto the basin of a glacial lake, its turquoise waters so opaque as to appear gelatinous. Roughly a mile in diameter at its widest point, Sheshnag lies in an amphitheater, sunk below the level of the upper valley and surrounded by perilously sheer snowcapped mountains. Although fed by the many streams that course down its retaining slopes, the glacial waters enter its imperturbable depths with no discernible movement—a stone cast into these waters would not, one imagines, make a splash or ripple but, rather, would slowly be sucked under, as through quicksand. Second only to the Amarnath Cave itself, Sheshnag is the pilgrimage's most important landmark and is sanctified as the lake on which Shiva sailed with Parvati; in earlier times, pilgrims used to wash away their sins en route to the cave by bathing in its forbidding waters.

Like many rivers and lakes in Kashmir, Sheshnag is also associated with local superstitious legends. A *nag* is one of the powerful old deities who dwell in the mountains and who from time to time creep forth, snakelike, through sinuous passages to emerge from a mountain spring or lake. Sheshnag means "seven

snakes," a reference to the seven peaks that encircle the lake and
to the multiheaded snake once employed by Shiva to evict an
annoying resident demon. The snake is still believed to reside in
the lake, and there was sudden excitement when an obscure object was spotted on its surface by the pilgrims. The crowd began
to increase as more and more people were beckoned over to behold this phenomenon, which George, observing it through
binoculars, reported to be a group of ducks.

The sun had long since been neutralized by the clouds. We
were at over twelve thousand feet, and the air was raw and cold.
The second camp lay only a mile or so distant, and the huddling
pilgrims began to trudge on. At one time, the second camp used
to be pitched on the floodplain of the amphitheater, a site now
deemed too inconvenient and, perhaps, too close to the lake's
haunted waters for nighttime comfort. We did not share these
scruples, however, and our small entourage descended the slopes
to the valley floor.

The most permanent dwellers in this lush, if sodden, enclosure were two families of nomadic shepherds, who had constructed rough summer huts and bouldered sheep pens. They
withstood the light but penetrating rain dispassionately, their
arms folded under their tattered dark cloaks, their heads covered
only with embroidered skullcaps.

As the rain increased, we pitched our tents and crawled inside,
venturing out again when it had cleared some hours later—
George to go fishing in the lake, I to take a walk to the mountains on the far side of our valley basin. The scale of the lake and
mountains exceeded the mortal range of perception, and what I
had judged to be a short walk across the plain took me over an
hour in each direction. The peaks of the barrier mountains were
blunted by the heavy clouds and drifted erratically with snow in
a manner that suggested no particular meteorological pattern
but, rather, an occasional and random dumping of its burden by
an indifferent heaven. The lower slopes were swept with the

dark green pasturage that carpeted the valley floor and were sil-
vered with coursing streams that either rolled directly into
Sheshnag or, like a *nag* itself, snaked across the floodplain from
the far mountains before eventually filtering into the unworldly
clouded-blue circle of the lake. Clearly, the place where I stood
now, and the land I had passed through, represented an embodiment of the Romantic ideal of Nature—wild, lonely, and formidable. But, perhaps because I was sensitive to my voyeuristic role
in this pilgrimage of an alien faith and had become accustomed
to view my circumstances with detachment, or perhaps only because I was tired and numb with cold, I felt a strange and disap-
pointing emotional neutrality, a state of mind well known to
Coleridge:

> *I see them all so excellently fair,*
> *I see, not feel, how beautiful they are!*

I was forced to recognize that, not unlike the pilgrims, I had
come expecting some wild transport of the soul, the poet's Brah-
man. Instead, I found myself roaming the saturated valley floor
as I thought about a warm fire and my dinner. Nonetheless, in
this prosaic state, a kind of purity of perception was forced upon
me. Incapable of possessing this scene through some personal
emotional transubstantiation—the Romantic poets' "Intellec-
tual Beauty"—I had to confront and contemplate it as it was,
unembellished by flights of poetic or even spiritual fancy: a remote and harsh world that endured magnificently although unseen by human eyes.

Dinner consisted of two trout that George brought back in
triumph to the tents and that we grilled over wood coals. Some
of the shepherds paid a visit but showed little real interest in us.
We were transient phenomena and would pass in less time than
it would take the clouds to clear.

At night, the rain returned and drummed on the tents without abatement into the morning. We waited without real hope

for a lull in the weather but eventually gave up and ventured out to break camp and join the other pilgrims. This day's march is the most fearfully anticipated, requiring a long climb up and over the Mahagunas Pass at nearly fifteen thousand feet before reaching the meadowlands of Panchtarni, the third camp.

Over the lip of the Sheshnag basin, we came upon Wawjan, the camp in which the pilgrims had passed the rainy night, a grim conglomeration of dripping canvas mired in mud. The *yatra* route had been churned by the feet of the laden pack mules and ponies into a bog too treacherous to negotiate, and so instead, the pilgrims were fanning out in bedraggled bands across the slopes that overhung the path, following the intricate traces of the myriad goat and sheep tracks that offered surer footing. The valley walls narrowed and the hill trails became more precipitous, but the main path below, swamped as it was by rivulets running off the mountain, was by now no feasible alternative. The shale slopes blended with the unremitting rain and lowering clouds in an all-encompassing gray fog.

The increasing altitude had combined with the devious routes of the goat trails and the inclement weather to slow the progress of the *yatra* considerably, and we had been walking through steady rain for some hours by the time we began the ascent proper of the Mahagunas Pass. A stiff wind arose, turning the rain into ice, and the clouds moved in yet closer, as if to smother any ray of hope that the day might still be salvaged. Looking about me, I saw no one, with the exception of George and myself, properly equipped for the weather. "Sufficient woollens, raincoats, umbrellas, waterproof boots/shoes and walking stick"—the pilgrims' efforts to follow the *yatra* organizers' advice were everywhere pathetically apparent: cardigans, sheets of plastic, garbage bags, and fold-up umbrellas were now vainly unfolded against this mere puff of Himalayan might.

An old man wearing a linen safari suit propped himself against the hillslope and spat into the mud, and men and women

crouched vacantly, catching their breath in the thin air. Hugging
her knees to her chest, a white-haired woman sat in sludge, a
sheet of dripping plastic draped over her thin sari. For us, too,
well fed and well equipped though we were, the trek had become
a slogging ordeal; yet, heroically, humblingly, all around us the
stream of pilgrims continued in an uncompromising flow,
clearly fueled by an inner fire that we did not possess. Bare feet,
flip-flops, plastic slippers, mud-caked socks, and canvas tennis
shoes slapped and slipped into the mire under carefully suspended polyester or cotton trousers and trailing saris. I had read
in earlier accounts that the Amarnath pilgrimage had exacted its
fatalities through the years, but these had seemed to me to be
exclusively what they were—reports from another century—
and it had never dawned on me that in the modern age a pilgrim
might not attain his goal.

Traditionally, on reaching the pass summit, each pilgrim adds
a stone to the piles left by those who have preceded him, thus
building a shelter for other pilgrims and the gods. Few people,
however, were taking advantage of these crude stone huts: At
least the prospect of a fire and warm blankets lay ahead if one
continued, whereas there was manifestly no comfort to be had
on this wind-and-rain-harried platform.

The pebbled moraines of the declining slopes on the other
side were now interspersed with grass and, to my amazement,
inappropriate as they were to the misery of the day, buttercups
and purple Himalayan poppies. The sleet eased to rain as we
clambered down the slopes, terraced by goat paths, towards the
broad meadowland of the open Panchtarni valley, which was
crisscrossed with rivulets and the stone-scattered remains of the
beds of rivers now extinct. Five streams, believed to be sacred,
drained this floodplain and were forded by makeshift bridges of
loosely assembled planks. The haphazard descent of the pilgrims as they spilled into the valley from all directions and all
levels of the mountain resembled some desperate refugee migra-

tion, and one was tempted to search into the distance behind
them for the sign of an enemy hard upon their heels.

Across the welcome flatland of the meadow, the third camp
had been set some distance back from a low embankment overlooking the farthest of the streams. Numbed to the bone with
cold, we impatiently pitched our own tents some distance in
front of this, on the embankment ledge itself. A kerosene stove
was lit and its flames allowed to soar outrageously under the ca-
pacious roof of Samson and Ahmed's tent, and by slow degrees
we dried off.

As the hours wore on, the rain abated, and towards sunset
George called to me from outside the tent to see the path to
Amarnath. Impossibly, the weather had cleared, and the sun,
slipping into the gorge that lay at the western end of the valley,
briefly caught the thin stream below us, flaring it with unstable
gold. By evening, the heavy clouds had dissipated and by night
only wisps remained in a sky that was crystalline black. The *yatra*
is timed so as to bring pilgrims to the cave on the day of the full
moon, which now illuminated the valley mountains, showing
them as the icons of unassailable might one believes the Himalayan peaks to be. In valiant contrast, during and after the rain,
from dusk till evening, the pilgrims continued to flow across the
plain; and as time wore on and the *yatra* trail thinned out, they
resumed a single-file formation. Awaking in the night, I saw, on
drawing back the tent flaps, snowdrifts gleaming on the towering black peaks and, a long way beneath them, a wobbly line of
light from the pilgrims' lanterns descending the far hills and
inching across the plain.

The final day's march to the Amarnath Cave, now just under
four miles distant, is traditionally begun before dawn. At four
o'clock, we rose to a softly clouded sky and a clear full moon,
and an hour later, having packed the tents, we made our way out
of the valley, following the golden river path of the evening
before. At the mouth of the gorge, the trail abruptly left the val-

ley bed in a sharp zigzagging defile into the mountains. The rising light revealed that the day was to be as flawlessly clear as that
on which we had begun our trek. Although accompanying the
main body of the *yatra*, we began to pass pilgrims who were already returning, at this early hour, from their worship at the
cave. For the first time, this mass migration, this stream of refugees, this confused dispersion, this unwieldy picnic assumed the
unmistakable solemnity of a spiritual event. The narrowness of
the mountain defile in the first instance ensured a genuine procession, although the rapt expressions of the returning pilgrims
bespoke the fact that this communal undertaking had slipped
into a new dimension. Hands clasped as if in prayer, eyes shining, and repeating a murmured chant, each returning pilgrim was
greeted in Shiva's name with marked reverence by those still en
route:

> *O Bhairavi! O Parvati!*
> *It is Sidhi-Lingam!*
> *It is Buddhi-Lingam!*
> *It is Sudhi-Lingam!*

At the top of the defile, the road leveled out into a narrow,
gloomy valley, bedded with snow that had drifted up in uneven
waves into the close shadows of its walls. In careful single file,
the pilgrims crossed the snowfields, working their way towards
the scattered light that filtered in at the far end of this passage.
As we emerged from the underbelly of the mountain, the blue
sky again widened above us, and one saw a river below; up ahead,
gaping in the side of the sunlit mountain to the left, was the
great gulf of the Amarnath Cave.

At the river, the pilgrim men stripped down to their shorts
and the women disappeared discreetly behind stone shelters to
undress. The stream of Amaravati descends from a glacier peak
to the east and is the stream by which Shiva bestowed immortality on the other gods. Thin sadhus, stout businessmen, sportily

dressed youths, and elegant women together laid aside their athletic tracksuits, robes, saris, shirts and ties, raincoats and jeans to wash away their sins in the river and so enter the cave purified. The Amaravati riverbed is rocky and littered with boulders, and the river valley, although it opens up significantly from the snowfields, is nonetheless restrictive and steeply banked, with its peaks on one side casting shadows across its slopes upon the other. Long drifts of snow and screes of dirt and rubble that had ebbed or avalanched down the mountains revealed the glacial dynamics of the valley. Some particularly zealous pilgrims were rigorously brushing their teeth in the sacred waters. Farther up the valley, a large *H* was formed on the ground with white boulders marking a helicopter landing pad; it seemed that the prime minister had beaten the other *yatris* to it, having arrived for the *darshan* of Shiva Lingam the day before.

A wasteland of massive boulders lay between us and the cave, which yawned above the sacred river, a deep, broad fissure at the "waist" of the seventeen-thousand-foot-high mountain face. *Amar* means "immortal," while *nath* is a term applied to divinities. It was here that lesser deities pursued by Death had implored Shiva for his protection. He obliged by bestowing on them the waters of immortality but disappeared shortly afterwards to his own abode. The prayers and petitions of the pilgrims at the cave represent the prayers of the distraught divinities; for mortals, Shiva's boon is a release from the fear of death, not from death itself.

In earlier days, pilgrims had manifested their obliviousness to the physical world by emerging naked from the sacred river and approaching the lingam clad only in birch bark. "One who achieves pleasure in this cave by engaging in the Tāṇḍava dance, will be considered pious and equivalent to a god," the *Amareshvara Mahatmya* states, in accordance with which devout Shaivists used to dance naked about the lingam. The mode of worship followed today presents a far more improbable sight—thousands of men and women standing patiently in a winding queue on rock-cut steps, at nearly thirteen thousand feet, amid snow-capped mountains, awaiting their turn in the carefully controlled access to the cave. Two iron guardrails spanned the cave's 150-foot-wide mouth to channel the entering and exiting crowds, and at the threshold, pilgrims were bade to remove their shoes and store them for safekeeping on a convenient rack that was overseen by two old men who acted as guards.

The damp stone was as cold as ice beneath our feet when we inched towards the deeper recesses of the cave. Although the pilgrims were packed together and by necessity virtually stationary, their faces conveyed an extraordinary impression of agitated, restless movement in the crowd: anticipation, trembling zeal, sheer bliss—the ferment of many souls was written nakedly on those expectant faces. A contained roar of voices and the clapping of hands made me turn; following the crowd's pointing fingers and uplifted hands, I saw pigeons sailing out from a niche in the cave roof some 160 feet above us and into the sunlight of the valley. These are the manifestations of Shiva and Parvati, which the ancient texts claim with confidence will play a part in each *darshan*.

We had ascended the steps up to a marbled stone platform before the entrance to the sanctum sanctorum of the inner cave, which was flanked on each side by sadhus—the one on the left engrossed in a holy book, the one on the right receiving cash offerings. At this point, a large bell was vigorously rung by each pilgrim on mounting the platform. Set some distance away from the steps was a small shrine consisting of statues of Shiva, Parvati, and a black stone lingam; before this collection, many, but not all, of the pilgrims prostrated themselves, touching each object with reverential hands. Higher up the marbled steps, in a niche between the cave and the platform, lay two more sadhus, sprawled in a web of orange scarves and paper money.

A high iron grille rose from the back of the platform, almost obscuring the ice lingam, which could just be glimpsed behind it. The old man immediately in front of me finally succeeded, after many attempts, in lighting a stick of incense with trembling hands. We drew even with the rail and at last confronted the miracle of ice—a milky yellow column some seven feet in height, festooned with scarves and tinsel and scattered with rose petals. Delicately preserved beneath its surface lay the offerings of past years—leaves and yellow, white, and red flower petals that had been trapped in the clouded ice by the thawing and re-formation of the lingam. Two soldiers waved us on: Eight thousand people are a lot to monitor, and the moment of religious ecstasy must be carefully rationed. Passing before the shrine, each pilgrim received the *tilaka*, the red forehead mark worn by the devout Hindu, from the hands of one of the soldiers.

Guided by the guardrails, we processed along the back of the cave, passing a long, low ledge of ice. The official story of the ice is that Shiva melted himself and then froze into a lingam for the amusement of Parvati, who worshipped him in this form. A more prosaic, and less suggestive, explanation is that several springs issue forth from the back of the cave and, because of the peculiar formation and pressure of their fissures, well up in a manner that forms the distinctive ice masses.

From the rock wall above the ledge of ice, a small group of successful pilgrims was busily chipping away souvenirs. Shoes were reclaimed and the custodians tipped. Outside, and looking back from the head of the sacred river, Amarnath loomed as a massive, unadorned black hole between heaven and earth. These glacial monuments! This fissure in the Mesozoic dolomite! This cave of ice! Better, surely, to rush disorderly and naked from the river than to worship in the rank and file of rock-cut steps and careful guardrails!

In the sunshine of the valley, many of the pilgrims now allowed themselves a well-earned break. Washing was done in the stream, food was unpacked, photographs were snapped, and naps were taken on patches of turf amid the boulders. Many, however, immediately commenced the long road home. This day's march was, in fact, the hardest, continuing back through Panchtarni to the camp at Sheshnag, in all a distance of nearly sixteen miles, and over the Mahagunas Pass. We arrived at our former glacial camp in the late afternoon, almost on our knees with exhaustion. But the night sky was as clear as the day's, and we were rewarded by the sight of milky Sheshnag under the clear full moon.

We encountered only a scattered remnant of the *yatra* on the next day's journey to Pahalgam. With their goal attained, the pilgrims could indulge in a leisurely pace, and the relatively few people we passed were strolling along easily or, especially if they were older, dozing in the sun on the grassy wayside. If indeed the *darshan* of Shiva Lingam brings an end to the soul's cycle of transmigration, then this was for them the end of the journey that would end all journeys.

WRITING TO HIS old friend Robert Southey, Coleridge, in a rush of nostalgia, suggested that "a Poet might make a divine allegory" of their parallel journeys through life. "O Southey ... a spiritual map with our tracks as if two ships had left Port in company."

The Amarnath *yatra* is the stuff of spiritual epic, and a poet could well make an allegory, divine or otherwise, of the parallel journeys made by the pilgrims and myself as we followed our different spiritual maps, like the song lines of unrelated tribes. And as the value of a map is determined by how ably it gets a person to his destination, I would have to allow the superiority of the pilgrims'—little else could account for the heroic completion of this arduous trek by the many elderly and frail men and women who, often by their own admission, under normal circumstances never walked so much as a straight mile.

Yet, in the grand picture, I am not convinced that the map of either of our tracks, or both together, adequately and completely describes the terrain we trod. The truest manifestation of the miracle of ice, bare of tinsel, guards, and patient crowds, may well be that which none of us will ever see. For which reason, when I build that cave of ice in my imagination, I envisage a winter journey, when the valleys would be white, Sheshnag lake an opaque frozen sheet, and Amarnath Cave drifted with snow and hung with ice beneath the sunny dome of the blue Kashmiri heavens; I see it as it must in fact appear during those iron months of winter when its paths are blocked and access is forbidden even to the hardy shepherds.

MOUNT ABORA
(and the Abyssinian Maid)

One of the books most widely read at the close of the eighteenth century, John Livingston Lowes tells us, was the Scottish traveler James Bruce's *Travels to Discover the Source of the Nile*, a work that has been called the "epic of African travel." Published in 1790, it is the highly romantic account of Bruce's six-year journey to and from the source of the Blue Nile in Ethiopia. Based on evidence in another of Coleridge's poems ("Religious Musings"), a Notebook memo, and his correspondence, we know this book made a great impression on him. The memo, for example, outlines his idea of using the search for the "fountains of the Nile" as a poetic motif. Bruce's description of the Ethiopian landscape and of his first sighting of the two fountains emerging from a "little island of green sods," a place held sacred by the local people, has, as will be seen, strong resonances with both Bartram's Florida and Kashmir, and it almost certainly motivated the conception of the "sacred river" of "Kubla Khan."

Abyssinia is referred to more directly, of course, in the weird and wonderful concluding cadenza of the poem:

> *It was an Abyssinian maid,*
> *And on her dulcimer she played,*
> *Singing of Mount Abora.*

It should be noted here that the earliest known version of "Kubla Khan," that of the Crewe Manuscript now in the British

Museum, differs in subtle ways from the version that was eventually published. One of these textual divergences is of crucial
importance to the issue at hand: In the manuscript, it is not
Mount Abora but Mount Amara of which the Abyssinian maid
sings, the later revision in all likelihood being made in the interest of euphony (Abyssinian/Abora).

We know, then, that Coleridge was, through Bruce, predisposed to things Abyssinian. It is therefore likely that another
memorable account of Abyssinia contained in Purchas's *Pilgrimage*—the work Coleridge had on his lap when he fell into the
reverie that brought the world "Kubla Khan"—would have
caught his attention; and in light of the manuscript evidence, it
seems reasonable to suppose that a chapter entitled "Of the Hill
Amara," based on a report by the Spanish friar Luys de Ureta,
particularly captured his imagination. This is all the more probable given Purchas's extravagant introduction:

> Many, many other Æthiopian rarities we might observe out
> of this Author; but (if it deserve credit) the Hill Amara after
> his description, may furnish you far and beyond all the rest of
> Ethiopia, as a second earthly Paradise.

Friar Luys, we soon learn from Purchas, never actually saw
Amara, and his account is taken from that of a fifteenth-century
writer who reportedly spent some time on the hill in the service
of the emperor of his day. By way of introduction to his report,
we are reminded by the author that, according to Homer, the
gods banqueted in Ethiopia and at this time bestowed on Amara
their collective gifts. Thus, the hill, "situate as the navil of that
Ethiopian body" on a great plain, is endowed with the choicest
of gardens, temples, and art. The hill is round and circular and
requires "a daies worke to ascend from the foot to the top." The
rock sides are cut so smooth and straight that it "seemeth to him
that stands beneath, like a high wall, whereon the Heaven is as it
were propped." A pleasant stream waters the gardens, leading

eventually to a lake. On the summit are thirty-four sumptuous palaces "where the Princes of the Royall blood have their abode," having been consigned to the hill fortress from the age of eight for the rest of their lives, so as to be safely out of the way of the ruling monarch and thus ensure "that one Sun only may shine in that Ethiopian throne."

Among the many features of Amara that would surely have appealed to Coleridge were the twin temples to the Sun and Moon, obvious material for his endlessly projected *Hymns to the Sun, the Moon, and the Elements;* the "sweet flourishing, and fruitfull gardens," which, burgeoning as they are with oranges, citrons, lemons, cedars, and palm trees, are reminiscent of Bartram's gardens of Nature; and, unmatched in the world, the wonderful library attached to the Monastery of the Holy Cross, a collection drawing upon the Queen of Sheba's private library, with lost works by such valuable authors as Solomon, Abraham, Job, and the Greek fathers.

The unconfirmed secondhand nature of Friar Luys's account becomes increasingly apparent as this wonderful narrative progresses, but there are, nonetheless, threads of truth woven into its glittering fabric. In 1270, the powerful northern Zagwe dynasty was overthrown by Yekunno-Amlak, who established in its place an Amharic "Solomonic" dynasty of his own. His death only fifteen years later precipitated a squabble for power among his many sons; and sometime between the years 1293 and 1299, Mount Amara was indeed established as a prison for princes of the ruling line.

In the early sixteenth century, invading Muslim forces under the command of Ahmad Gran swept down from the Shoa plateau into the mountainous passes that led into Amhara, where the royal forces had made a last retreat. In the years subsequent to the Solomonic dynasty's rise to power, Amhara had served as the unofficial capital of an increasingly strong Christian empire, and as such, it now bore the brunt of Ahmad's anti-Christian hostility. All the great churches and thriving monasteries were sacked and their manuscripts, art, and treasures burned or looted. Muslim chronicles of the time report an attempted siege by Ahmad's forces of the rock citadel of Amara, on which could be seen "a thousand palaces." The mountain citadel, after holding out for months, succumbed at last and its buildings were burned to the ground. It was the last time that Mount Amara served as a royal prison.

Its use as a monastery, however, continued, and over the centuries successive replacements of the mountaintop churches of which Coleridge had read in Purchas were safeguarded by battalions of priests of the Ethiopian Orthodox Church, a distinctive and ancient branch of Christianity, most closely related to that of the Copts. Whether there remained any relics of the royal past, or of the days when the gods banqueted on the heights of Amara amid gardens and fountains, or of the matchless treasures of its library, I had yet to discover. But from what I could gather, an isolated monastery was still in existence on the summit of Gishen Mariam, as the Hill of Amara is now called, in the remote and desolate tablelands of north-central Ethiopia. This and the fountains of the Blue Nile were my next two destinations.

AS PURCHAS INDICATES, the land of the Ethiopians was known as far back as Homer's *Iliad*—one theory for the origin of its name is a derivation from the Greek *aithein ôps*, meaning "to burn the face." With a total area of over 470,000 square miles, Ethiopia is the tenth-largest country in Africa. Its boundaries are shared in the south with Kenya, in the west with Sudan, and in the east with both Djibouti and, traditionally a troubled border, Somalia. Following the outcome of a lengthy secessionist war, which ended in May 1991, its northern border is now with independent Eritrea, formerly its northernmost province.

Unique in sub-Saharan Africa, Ethiopia has never been colo-
nized: An invading Italian army that attempted to stake a claim
on the country in 1896 was resoundingly beaten by indigenous
forces led by Menelik II—winning Ethiopia marked prestige
throughout the rest of the continent—and had to content themselves with the country's most northerly tip, which they established as the separate colony of Eritrea. The country was briefly
occupied, for six years, by the Italians during World War II.
Modern Ethiopia did not come into existence until the mid-
nineteenth century; prior to this, it had been divided among different petty kingdoms. Its earliest recorded civilization dated
from the second millennium B.C.: the kingdom known as Punt to
the ancient Egyptians. The aboriginal inhabitants of the land are
believed to have been of Hamitic stock, related to the Berbers of
North Africa and the ancient Egyptians. In the sixth century
B.C., a south Arabian Semitic people immigrated to Ethiopia; for
the next seven centuries, this Sabaean culture was the dominant
influence. Amharic, the national language of modern Ethiopia, is
a Semitic tongue.

In the second century A.D., the powerful kingdom of Aksum
arose in the north, founded, according to tradition, by Menelik
I, the offspring of Solomon and the Queen of Sheba, and characterized in many important respects by the Judaism of that time.
Christianity was brought to Ethiopia in the fourth century A.D.,
and in spite of Islamic incursions that began in the seventh century, it has remained strong to the present day, constituting one
of the longest unbroken histories in Christendom. As a Christian stronghold in a continent that, in European eyes, was otherwise inhabited by pagans and Muslim infidels, Ethiopia came to
be romantically regarded as the lost kingdom of the legendary
Christian ruler, Prester John. Isolated from the mainstream of
their respective faiths by an enveloping hostile Arab presence,
bloody political infighting, and the country's mountainous terrain, Jewish and Christian sects evolved their own unique, Ethi-

opian character. The religious practices of the Falasha, or Ethiopian Jews, appear to derive directly from the patriarchal traditions of the Old Testament; the Ethiopian Orthodox Church
believes in the Monophysite, or single nature of Christ, as opposed to the more widely held doctrine of his human/divine
duality.

The Portuguese were the earliest Europeans to gain a foot-
hold in Ethiopia, largely through the agency of missionaries who
were bent on converting the country to a more orthodox—that
is, exclusively Catholic—form of Christianity. The Jesuits were
expelled in 1633, but a Portuguese presence remained influential
throughout the Gondar period, so named from the powerful
city-state that dominated Ethiopia from this date until 1855.
Modern unification of the kingdom's disparate and contentious
factions began at the close of the Gondar period and continued
until the death of Menelik II in 1913. The country's internation-
ally best-known ruler, the Emperor Haile Selassie ("the Lion of
Judah," "the King of Kings"), came to power as regent in 1917
and as emperor in 1930.

After World War II, Selassie resumed his attempts to mod-
ernize his kingdom. His attention, however, was largely focused
on the urban centers, while the countryside remained in the
thrall of a virtually feudal system. In 1973, a famine in the northern provinces that resulted in the loss of at least 100,000 lives
served to fuel increasing discontent with the country's leader-
ship. In the wake of a succession of popular strikes and mutinies
within the army, Selassie was deposed in 1974. A governing national committee called the Derg (literally "committee" in Amharic) was established, its membership drawn from military
personnel. Members of the old imperial guard were spirited
away, to imprisonment and often death. The emperor's murder
followed in 1977, according to most sources by the command, if
not the actual hand, of his eventual successor, the sinister Col.
Mengistu Haile Mariam.

of ways of getting to Bahar Dar, my first destination and the town closest to Lake Tana—by air or a two-day bus journey, for example—but the extra leg to Gishe Abay was more problematic. Petrol supplies in Bahar Dar were unreliable and there could be no guarantee that I would find local means of reaching the Nile fountains. As for Gishen Mariam, four-wheel-drive transportation of some kind was an absolute necessity, the mountain road being by all reports rough at the best of times and currently in a very poor state of repair. Again, local transport could get me as far as Dessie, the capital of the Wollo district, in which Gishen Mariam lay; transport—and petrol—from Dessie to the monastery, however, proved impossible to requisition in advance. All local four-wheel-drive vehicles were in the possession of the several relief agencies that operate out of Dessie, and their priorities, reasonably, did not include day trips to mountaintop monasteries of poetic interest. Nor was it possible to rent a vehicle in Dessie itself, which meant that my best bet was to finalize all transactions beforehand in Addis.

The transportation dilemma is worth spelling out in detail because it is illustrative of Ethiopia's very basic infrastructure problems and it helps to explain its earlier attitude to tourism. In the past, a visitor had to submit every aspect of the most modest itinerary to the scrutiny of a single government agency, the notorious National Tourist Organization, or NTO. Even a short excursion within the Addis city limits would require the presentation of a list of specific destinations and advance payment at an extortionate rate for a car and driver for a specified block of time. Individual tourism anywhere outside Addis was also made as difficult and as expensive as possible, and it required a battery of official permits for preapproved routes. Today, one can travel freely from district to district with a minimum of bureaucratic hassle. Rented transportation is still astronomically expensive but, one has to acknowledge, understandably so: In spite of the rough terrain and roads, there are few four-wheel-drive vehicles in the country in the first place, and the petrol supply is a chronic problem, especially in view of the daunting number of uses to which it must be put in the interest of rebuilding this battered nation. As a result of this new attitude towards tourism, envisaged as a not-unimportant component of the rebuilding effort, a number of private tour companies have opened up, breaking the NTO monopoly. After extensive inquiries, a small company called Caravan Tour and Travel looked the most promising; unusually, it was run by a woman.

Samia Saleh Kebire was a beautiful, extremely elegant woman in her mid-thirties, with a face that radiated intelligence and a manner that indicated a can-do entrepreneurial talent. In addition to running her business, she had three children to raise from a marriage her parents had arranged for her at the age of seventeen to a considerably older man, who, for his part, had determined to make her his wife when he had first met her four years before. This matrimonial method had, in Samia's case, something to recommend it, for seventeen years later the marriage was clearly a very happy one. A photograph I later saw of Samia showed her in traditional Tigrayan dress—robed, veiled, her eyes heavily kohled, and wearing a sweeping gold ring through her nose. She was excited and intrigued by my trip, never having heard of, let alone been to, my specific destinations. Her enthusiasm visibly increased with each meeting, and I knew that she was doing extensive homework behind the scenes. Having put myself in her hands, I was told to relax and look around the city while she negotiated through her considerable network of contacts for petrol supplies, drivers, and boat time on the lake.

"I am thinking it is better that I go with you to Bahar Dar," she said with studied nonchalance a few days later. "That way, I can see that everything is in order. Because this is special, I do not want to leave it to the boys." The boys, it would turn out, were her string of grown male employees.

Relieved of all responsibilities, I passed a few desultory days in Addis, taking in all the "sights"—the National Museum housed in Haile Selassie's former palace, the market, the shops, the grandiose Soviet-style Revolutionary Square—and pacing the streets, often in the drizzle. The swimming pool at the Hilton was built over a hot spring, and I availed myself of this amenity on a daily basis. It was in the nearby coffee shop that I came across a television schedule and learned that CNN was available around the clock and that Agatha Christie's *Death on the Nile* was being shown that night.

I was staying in a rambling, pleasantly seedy colonial-looking hotel set among gardens and conveniently central to the town. The somewhat gloomy lobby was invariably filled with crowds of foreigners, mostly on business. The majority were lone Europeans, whose eyes tended to search out each new white face, looking for possible contact, or, alternatively, to avoid it studiously. A caftaned West African strode in, escorted by a flotilla of enormous turbaned women, who were jointly received by the Ethiopian hotel staff with noticeable distaste. A professionally charming Rasta man held permanent court, usually either waiting for or entertaining journalists: Ethiopia is, of course, the Rastafarian Zion, and there is a small settlement of Jamaicans south of Addis. More and more visitors arrived—who were all these foreigners crowding Prester John's lost kingdom?

In the hotel lobby, I also learned of the curious fate of a local hermit, one of the many holy ascetics who live the life of a biblical prophet in various parts of the Ethiopian wilderness. The man in question was on the eve of departure for the United States, having had the dubious good fortune to have been the object of a Californian woman's visionary dream. She was certain she had found the very prophet of her dream—or so she claimed—the one who would be her salvation and that of a great many other people. Abandoning her Pentecostal Church, she had converted to the faith of the Orthodox Abyssinians, coming to Ethiopia on a dream and a prayer to take the hermit home with her to California; to do what, no one knew, as she spoke no Ethiopian language, and the prophet no English.

In Addis, the Ethiopians I met were well informed about the West; all who could had followed the Gulf War on CNN with passionate attention, and they were remarkably up-to-date on the upcoming American presidential election. I, on the other hand, became increasingly aware of my cursory knowledge of Ethiopian history—there had been Haile Selassie, and of course the Italians, and some very bad years, and now things were much better. And so again, in Prester John's legendary realm, I found the tables turned. "The new countries do not interest me so much," Samia would later tell me, wrinkling her nose. I had asked whether she had any desire to visit the United States. "Me, I prefer the ancient cultures, like in Italy. I adore Italy. Have you been to Cortona? No? But it is so near Florence. It is one of my favorite places in the world."

ON THE MORNING of our departure, I was awakened by a woman's voice, strident, indignant, and English, rising from the garden below my window. "What do you mean you don't know what it is? It's your national *bird.*"

In the breakfast room, every window table was taken by a solitary European with a book propped up in front of him. At the center tables, Africans sat in couples, animatedly talking business, or in family groups.

After breakfast, while buying postcards at the small hotel gift shop, I ran across the owner of the voice that had awakened me, a thin, drawn-looking Englishwoman who was taking her leave, reluctantly it seemed, of the Ethiopian woman who ran the shop.

"Yes. Well, I enjoyed the coffee," she said in a somewhat haughty, piercing English voice.

"You can come back. Don't worry, we can do it again," the

proprietress replied languidly, cutting through the shrill diffidence to the lonely, displaced core.

THE ARRANGEMENTS MADE by Caravan Tour and Travel on my behalf included flying to Bahar Dar from Addis. At the airport, the sky was lowering and stormy. When our flight was announced, Samia and I filed out with the other passengers onto the tarmac, where two planes were awaiting, their gangways down. One was absurdly small and propellered, the other a tidy miniature jet. I marched decisively towards the latter.

"It is this one over here," Samia called to me from under the wings of the first plane, where the eight other passengers were regarding me curiously from the gangway ladder. We were delayed from takeoff while attempts were made by the land crew to hunt down a spare Ethiopian Air official to enact the duties of flight attendant on the spur of the moment. Wise men all, they had placed themselves well out of sight, and an hour passed before a candidate was driven up the gangway and the plane's tiny door closed inexorably behind him.

The weather was judged to be holding and we were cleared for takeoff, although there was the chance that an in-flight route change might deposit us someplace other than the scheduled destination. Bad weather made this standard rainy-season procedure.

"Ethiopian Air is the best airline in Africa," I recited to myself as we took off, an incantation that was, in fact, true. Outside Addis, the mountainous slopes that fell away from the city were thickly wooded and I realized with a start that this forest coverage had once been extensive—that this was what, in a more generous age, the entire land had looked like where it was now plucked bare. The plane danced and slipped in the sky and I cast a covert glance at Samia, who was leaning back in her chair composedly, albeit with her eyes closed. I was quietly sick in my airline bag, something I had never succumbed to before.

"It is because we are sitting near the front of the plane, over the propellers," I explained to Samia, who raised her eyebrows and nodded slowly. Below us, under thunderous, careering shadows, the earth was parched and brown, rent here and there by massive abyssal clefts and canyons whose depths showed only as dark patches from the clouds. An eternity later, I opened my eyes, to find that the day had become brisk and sunny and that we were skittering towards a great lake.

I leaned towards my window, hoping to catch a glimpse of the Nile, here at the commencement of its 2,750-mile course to the Mediterranean. A dirty brown but nonetheless impressive river could be seen winding across the plain that spread outside the town we were now approaching. Skirting its shore, our flight revealed that the water of Lake Tana was—truly—eau de nil, pea soup turning abruptly to deep coral-reef blue around its jagged jetties of land.

What is wrong with this picture? I wondered to myself as we touched down and coasted towards the terminal building. Its right side was slouching and it was in general poor repair, but there was something else amiss that I could not immediately put my finger on. As we drew closer, the "building" was revealed to be a lone facade; behind its one surviving wall lay only charred rubble.

"The fighting was very bad here, all around Bahar Dar," said Samia. "The people really suffered." The airport had been bombed and all that remained usable was the runway on which we had landed. While we talked, the plane's luggage was unloaded and piled onto a cumbersome trolley, which was then manually and laboriously dragged up the road leading from the airport. The laborers in question were not in uniform, but I assumed these were official duties they had undertaken; even the formality of a luggage trolley seemed a miracle of courtesy under the circumstances.

A group of cars and vans waited some distance up the road to claim the passengers—another token of unorthodox efficiency.

The van Samia had requisitioned was among them, and two of her "boys" were on the lookout for her. I sensed affectionate deference to her in their greeting.

The land was now very flat and the heat fierce, or perhaps it only seemed so after Addis. There was little traffic and the roads were used less by cars than by pedestrians, most of whom were dressed in shabby Western clothes and barefoot. Some of the men had draped their heads with long bands of cloth resembling clumsy turbans, presumably as protection against the heat.

Bahar Dar lies on the southern shores of Lake Tana and has historically been one of the obligatory stops on a typical visitor's itinerary—assuming, of course, that the current political situation made such visits feasible. Its major attraction is the lake, but the town itself is not unattractive. Its outskirts are fringed with high grass, palms, eucalyptus, and banana trees. The simple mud-brick houses and shops are brightly painted, the roads wide and clean, and the central road, at least, well paved. On entering the town, one is confronted by an enormous billboard with crude but effective paintings of a distraught woman, a broken human body, and the head of Mengistu. One did not have to be able to read the lurid Amharic subscript to know that this was a testament of outrage over the torture and murder of thousands upon thousands by the Derg forces. The toll in Bahar Dar was by all reports especially bad. Everyone seemed personally to know of someone who had suffered.

The first day's program included a tour of the town and then a drive up into the nearby hills, along a snaking road shaded by jacaranda and other flamboyant trees and scattered with their lavender and red petals. We came to a halt in a sweeping circular drive adjacent to a promontory that looked out over the Blue Nile valley and Lake Tana some distance to the east. The drive behind us, as it turned out, marked the entrance to a grand house, guarded by an armed sentry and iron gates, that in happier days had been Haile Selassie's residence.

Below us, a band of lush grass on either side of the river

marked its floodplain. On the far shore, a faint haze of wood smoke hung over the trees and villages, blending easily into the benign gray twilit sky. In the light wind, the river surface was roughened into silver scales but showed no movement at all of its own—without reference to the lake, one could not have guessed in which direction it was flowing; but in a different time of year, between November and March, this same river would be raging over the valley. While the White Nile, which has its origin in Lake Victoria in Kenya, is the longer river, the Blue Nile accounts for over 70 percent of their combined water volume, a fact that gives one an idea of the extent of its full rainy-season strength. In 1990, this peaceful scene had been marred by a battle. The bridge leading to Bahar Dar had been blown up by guerrilla forces and some of Mengistu's troops who were left stranded on the far shore had attempted to ford the river at its height. Mired by mud, overwhelmed by the deceptively powerful current, and for the most part incapable of swimming, as many as three hundred men are thought to have drowned, and their bodies still lie somewhere on the bed of the Blue Nile. Indeed, the promontory, backed as it is by the Lion of Judah's "palace," puts one in mind of the kind of platform from which a latter-day Xerxes might survey his troops. One could well imagine the little emperor's somber pride and satisfaction in surveying this scene—one of the world's mighty rivers at his feet and the sound of his subjects' voices rising as shrill as a bird's cry from the plain.

There was time enough before dark to drive to the lake, where we found fishermen congregated under the boughs of an enormous friendly tree, chatting together in the dusk. Their boats, made of bundles of papyrus reed, had been dragged onto the shore and overturned to dry out overnight—each boat has a life span of about three good fishing days. Two little boys who had followed us to the boats stepped forward to report with some eagerness that historians now believe the ancient Egyptians learned the art of making their papyrus crafts from the Ethiopians, and not, as was formerly held, vice versa; this same information was to be conveyed to me on a number of occasions, and so it is clearly a matter of national pride. Papyrus reeds had also been used to build the rough shacks in which some of the lakeshore people lived. Lines of mules were being laden with corded bundles of cut wood that had been ferried over by these lightweight boats from the other shore. By the time we left, the night air was heavy with the scent of wood fires, a *textured* scent, resinous and grainy like good honey, that I have always associated with nightfall in Africa.

I had been booked into the Ghion Hotel, one of the two lakeshore establishments. The small complex of low buildings had been built by the Italians and used as their regional headquarters during the period of their occupation. It had been "destroyed," I was told by a local resident, around 1989 by the fighting, and so the mustardy yellow and green walls, the central tiny garden, the swept paths and flower beds were all evidence of its valiant resurgence.

In the forlorn, dark television room, the television was tuned to the national station, which repeatedly broadcast news relating to the recent unthinkable events. It was rumored that in the final, increasingly paranoid months of the Derg's regime, tens of thousands of youths—men between the ages of eighteen and thirty and considered by the authorities the most likely to engage in "subversive" activities—had been taken from their homes in house-to-house searches and killed. Like other inquirers distanced from the reality of other holocausts, I was aghast and uncomprehending: If people had *known* their houses were going to be searched, why had they not hidden? Why—with sudden inspiration, thinking of the silent, lightweight papyrus boats— had they not gone across the lake at night and hidden out on its wooded islands? Patiently, it was explained to me that if the sons had not been at home when the authorities called, their whole families would have suffered; that they arrived without warning; that if your neighbor was taken, you said to yourself: He must, perhaps, have done something to deserve this—for how else could it be allowed to happen? I recalled the numerous barefoot pedestrians, the roads empty of cars. How far can one flee on foot, alone, in a paranoid country?

The national television had been put to a novel and cathartic use. The survivors, the bereft relatives, the returned exiles, virtually everyone who was willing, had been invited to come forward and tell the country what they had witnessed and suffered.

"Two nights a week," said Samia, "you sent your children to bed. You did not eat dinner, but sat with the rest of your family before the television with a bath towel on your lap, because you knew there would be that much weeping."

From a cynical point of view, this could be regarded as a clever political ploy by the new government to rally a people, united in their outrage, to its flag. Yet few other possible means of dissipating pain and bitterness so constructively come to mind. Some of the survivors, however, are beyond reconciliation. One of the hotel guests translated for me the speech of a young woman who had returned from exile, where she had fled after having been tortured.

"I come back to kill you—and you and you," she said, pointing to the crowd and the camera. "You did nothing. Because of you, I suffered. I have come back to kill you all."

Bahar Dar, like Gondar, Aksum, and Lalibela, had been closed to all visitors for over a year. The few tourists who came to Ethiopia came for "adventure" and went south to the game parks near the Kenya border and to Omo, where the women wear wooden plates in their lips. With these inescapable facts continually in mind, I found myself, while sitting on the restaurant porch or on a stone bench by the water, regarding the revived hotel rituals with increasing awe. The bottled water; the coffee and tea served on a little tray with embarrassed apologies for there being no milk; the carefully handwritten daily menu, enclosed in a plastic folder and each day stating that dessert would be "fresh bananas"; the waiter's dignified walk across the lawn to take an order (more likely from an Ethiopian customer than from a European); the worn but clean tablecloths: How— in an isolated lakeshore town essentially surrounded by villages and bush, amid a population diminished by war and ravaged by grief and dispossession—how is one to regard these proceedings? As ludicrous? Or incalculably heroic?

LAKE TANA STANDS at an elevation of six thousand feet above sea level. From its southern tip, the Blue Nile flows forth in a southeasterly direction for some ninety miles before executing a slow curve and then winding north into the Sudan. At Khartoum, it joins with the White Nile, and for a few months from January onwards, the two rivers flow side by side, their respective currents neither strictly white nor blue, but distinctly discernible nonetheless. From this point, the united rivers are simply the Nile. Between its highland outflowing from Lake Tana and the junction at Khartoum, the Blue Nile drops five thousand feet, plunging through gorges so precipitously deep that they were not systematically explored until 1960, when an American survey team sounded their depths using helicopters.

Some seventy miles to the south of Lake Tana, in swampy ground near the village of Sekela, a small and unremarkable stream filters out of the ground and wends its way into the lake. Insignificant as it may appear by virtue of size and the fact that its actual entrance into the vast one-thousand-square-mile reservoir of Lake Tana makes scarcely any impression whatsoever, it is held to be the true source of the Blue Nile. This river is called Gishe Abay, or "the Little Abay," Abay being the indigenous name for what the West has termed the Nile.

The "discoverer" of the fountains of the Nile in the swampland of Gishe Abay was James Bruce, an aristocratic and wealthy Scotsman who in 1768, at the age of thirty-eight, embarked on his arduous quest for the solution to this most ancient of geographical puzzles. Little was known to the outside world of any of the realms through which Bruce would pass—Sudan, Ethiopia, even Egypt, whose great ancient civilization had in the eighteenth century yet to be rediscovered. A very few Europeans had penetrated these blank areas of the maps, the most important, for Bruce's story, being the Portuguese Jesuits who had lived and traveled in Ethiopia in the early seventeenth century and a French doctor named Jacques Poncet, who, at the end of the same century, in the capacity of ambassador to the king of France, had accompanied one of the priests as far as Gondar, just above the eastern shore of Lake Tana. The descriptions furnished by these travelers enabled cartographers to chart with general accuracy the location of Lake Tana and the Blue Nile; its relation to the White Nile was, of course, unknown at this time.

Very little that Bruce had previously achieved could have been considered helpful to him as an explorer. His most important assets appear to have been a facility with languages and an unshakable self-possession. Six foot four, powerfully built, and red-haired, he was a man who would have commanded attention in locales less unlikely than the highlands of Abyssinia. His consciousness of his own worth was very great, and in his eventual five-volume account of his travels, he allows himself much scope to assert his character. His style is somewhat Thucydidean in that it is punctuated by purportedly spontaneous speeches of suspect fluency in awkward situations. Arriving in Massawa, the Red Sea port and threshold of Ethiopia, Bruce confronts the sinister Naib (essentially a tribal chief) who has previously threatened him with imprisonment, starvation, and death, as well as denying him the authority he sought to journey inland.

" 'Whatever happens to me must befal me in my own house,' " Bruce reports himself as saying. " 'Consider what a figure a few naked men will make, the day that my countrymen ask the reason of this either here or in Arabia.' I then turned my back, and went out without ceremony. 'A brave man!' I heard a voice say behind me. *'Wallah Englese!* True English, by G-d!' "

Bruce eventually made his way to Gondar, at that time the most powerful city in the land, staying at the court of Tecla Haimanout, the fifteen-year-old boy emperor of Ethiopia. The country was at this time embroiled in a chronic state of petty but savage feuding and tussling for power, and life at court exposed Bruce to some of the more unspeakable aftereffects. On the day of his arrival, forty captured rebels had their eyes torn out before being banished from the city to meet their fate in the wilderness. One of the king's chief rivals was flayed alive and his skin stuffed and hung from a pole. Even peaceable court life was bloody, and Bruce describes in appalling detail feasts in which the meal's steaks were cut from a living, bellowing cow and eaten raw while the victim slowly expired at the company's feet. As Alan Moorehead writes in *The Blue Nile,* "There is an air of nightmarish fantasy about affairs in Ethiopia at this moment." It is highly probable that one of the incidents Bruce witnessed while in the company of the king (on his return from Gishe Abay) was worked into the final stanzas of "Kubla Khan":

> [The king] had desired me to ride before him, and shew him the horse I had got from Fasil. . . . It happened that, crossing the deep bed of a brook, a plant of the kantuffa hung across it. I had upon my shoulders a white goat-skin, of which it did not take hold; but the king, who was dressed in the habit of peace, *his long hair floating all around his face,* wrapt up in his mantle, or thin cotton cloak, *so that nothing but his eyes* could be seen, was paying more attention to the horse than to the branch of kantuffa beside him; it took first hold of his hair, and the fold of the cloak that covered his head . . . in such a manner, that . . . no remedy remained but he must throw off the upper

garment, and appear . . . with his head and face bare before all
the spectators.

This is accounted a great disgrace to a king, who always
appears covered in public. . . .

With a great show of composure, the king had calmly asked
for the *shum*, the governor of the district. "Unhappily," writes
Bruce, "he was not far off":

> A thin old man of sixty, and his son about thirty, came trot-
> ting, as their custom is, naked to their girdle, and stood
> before the king. . . . There is always near the king, when he
> marches, an officer called Kanitz Kitzera, the executioner of
> the camp; he has upon the tore of his saddle a quantity of
> thongs made of bull hide . . . this is called the tarade. The
> king made a sign with his head, and another with his hand,
> without speaking, and two loops of the tarade were instantly
> thrown round the Shum and his son's neck, and they were
> both hoisted upon the same tree, the tarade cut, and the end
> made fast to a branch. They were both left hanging. . . .

As Lowes says, this is not the sort of tale one forgets. And in
it surely is the inspiration for the lines

> . . . *Beware! Beware!*
> *His flashing eyes, his floating hair!*

Bruce spent eight months at the Gondar court before setting
out in October of 1770 for the Nile fountains. His description
of the countryside is familiar: There are forests in romantic
situations, a grove of magnificent cedars, suggesting a cover for
some savage creature. He reminds his companion that the Nile
water is enchanted. As they come near to the cliff of Gishe, the
ground slopes away in an easy descent, covered all the way with
fine grass. Melding with the imagery of the mountains of Kashmir, this is the landscape of Xanadu:

> *But oh! that deep romantic chasm which slanted*
> *Down the green hill athwart a cedarn cover!*
> *A savage place! as holy and enchanted*
> *As e'er beneath a waning moon was haunted*
> *By woman wailing for her demon-lover!*

Finally, on November 4, 1770, Bruce reached the elusive fountains, which he first glimpsed, following the direction of his guide's outstretched arm, from a hill on which stood a little church. Throwing off his shoes, Bruce ran down the hill to the edge of the marsh:

> I came after this to the island of green turf, which was in the form of an altar, apparently the work of art, and I stood in rapture over the principal fountain that rises in the middle of it.

Thus in Abyssinia, Coleridge discovered yet another "wilderness-plot, green and fountainous," and moreover in a place savage, holy, and romantic.

TWO DAYS AFTER our arrival in Bahar Dar, Samia and I waited in the lobby of my hotel, along with her two aides and a driver, for the car which would take us to Gishe Abay. Samia was wearing a light sweater of silky turquoise cotton over a slim floral skirt, open-toed canvas boat shoes, and sunglasses. I was aggressively dressed in a long, full *Out of Africa* skirt, a sensible loose cotton T-shirt, ankle socks (to guard against thorns), and tennis shoes. Caravan Tour and Travel might be my means of conveyance, but I was, for all that, going to the fountains of the Nile.

The way south to Sekela was over a modestly undulating plain, set against a background of more distant mountains. There were few trees, but the land was otherwise astonishingly lush; green and clipped by grazing, its wide tracks of hoed soil rich brown and moist—in every respect unlike the parched, desolate dust bowl that had been the predominant image of the Ethiopia of my imagination. Although the road took us, naturally enough, through the most inhabited places, the emptiness of this apparently fecund land, the sense of generous space beyond the roadside villages, was striking. One of the policies of the previous government had been the collectivization of settlements, which entailed the forced abandonment of traditional villages: An incongruous sight were the villages in which remnants of a hammer-and-sickle banner or, stranger yet, the face of Lenin still hung. Another factor accounting for the miles of uninhabited space was that in recent years people had simply fled as far from the roads as they could so as to be out of reach of the factional fighting.

That this road had once been used by troops was apparent from the number of burnt-out or simply abandoned tanks that had been left to rust along the edges; outside one village, they were being used by children as a playground. Several times, we were flagged down by strolling soldiers. Our driver hesitated and then resolutely barreled on; how seriously does a request for transportation have to be taken, I wondered, when the soldiers are clearly armed?

For many miles beyond Bahar Dar, the villages we passed were humble and traditional, consisting of conical-roofed dried-mud huts and occasionally cinder-block houses. In spite of the relative dearth of settlements, we passed files of people, the women usually shaven-headed, the men wearing their precarious turbans. The destinations of these endless lines crisscrossing the plains were the markets that overflowed at various points. The men and women commonly wore long white cloaks wrapped about them like full-length shawls, banded with red or green and, given the use they were put to, invariably grubby. The markets seemed drab affairs, peopled with indistinct figures carrying wares bound in sacking—a muddle of brown, gray, white, and tan so closely pressed together that one could make out neither the goods being sold nor when a transaction had taken place. The only immediately distinguishable commodities were the chickens, hung live and upside down from carrying sticks, all else being concealed in mysterious bundles.

Life from the villages overflowed into the road even where there were no markets. A roadside tailor was doing business underneath an umbrella he had strapped to his chair; a man ironed his shirt on the threshold of his hut with an iron hot from the coals in front of his door; a well-dressed cripple crawled on his hands and knees beside the road.

"Are you fond of Strauss?" Samia asked from the backseat. "I have a tape with me." We had thus far made our journey to the accompaniment of an assortment of African rock tapes provided by the driver, neither strictly rock nor strictly African. I replied that I did but that this would not make us popular with our companions.

"That is all right," she said with her winning smile. "We have supported their music now for some time."

At the edge of a trim village called Derbete, the road crosses the Little Abay, in this season a substantial russet-colored river. When the rain comes, it is "the color of water," one of Samia's two associates told me. There is in the bare landscape of the plains an air of contentment. The mountains are so far in the distance that they do not present themselves as obstacles or barriers, and one presupposes a way of life that has no need of their protection. The grass seemed even greener now and was embellished by clusters of low-lying yellow flowers. Trees, usually acacia, were still infrequent; of this same area, Bruce had commented that it was in his time being denuded of trees for firewood. Grazing cattle and goats abounded, and the conical huts we passed were neat and looked prosperous, a few of them walled or, less frequently, hedged.

The road skirted a sudden line of hills and then dipped behind them into a low valley. We continued through this pastoral scenery until the road deposited us at the end of a gentle ascent, beside a dark grove of trees walled around with stone. A large, elaborately thatched conical roof could be seen above the trees. This was the roof of St. Michael's, the church beside which Bruce had stood to view the Nile fountains.

Banging the van doors behind us, we disembarked, Tecla, Samia's chief aide, commandeering my small day pack: Clearly the order had been given that madame was to make her explorations unencumbered. A crowd of village children instantly gathered to form a horseshoe around us, and across the plain and dipping hills, herdsmen could also be seen approaching. From Bruce's description, I knew that the Nile fountains lay at the foot of the hill, but my view of them was obscured by a tree nursery down to my left and a small but dense grove of trees directly ahead. Samia explained to the crowd what I wanted, and they nodded approvingly, indicating no surprise at my request. The children scrutinized me thoroughly and seriously, with no childish giggles or squirming; but if any one of us spoke or smiled in their direction, they broke into enormous grins in such perfect unison as to appear choreographed.

As in Bruce's time, the local belief is that Gishe Abay first arises from its underwater course in the depths of mountains some miles hence but that it breaks into the open only here in the marshy land beside the village. There are two "fountains," or specific points where the underground water rises, both hard by the grove of trees at the bottom of the hill. One of them, we were told, lay in a "church," the warden of which would have to be fetched. The sun was high and intense, and Samia produced two small collapsible umbrellas to use as sunshades; under the shade of these parasols, we strolled down the hill, escorted by the moving horseshoe of children.

We were soon joined by the warden, who was an old man dressed in tattered trousers: Africa keeps one on one's toes, as a person's importance cannot be reliably judged from his clothes. An arched wooden gate, rather like the entrance to an English country churchyard, opened onto the grove. Across its stone threshold, a short beaten path led through the green light of the trees to a small pond that was enclosed in a kind of bower. Samia had not joined me, but had remained on the threshold, talking to the crowd; she was, as I would discover in the course of the many experiences we eventually shared, an intensely charismatic person, radiating both authority and a kind of maternal competence that drew people to her. Tecla, however, had come along, both out of curiosity and a concern that I might require something of importance from my rucksack: a notebook and pen, for example, or my hat for the African sun, my sunglasses, my head scarf to be worn as protection from the heat, my camera and extra film, perhaps, or my sunscreen, water bottle, Kleenex, extra socks, or Band-Aids. The pool bottom was dark with leaf mold, but the water itself was cool and clear, as befits a Nile fountain.

Outside again, we proceeded to the second and primary "source." Whereas the water in the grove had formed a still pool, that of the second fountain seeped forth to form a rivulet whose course could be traced across the plain on the outskirts of the village, very gradually widening and gaining in significance. This, the true source, remains very much as Bruce described it—a dark hole in the middle of a small hillock of sodden turf enclosed by a double ring of small stones, which Bruce termed an altar. If one stamps the ground from the edge of the marsh, the small dark hole of water shakes, as if the whole hill were floating on a river.

An impressive crowd of men and children—no women—watched me fixedly as I made my way towards the circle of stones. I had taken off my shoes so as not to get them wet, and this, too, they had watched with intense interest. Samia asked whether I wanted a photograph taken—well, why not?—and I assented. The children were extraordinarily well mannered, scuttling aside so as not to spoil the picture, but beaming delightedly if asked to pose.

At the end of our excursion, we returned to look at the church, which stood in its overgrown stone-walled enclosure. Architecturally, it derived from the humble village hut, being a mud-brick rondavel covered with a thatched conical roof, but its size and the intricacy of its thatching made it a commanding structure. It was firmly locked up behind closed wooden doors and shutters, which, together with the untended grass, suggested that the church was defunct; I was assured, however, that it was opened regularly for services. There are a great many of these distinctive churches throughout the country—the islands and peninsulas of Lake Tana are particularly noteworthy in this respect—often containing strikingly brilliant frescoed walls, dating back centuries, a testimony to the vigilant maintenance on the part of the priests.

A still-larger crowd had congregated to observe my perambulations around the church and its yard, and when I came to leave, many people stepped forward to smile and shake my hand and wish me a good journey. On the return trip, we stopped to have a late-afternoon picnic that Samia had prepared, sitting at leisure on fine grass in the shade of a wild orchard of low, twisted trees.

"This part of the country is beautiful," remarked Samia. "But it is a shame. I do not think I could take a tour group here. Three hours out, and three hours back—it is a long time for most tourists to see so little. They are not like you, who loves to see beautiful Nature."

As we approached Bahar Dar, the driver and Tecla began to laugh amongst themselves, and Samia turned to me to translate.

"They are saying the people of the village are so superstitious. As you were leaving, the people were saying that they could no longer use their water."

I looked puzzled.

"Yes. They believe, Caroline, that their water is holy and that a woman's touch will defile it. Many people come to the water to get healed. But now," she said, laughing, "they say it will not work."

With dawning comprehension, I recalled how Samia herself had always stood back on the perimeter.

"No," she replied to my unspoken question, "they would never have let me enter. But you were a visitor."

This incident was emblematic to me of Africa's at once great strength and great weakness; its people would endure to see their holy places trodden underfoot rather than be impolite to a stranger. It was too late to turn back and tell the villagers I had not known.

IN ADDIS, WHERE I was to spend a few days before departing for Dessie, the rain was harder and heavier than before I had left for Bahar Dar. The unpaved roads were swimming in mud, and those that were paved seemed on the verge of cracking open. People walked resolutely bareheaded through the rain or stood flattened against buildings and trees in an attempt to stay dry.

Back at my hotel, I attempted to get tea and something to eat at teatime, but the coffee shop, bar, lobby, restaurant, and room service were either closed or otherwise engaged, and I left for my room discouraged. Some hours later, however, as I was going out for dinner, I was accosted by the young woman who ran a small business center within the hotel.

"I have heard you were looking everywhere for tea," she told me urgently. "Please, next time come to me. I am always here, and I can give you tea *and* cake."

EARLY ON THE morning of departure for Gishen Mariam, Samia arrived at my hotel with the jeep and driver she had organized. The plan had been that we would drop her off at her home before setting out for Dessie. I was, therefore, somewhat confused when we drove out of the city limits and I saw that the driver gave no indication that he intended to stop anytime soon. Concerned, I turned to ask whether we had overshot a turnoff.

Samia's eyes were brilliant. "I cannot help it! I have to come with you! I couldn't sleep all last night, and my husband said, 'Samia, you must finish your adventure!' "

My impression from the air on arrival in Ethiopia had been of a barren land, a terraced palette of brown hues ranging from mahogany to sable that appeared to have the gently nubbed texture of worn felt. One did not imagine that this land was overgrazed, which admitted the unthinkable possibility that it had previously been green; rather, one accepted it as a specific form of terrain whose nature did not permit growth of any kind. Viewing other parched lands from the air, I have had a sense of settled, if beaten, communities, but Ethiopia, on first glimpse, seemed a land of almost biblical character—conducive only to nomads, to restless, weary, uprooted wandering in search of a place in which life of any kind might conceivably be supported. On the ground, this impression is both contradicted and substantiated, depending upon what region one visits and at what time of year. The land around Lake Tana, for example, had clearly belied it. But the harsh, rugged mountainscape in which Gishen Mariam lay seemed to have been fashioned expressly to test the limits of human endurance.

The countryside immediately outside Addis was dramatically mountainous and, under the lifeless sky of this early rainy season, somber. Apart from clumps of windblown blue gum trees, the land that rolled away on either side of the road was as featureless as a prairie, and, to my astonishment, extensively cultivated. Dark brown acre upon acre of meticulously turned soil but only a handful of huts were passed—where was the workforce that had so painstakingly transformed so many miles? The vast majority of Ethiopia's estimated population of over 50 million live in rural areas, while four-fifths of the workforce are engaged in mostly subsistence agriculture. But again, the recent wars had driven many of the people away from roads to safer, less accessible areas.

Gradually, the arable land gave way to more rugged terrain, and about eighty miles outside of the capital the road tunneled through a sheer cliff, emerging on the other side to overlook a spectacular and unexpectedly luxuriant upland valley whose terraced slopes and floor were patchworked with the colors of its various crops and fields. Here the air was bluff and cool; but on the other side of this, after some hours of further descent, we found ourselves crawling across the floor of a murderously hot valley of a very different nature; its naked walls were crumbling and powdery, the leaves of all its trees wilting, and even the desert-hardy aloes had dried out, uprooted, and keeled over. The desiccated bush sang like a live wire with cicadas.

Streams of people appeared, more than we had seen in one place anywhere else, walking barefoot on the tarmac road, or, if they were children, skipping and running and waving at us as we passed. Every male, of whatever age, was possessed of a long stick, which he walked with, carried over his shoulders, used to herd animals, or propped himself on when standing. The young girls were strikingly beautiful, their hair worn in thick, glossy shoulder-length braids that streamed behind them as they ran and large silver medallions flashing from their necks. But for all the life and energy exhibited, one was indignant for them—why live here when only miles away there lay lush highlands?

The huts one saw now were not even shacks, but haystacks, slipping piles of straw into which human beings burrowed to eat and sleep. Farther along, I noted with a kind of horror that the dry cliff face abutting the road had been terraced for crops. As if to make it definitively clear that we had entered a different land, two camels sauntered out of the scrub and ambled unattended down the road. There was a glint and shimmer from the river floodplain that paralleled the road, not of water, for the riverbed was dry, but the reflection of rocks under the bare sun. Later, we came upon a knot of people washing and sitting like blissful hippos in a thin, terrible trickle that had somehow appeared among the parched river stones. By imperceptible degrees, this stream must have gained strength, for farther down, the valley floor suddenly was transformed again, the floodplain now green and grazed by numerous cattle, watered by real rivers—and one's very soul drew a deep sigh of relief.

The town of Dessie made its first appearance as a ramshackle congestion of huts and houses slipping down the sides of a mountain. Within its bounds, narrow potholed streets led the way between lines of crooked buildings valiantly painted in cheerful colors—green, turquoise, pink—beneath their battered roofs. One felt that some deep force underlying the whole range of encircling mountains had recently shrugged and sent a ripple through the entire town that had made it slightly cockeyed. Balconies and terraces slanted dangerously and whole buildings were askew.

A number of signs indicated the presence of relief organizations. Between 1984 and 1985, Dessie was the site of one of the most desperate droughts and famines to strike the country in a century. In 1984, by outside reckoning, 7 million Ethiopians faced starvation, principally in the northernmost provinces of Tigré, Eritrea, and Wallo. The causes of this disaster were manmade as well as natural. The northern provinces have historically been so overcultivated that the soil has been depleted, and deforestation and loss of vegetation coverage have been so drastic as to produce a climatic change—the annual precipitation in these regions is calculated as being less than one-half of what it was ten years ago, a fact attributed by environmentalists to the loss of oxygen-producing greenery.

Coupled with this environmental desolation were the disastrous "reforms" mandated by the previous government, such as the collectivization of villages in conformity with socialist practice. Another human contribution was more sinister. The hundreds of thousands of tons of grain that had been airlifted from nations around the world were kept from being delivered immediately—and sometimes at all—to the most desperate areas. Supplies were diverted to pay off army troops and fell into the hands of high-up government and military officials, who could later profit by their resale. It is the belief of many people in the country that the ongoing border hostilities between Ethiopia and Somalia, which together with the secessonist wars with the northern provinces created 2 million refugees, had been deliberately exacerbated by the Ethiopian government so as to distract the attention of the world community from its domestic crises. Although there is currently no famine in Ethiopia, the afflicted regions have not recovered from their recent tribulation, which upset the traditional rhythm of food production and brought on its heels livestock and agricultural diseases.

Samia and I checked into Dessie's cheerless government-owned hotel. The dust from the road had made us both several shades darker than our respective natural colors, but there was no running water available and we had to make do with bucket showers.

In the middle of the night, I awoke, to hear distant gunfire; at breakfast the next morning I asked Samia about it.

"Yes, I heard it, too. But the weapons, they were not very modern." She laughed. "You see, we have all become arms experts over the years." In Addis, there had been long periods in which gunfire had been part of daily life. During one grim period, city residents on their way to work in the morning had routinely confronted the victims of the night before laid out in the streets with warning signs nailed to their corpses.

After breakfast, the driver, who had stayed with relatives, took Samia and me and a local friend of hers named Esewbalu to the market to buy food for the long journey to Gishen Mariam. Esewbalu was an earnest, pleasant young man who worked for the Ministry of Sports and Culture and who had taught himself English, as so many young people in Africa do, primarily by listening to English-language radio. The market here at least was well supplied, with papaya, sugarcane, bags of herbs, potatoes, and chickens ferried in and out by bellowing camels and heavily laden women. Our driver was a small, dainty-featured man who maintained a serene and distant smile throughout the hours of arduous driving. Although he clearly understood Samia and me when we spoke in English, he himself said very little. Now, however, seeing that I was intrigued with the market, he volunteered his observations, at the same time revealing that there are fonts of English instruction other than the Voice of America.

"You notice it is crowded?" he asked. "Many people have come here because of the relief. There is no work, and many people are filling the town. There are loiterers. There are thieves, vagabonds, and brigands."

GISHEN MARIAM, HIGH in the Ambasel range, is only forty miles or so north of Dessie on a map, but the drive would demand five hours, owing to the brutally rugged road. The monastic tradition in Ethiopia is ancient and widespread, dating from the fifth century, when it is said to have been introduced by Syrian monks. Under Haile Selassie, the Ethiopian Orthodox faith was decreed the state religion, a status it lost under the Marxist regime. Although Gishen Mariam is today still the focus of an annual pilgrimage, it is by no means one of the better-known monastic sites. The legendary rock-hewn church of remote Lalibela, dating from the twelfth century, is probably the most famous; the most intriguing may be St. Mary's Church at Aksum, which claims possession of the original Ark of the Covenant, said to have been taken out of Israel in the tenth century

B.C. by Menelik I, the son of Solomon and the founder of the
Ethiopian royal line. From everything I had heard and read, the
modern priesthood, which was particularly strong in the countryside, represented an ancient, venerable, and well-schooled tradition, which had successfully preserved its church's lore and
musical and liturgical practices throughout centuries of tribula-
tions. The priests are honored as prophets in their own country,
where there are today 18.5 million people of the Ethiopian Orthodox faith.

A north-going road from Dessie led us into a worn-out valley
etched by what in another season might be a river. At an oppor-
tune point, we lurched across, picking up the road on the opposite bank, which crawled around the crumbling mountains.
Road, river, mountains—all were the color of sand. Here and
there in the riverbed, one could spy pools of rushes or greenery,
but elsewhere only scraps of herbage survived, loosely rooted in
the soil. An hour or so out on the mountain road, we found the
way blocked by a giant cactus tree that had fallen from the overhanging cliff. Disembarking from the jeep, we began to dismem-
ber it, pulling its spongy limbs away after only a few chops of a
machete. Surprisingly, the sun, which was high and direct, was
not unduly hot, and a vigorous wind blew past the mountain and
down the valley.

So far, since leaving Dessie we had passed only a scattering of
huts, usually standing just below the road, with the tips of their
conical thatched roofs protruding above it. Now a man and a
young boy appeared in the dust, dressed in rags and walking
heavily under headloads of wood. Seeing us, they stopped and
unloaded, and with scarcely a word exchanged, they began hack-
ing at the tree with their knives. Samia and I, as the patrons of
the journey, were waved aside, and Esewbalu, presumably as an
educated man and therefore unworthy of manual labor, withdrew, and so we stood together, uselessly regarding the proceedings. The young boy, at nearly six feet, was strikingly tall for his

age and had seemed slender as he approached us on the road. Now I observed with shock that his long legs did not vary in width—that from ankle to upper thigh, they were no thicker than my fist. When the tree had been successfully dragged off the road, our two volunteers immediately took up their head-loads and started on their way; they had expected neither a ride nor payment, and we had to chase after them to offer our thanks.

Somewhat farther on, we came to a solitary branch in the road that was marked by a dented sign bearing the words GISHEN MARIAM in Amharic and Roman letters and an arrow pointing up the higher track. From this juncture to just below the summit, where we parked, the road was almost unnegotiable, steeply angled and drifted with rocky landfall, and on more than one occasion we had to get out and walk behind the grinding jeep. Unfolding below us, as we rounded each progressively higher curve, was a vast plain pillared with flat-topped massifs, called *ambas*, each so regularly etched with identical lines of sedimentation as to have clearly belonged, in ages past, to a single all-encompassing tableland. Disconcertingly, as if the disparate bluffs had only moments before been rent asunder, the mind's eye strove to piece them back into their proper unity.

We rounded another bend, and in the distance above I saw what could at first glance be taken for a man-made fortress, a mountain whose blunt panoramic summit was rimmed with a peculiar stratification of rock that lent it the appearance of an encircling battlement. Of all the mountains on the plain, I felt this had to be Mount Abora.

Our spiral up the mountain ended with the road, beside a group of huts situated on a small level bluff. Worn in the rock-face to our left, a narrow path, like a goat trail, zigzagged a short distance up the mountain, where it intersected a giddying flight of rock-cut steps. Surmounting these were the iron gates that guarded the only entrance to the citadel, imposing and fringed overhead by tassels made of tin that fluttered and rang like flimsy bells in the raking wind. A white-robed gatekeeper bowed

elaborately as we passed, his outstretched arm sweeping us on to
the platform of the summit.

The mountain takes the form of a rough cross, and we had
entered onto one of its transepts. A lean-to hut and bare flagpole
were the only outstanding objects on the barren rock plateau,
but farther on we confronted another, shorter flight of steps
running beside a thatch-topped retaining wall, which half hid a
group of huts. A line of curious children trickled out to watch as
we approached a church enclosure, which appeared directly
ahead of us, but at the sound of an angry woman's voice from
one of the huts, they vanished behind their wall again.

Kidrai Maryam, or the Church of Holy Mary, was an octago-
nal stone building capped by a swooping conical tin roof and
cheerfully embellished by a colonnade of pale blue pillars, towering red wooden doors, double-arched windows, and crocus
yellow walls. A young boy who had trailed behind us into the
churchyard volunteered that the church was kept shut but that
he would fetch the priests to let us in. After he had darted off,
we settled on the church steps and enjoyed the calm of the enclosure, which was set within a grove of blue gums and encircled
with juniper. The wind, the tintinnabulation of the tinny fringe,
and one lone bird were the only sounds to be heard.

A new messenger arrived shortly to tell us that the priests
would meet us at yet another church that lay nearby, and obedi-
ently we rose and followed our guide. The second church
proved an unexpected sight, being shaped like an oversized bar-
rel with tubby transepts, painted brilliant white and decorated
with crimson and gilt arabesques, paisleys, and other florid
motifs unambiguously borrowed from the Muslim world.
Crowning this phenomenon was a handsome conical tin roof
surmounted by an ornate cross that resembled a giant Christmas
snowflake. Set as it was on this remote mountain summit in a
desolate plain, in an area elsewhere reeking of poverty, it was a
resplendent, if incongruous, apparition.

The small crowd that had drifted into the enclosure to watch us now became very agitated, beginning to bow and genuflect in anticipation of the priests, who, sure enough, soon appeared, led by the abbot himself, a handsome, bearded patriarch, wearing over his slacks and tennis shoes a white robe that swirled in the wind. The lesser priests behind him were scrappier versions of the abbot, thinner, scantier of beard, and clad in grubby robes. On catching up with the abbot, they began an elaborate ceremony of reverential greeting, although they had essentially arrived with him. The abbot received his acolytes in a manner befitting a pope, gazing into the distance while each priest bowed before him and ritualistically kissed a heavy iron cross that he carried apparently for this sole purpose. First the forehead, then the lips were touched with the cross, which was next reversed with a practiced flip of the abbot's wrist, then the lips again: forehead, lips (flip), lips; forehead, lips (flip), lips. The abbot was adept enough to conduct this rite while looking skyward with an abstracted air. When the priests had been dealt with, a few of the bold ventured forward from the watchful, bobbing crowd to receive the cross themselves, and a couple of little boys approached the church to prostrate themselves on its threshold, kissing the steps and then the lintels. Finally, everyone was finished, and the priests and abbot looked around and rested their attention on us.

Samia and I greeted the abbot with respectful bows and Samia explained that we wished to see inside the church. The abbot replied that this was the church under whose floor was guarded the True Cross of the Crucifixion, and that no women were allowed inside, a pronouncement that was not entirely unexpected, this being the practice of many of the churches in the country. I now noticed that there were no women, or even little girls, among the people who had gathered to watch our reception.

"Oh well," I said resignedly.

"Go closer, Caroline," said my trusty guide.

I stepped tentatively towards the church.

"You can go closer," Samia directed. The abbot, however, called out to her.

"He is saying that you must stop at the stones," said Samia, referring to three large blocks that formed a kind of altar. "But pretend you do not understand. Go closer."

I stopped uncertainly by the altar.

"Closer, Caroline," said Samia as the priests called out again and began to address her excitedly.

Samia giggled. "These priests say that last year two women tried to enter the church. One became a stone statue and the other fell into a hole that opened at her feet." Samia turned back to the priests and then reported to me.

"I asked them how could that be? Before they arrived, we ate our picnic here on the church steps and nothing happened. Go closer, Caroline."

I stepped past the altar, and the abbot intervened.

"He says you can go a few steps past the altar. Closer, Caroline." Behind me, more words followed, but I sensed, without looking, that a tide of sorts had turned. Samia was interrogating and the priests were confusedly answering.

"I have told them that you have traveled thousands of miles to write about our country and that you will tell the world that in Ethiopia the priests keep their churches locked to the people. In addition, their road here is in terrible condition. Closer, Caroline."

Behind me, a directive must have been given, for a priest strode past me to the church, unlocked the doors and threw them open, and then vanished into the shadows of the interior. Moments later, a sudden flare of light revealed him standing to one side of the door, holding a flaming taper above his head. Dimly, I could make out a patterned backdrop of some kind.

"I have told them you need to take pictures," Samia called. "Go closer, Caroline. Pretend you cannot see."

I edged my way uneasily forward, waving my camera. I could now make out a large drum lying on its side on a carpeted floor. More words had been exchanged behind my back, and Samia called out that I should ascend the steps to the threshold, which I did, with no comments at all from the priests.

"All the way to the top step, Caroline. Can you see what you want, or should we get you inside?"

In fact, I could see all that I needed to. The back wall was hung with European religious pictures of a sentimental nature, flanked by worn floral curtains, which the taper-bearing priest had pulled aside for my inspection. According to tradition, it was under this inner shrine that part of the holy cross, brought from Jerusalem in the late fourteenth century, is safeguarded: Other scholars might speculate that the tradition of the church's name arose from the rough cruciform nature of the *amba.*

Of the estimated two hundred individuals residing on Gishen Mariam, seventy-two were priests. With few exceptions, all were locally trained, meaning they had essentially lived their lives on Gishen Mariam's summit. *Priest,* it soon transpired, was a kind of code word for "adult male resident," all males on the mountain belonging to this brotherhood.

I told Samia and Esewbalu to ask a knot of children who followed us around the *amba* what they wanted to be when they grew up.

"Priests," said the little boys, one and all. But the little girls said nothing.

"What about a pilot? What about a doctor?" Esewbalu asked them.

"What's a pilot? What's a doctor?" they answered. The priests are not required to remain celibate, and so most of the children on the mountain are their offspring. The boys, on attaining manhood, will be inducted by their older brothers and taught the priestly ritual secrets, such as opening the church each morning, sweeping it out, kissing the cross, beating the ritual drums, and chanting the liturgy. They do not necessarily have to learn to read and write, and there are no schools on the mountain. The girls, on attaining womanhood, essentially become the servants of the men—thus increasing the duties they are expected to perform—and produce more priests.

"And why not be a priest?" as Samia said. "And why not be treated like a king?"

The structure of many of these monastic churches—a rondavel with a narrow interior peristyle encircling the sanctum sanctorum—essentially precludes interior congregational services. Groups of worshippers of any size must be preached to outside, thus ensuring that the churches remain the exclusive domain of the priests. The churches are kept locked throughout the day and night and are normally opened only for cleaning in the morning, "when the people are away," as the abbot said. There are currently three churches on the mountain; a fourth is in the process of being built.

"Why do you not build schools? Why do you have no clinic?" Samia scolded the abbot.

"The people want churches," the patriarch replied with dignity.

Ethiopian Orthodox services incorporate a great deal of music and drumming in their liturgy, an aspect of worship that has its roots in the Old Testament. Gishen Mariam caters to its largest crowd at Maskal, an annual festival celebrating the original discovery of the cross in A.D. 326, by the Empress Helena, and an occasion that attracts hundreds of gift-bearing pilgrims. The pilgrimage offerings were stored in a "museum" near the church, to which we were led by a bleary-eyed priest, redolent of beer.

At the top of a flight of shaky wooden steps, a door opened onto a kind of loft, which was filled with neatly folded and piled-up rugs, row upon row of ornate prayer umbrellas, and, as in an opera chorus's changing room, a rack of sumptuous

silk and lace cassocks. A shelf of dusty leather-bound books—
sacred texts—stood to one side, while in pride of place at the
center were stacked religious icons apparently culled from gift
shops in holy places around the world. The treasures included
metallic wall clocks depicting the Last Supper, doormats woven
with the face of the Mother of God, posters, and other religious
curios.

"Cultural history," Esewbalu whispered, lowering his voice as
in a church. During our interview with the abbot, Esewbalu had
busily applied himself to writing down the holy man's *ipsissima
verba* as they fell from his lips. The pilgrim offerings provide the
priests with their livelihood, our guide explained, and from time
to time choice gifts are selected for sale down the mountain.

On leaving, I complimented the priest on the beauty of his
church, noting its unusual facade. He looked pleased and nodded, explaining that some one hundred years or so ago, in the
time of Menelik II, one of the priests had been abroad and seen
the gorgeous decorations on the mosques; he had subsequently
arranged to commission two Arabic craftsmen to decorate the
newly built church. When, after several years, they had completed their work, the priests took them aside and chopped off
their hands, for, as infidels, they could not be allowed to walk
away free after laying their hands on the church of the True
Cross. This story, whether true or not, may also reflect the tradition, reported by a sixteenth-century traveler, that any stranger
attempting to enter the royal citadel of Mount Amara was pun-
ished by having his eyes put out and his hands and feet cut off.

In the early evening, we made our way back down the mountain, the driver carefully carrying a bottle of dirty water and
some soil that the priests had blessed and sold to him. The wind
had become stronger as the day wore on, and the tin tassels
above the summit gateway were now jangling frenetically.
Beyond the gates, we met on the narrow rock steps an old
woman bent so low under her backload of wood that her elbows

almost touched the ground. Her eyes were staring and she was gulping for breath.

"Take your time, mother," said Esewbalu as she tried to step aside for us. "We will pass when you are ready."

"You are kind; you are kind," she replied, leaning heavily against the rock balustrade.

"You have come far, mother," said Samia.

"Yes," she replied. "It would not be so bad, if there were only water at the top."

"If the priests had to carry their own wood and water, I do not think they would live so high on the mountain," said Samia when the woman had lurched past.

We had left our departure too late. The valley, at a thousand feet below, so steep that its floor had earlier been lost in its own shadow, was now wrapped in a dull haze, behind which the sun was already slipping. It was well into night when we arrived in Dessie, our valiant driver having had to negotiate the treacherous return journey more or less in the dark.

"The way was long and dangerous," he summarized, turning off the ignition. "But we are all happy. Everything on the program was a success."

JAMES BRUCE RETURNED to England in 1774, ten years after his departure for Africa, with the expectation of a hero's welcome and a possible baronetcy from King George. In Paris, where he had dallied for some time before coming to London, the story of his travels and his bulky portfolio of sketches, botanical specimens, linguistic studies, charts, and anthropological observations were received with much acclaim. But a very different reception awaited him in London.

The sights and events that Bruce had witnessed in Africa were barbarous and strange beyond belief to polite London society, and Bruce was received at dinner tables and in salons not as a returning hero but as an amusing, somewhat pompous curiosity. In addition to the general bemusement he met, fate dealt him an even more damning blow: Of Bruce's many accomplishments, the one that in his own eyes justified and outshone all the others was, of course, his discovery of the fountains of the Nile. Now, as it happened, in 1618, approximately 150 years before James Bruce, a Portuguese priest named Father Paez had visited many of the places in Abyssinia recorded by Bruce, including that unprepossessing patch of marshy land hard by Sekela. A description of this site, moreover, was published some twelve years later in 1630 by a fellow Jesuit, Father Jeronimo Lobo; it is unclear whether Lobo himself also visited the fountains or if he merely based his written account on Paez's manuscript. In either case, Father Lobo's work, which overtly refers to Paez, was available to Bruce in English. In 1735, some forty years before Bruce's reappearance on the London scene, a translation had been made of Lobo's book from a French version of the lost Portuguese original, entitled *A Voyage to Abyssinia*; it was Bruce's ill fate that this translation had been rendered by none other than Samuel Johnson, author of *The History of Rasselas, Prince of Abyssinia* and the man regarded as the supreme authority on things Abyssinian, as on all else. Johnson's preface to the translation was, moreover, when read in light of objections that would be made, forty years later, to Bruce's extraordinary claims, presciently pointed:

> The Portuguese Traveller [Johnson had written in 1735], contrary to the general Vein of his Countrymen, has amused his Reader with no Romantick Absurdities or Incredible Fictions. . . . He appears, by his modest and unaffected Narrative to have described Things as he saw them, to have copied Nature from the Life, and to have consulted his Senses not his Imagination; He meets with no Basilisks that destroy with their Eyes, his Crocodiles devour their Prey without Tears, and his Cataracts fall from the Rock without Deafening the Neighboring Inhabitants.

Johnson's view of Bruce was that a man whose major claim to attention was manifestly founded on falsehood deserved little sympathetic hearing in anything else, a pronouncement that served to vindicate the increasingly prevalent opinion in London that Bruce was a teller of romantic tales. A supplement to the comic story of the extravagant "travels" of the fictive Baron Münchhausen was published and "humbly dedicated to Mr Bruce the Abyssinian traveller." The charge was even made that Bruce had never set foot in Africa but had hidden out instead in Armenia for all the years of his absence. Bruce's claim to have discovered an ancient painting of an Egyptian harp in a rock tomb in Medidnet Habu was singled out for special ridicule, largely on account of its popular conflation with his dissertations on Abyssinian musical instruments and on an unkind pun of *liar* for *lyre*. Egyptian harps, Abyssinian lyres—somewhere in this soup of associations surely lies the inspiration for the Abyssinian maid with a dulcimer in the final, "Ethiopian" stanza of "Kubla Khan."

In disappointment, disgust, and bitterness, Bruce withdrew to Scotland. He married, occupied himself with his estate, and locked away his voluminous Ethiopian material. In 1785, his beloved wife died, and it was perhaps this loss, which he felt keenly, that eventually rekindled a concern for his reputation and honor. At any rate, it was not long afterwards that Bruce turned his attention back to his old journals and embarked on the writing of a memoir of his Abyssinian experience. Although he had notebooks, letters, charts, and logbooks to work from, he preferred to work—at this distance of so many years—from his memory; and moreover, in preference to doing the writing himself, he chose to dictate to an assistant who struggled to keep pace with his flow of words. Unhappily for Bruce, the publication in 1790 of *Travels to Discover the Source of the Nile* only succeeded in reawakening the ridicule of the years before.

"The world makes a strange mistake when it supposes that I would condescend to write a romance for its amusement," Bruce is reported to have said to his daughter. In his lifetime, he never received the vindication he desired and deserved, and to the end of his life he was held to be something of an eccentric. After his death in 1794, however, little by little, different aspects of his account were confirmed by scholars and explorers. And in the early nineteenth century, in the rock tomb of Ramses III at Medidnet Habu was found a delicate painting of an Egyptian harp—and Bruce's name scratched on the rock surface beside it.

COLERIDGE, IN A passage from one of his more discursive late writings that could have been modeled on Bruce's story, tells a parable about "a poor pilgrim benighted in a wilderness or desert, and pursuing his way in the starless dark with a lantern in his hand." By happy chance, the pilgrim stumbles on an oasis of surpassing beauty. "Deep, vivid, and faithful are the impressions, which the lovely imagery comprised within the scanty circle of light makes and leaves on his memory." Frightened by a noise, the pilgrim

> hurries forward: and as he passes with hasty steps through grove and glade, shadows and imperfect beholdings and vivid fragments of things distinctly seen blend with the past and present shapings of his brain. Fancy modifies sight. His dreams transfer their forms to real objects . . . and when at a distance from this enchanted land, and on a different track, the dawn of day discloses to him a caravan, a troop of his fellow-men, his memory, which is itself half fancy, is interpolated afresh by every attempt to recall, connect, and piece out his recollections. His narration is received as a madman's tale. He shrinks from the rude laugh and contemptuous sneer, and retires into himself.

There are few better examples than James Bruce to illustrate the difficulties inherent in attempting to revive the symphony and song of an experience. Bruce's extraordinary adventures, generally, were confirmed, but much could—and has—been said of the manner in which he rendered his personal account. Bruce himself had been well aware of the earlier journey of the Portuguese priests, but his zeal for his quest, his desire to distinguish himself in some great way, his vanity, and his morbid hatred of Catholicism conspired to blind him, one feels genuinely so, to their prior claim. His description of Tissisat Falls, the Blue Nile's first major cataract, is entirely, perversely flavored by his determination not to see it as his Jesuit predecessors described it. And at Khartoum, where the Blue and White Nile join forces, how could he have avoided the apprehension that there was "another Nile" and consequently another fountain that had yet to be discovered?

All of these shortcomings serve to indicate the extreme difficulty of making objective observations about one's travel experiences in the first place, and of recalling them objectively in the second. And there is a further difficulty. Like most literary genres, travel narration is determined, if not to a great degree defined, by conventional dictates. For example, all personal accounts of this kind traditionally require a hero; specifically, they require a single hero, which assuredly explains why the European companion of Bruce's adventures—the gifted young Italian architect and draughtsman Luigi Balugani, who was present throughout the major part of Bruce's travels, and in particular when Bruce ran down the grassy hill at Gishe Abay—has been completely and utterly expunged from Bruce's story.

Moreover, travel narrative is by tradition an inherently romantic genre, in the original and strictest sense of the word, which was coined in the mid-seventeenth century when French heroic and medieval romances had widespread popularity in England. *Romantic* meant, literally, "like the romances," which were in turn characterized by "improbable adventures remote from ordinary life." Invariably, in the course of a journey one will en-

counter situations that, gratifyingly, fall within the compass of
this definition; but, increasingly, the realities of modern travel
cannot be relied upon to yield experiences that meet the old romantic expectations. And as one does not read travel literature
simply in order to relive the familiar and mundane experiences
of one's own "world" in an unfamiliar setting, the temptation is
very great, when playing the hero of one's own story, to dismiss
and edit away all elements that do not measure up. All good
travel narratives feature a trusty native guide, but he should be
dressed in flamboyant traditional robes, or, alternatively, in rags,
and it is distracting if this guide is a chic, sophisticated woman;
and it is downright jarring if the guide is unabashedly a tourist
agent. Similarly, one may not wish to read about how difficult it
is to find a car, about wretched hotels, or about flights to Bahar
Dar. No, a hero should set out from a tent or mud hut or pasha's
court, and the reader should be spared these tedious details. Historically, the hero of a travel story has presupposed a cultural
superiority to the country visited and a global access denied indigenous people; but now when the distant traveler arrives in
Prester John's kingdom, he may find that, courtesy of CNN,
much about him and his world is already known.

Neither the world nor our perception of it has yet changed so
much since Bruce's time that romantic stories cannot still be
written. The ingredients are usually there in most travel "experiences" and only require judicious editing. Certainly, I could have
given a more palatable, traditional account of a journey to the
fountains of the Nile. There had been some instances of sniper
activity, for example, and I could surely have played up these
dangers. I could have skipped the plane ride altogether and simply arrived in Bahar Dar. The Ghion Hotel on Lake Tana's
shores, with its flocks of kingfishers, herons, fish eagles, and iri-
descent starlings, with its frangipani, jacaranda, hibiscus, and
magnificent strangling fig could surely have been made more exotic. "Native" life in the roadside villages could have been made

to seem either more savage or more mysterious—and I could have referred to my driver but made no mention of my guide. In real desperation, it is of course possible to contrive difficulties. I could have insisted on hiring a mule for the last mile of the journey, or, alternatively, made my trip deep into the rainy season when I would have had to do so. I could have sought out the worst possible lodgings and then dwelt on my discomfort. In short, while the old epics belong to an age when the world was glamorously inaccessible, an acceptable modern mini-epic could still have been devised. The question is, Can one in good faith deny a country its painfully acquired progressions? Can one's experience of a country be tailored to the exigencies of one's own romantic quest?

The modern traveler will inevitably find himself walking self-consciously in the footsteps of an earlier, more illustrious predecessor, compared with whose adventures his own may seem prosaic and dull. Yet, for all that, even in an age when it is possible to take a day trip to the fountains of the Nile, I do not believe that making journeys even to regions increasingly less and less remote from one's ordinary life will cease to allure and fascinate or that accounts about these journeys will lose their charm. I do believe, however, that it will become increasingly difficult for the traveler to cut the dashing figure of the old romantic epics, or, like Bruce, to pretend to himself that he has done so.

ETHIOPIA WAS THE last of my destinations. My travels had awarded me glimpses—albeit scattered—of the landscape of Xanadu. Now, nothing remained for me but to turn to the place where it had been conjured up and to the poet who had dreamed it.

EXMOOR

*E*arly in the year 1797, Coleridge established himself and his small household at Nether Stowey, a village at the foot of the picturesque Quantock Hills on the southwest coast of England. His fantasy of a pantisocratic existence had by this time been abandoned, but it was his hope that in the isolation of the Somerset-Devon borderland he would be able to replicate something of the essence of his Utopian dream without a company of comrades. The move to Stowey also amounted to a renouncement of the other pursuits with which he had previously toyed—such as teaching and practicing as a dissenting preacher—in favor of a serious and single-minded dedication to his writing. His first child, Hartley, had been born in September of the preceding year, and this event seems to have acted as a strong inducement for him to rethink and refocus his life.

Financial realities, an uncomfortably small and ill-furnished house, and the dawning awareness that his passive wife, Sara, was not the perfect mate were a few of the concerns that prevented the actualization of Coleridge's dream of rustic tranquillity and productivity. His literary output was for the most part fragmentary. On the other hand, in keeping with his poetic master plan, he was reading voraciously.

"I should not think of devoting less than 20 years to an Epic Poem," Coleridge wrote in a letter to his publisher, Joseph Cottle.

Ten to collect materials and warm my mind with universal science. I would be a tolerable Mathematician, I would thoroughly know Mechanics, Hydrostatics, Optics, and Astronomy, Botany, Metallurgy, Fossilism, Chemistry, Geology, Anatomy, Medicine—then the *mind of man*—then the *minds of men*—in all Travels, Voyages and Histories. So I would spend ten years—the next five to the composition of the poem—and the five last to the correction of it.

These "Travels, Voyages and Histories" would, of course, be important to "Kubla Khan."

On a summer evening in early June of 1797, while returning to Stowey from Bristol after delivering some poems to his publisher, Coleridge made a detour to visit a young North Country poet called William Wordsworth and his sister, Dorothy, who were living at Racedown, in Dorset. Although the two men had met briefly in August of 1795 and had been corresponding and reading each other's work since that time, their friendship was not established until this memorable visit, which stretched on for weeks. Coleridge's enthusiasm for the Wordsworths was literally transporting, as he swept them along with him first to his own inadequate cottage and then more permanently to a country mansion in Alfoxden, some four miles west of Stowey. Once safely ensconced within the same neighborhood, the three friends embarked upon a kind of abbreviated pantisocratic existence, communing with nature in the course of long walks, conversing, and sharing their poetic interests. Both the letters of this period and Dorothy Wordsworth's delicate but incisive journal suggest that Nature served as a kind of fourth companion during this summer idyll—certainly more of a real presence than was Sara Coleridge, whose domestic duties tended to keep her indoors at the Stowey cottage. The weather, the landscape, and the different tones of the different hours of the day were reverently noted, discussed, and described in exquisite detail by the threesome, and it is not difficult to imagine that this cultivated hypersensitivity to the natural world predisposed Coleridge to retain and savor in his prodigious memory particular images of nature culled from his extensive reading.

Sometime in early October, at the close of this happy summer of invigoration and inspiration, Coleridge took a long walk along the north Devon coast to Lynton, some twenty-four miles distant, this time alone and without the companionable conversation of his two friends. On the return trip, he was struck ill "with a dysentry," as he later recorded in a footnote to the earliest manuscript account of this event (not to be confused with the later *published* account that prefaces the poem), and halfway home he turned aside to Ash Farm to spend the night. At least since the spring of 1796, Coleridge had fallen into the dangerous habit of taking opium, often for extended periods, in times of illness; now, at Ash Farm, as he later reported, he took two grains of opium to check the dysentery and then fell into the reverie in which he composed "Kubla Khan."

Ash Farm is, as Coleridge wrote in his manuscript account, "between Porlock & Linton, a quarter of a mile from Culbone Church." Porlock, village of ill-repute whence came the "visitor on business" who interrupted Coleridge's transcription of his dream, is a tiny community of neat stone cottages and steep, narrow streets, close to the sea. Its main hotel, the Ship Inn, is where Coleridge reputedly used to go to smoke, or so I was told by its manageress, who, spotting me as yet another tourist on a Coleridge pilgrimage, took a perverse delight in attempting to puncture any illusions I may have wished to cherish about the poet:

"Of course, by the time he ended up here, he was potty with drugs and as likely to be found rolling around in a ditch."

Turning inland on the old toll road from Porlock, I met another, more genial local historian in the person of the toll keeper, an engaging elderly man who had himself walked through Coleridge's local paces. He had also taken opium, when hospitalized many years before, and still retained a vivid memory of the ensuing dream, in which he had seen himself sailing down along the most westerly Scottish isles.

"I've never in my life seen them," he said, "but I *knew* that I was there. The man in the bed beside me was from Scotland and had told me about them."

Past the tollgate, the road leisurely unfolded through forest, which, on this defiantly brilliant day, presented itself less as a collection of trees than as a golden green ethereal glow, an enveloping fairyland ether more than a mere prosaic forest.

Ash Farm is in a lonely position, far removed from other dwellings, and reached by a lengthy lane that runs narrowly through hedges. On this day of summer glory, there could be nothing sinister about this isolation, but one could imagine how in bleaker weather, such as that in which Coleridge had most likely been forced to pay his visit, it would present a different aspect. Exmoor is, after all, Lorna Doone country, and the darker moods of its hills and moorlands are notoriously disquieting. An Esshe Farm is listed in the Domesday Book, and indeed the snug, newly painted farmhouse gave the impression of being anciently established in the landscape. On the opposite side of the hedge, a sheep baaed at me and blinked. For miles beyond, the grazed fields swelled and dipped.

At the house, I was greeted by an attractive woman with black hair and ivory skin who did not look at all the country farmer's wife. To my joy, it was possible to get a room for the night in the old farmhouse, and the next morning I was pointed in the direction of Culbone Church, along a path that rolled down the steep slope of the farm's sheep-grazed field into a copse of forest nestled in the valley.

The roof of the little church is first seen from the height of a ravine within the forest, and scrambling down the sheer path I found it to be set delicately in its own long-grassed valley. It is the smallest complete parish church in England, and its walls date from at least the twelfth century. The evidence inside was that the church, with its handsome bossed ceiling and intricately paneled pews, was still affectionately cared for, its minuscule congregation notwithstanding. Seen through the clear diamond-patterned windows was the forest, and it would be a devoted worshipper indeed who could keep his attention inside the church on a day such as this, when the green leaves and blue sky were in such radiance. But the principal feature of Culbone Church is its raw setting. Reputedly, it stands on what was once a Celtic religious site; and even if this was not the informed opinion, one would surmise that this was ancient sacred ground. The forest slopes darkly and abruptly down the close-pressed valley walls that confine the little glen, manifesting a wild, primal beauty that is completely unrestrained by the gray delicacy of the little Christian icon. Indeed, there was something helpless and forlorn about the very existence of this emblem of a centuries-old attempt to domesticate man's instinctive religious impulse. The little monument—so tiny because this was all the space the deep valley walls allowed it—only highlighted one's sense that tremendous, uncontainable forces permeated the woodland. Centuries ago, the parish woods had been inhabited by charcoal burners and a colony of lepers—a place holy and, in this weather, enchanted but not unsuggestive of archaic savagery.

Departing from Culbone, my pilgrimage continued, in reverse, to Lynton, which towers over the ravines and East and West Lyn rivers from its clifftop perch. Since the early eighteenth century, it has attracted visitors, and the economy of it and Lynmouth, its seaside "sister" village below, is today greatly dependent on tourists. The architecture of this spectacularly located town hardly suggests a summer resort, however, being heavy, oppressive, monumental, and Victorian—more evocative of a prison or workhouse than of anyplace one might voluntarily go for recreation. And yet, unlike the dainty and inadequate church, these buildings seemed in some weird way to echo the land's own force, which is darkly somber here, even on a soft July evening in golden dying light. Beside the village, the West Lyn comes pouring down from the cliffs into the boulder-beached sea. There are a number of trails mapped out for visitors that parallel Lynton's more picturesque streams and cascades, but in Coleridge's day these would have been left to one's own discovery.

West of Lynton lies some of the most dramatic coastal scenery in England. A perilous cliff line, swept to its edge by moorlands, overlooks the forboding Valley of the Rocks, which sprawls and spills into the sea. Strangely, the sea on this blue day seemed flat and dull, an impression that was perhaps exaggerated by its contrast to the marked energy of the convoluted rubble of boulders for which the valley is named—naked manifestations of the earth's latent forces. Without question, if Professor Lowes had never written his acclaimed book, one would turn here, to the scenery of Exmoor—the scenery, after all, last experienced by Coleridge before his reverie at Ash Farm—for the inspiration of Xanadu. Even the tourist brochure (which, by the way, makes no mention of Coleridge) written to guide the visitor around the charms of Lynton inevitably falls into language worthy of "Kubla Khan": "The wild and fantastic heights, making for precipitous hills, valleys and gentle streams, combine to make the whole area a paradise . . . while the romance of the place makes it a number one place for honeymooners." Or, more aptly, for women wailing for demon lovers (as a footnote, it is worth mentioning that the essayist and critic William Hazlitt, in a reminiscence of making this walk from Stowey to Lynton in Coleridge's company some eight months after his reverie at Ash Farm, recalls the "screaming flight" of the gulls in the Valley of the Rocks—perhaps the inspiration for a woman wailing in a savage, romantic chasm).

Coleridge himself gave various dates for the composition of

"Kubla Khan." In the Crewe Manuscript, he cites "the fall of the year, 1797"; in the published preface, it is "the summer of 1797." In his Notebook of 1810, he recalls the spring of 1798, while in "retirement between Linton & Porlock," as the first occasion on which he had "recourse to Opium," a statement that is manifestly false, unless, as his biographer Richard Holmes suggests, by "recourse" Coleridge meant his first use of the drug "for nonmedicinal purposes." Scholars today tend to support the October 1797 date as being most probable, although Lowes's preferred date was the summer of 1798. In either case, there is no reason to doubt the essential inspirational sources for the poem—the travel books cited in the Notebooks and the wild Exmoor landscape.

Between the date of composition and the poem's actual publication in 1816, there are strikingly few references, by Coleridge or others, to this most famous of poems. The earliest is found in Dorothy Wordsworth's journal for October 1798, when she and her brother were with Coleridge in Germany. This historic first mention is hardly illustrious, being based on a bad pun: She speaks of carrying *"Kubla* to a fountain"—that is, a *khan,* or watering "can" (evidently, Coleridge's pronunciation of the word rhymed with *ran*). Sara Coleridge refers to the poem in a letter as "Koula Khan."

More compelling is the description of Coleridge's recitation of the poem, before its publication, at one of Charles Lamb's famous Wednesday-night parties. In this account, Coleridge appears to have almost subsumed the role of the inspired, visionary bard of his own final stanza:

> There [at Lamb's] Coleridge sometimes, though rarely, took his seat; and then the genial hubbub of voices was still: critics, philosophers, and poets, were contented to listen; and toil-worn lawyers, clerks from the India House, and members of the Stock Exchange, grew romantic while he spoke. . . . Al-

though he looked much older than he was, his hair being sil-
vered all over, and his person tending to corpulency, there
was about him no trace of bodily sickness or mental decay,
but rather an air of voluptuous repose. His benignity of manner placed his auditors entirely at their ease, and inclined
them to listen to the sweet, low tone in which he began to
discourse on some high theme. Whether he had won for his
greedy listener only some raw lad, or charmed a circle of
beauty, rank, and wit, who hung breathless on his words, he
talked with equal eloquence; for his subject, not his audience,
inspired him. At first his tones were conversational; he
seemed to dally with the shadows of the subject and with
fantastic images which bordered it; but gradually the thought
grew deeper, and the voice deepened with the thought; the
stream gathering strength, seemed to bear along with it all
things which opposed its progress, and blended them with its
current; and stretching away among regions tinted with
ethereal colours, was lost at airy distance in the horizon of
the fancy. . . . Coleridge was sometimes induced to recite por-
tions of "Christabel," then enshrined in manuscript from
eyes profane, and gave a bewitching effect to its wizard lines.
But more peculiar in its beauty than this, was his recitation of
Kubla Khan. As he repeated the passage

> *A damsel with a dulcimer*
> *In a vision once I saw:*
> *It was an Abyssinian maid,*
> *And on her dulcimer she played,*
> *Singing of Mount Abora!*

his voice seemed to mount, and melt into air, as the images
grew more visionary, and the suggested associations more
remote.

The year 1797, which has been fairly called Coleridge's *annus
mirabilis,* also saw the composition of "The Rime of the Ancient

Mariner," and the first part of "Christabel," as well as "This Lime-Tree Bower My Prison," one of his most successful "conversational" poems. In 1798, Coleridge and Wordsworth jointly published *Lyrical Ballads*, a landmark of Romantic literature and of English poetry in general. Although Coleridge's role in this venture was at Wordsworth's instigation later cruelly curtailed, the original inspiration had been for the two poets to divide the poetical province, with Wordsworth taking commonplace subjects and Coleridge the supernatural.

Shortly after the publication of *Lyrical Ballads*, in the same year, Coleridge, initially accompanied by the Wordsworths, departed from Nether Stowey for Germany, intent on learning German and philosophy, which "philosophizing" was to shape to a great extent his subsequent views on metaphysics and religion. He remained abroad some ten months, and on returning in 1800, he brought his family to Keswick in the Lake District, not far from where the Wordsworths had settled.

Coleridge's health had by this time broken down, his most serious afflictions being rheumatic fever and opium addiction. Although expansive on the topic of most of his ailments, he refused for a long while to acknowledge his drug addiction, maintaining, to himself as well as others, that his use was only medicinal. He now made other excursions abroad, to Malta and Italy, principally in quest of better health and spirits—a quest that would consume the rest of his life. On his return to England in 1807, he at last separated from his long-suffering wife.

Henceforth, his time was for the most part spent in giving lectures and writing—or planning to write—for the sporadic periodical he had founded to treat "Principles of Political Justice, of Morality, and of Taste," entitled *The Friend*. The year 1810 saw a breach in his long friendship with Wordsworth, the cause of which was a criticism of Coleridge made by Wordsworth in confidence to a mutual friend, who irresponsibly passed it on, according to Coleridge, in the following form: "Wordsworth has commissioned me to tell you that he has no hope of you, that you have been a rotten drunkard and rotted out your entrails by intemperance, and have been an absolute nuisance in his family." Undoubtedly, as Wordsworth subsequently took elaborate pains to state, a well-intentioned observation had been severely garbled, but the incident does nonetheless highlight certain truths about Coleridge's condition. In order to counteract the depression that followed his opium bouts, he had resorted to the "stimulus" of alcohol. In the same year, the ever-loyal Dorothy Wordsworth had written to a friend that Coleridge "lies in bed, always till after 12 o'clock, sometimes much later. . . . He never leaves his own parlour except at dinner or tea and sometimes supper, and then he always seems impatient to get back to his solitude—he goes the moment his food is swallowed. Sometimes he does not speak a word."

At last, in 1816, Coleridge made a brave move and, acknowledging the extent of his drug addiction, placed himself under the care of a doctor in Highgate, then a village north of London.

"For the first week I shall not, *I must not be permitted* to leave your House," Coleridge wrote to Dr. Gillman, prior to his admittance to his charge. ". . . Delicately or indelicately, this *must* be done: and both the Servant and the young Man must receive absolute commands from you on no account to fetch anything for me. The stimulus of Conversation suspends the terror that haunts my mind; but when I am alone, the horrors, I have suffered from Laudanum, the degradation, the blighted Utility, almost overwhelm me."

Although he intended to remain in Highgate for only a month, his sojourn there lasted for eighteen years, or until the end of his life. It was in the summer of 1816 that two of his poetic masterpieces—"Kubla Khan" and "Christabel"—were finally brought to publication, along with the lesser "Pains of Sleep." This latter poem, it has been suggested, depicts the flip side of an opium high—the junkie's night terrors. As noted earlier, the published version of "Kubla Khan" differed in subtle but often important respects from that of an earlier manuscript, a fact that suggests that the original "dream-poem" received revisions over the years in the course of its recitations. Some scholars believe that the concluding stanza, differing in subject, metrics, and mood from the rest of the poem, was the most revised, if not an altogether later addition. A yet more extreme view is that the poem was a self-consciously crafted conventional work to which Coleridge added the romantic preface as an excuse for its incompleteness. But most would feel, as Lowes says, that "nobody in his waking senses could have fabricated [the] magical [final] eighteen lines."

The poem was by no means received with universal acclaim upon its publication. Hazlitt lambasted it in the *Edinburgh Review*, pouncing on Coleridge's self-effacing statement in his introduction that as far as his own opinions were concerned, he was publishing the poem "rather as a psychological curiosity, than on the ground of any *poetic* merits."

"In these opinions of the candid author," Hazlitt wrote, "we entirely concur," and he goes on to add that the lines "smell strongly" of the anodyne of laudanum and, citing the sedative powers of the anodyne, suggests that "a dozen or so lines . . . would reduce the most irritable of critics to a state of inaction." On the other hand, "Kubla Khan" had its strong champions, perhaps most notably Lord Byron, at whose request, according to Coleridge, this most Byronic of poetic works was published.

A few of the scattered images of the fragmentary poem turned up, some two years after its composition at Ash Farm, in a trivial work, first published in the *Morning Post*, entitled "Lines Composed in a Concert-Room":

> *Dear Maid! whose form in solitude I seek,*
> *Such songs in such a mood to hear thee sing,*
> *It were a deep delight! . . .*

And in his rambling prose essay in defense of Trinitarian Christianity, entitled *Aids to Reflection*, published in 1825, the familiar imagery of fountains, "odorous and flowering thickets" opening into "spots of greenery," grottoes, and caves is worked into a rather confusing "allegory of the Mystic." But apart from these weak reverberations, "Kubla Khan" left no impression on Coleridge's own later works. His summer day of poetic inspiration was in any case short-lived, his last poem of any note, the blank verse "To William Wordsworth," being composed in 1806. Coleridge's literary critical masterwork *Biographia Literaria,* published in 1817, was his last important literary work of any kind.

In 1833, the breach with Wordsworth was patched up and Coleridge returned with his old friend for a tour of Germany and the Low Countries. And in September of the following year, he died at Highgate. An autopsy revealed that his lungs had been compressed between an abnormally large heart, exacerbated by early rheumatic fever, and a massive cyst in the right side of his chest. Coleridge's sufferings, about which many friends had grown skeptical, had, then, been real enough, and his characteristic and maligned "indolence" as well as opium use, therefore, somewhat vindicated.

One of the dangers of some critical treatments—as, perhaps, of this one—is that they can be taken to imply that the "phenomenon" of "Kubla Khan" was the inevitable result of a combination of opium and eclectic reading—that drug plus travel literature equals masterpiece. But whatever the stimulants, the creative process took place within the uniquely teeming, fertile, dreaming mind of Samuel Taylor Coleridge. That this armchair Odysseus had ranged over so many interior landscapes, "seeing the towns and learning the minds of men," was itself an expression of his most characteristic passion to know all things of the world, to journey to the furthest horizons of intellect and imagination. He was, as Wordsworth is reputed to have said, his voice breaking, "The most *wonderful* man I have ever known."

In a postscript to his exemplary biography of Coleridge, Richard Holmes poses the interesting question of how Coleridge would have been perceived by posterity if he had died in the course of his Mediterranean "exile" in Malta and Italy—as indeed his friends half-expected he would—and posits that "he would be seen as part of that meteoric, Romantic tradition of young writers, like Keats, Shelley, or Byron . . . who lived and died in a blaze of premature talents." Coleridge was, one must remind oneself, only twenty-five years old in 1797, his *annus mirabilis.* "Kubla Khan," Holmes suggests, unpublished at this date, might have existed only as an "oral memory, uncommitted to manuscript, a true piece of Romantic folklore." As it is, Coleridge's poetic output is seen within the context of a relatively long life of ill-conceived and half-finished projects, and he himself as possessed of a genius that, like his famous poem, was filled with scattered images, fragmented and incomplete. One cannot help wondering whether in later years, when paralyzed by doubt and an inability to actualize his many projected schemes, Coleridge looked back with longing on that day when his poetic powers had unfolded with such miraculous lack of effort.

Significantly, there is in "Kubla Khan" a manifestation of the fear of creative impotence that would torment Coleridge throughout his life: The conditionals *could* and *would* of the mystic/poet's desire to revive symphony and song in this case speak legions. Thus while "Kubla Khan" represents Coleridge's summer kingdom of enchantment, its dome of pleasure is already overshadowed by a dark foreboding.

WHERE, ONE ALSO has to wonder, would the "lost" 150 or so lines have taken the poem? Coleridge addressed the incompleteness of "Kubla Khan" at the conclusion of its published preface: "From the still surviving recollections in his mind, the Author has frequently purposed to finish for himself what had been originally, as it were, given to him. [*Aurion adion asô*]," Coleridge wrote, paraphrasing Theocritus ("Tomorrow I shall sing more sweetly"): "but the tomorrow is yet to come."

Coleridge and the companions of his romantic walks could

not have guessed at the changes that have been wrought in the world since the "glad morning" of their youth. And whether it is the world that has most changed or our perceptions of it, we do know this: It is unlikely that, ever again, a Xanadu will be yielded from contemporary descriptions. We know now that the tomorrow will never come.

I had imagined that on completing my journeys I would re-turn to "Kubla Khan" with a heightened poetic vision—indeed, with something approximating the vividness of the original opium dream; and it is, perhaps, a testimony to Coleridge's tran-scendent genius that I did not. As the opening lines unfold, the same images rise in front of me as before—a place dark and craggy, with perhaps more of Florida's shaggy greenery than of anything else, but essentially reminiscent of nowhere I have seen.

Ironically, I was, after all, left with an enduring and unex-pected memory of Xanadu. It harbors few images at all, just the bare bones of Shangdu's ruined vanished city, with light and geese above and somewhere down below the outshine of a limit-less plain of golden grass—nothing more to fill that magnificent, plundered void, that wasteland of a palace, those fallen walls and towers.

BIBLIOGRAPHY

COLERIDGE

Chambers, E. K. *Samuel Taylor Coleridge: A Biographical Study.* Oxford, 1938.

Coburn, Kathleen, ed. *The Notebooks of Samuel Taylor Coleridge* (especially vol. 1, 1794–1804). New York, 1957.

Coleridge, Samuel Taylor. *The Complete Poetical Works of Samuel Taylor Coleridge*, edited by Ernest Hartley Coleridge. Oxford, 1912.

———. *The Complete Works of Samuel Taylor Coleridge*, edited by W. G. T. Shedd. New York, 1884. ("Aids to Reflection," the essay referred to in the last two chapters, comprises vol. 1 of this seven-volume collection.)

Griggs, Earl Leslie, ed. *Collected Letters of Samuel Taylor Coleridge.* Oxford, 1956.

Holmes, Richard. *Coleridge: Early Visions.* London, 1989.

Lefebure, Molly. *Samuel Taylor Coleridge: A Bondage of Opium.* New York, 1974.

Lowes, John Livingston. *The Road to Xanadu.* Boston and New York, 1927. (Much quoted in, and the basis of, my book.)

Noyes, Russell, ed. *English Romantic Poetry and Prose.* New York, 1956. (A good basic anthology of Romantic literature, and handy for giving an introduction to Coleridge through the eyes of his contemporaries. The description of Coleridge's recitation of "Kubla Khan" in the last chapter is given by Sir Thomas Talfourd. Full references to contemporary writers are found in the bibliographies of Holmes and Chambers.)

Suther, Marshall. *Visions of Xanadu.* New York, 1965. (Anti-Lowes: echoes of "Kubla Khan" culled from Coleridge's own writing, thus indicating a predilection for Xanaduesque imagery. Provocative but far-fetched.)

INNER MONGOLIA

Boyle, John Andrew. "The Seasonal Residences of the Great Khan Ögedei." *Central Asiatic Journal* 16 (1972): 125–31.

Bushell, S. W. "Notes on a Journey Outside the Great Wall of China." *Proceedings of the Royal Geographical Society* 18, no. 2 (1874): 149–68. Also see "Notes on the Old Mongolian Capital of Shangdu." *Journal of the Royal Asiatic Society* 7 (1875): 329–38. Also *Journal of the Royal Geographical Society* 44 (1874): 73–97.

Campbell, C. W. "A Journey in Mongolia." *Great Britain Foreign Office Report, China* 1 (1904): 11–12.

Cleaves, Francis Woodman. "The 'Fifteen "Palace Poems" ' by K'o Chiu-ssu." *Harvard Journal of Asiatic Studies* 20 (1957): 391–479.

Gerbillon, Jean François, "Voyage dans la Tartarie Occidentale, par l'ordre de l'empereur de la Chine ou à sa suite, en 1688 & 1698," in *Histoire generale des voyages* . . . edited by Antoine François Prévost, vol. 9, p. 469ff.; vol. 10, p. 70ff. La Haye, 1747–80. Also published as "Travels into Western Tartary, by Order of the Emperor of China, or in his retinue, between the Years 1688, and 1698," in *A New General Collection of Voyages and Travels,* edited by John Green (the Astley Collection), vol. 4, p. 664ff. London, 1747.

Harada, Yoshito, ed. *Shang-tu: The Summer Capital of the Yüan Dynasty* (mostly in Japanese). Tokyo, 1941.

Impey, Lawrence. "Shangtu, The Summer Capital of Kublai Khan." *Geographical Review* 15 (1925): 584–604.

Morgan, David. *The Mongols.* Oxford, 1986.

Polo, Marco. *The Travels,* translated by Ronald Latham. London, 1958.

Pozdneev, A. *Mongolia e Mongolij.* St. Petersburg, 1898. (Quoted passages were translated from the Russian by Gina Kovarski.)

Rashīd al-Dīn. *The Successors of Genghis Khan,* translated from the Persian by J. A. Boyle. New York, 1971.

Rossabi, Morris. *Khubilai Khan: His Life and Times.* Berkeley, Calif., 1988.

Steinhardt, Nancy Shatzman. *Chinese Imperial City Planning.* Honolulu, 1990. (Professor Steinhardt is the principal source for information on Mongolian imperial architecture for this book. In particular, she is to be credited for the suggestion that Shangdu was used by the khans for recreation and hunting after 1262, the foundation date for Dadu.)

———. "Imperial Architecture Along the Mongolian Road to Dadu." *Ars Orientalis* 18 (1988): 59–93.

———. "The Plan of Khubilai Khan's Imperial City." *Artibus Asiae* 44 (1983): 137–58.

A great deal of poetry was written during the Yuan dynasty by Chinese envoys and officials in the Khan's court describing their visits to, and impressions of, Shangdu, or the Upper Capital. Poems quoted in the first chapter are to be found in the following works:

Liu Guan (1270–1342). Excerpts from the *Shangjing jixing shi (A Poetic Diary of the Upper Capital).* Beijing: Gugong bowuyuan (Palace Museum), 1930 (a photolithographic reprint of the early fifteenth-century woodblock), 6a–7a.

Yuan Jue (1262–1327). "Miscellaneous Songs on the Upper Capital," in the *Qingrong jushi ji (Collected Literary Works of the Lay Buddhist Who Keeps His Form Pure),* Sibu beiyao ed., 15:5a–6a.

Zhou Boqi (d. c. 1367). Excerpts from the *Bowen jinguang ji (Collected Poems by Bowen [Zhou Boqi] Composed in Proximity to the Light [of the Emperor]),* in the *Yuan shixuan, chuji.* Taipei: Shijie shuju (1962 reprint of the 1751 ed.), pp. 1857–65.

The poems are so evocative that I regret not having been able to place them all in my work. Most of the poems have never been translated. All English translations appearing here were made by Dr. Richard John Lynn, who, as a result of this "assignment," is working on a forthcoming collection of poems about Shangdu translated into English.

FLORIDA

Adicks, Richard, ed. *Le Conte's Report on East Florida.* Orlando, Fla., 1978.

Bartram, William. *Travels Through North & South Carolina, Georgia, East & West Florida, the Cherokee Country, the Extensive Territories of the Muscogulges, or Creek Confederacy, and the Country of the Chactaws.* Philadelphia, 1791. (Reprint by Penguin Nature Library, New York, 1988.)

Cabell, James. *The St. Johns River: A Parade of Diversities.* New York, 1943.

Essoe, Gabe. *Tarzan of the Movies.* New York, 1968.

Glunt, James, and Ulrich Phillips, eds. *Florida Plantation Records, From the Papers of George Noble James.* St. Louis, 1927.

Hodges, Frederick W. *Spanish Explorers in the Southern States.* New York, 1907.

Motte, Jacob Rhett. *Journey into Wilderness; Account of an Army Surgeon's Life in Camp and Field During the Creek and Seminole Wars, 1836–1838,* edited by James F. Sunderman. Gainesville, Fla., 1953.

Muir, John. *A Thousand-Mile Walk to the Gulf.* New York, 1916.

Olschki, Leonardo. "Ponce de León's Fountain of Youth." *The Hispanic American Review* 21, no. 3 (1941): 361–85. (In a striking coincidence, the two principal poetic strands that apparently combined to shape this legend were the *Letter of Prester John* and the *Roman d'Alexandre,* two medieval works that refer to India and Ethiopia—the two other places that inspired the imagery of Xanadu.)

Ribaut, Jean. *The Whole & True Discovereye of Terra Florida* (facsimile reprint of London edition of 1563). De Land, Fla., 1927.

State of Florida, Geological Survey. *The Springs of Florida.* Tallahassee, Fla., 1977.

Tebeau, Charlton W. *A History of Florida.* Coral Gables, Fla., 1971.

Whitman, Alice. "Transportation in Territorial Florida." *Florida Historical Quarterly* 17 (July 1938): 25–53.

KASHMIR

Ahmad, S. M., and R. Bano. *Historical Geography of Kashmir.* New Delhi, 1984. (A catalog of ancient references to important sites.)

Anonymous. *Phallic Miscellanies; Facts and Phases of Ancient and Modern Sex Worship, as Illustrated Chiefly in the Religions of India.* London (?), 1891. (A curiosity, and chiefly valuable for its description of early rites of lingam worship.)

Bamzai, Prithivi Nath Kaul. *A History of Kashmir: Political, Social, Cultural, From the Earliest Times to the Present Day,* rev. ed. Delhi, 1973.

Bernier, François. *Histoire de la dernière révolution des états du Grand Mogol.* Paris, 1670–71. Also published as *Travels in the Mogul Empire, A.D. 1656–1668,* translated by Irving Brock, edited by Archibald Constable, 2d rev. ed. London, 1914.

Beveridge, Henry. *The Tûzuk-i-Jahângîrî* (Jahangir's autobiography), translated by Alexander Rogers. London, 1909 and 1914.

Crowe, Sylvia, Sheila Haywood, Susan Jellicoe, and Gordon Patterson. *The Gardens of Mughul India.* London, 1972. (A work of scholarship and love; sheer pleasure.)

Hassnain, F. M., Y. Miura, and V. Pandita. *Sri Amarnatha Cave.* New Delhi, 1987. (A pilgrim's "manual" to making this holy journey.)

Lamb, Alistair. *Kashmir: A Disputed Legacy, 1846–1990.* Hertingfordbury, Hertfordshire, England, 1991.

Lawrence, Walter R. *The Valley of Kashmir.* London, 1895. (A comprehensive description of the valley, including its geology and flora, and the political and social history of its inhabitants.)

Maurice, Rev. Thomas. *The History of Hindostan; Its Arts, and Its Sciences, as*

Connected with the History of the Other Great Empires of Asia, During the Most Ancient Periods of the World. London, 1795.

Morgan, Kenneth W., ed. *The Religion of the Hindus.* New York, 1953. (An informative and readable treatment of a complex subject; I was also helped by the more concise discussion and bibliography in the *Encyclopaedia Britannica*'s chapter on Hinduism.)

Pandit, Ranjit Sitaram, trans. and ed. *Rājataraṅgiṇī: The Saga of the Kings of Kas'mîr.* New Delhi, 1968.

Rennell, James. *Memoir of a Map of Hindoostan; or the Mogul's Empire,* 3d ed. London, 1793. (Reprinted by Editions Indian, Calcutta, 1976.)

Zaehner, R. C. *Hinduism,* 2d ed. Oxford, 1966. (Scholarly, and systematic. A good reference but a somewhat heavy-going cover-to-cover read.)

ETHIOPIA

Alvarez, Francis. "The Prester John of the Indies: A True Relation of the Lands of Prester John, Being the Narrative of the Portuguese Embassy to Ethiopia in 1520 Written by Father Francisco Alvarez," in *Hakluytus Postumus, or Purchas His Pilgrimes,* vol. 7. Glasgow, 1905.

Bruce, James. *Travels to Discover the Source of the Nile in the Years 1768, 1769, 1770, 1771, 1772 and 1773.* Edinburgh, 1790. (A complete edition, outside of a special collection, is both hard to find and a momentous undertaking. A good excerpted edition is that selected and edited by C. F. Beckingham, Edinburgh, 1969.)

Budge, Sir E. A. Wallis. *A History of Ethiopia, Nubia and Abyssinia.* London, 1928.

Cheesman, R. E. *Lake Tana and the Blue Nile: An Abyssinian Quest.* London, 1936. (An account of the first successful attempt to chart systematically the Blue Nile's course.)

Greenfield, Richard. *Ethiopia: a New Political History.* New York, 1965. (Focuses on twentieth-century Ethiopian history, particularly Haile Selassie's reign up until the coup attempt and its aftermath in the early 1960s.)

Lobo, Father Jeronimo. *A Voyage to Abyssinia, By Father Jerome Lobo,* translated from the French by Samuel Johnson. London, 1735. (Also included in this volume is a translation of Father Paez's earlier description of the Nile fountains, from which Lobo's account is almost certainly derived.)

Moorehead, Alan. *The Blue Nile.* London, 1962. (The great river, from start to finish.)

Purchas, Samuel, ed. "Africa. The Seventh Booke. Relations of Ethiopian rarities, collected out of Friar Luys a Spanish Author," in *Purchas His Pilgrimage.* London, 1617. (See especially p. 843ff., "Of the Hill Amara.")

Reid, J. M. *Traveller Extraordinary: The Life of James Bruce of Kinnaird.* New York, 1968.

Taddesse Tamrat. "Ethiopia, the Red Sea and the Horn," in *The Cambridge History of Africa,* edited by Roland Oliver, vol. 3. Cambridge, 1977. (Includes an account of the institution and fall of Mount Amara.)

Thesiger, Wilfred. *The Life of My Choice.* Glasgow, 1987. (Includes, among much else, an account of Thesiger's boyhood in Haile Selassie's Ethiopia and travels in the country's wildest reaches. A portrait of Abyssinia as it was and will never be again, by the last great traveler of our age.)

A NOTE ABOUT THE AUTHOR

Caroline Alexander was born in North Florida and has lived in Europe, Africa, and the Caribbean. Following a Rhodes Scholarship at Oxford, she was a lecturer in classics at the University of Malawi for two and a half years. In 1991, she received a doctorate in classics from Columbia University. She now lives on a farm in New Hampshire and is a regular contributor to *The New Yorker*.

A NOTE ON THE TYPE

The text of this book was set in a digitized version of Centaur. Originally designed by Bruce Rogers in 1914 as a private type, it was named for the book in which it was first used (*The Centaur*, by Maurice de Guérin). Monotype made it generally available in 1929.

Rogers based his design upon the 1470 font of Nicolas Jenson, the Venetian printer, introducing refinements lacking in the original. Typographers consider Centaur to be one of the finest roman types currently available, a superb revival of the Jenson letter which has served as an inspiration for all designers of roman type.

Composed by ComCom, a division of Haddon Craftsmen,
Allentown, Pennsylvania
Printed and bound by Arcata Graphics/Martinsburg,
Martinsburg, West Virginia
Designed by Robert C. Olsson

HERB SEASONING

Also by Julian F. Thompson

HERB SEASONING

JULIAN F. THOMPSON

**SCHOLASTIC
HARDCOVER**

Scholastic Inc.
New York

Library of Congress Cataloging-in-Publication Data
Thompson, Julian F.
  Herb Seasoning / Julian F. Thompson.
      p.   cm.
  Summary: Teenager Herb Hertzman embarks on an Alice-in-Wonder-
land-like journey in his search to find out what his life is all about.
  ISBN 0-590-43023-8
  [1. Self-perception—Fiction.] I. Title.
PZ7.T371596He   1990   89-10630
[Fic]—dc20   CIP
                                                                        AC

12 11 10 9 8 7 6 5 4 3 2 1   0 1 2 3 4 5/9

                         Printed in the U.S.A.   37
                  First Scholastic printing, March 1990

Whatever it turns out to be,
this book's for Polly, lovingly.

HERB SEASONING

1
BACKGROUND
INFORMATION

From *The New York Times*, Tuesday, December 29, 1987:

> *As it happens, 1988 will arrive a little late this year — one second late, to be exact — and thereupon hangs a tale.*
>
> *By international agreement, the world's time-keepers, in order to keep their official atomic clocks in step with the earth's irregular but gradually slowing rotation, have decreed that a "Leap Second" be inserted between 1987 and 1988.*
>
> *So at precisely 11:59:60 P.M. on New Year's Eve, there will be a one-second void before the onset of 12:00:00 A.M. New Year's Day . . .*
>
> *For various reasons — the sloshing molten core, the rolling of the oceans, the melting of*

*polar ice and the effects of solar and lunar grav-
ity — the planet rotates on its axis at irregular
rates, and on average has been slowing down by
about one-thousandth of a second per day.*

*Thus, every few years a full extra second is
accumulated on the clocks. So periodically, to
get the clocks back in step with earthly rotation,
a leap second has been inserted to remove the
extra second from the clocks. Without much fan-
fare, it has happened 14 times since 1972 . . .*

Here's what Dr. Dennis McCarthy, an astrono-
mer at the Naval Observatory, had to say about the
meaning of a second, according to the same *Times*
article:

> *"A second is a relatively long amount of time.
> If you're flying a plane by instruments, and
> you're off by one second, you're going to miss the
> runway by nearly one-fifth of a mile."*

Unbeknownst to him, or anybody else, Herbie
Hertzman was born during a "leap second," the one
that happened more than sixteen years ago.

So, you *could* say that he wasn't born *at any time*.
You *could* say that he missed the runway, that he
wasn't *ever* born.

2
AUTHOR'S DISCLAIMER

I'm not saying any of those things. You're going to have to make up your own mind about this character, and about the larger question of whether people can occur — can be allowed — with no time on the clock. Or whether they should be like baskets in a game of basketball, which only count if they have left the shooter's hand with time still showing. But otherwise are disallowed. I leave that up to you.

I don't know. A lot of Herbie Hertzman's story sounds incredible to me, but yet I still believe it. It's possible that that's because I'm just about as gullible as . . . well, old Herbie is, or was, or might have been. You, I wouldn't know about.

3
T.K.

To the extent that it's possible for anyone to learn anything in high school, Herbie Hertzman probably learned that Tyche was the Greek goddess of luck in Miz Potemkin's History of Western Civilization class, required of all sophomores.

And, if boys like Herbie remember anything important for more than fifteen minutes, which his putative mother almost surely doubted, he still retained that information twenty-four months later.

The memory would be, and was, a little flawed, however. Western Civ is hard to get down pat. It's full of words that almost everyone misspells, like "peasants" and "cavalry," and others that are tricky to pronounce, for instance, "Arkameedeez" and "Cardnal Rishloo." Not to mention those you don't remember what they mean, like "putative."

Fall of sophomore year, Herbie wrote down

Tyche in his notebook just the way that Miz Potemkin mizpronounced it: "T.K." Ever after, he imagined T.K. as a youthful, perky, fun-type goddess in an extra-short, white, silky tunic.

"T.K.," Herbie wrote, that time. And then he wrote, "Good luck."

4
TWO YEARS LATER

By the time he was a senior, Herb was seventeen
and six feet two, with a fine, round head of shiny
coal-black hair cut close to it in ringlets, like you see
on ancient statues of Apollo. In general, he had a
mildly puzzled look in his surprisingly blue eyes.

Most days he wore a collared long-sleeved shirt
to school, with blue jeans and a dark brown leather
vest, and he always had his big, wide, buckled belt
on upside down. Can you imagine that? When he
was little and his mother dressed him, she would
slide his belt in from the wrong direction, upside
down. She wasn't being mean or careless; some people *don't* know any better. So, of course, the buckle
wasn't ever on the proper side, and he, both young
and ignorant, always kept it that way. And naturally
he drew a lot of stares at school, whether he was
there or not.

He also, more than ever, *hungered* for good luck. He believed that with good luck a person might attain the two things that, it seemed to him, were key to being happy:

1. Love (he always put that #1, so's not to seem a grubber, or insensitive), and
2. Money

He also knew there were some other means that lead to one or both of those same ends, supposedly. The ones you hear the most about are:

a. Natural Ability, and
b. Hard Work

And of course you also hear people say that the surest way to find Love is to have:

1. Money

And the only way to be sure of having Money is to have:

1. Rich Parents

Well, Herbie knew he didn't have Money or Rich Parents. And when it came to Natural Ability, it seemed as if the evidence was mostly on the side of . . . undecided. As a rule, he "got" things right away, but he didn't always seem to *keep* them. Or, put it this way, he'd retain a lot of stuff he didn't even need (like where both Holden Caulfield and that Frank Viola went to school, and who the hylozoistic monists and Bailey Quarters were), and then forget how to extract the square root of 237. It seemed to him the things he learned just on his own had a way of hogging all the airy, light, high-ceilinged rooms up in the front part of his brain, and of forcing certain school "material" to stay in narrow closets with the bulbs burned out.

Herb couldn't figure out if he was "college

bound," or not. He didn't like the *term* at all. It made him think of "snowbound," which he knew was *trapped*. But at least it was okay, an accepted thing to do. He hadn't ruled it out. What he needed was some reason he could use to rule it *in*.

Older people more or less encouraged him, but not that much. "You've got a real good head on your shoulders" is something that a lot of parents tell their kids, some of them named Herbie. They almost have to, though. Face it, he is *theirs*, a mixture of their genes, and if he doesn't, how do they explain it, short of saying they're a pair of dullards, too?

"You are perfectly capable of being a B + student in this course" is more what *teachers* feel compelled to say, because they know that if they're doing even a quarter-way decent job, a bowl of bread dough could make C, by simply being plopped down in the room, most days.

I think the truth of the matter is that Herbie was or is or might have been acutely smart, but like you and me and the lamppost, he didn't really know exactly what that meant, so he couldn't get a lot of satisfaction out of it. He couldn't count on it to bring him Love or Money.

Not the love of Tyree Toledano. Not its equivalent in money, say, the contents of the U.S. Mint.

So, he told himself, he'd probably be smart to put his faith in T.K.

"But what about Hard Work?" someone in the room will always say. And not *just* to prove he was paying attention a while back. There's a certain type of person who will *always* drag that concept in. *Hard Work*. Even people with so much natural ability you'd like to *kill* them try to act as if it's really ol' Hard Work that got them to whatever pinnacle, or pedestal, they're up on. Also, once you get to be a certain age, it seems as if you've got to shove your way into the world of youth and put up lots of verbal temples to this boring, sweaty god.

Herbie wasn't sure that he was ready for it, though, this Hard Work deal. He *wished* he was, or would be. He wasn't afraid of the stuff, he didn't think; it was more a question of . . . well, if he *could*, or not. So far, there'd always been resistance, coming from a yawn mine deep inside his system. He hadn't managed to produce Hard Work on anything for more than maybe forty minutes, tops.

No, T.K. seemed more likely than Hard Work to get him what he wanted, needed, *had to have*, if he was ever going to be a happy fella. You remember: Love and Money.

Not that Herbie Hertzman was, like, notably *un*-happy, either; please do not misunderstand. He was, like many of the rest of us, more in-between, like, *there*. If, years and years from now, he lives or dies peculiarly, or marries in a way that calls for national attention, and members of the media go digging up his past, I bet they get a lot of "Herbie Hertzman? Sure. He was in my bio class, I think. He seemed to be a sort of easygoing guy, I guess. What's that? No, nothing special, really. . . ."

But meanwhile, at the age of seventeen, he had his ordinary daily life to lead. And that included dealing with the question everybody seemed to ask about his future:

"WHAT *ARE* YOU GOING TO *DO*, LIKE, WITH YOURSELF?"

9

5
GETTING GUIDANCE

The best place to head for in any high school, if you're trying to figure out what you're going to do with yourself, is *not* the boiler room, not anymore. It's generally locked, for one thing, and even if it isn't and the custodian is there, the chances are he may not be as wise and caring as the old *janitors* used to be — the "After all, they're only kids . . ." guys. Vocations are way down, and lots of modern ones are in it for the benefits, from what I hear.

Because he knew that, Herb decided he would try the Guidance Office, first. He was pretty desperate. He set up an appointment with his counselor, as he had done at other times, in other years, for other reasons. The very first time he'd done so, he'd expected to meet someone who'd be pretty much like his *camp* counselor, whose name was Quint, and who was on the JV tennis team at Yale. In fact,

Herbie'd almost expected that the guidance counselor's office would have a bunch of bunks in it, and he would lay around on one, and his counselor on another, and they'd sort of shoot the bull about the pennant races or the difference between being intense and a bad sport, before they got around to what he'd scored in first-year algebra.

It hadn't been like that at all, of course. Not then or any other time. And it wasn't just the lack of bunks. The way that Herbie finally figured it, "camp" and "guidance" were completely different kinds of counselors, the way that "baseball" (say) and "window" are two different kinds of fans.

"Hey! Herbivorous!" said Mr. Alexander Rex, his guidance guy, that day. Mr. Rex — when you said the name, it *had* to come out "Mister X" — had wraparound dark glasses on, and high-top silver sneakers covered with tiny mirrors, and a great big knitted purple sweater with a huge, white, knitted question mark right in the middle of the front of it. Everybody knew he was the shortest, smartest, blackest member of the guidance staff. He did his hair the way that Ziggy Marley does, and he was five feet four.

"COME-Come-come," he said to Herb and took him to a half-partitioned cubicle. He went behind the small, plain desk and sat. Herb took the chair that faced it. On the floor, beside the counselor, there was a topless wooden box — or file drawer, possibly — that seemed to hold a lot of folders, maybe student records.

Mr. Rex then cocked his head a little — up, as if in thought. Because of the very dark glasses, Herbie

11

couldn't tell where he was looking. But suddenly the shaded eyes came down to level, and Mr. Alexanderex commenced to give out guidance, *à la* Socrates.

"What you be going to do with you, young blood?" he asked. His head jerked back and forth, and he spoke fast and with a boppin' beat. "What's shakin' in between Ol' Lady Want and Mister Should?" The students didn't know it, but he talked like that to keep from getting bored.

"Well, as a matter of fact," said Herbie, shaking his own head and allowing himself a small, self-deprecating smile, "that's kind of what I want to talk to *you* about. I know I'm expected to *make* something of myself, but I don't know exactly what that is. Everybody's asking me what I'm going to *do* with myself" — Herbie pulled his handsome, longish nose and shook his head again — "and I'm not sure at all. Maybe that's because I don't know what I want to *make*, yet. Of myself, I mean. Other than, well, something different than whatever I am now." Another sigh, this one ending in a totally self-conscious chuckle. "But I'm sure I'm not too clear on all the possibilities. What I might be *suited* for, or anything like that."

During the last part of that speech, the guidance guy leaned over to his right, twisting his body and reaching for the hanging files and folders in the open box. This was a real familiar sight to Herb. In fact, it happened every time he went for guidance. And always with the same result.

As Mister X's fingers did their walkin', he began to rap, again.

"I be tryin' to find you' RECORDS-Records-

records, man," he said. "You' grades which whisper what you' *done*, you' test scores screamin' what you *can*."

Finally, however, he sat up again, and empty-handed; no telling what was in his eyes. His head shook back and forth.

"Somebody musta *borrowed* them," he said, no longer upbeat. "Somebody *always* borrowin' my records. Make me sick, I tell you, bro'. Can't sing without my music on, y'know."

Herbie swallowed hard. The situation seemed acutely serious. High school wasn't everlasting; it would soon be over. You didn't have to *do* stuff with yourself in high school; stuff was done *to* you, by *it* — or sometimes *them*. But sooner than he liked to think, all that would change. If he didn't do some *something* with himself, he wouldn't be a player in the game of life. He'd be a nobody, a man without a number.

"Well," he said. He'd try to be a good sport, anyway; Quint had counseled him on that. "I guess there isn't anything that anyone can do. . . ." He started to get up.

"No, wait," said Alexander Rex. He said it in a hoarse, but somehow friendly, whisper. He slid out of his chair and, crouching, put his ear to the partition on his left. Then, very slowly, he stood up; when he was up on tiptoe, he could just see over it. He nodded, then crouched down again and did the same thing on the right partition. When he was seated in his chair again, he flicked a switch atop the little speaker on his desk. Cheerful background music issued forth, the kind that gives you something to despise when you are put "on hold," sometimes.

Then he leaned way forward, elbows on the desktop.

"There is a place," he said. His voice was very different now. He'd dropped his role, his cover; this was undiluted Alexander Rex, a human being stripped of pretense and disguise. He'd decided to risk everything he'd carefully assembled through the years, his pension, for the sake of this mere high school kid, a person of no consequence whatever.

"Here," he whispered. He took a fountain pen and a mini-pad from out of a secret drawer and scribbled an address in purple ink on a tiny slip of paper. "Memorize it." Herbie did. "Now, eat it!" Herbie hesitated. "Hey, don't worry," Mr. Rex assured him. "It's all completely pure and natural. The ink is Concord grape juice, no preservatives." Herb did as he'd been told. It really wasn't bad. The paper had a vaguely nutty taste to it; it turned (returned?) to pulp inside his mouth quite quickly.

"The person that you'll see is, like, a consummate professional," continued Rex. "You'll be presented with a range of options to consider. You won't be pushed or pressured into anything."

Herbie raised a finger, had a question, but the counselor had read his mind.

"Your parents needn't ever know," he said. "It's up to you to tell them, if you choose to. Myself, I think it's better if you can, and do. But as I said, it's up to you."

Herb cleared his throat in some embarrassment. "Money," he croaked out. "Is there a fee? I haven't got but maybe three-four dol — "

"No," said Mr. Rex. "The services are free to those who can't afford them. Their funding comes from God knows where." He sighed. "We'd do what

14

they do, here in school, except that you-know-who put in those regulations saying that you can't *do* certain things with public money." The guidance person and the newly guided boy both shook their heads, together.

Then Rex pulled down his shades enough so Herb could see him raise his eyebrows. "Is that it?" they clearly said. Herb nodded. Rex flipped off the music and stood up.

"So, keep your nose clean, just say no, my man," he boomed, "an' instead of 'It's too hard,' tell homework, 'Hey, I can!' "

Herb found his own way out. As usual, he hoped he might run into Tyree Toledano.

6
TYREE TOLEDANO

The trouble was: Tyree was not that sort of person, the kind you always happen to run into. She was made of airier, more insubstantial stuff, the stuff that dreams are made of.

That's why she never did attract attention at the places Herbie saw her, even if she was more beautiful than any girl he'd ever seen.

She came into a class of his one time, and he'd just sat there staring at her for the entire period, although nobody else seemed to notice her at all. She had intensely dark, thick eyebrows, and huge dark eyes, and a mouth that seemed, to Herbie, wide enough to slide a half a bagel into — halfway, anyway. Her dark brown hair was soft and wavy, and it settled on her shoulders, either side. That day she had a buttoned woolen sweater on, but not a shirt — a smooth, light tan one made of cashmere, Herb was pretty sure. She hadn't done the top two buttons, though, and on a fine gold chain around her lovely neck she wore a curious black amulet, shaped like . . . well, a cough lozenge. Mr. Roland didn't call on her all period, and she never came back to that class again. Herbie didn't blame her.

Another time, he saw her doing cartwheels in the hall in school, barefoot in a minimal blue leotard, her straight blonde hair pulled back and knotted in a dancer's bun, her lower lip between her teeth, and her blue eyes focused on some distant, but important, goal. Herb watched her then until she reached the Girls' Room door, through which she disappeared.

One other day, she came toward him on the street, with a small smile playing on her frosted lips, and her flaming hair tied loosely just behind her neck by what he took to be a multicolored silk bandana. She wore a pale green shirt that afternoon, and very tight, white, narrow-legged pants and bright red patent leather pumps with spiky heels. After she'd gone by him, and he'd turned to watch her slender gracefulness some more, he was surprised to find she'd disappeared. It was as if the ground had opened up and swallowed her, or she'd been magically transformed into a bus stop sign, two women pushing strollers, or that leggy Irish setter, there.

Not seeing Tyree anywhere inside, or just outside, the school that day, Herb decided that he might as well head home. It was, perhaps, a little late to go to the address that Mr. Rex had given him. And anyway, before too awfully long, it would be suppertime.

7
A YOUNG PHILOSOPHER
WALKS HOME

Herb always liked his journeys home. He didn't
have a car and didn't like to ride his bike. He walked.
And thought about . . . well, things. Sometimes —
after he had passed the window of Belinda's Lin-
gerie, for instance — his thoughts were fairly junky.
But at other times they were extremely philosophical, he thought. For example (from some thoughts
he'd had while walking home two weeks before):

A person's life is somewhat like the wardrobe in
his closet (Herbie thought). Most of it is everyday:
not too great, but not real bad. And the extremes,
they balance one another out. For every real sharp
jacket (the equivalent of hearing that you've made
somebody very, very proud or happy), there is also
a disgusting pair of stupid checkered pants with a
spaghetti stain on them (which are like finding out
you totally destroyed the social studies final).

What that means is that a wise man *must* remember that his life and wardrobe never stay the same for long. Things go back and forth from good to bad and back again. And as they do, it is important (he decided) to *appreciate* the goods, and not just curse and moan about the bads, the way so many people seem to do.

And so he'd made a resolution that he'd try to do exactly that, and more. Every time he had good fortune, he'd not only take the time to notice and enjoy it, he would also thank the source of it: T.K. (or her present-day equivalent; Herb didn't think names mattered much). He could and did imagine perky little T.K. smiling when she saw him being grateful. And maybe even taking notes about him on a pad of old papyrus that she had right by her hot tub. High up on the slopes of Mount Olympus.

So anyway, on that day Herbie strolled along quite happily, just Doing Nothing With Himself but stepping over cracks, admiring some passing cars, and thinking, oddly, of the first line of *The Handmaid's Tale:* "We slept in what had once been the gymnasium."

But then he couldn't help but notice some excitement, up ahead. There were some twenty, maybe even fifty, people gathered on the sidewalk just outside a church, with others partway up its steps.

"Frank Pizarro," Herb said merrily, out loud, invoking (as he did) the memory of that *other* great discoverer/explorer. "What's all this about?"

Apparently "all this" was all about the stuff that happens after lots of weddings. As Herb got closer, he could see the bride and groom were posing on

19

the church's upper steps, while people took their picture. Beside the curb there was a long, white limousine.

When he was *very* close, Herb realized that hardly anyone was speaking, but that many people in the crowd were saying things in *sign language*. ("Hey, Vic! Hey, Vera! Smile!" presumably.) The newly married couple were a prematurely balding fellow with a short black beard and a pleasant-looking girl who wore blue sequined glasses. Because they, too, were signing ("Cheese!"?), Herb figured that they also didn't hear too well, the same as many of their friends.

Herb mingled with the people on the church's steps. One thing about him was, he really *did* like almost everyone, all different kinds of people. In hardly any time at all, he felt a part of this occasion and was happy for this happy-looking couple. Vic and Vera both looked very nice to him. If Vic became completely bald in another three-four years, so what? Herb was sure that Vera'd go on loving him.

Just then he noticed that the fellow he was standing next to on the steps was talking and laughing with the person on his other side, *while also signing at the couple up above*. Herb thought that *that* was pretty special. This guy, with just one brain, could carry on two different conversations at one time!

"Excuse me," Herbie said to him, interrupting both of them, "but could you show me how to sign something?" He thought a moment. "Like, 'I hope you have a really happy life'?"

The fellow, confident enough to have on cowboy

boots, said, "Sure," then smiling in a very friendly way, he made about a half a dozen movements with his hands, which Herbie duplicated perfectly, the first time that he tried them.

"Boy, you got it," cowboy boots informed him. "Perfect." And he clapped Herb on the shoulder, communicating further friendliness.

"Great," said Herbie, "thanks." And he did the movements with his hands a second time. He felt as if he'd learned another language, which'd be his third, if you included Spanish, which he'd had in school three years. He wondered if the hand gyrations that this guy had taught him meant the same in Spanish.

"Here, show my friend." Cowboy boots was tapping Herbie on the shoulder, the same one that he'd clapped, before. "Hey, Vinnie, look what I just taught this dude to say to Vic and Vera. Go on," he said to Herbie, who then did his sentence still another time: "I hope you have a really happy life," or as Herbie told it to himself this time, as he was doing it: *"Espero que ustedes tengan una vida muy contenta."*

But Vinnie didn't nod and smile and clap Herb on the shoulder. Instead, he grabbed the two of Herbie's hands in his own pair, while glaring, at the same time, at the guy in cowboy boots.

"What's the matter with you, Elmer, anyway?" he snarled, and clearly he was not amused, no way. He switched his eyes, now back to Herbie. "Look, you just forget that, kid, okay? My buddy here's a wise guy — see? — a real *jerkisimo.*"

"Well, what?" said Herbie, puzzled, looking at

21

his captive hands. The Vinnie guy still had him muzzled. "I asked him how to say 'I hope you have a really happy life.' "

Vinnie looked from side to side, then bent his mouth toward Herbie's ear.

"What you were going to say," he said, "was, 'Hey, I think you both look like a pair of jerks.' " Except, instead of "jerks," he said a vulgar word you seldom hear at weddings — even if it may be thought by former boy- or girlfriends of the bride or groom.

"*What?*" said Herb. He turned back to the cowboy-booted man. "That's really rotten of you, Elmer." Now he wanted to get out of there. He tried to think of something else to say, an exit line.

"Your mother ought to wash your hands with good strong soap," he sneered.

Halfway home, he thought he'd better stop and get some offerings for T.K. Luckily for him, he hadn't left the real America; there was a fast-food place a half a block away.

8
OFFERINGS

Magdalena Orgalescu, Herbie's mother, had married Big Ben Hertzman eighteen years before. Ben wasn't all that big; although he did stand six feet three, he was and is quite slender. It was more that "Big" and "Ben" are words that go together in a lot of people's minds, just like "Ho" and "Jo" and "Squirmin' " (I am told) and "Herman."

Lena (short for Magdalena), *she* was big, however. For a while, that is, when she was younger. She'd come over from Romania at the age of twelve, and in the first ten years she was here, she more than doubled what she weighed.

You couldn't really blame her, though. Romanian immigrants are apt to eat most everything in sight, when they are able to. Although it's one fantastic country, and the homeland of a lot of dandy human beings, some of whom are gypsies, Romania hasn't done real well, in certain ways, since World War II. There have been a lot of shortages, for instance. Of almost everything, some say, but especially of food that's fun to eat. Butter, milk and bread are rationed to this day; salad at a restaurant is often just four pickles on a plate. The Fudge Banana Brownie is endangered, possibly extinct, in Bucharest.

But once she was completely Americanized, and had started to make something of herself, Lena got into serious dieting. She cut her weight in half and met Ben Hertzman. Then she married him and sometime later Herb was either born, or not. There isn't any question that she *could* have given birth the day and month and year that Herbie called his birthday. Even that "leap second." Nowadays, Ben Hertzman sometimes says that Lena has a "perfect" figure; other times he'll say that she is "skin and bones." It all depends on whether he's kidding around or not — which is almost impossible to tell. Even Lena says she doesn't know, herself; that's rare for a Romanian.

"Hey, Mom! Hey, Dad! Anybody home?" called Herbie, coming in the door.

"Hi, honey," Lena Orgalescu Hertzman answered. "In the kitchen. With good news."

"Hey, Mom," said Herb again, arriving in the kitchen. He bent and kissed her cheek.

"You're late," she said, but not complainingly. She was wearing an embroidered robe and sitting at the kitchen table. In front of her there was an almost empty teacup and a deck of cards. She'd been relaxing after work. By day, she was a stockbroker.

"I was at the windup of a wedding," Herbie said.

24

"And I made a pit stop, after, at Phast Phil's. Tell me some good news."

"Two things," she said. "The first one is, your Uncle Babbo wrote. He's coming for the weekend, and he wants to talk to you. He's got some thoughts about your future, possibly a proposition, I believe." She smiled. "The second is" — she looked down at her teacup — "an idea that came to me a little while ago. It's another line of work you might look into, if you don't get into college." She held out a clipping to him. "Take a look at this."

It was from a magazine. He looked at it. It was an ad that also had a picture in it. The picture was of twelve young men, all dressed the same. They were wearing light blue leather boots, the soft and floppy kind, and light blue trousers, sort of pirate's pants, with white scarves looped around their necks and little blue boleros. They were members of a dance group called "The Wedgwoods" who, the ad explained, "performed on stages coast-to-coast, as well as for the heads of state of many foreign governments, abroad."

"What?" said Herbie, grinning in surprise. "My mother wants that I should be an *entertainer*?" He shook his head. "That's crazy, Mom. I'm not a fun-type guy. And I'm a *lousy* dancer. Just ask . . . anyone."

"It's just a thought," his mother said, and shrugged. "You've got a lot of dancing in your blood, your *genes*. And you've got the looks, like all the Orgalescus. Did you know your Uncle Babbo was a model, once? But just the very top part of his head, and pictured from above. He was the 'after' in a hair restorer ad."

But Herbie only shook his head again. His mother's brother, Babbo Orgalescu, was extremely dark and hairy. Sometime after his arrival in America, he'd come upon the motto that he'd lived by, ever since: "Use it or lose it." The last that Herbie heard, he was involved with something by the name of "Your Mane Man: The One Complete Hairstyling System."

"I don't know, Mom," Herbie said. "I guess I'll have to sleep on this one. I'm not sure I'm right for it. I see myself as more the sedentary type. More of a thinker, a philosopher." He grinned. "A guy who's into finding out the answers to Big Questions. Like, 'Why *can't* I put my dirty dishes in the sink?' " He tried to laugh it off.

His mother picked up the deck of cards and began to deal them out in four rows on the table. Herb knew that might be solitaire, but maybe not. He also knew he probably would hear some more about "The Wedgwoods."

"Pan Am was up five-eighths today," she said. "Does that say 'journey' to you, maybe? Or, even like a *tour* — from 'coast to coast'? And possibly 'abroad,' to where the heads of foreign governments are found?" She took a glance up at his face. "I know, I know — to you that sounds like superstition. 'How could the New York Stock Exchange have anything to do with *me*, my future line of work?' you ask. *But*" — she smiled at him and closed one eye — "I tell you dis: Stranger t'ings haff happened."

"Right," said Herbie, thinking of the food he'd bought while coming home. "I'll think about it, Mom. Upstairs." When his mother put the accent on, he knew that it was time to split.

26

* * *

When Herbie got up to his room, he lost no time in setting up the offering to T.K. It meant more if he did it at a time when he was really hungry, like right then.

The ruling principle, the one that animated quite a few of Herbie's dealings with the goddess, was simplicity itself. He believed the letters T and K had magic properties, at times, at least for him. When they were found in certain words, and in that order, those words become the names of lucky *things* (he had decided). And so, for instance, TiddlywinKs would be a pastime favored by the goddess and would be a lucky game for him to play, compared to baseball, say. BasKeTball, which had "the letters" in it, but *reversed*, was almost certainly a no-no — as were KilTs and sKirTs (at least for him). In order to be realistic (also fair and open-minded), the boy permitted some *exceptions* to the rules, as in the case of KiTchen. *It* could be a *very* lucky room, as on the nights his mother cooked roasT chicKen.

But he only made these offerings to T.K. on *extremely* rare occasions, special times when he had special needs for great good luck. And he always made them properly, with ceremony, the way he did right then. First, he'd TaKe a shower, to get clean and worthy. Then, he'd put fresh sweaTsocKs on, and nothing more — hence, nothing hidden from the goddess, up his sleeve or anywhere. After that, he TooK Ten nicKels, and he put them in a circle just a foot across. (In Brazil, they make the magic circle out of candles, and you can see where *that* has gotten *them*.) Inside it, went the offering

27

itself, always just two items: a TurKey sandwich and a real ThicK chocolaTe shaKe.

With all that finally done, Herb sighed contentedly and smiled, and lay down on his bed. For luck next day, he decided that he'd wear his deersTalKer, and TaKe his TomahawK.

He checked the magic circle and the food inside it. A quarter of an hour had gone by. He thought that T.K. *probably* was done with it by then, although mere mortals like himself could not (of course) be sure. The sandwich and the shake contained a lot of different nutrients, as everybody knew: protein, carbohydrates, vitamins and minerals. And also "nectar" and "ambrosia" (less well known), which were what a goddess drank and ate. Herb believed that T.K. would extract those parts of what he offered, and then leave the rest behind. The food would *look* the same, of course — just as it will do if you take all the vitamins away (the way the human processors still do, sometimes). So he could only go by time, to tell when she was done, and it was time.

His job was (then) to properly dispose of all the "scraps" (as he called them in his mind). He couldn't let them sit there on the floor. Mice would be attracted by them, surely, mice *and* roaches.

And so, Herb dressed and then sat down and ate the "scraps" himself, praising T.K. as he did so. After which he hurried down to dinner.

28

9
ON THE WAY TO CASTLES IN THE AIR

The address that Herbie'd memorized the day before was seven-dash-eleven Sunset Strip, and when he left his house to head for it, at 10 A.M. next morning, he realized he didn't know where he was going, where Sunset Strip might *be*. Not even more or less.

"Is this the story of my life, or what?" he said out loud.

He stood there for a minute, puzzling. The only thing that he could think to do was . . . well, *eliminate* the parts of town he was familiar with, and go to all the others, one by one, until he hit the right one. The thing that made *that* hard, confusing, was that he thought he'd been all over town, before.

The name of the — what would you call it? — *service* he was seeking was, according to what Mr. Rex had scribbled down, "Castles in the Air." That's

29

all the counselor had written on that tiny slip of paper: "Castles in the Air, 7-11 Sunset Strip." That *sounded* fairly classy, Herbie thought, but he also knew that names could be deceptive. "The Church of the Supreme Transmogrified Redemptor" was a rather shabby storefront, and "Nathaniel's One-Step Quickie and Immaculate Dry Cleaning and De-Staining Empire" was not a place to go (he'd heard his mother tell a friend) with any dress you planned to wear again. Herb could only hope that "Castles in the Air" would be more solid and substantial than its name implied. He started out, as usual, with hope (but not prejudgment) in his heart.

A few miles later, he was finding unfamiliar streets, all right, and they were lovely; one of them was Sunset Strip. As Herbie walked its gently curving way, however, he seldom saw a house. *Driveways*, he could see; driveways made of gravel and of blacktop and of white crushed stone were nicely spaced, but plentiful. *Gateposts*, he could see, and also sometimes gates and even once a gate*house*, he could see. *Signs* with names of people or of properties were also common: B.D. SWIGOTT or THE LARCHES. He saw some other signs, as well, with messages such as NO ZEALOTS and PLEASE DON'T FEED THE GRYPHON.

Human beings seemed as rare as houses. In fact, the only person Herbie saw close up in all the miles he walked on Sunset Strip was this one fellow who was standing by a driveway with a large sign reading PRIVATE ROAD beside it. Herb thought he was a few years older than himself, and he was wearing a short haircut and a leisure suit that still had the price tag, as well as other labels, hanging from one sleeve.

"Who are you and what's your business, here?" he said to Herb, quite sharply.

"Herbie Hertzman," our young man replied. "I'm not in business, yet. I'm looking for a place called 'Castles in the Air.' Who wants to know, just out of curiosity?" He let the fellow see his tomahawk, ran a finger right along its business edge.

The stranger jerked a thumb toward the sign. "I'm Private Road," he said. "Private Buford 'Buddy' Road. I just came home on furlough for a week, to check on my estate, here. 'Castles' is a ways up there, someplace. Keep going, you can't miss it. And if you take my best advice, you won't ask anybody else you meet for any more directions. We've got some all-world goofballs living in this neighborhood, and two of the rock-bottom worst, I'm sad to say, are in my line of work: Corporal Punishment and General Nuisance. They're making it real hard for me to be all that *I* can be, I'll tell you that much. I'm pretty sure that I could find my future in the army, if they'd stop ordering me around. And they're apt to do the same to you, if you should cross their paths."

He looked Herb over, top to toe to top again. "And how do you keep hand and mouth together, Sherlock?"

Herbie thought that instead of "hand and mouth," he'd probably meant either "body and soul," or "realistic expectations and utopian dreams," or "old paperback books," or "families that don't play," but he decided not to take his chances with eccentric, snappish, Buford "Buddy" Road.

"Oh, fork *or* chopsticks," he said quickly, with an

31

easygoing smile. "It all depends what sort of mood I'm in, I guess. I can bring the bacon home with either one, heh-heh. But have a nice day, won't you?"

And with that he headed off, politely but with tomahawk still swinging in his hand.

A few miles farther on, Herbie finally reached a driveway with an *extremely* welcome sign right at the foot of it: CASTLES IN THE AIR. He paused again to check out his surroundings.

For the most part, they looked good; they even *sounded* good. The drive was white and crunchy — also smooth, devoid of potholes, pits or puddles. There were two sturdy fieldstone gateposts, columns really, flanking it — but no gate to block his way. Outside the posts, however, was a tall, black iron fence, made of slender eight-foot pieces up and down, and set about a half a foot apart. They were also curved a little on their upper ends, and sharply pointed, there.

Tied onto this aristocratic fence with bright red twine were half a dozen crudely lettered signs, bearing rather hostile messages, considering the neighborhood. IMPRACTICAL IDEAS ARE PRACTICALLY REPULSIVE, STUPID, said one. Another read HONK IF YOU'RE NOT DAYDREAMING. Two others were: CASTLES IN THE AIR IS FULL OF GOONY BIRDS, and KEEP KNOWLEDGE OF THE WORLD WHERE IT BELONGS, IN SCHOOL. Behind the fence, however, gentle rhododendrons grew, in some profusion.

Peering up the drive, Herb could see a slate roof in the distance, with a tower sprouting from one corner of it. He felt sure that he was seeing Castles in the Air itself, a building firmly grounded in a better part of town.

"Well, I guess it's not a storefront," Herbie said out loud, as he began to walk up toward the place.

Before he'd gone three steps, he was startled by two voices coming from his left, just past the gatepost on that side.

"Ahem," said one of them. "Ahem. Kaff-kaff-kaff-kaff."

"Chivvy-chivvy-chivvy-chivvy-chivvy," said the other one, and very sharply, too.

"What?" said Herb. He couldn't see the speakers — anyone, in fact. The voices seemed to come from somewhere in the rhododendrons. "Who's there? You want to speak to me?"

" *'What? Who's there? You want to speak to me?'* " That second voice was, clearly, making fun of his. "Yes, we-want-to-speak-to-you, you idiot. Who else would we be speaking to? You think we're out here for our health, or something?"

"To be honest with you," Herbie said, "I wouldn't know. It seems to me that this would be a pretty good environment — in terms of health, I mean. Actually, I barely know what *I'm* here for, myself. But — could I ask? — are you from Castles in the Air? You wouldn't be, like, *yeomen* of some sort — or would you?"

" *'Like-yeomen-of-some-sort-or-would-you?'* " It was that same sarcastic voice, mocking him again. "No, we're *not* like-yeomen-of-some-sort. Or yes-men-of-some-sort, or even *no*-men-of-some-sort. You don't have eyes, or something? Don't you know *pickets* when you see them? I suppose you're going to say you didn't see our signs."

33

"Perhaps you thought," another voice chimed in, "that you could just come waltzing in as if this was a disco, or a *dance* hall. As if it was some stupid *mall*. Or Constitution *Hall*."

"Look," said Herbie, "there's been some mistake, I think. What I'm doing here is completely consistent with the whole idea of a pluralistic, democratic society (with a well-established and accepted labor movement) in which every person regardless of race, color, creed, or rational origin can totally self-make himself in almost any way he chooses. Provided he can figure out what choice he wants to make, out of all the choices there might *be*, as well as counter work. Like, well, to give you one extreme example I can think of — and I'm not saying this is necessarily the choice that I'm about to go for, *but* — well, like, hey, I *could* be President, someday."

"The hell you *could*," said one of the first voices, the most vicious and sarcastic one. "There's laws to keep absurdities like that from happening, thank God. And what there also are is *ruts* for kids like you to settle down in and shut up, you follow me? You think you're better than your parents? They did what they were told, or else, I'll bet. And you, you'd better do the same."

"Oh, yeah?" said Herbie, getting just a little miffed. "Well, I've got news for *you*. This is a *real* free country we've got going here, and it's up to me to make my own decisions . . . er, once I find out what the choices are, that is. In fact, that is *exactly* what I'm going up to Cas — "

"Son," a voice said, interrupting him. It was a new and deep and southern kind of one. "We're not askin' you all this, we're *tellin'* you. We're just

34

about to give you your instructions, boy. Lak judges do with juries, we got, lak, a *charge* to lay on you, a *pickets' charge*. So you just listen up and mind. You ready, boys?" he said. " . . . two, three, four. . . ."

And then the charge came rolling out from deep inside the rhododendrons, line after line after line:

> "We will tell you what to think,
> we will tell you what to do.
> Don't you dare to make a stink,
> or things will go real bad for you.
> And, above all, you little jerk,
> don't expect to like your work."

It wasn't any fun for Herb to stand there, in the open, hearing that — *exposed* to it — a threat, an existential horror of that magnitude. He didn't know if there was anything that he, a teenaged kid, could do to check it, counteract it.

But something told him that he'd better fire back a salvo of his own, and hope that it connected. And so he faced the rhododendrons squarely, with his shoulders back.

"Your threats won't work," he managed to blurt out. "I'm not that dense. I don't take orders from a fence."

With that, he turned his back on them and marched straight up the driveway. He hoped the pickets couldn't tell, from looking at his back, how all that talk of "ruts" and not expecting to enjoy what he was going to do had scared him.

Behind him, there was only silence. Except, of course, for groans.

35

10
BLAST OFF

For the most part, Herb wasn't into preconceptions. He took both things and people as they came, instead of working out beforehand how they might or ought to be, and having expectations of them. Some people call that "being philosophical"; others say it's more like bland, or dumb, or lazy. If asked what *he* thought, Herbie would have put it this way: "Pretty much, I trust to luck, I guess."

And so, he didn't think much of the fact that when he topped a final little rise of ground, he saw his destination was this enormous gray stone building with only slits, high up, for windows, connected to a big round tower with a battlement on top. Or that it had a nice wide moat around it, and a drawbridge that was open — down — with a sign on it which read not only CASTLES IN THE AIR, but also BED AND BREAKFAST — HOMEMADE FRENCH TOAST. Or that there was a woman in a wide straw hat kneeling by the flower garden running 'round the moat, and pulling weeds from it. Which weeds and other garden debris she was tossing into a two-wheeled cart beside her. He just accepted all of that, convinced that this was going to be his lucky day.

It seemed the woman must have heard Herb crunching up the driveway. When he was still about four bowling alley lengths from where she worked, she turned and waved at him and then, with sweeping motions of one arm (the one that ended in a trowel) she urged him to approach, to come across the close-cropped lawn and join her. Even at that distance he could see that she was laughing to herself, quite merrily. Herb, himself, had never found that doing garden work was that much fun.

When he got close, and doffed his double-visored cap, the way he always did when he was wearing hats and meeting ladies, she turned her head around again and peered at him.

"Great Hebe's junior jeebies!" she exclaimed. "You must be Herbie Hertzman!" And while he nodded "yes," she picked one knee up off the ground and, using it to push on with both hands, she made it to her feet.

"Sandy said you might be coming by," she said to Herb. "I'm Sesame deBarque." She pulled a muddy glove off her right hand and offered it to him, laughing much as if she'd just exposed a rabbit, or a squid.

Herb shook the hand enthusiastically. Sesame deBarque was older than his mother, also shorter, rounder, fair instead of dark. Wisps of blondish hair escaped from underneath her picture hat, and her full, strong-featured face was ruddy. She wore — indeed, she was enveloped by — a shapeless tentlike sundress cut from some material that would have made a cheerful cover for a couch, patterned as it was with large green leaves and ample yellow flowers that looked much like cabbages. This garment ended just above her knees on which were strapped two rubber kneeling pads; below them, her pink, sturdy calves were bare, as were her ankles and her feet. Her toenails gleamed bright emerald.

"Sandy?" Herbie said.

"Alexander Rex," she answered. "Cunning little devil, isn't he?" And then she laughed again, and slipping one hand under Herbie's arm and grabbing her cart's handle with the other, she began to walk both cart and boy toward the open drawbridge.

Unsure of how to answer that, or even if he should, Herb pointed at the sign tacked to the drawbridge.

"You know, it isn't really either bed *or* breakfast that I'm looking for," he said. "I thought I'd made that clear to Mr. Rex, although sometimes it's quite easy not to understand another person. But anyway, it's actually more something to *do* I'm hoping to find out about. With myself, you know? Although, to be completely honest, I've worked up quite an appetite from all the walking that I've done today." He paused and thought it over. "And I really like French toast a *lot*," he said, quite truthfully.

Sesame deBarque threw back her head and laughed again.

"And Russian dressing, too, I'll bet," she said. "But Herb, I know *exactly* why you're here. That sign is just to throw them off. The tourists and the

38

busybodies — all the unbelievers. And, as far as cooking is concerned, it's all that I can do to toast *myself*, before an open fire. That's why I always have the other sign on, too. The little one above the archway, there." She pointed.

Herbie looked where she was pointing and sure enough, above the large main entrance to the castle was a small pink neon sign. NO VACANCY, it blinked, in Gothic script. It fit in very nicely with the architecture, Herbie thought.

"But," she added, "we can have a snack before we settle down to work. Just let me toss this junk out, first."

With that, she let go of his arm and pushed the cart up to the water's edge and dumped its contents into the moat. Herb was surprised at that. The driveway and the grounds were so well manicured, it seemed peculiar, out of place, to see this garden refuse floating on the moat's clear water.

His hostess must have seen the look on Herbie's face.

"Don't worry. Watch," she said. They'd crossed the drawbridge to the castle side, and there she seized the handle on a chain that hung down just outside the door and gave the thing a yank.

At once, the water in the moat began to move, from right to left as Herbie turned to look at it, and faster all the time until it was as speedy as rapids or a whirlpool. The water level kept on lowering, as well, until the last few inches swept from view and disappeared some place beneath the castle with this most enormous "Glug!" — after which fresh water gushed into the moat again. Herb stood there, staring, stupefied.

Sesame deBarque, however, clapped her hands delightedly.

"Isn't that a ring-tailed doozie, now?" she raved. "A scientific and hygienic miracle? This is the first one ever made, by the Arab prince, Walid Caliph, in 1323 A.D., and installed around his castle in North Africa. Do his initials ring a bell with you, by any chance? You bet they do." She nodded. "Then what happened was some movie mogul saw it over there in 1951, still working perfectly, and fell in love with it. He bought the whole shebang the way they do — castle, moat, the works — and moved it stone by stone to this location. But some years after that there was an awful . . . incident. Someone pulled the chain during a party — accidentally or on purpose, who's to say? — and a half a dozen starlets and a man named Sid were never seen again. The mogul sold the place to me and moved to St. Tropez with someone by the name of Bijou." And she shook her head. "Some say he got away with murder, that he'd had it in for that guy Sid for years. They say he planned it all, even to the choice of weapon. According to that theory, the starlets were . . . unlucky, you could say. In the wrong place at the very worst of times."

"Gee," said Herbie. "That's some story, Ms. deBarque."

"Please," she said. "I'd rather that you called me Sesame, or Ses. Or SDB, if you prefer initials." She winked and clapped him on the back. "So. How about we get ourselves a snack and go to work? Okay?"

"Terrific," Herbie said. She flung the portal wide and went on in ahead of him to turn the lights on.

* * *

"Sandy Rex and I did Outward Bound together, years ago," Ses deBarque was saying as she and Herb went down another vaulted corridor, one peanut butter sandwich later. "He was a great kid to have in your group, a real team player, but he had a terrible sense of direction. Put him in the woods without a compass and he'd just go 'round and 'round. That's probably why he went into Guidance. He'd have, like, perfect empathy, you know? I mean, he'd know the questions from the inside out. Like, 'Where am I?' and 'How do I get out of here?' "

"Yes, or 'What am I going to do with myself?' " said Herbie. "Which is my main question and the reason Mr. Rex suggested I come up here. What he didn't tell me, though, is how you possibly could help me."

"That's not surprising," she replied. "You see, he doesn't know. Nobody does, except for me and all the clients that I've served. And with them I have, like, an agreement."

They came to a door at the end of the corridor. She opened it and motioned Herbie in ahead of her.

He gasped. It was a gorgeous room. The words that came to Herbie's mind were "huge baronial hall." That is to say, the place was barnlike in dimensions, with those slits of windows high up in the walls on either side, and lots of banners, pennants, ensigns, streamers, flags, gonfalons and the like hanging from the noble rafters or jutting from the walls on staffs. Herb recognized the logos on a lot of them, and saw that many of them were from very major corporations and professions including, to his mixed emotions, all of these: Toyota, and McDonald's; IBM, the Minnesota Twins.

A huge refectory table, flanked by maybe forty high-backed chairs, ran down the middle of the room. At the far end of it was a handsome walnut desk, with swivel chair behind it and a client's chair in front. And against the farthest wall there was a huge, and most amazing, wheel!

The thing was twenty-five-feet high, at least, and flat, its surface sectioned off in pie-shaped pieces, eight of them, all in different bright, exciting colors. And each of those eight sections had some words in it. Here is what it looked like, provided you imagine all the different colors on the thing:

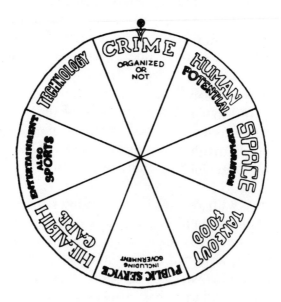

At the top, there was an arrow that would point to something if the wheel were spun and then allowed to stop.

"Let's get the paperwork all taken care of, first," Herb's hostess said. She led him past the big long table to the desk and took her place behind it in the swivel chair. He sat across from her and crossed his legs. It seemed to him that that would be the sort of thing a person taking care of "paperwork" would do.

"This is our basic 'dinner plate' agreement," Ses explained. She'd pulled out a loose-leaf notebook more or less three inches thick.

"Dinner plate?" said Herb.

"Yes, isn't that absurd?" she said. "It's something that we *say*, these days; don't ask me why, for heavens' sakes. Unless it's because it can hold four hundred and thirty-seven helpings of 'the parties of the first and second part,' and eighty-six side orders of 'whereas.' But anyway. We also have the short form, if you want to save some time."

She handed him a single sheet of paper that read: "I agree that I can't have it all.*" Below that was a line for him to sign on; it was dotted.

At the bottom of the page, beside another asterisk, it said: "Just thank your lucky stars for anything you get, and swear you'll never mention any part of this to anyone, so help you Hannah."

"So," said Herb. He signed the thing and sat back in his chair. So. He had agreed. To what, though? Really?

"I guess I'm set," he said. "But still. The one thing I don't understand is . . . is what it is you're going to do for me."

Sesame deBarque just stared at him a second, blinking. But then she wrinkled up her nose and shook her head, and started making sounds of comic self-disgust, while laying open-handed swats on top of her straw hat.

"Absentminded Minnie Thaw," she seemed to say. "I haven't told you . . . *anything* — now, have I? Well . . . " She reached across the desk and patted Herbie's hand.

"Here's the way it works," she said. She rose and went to stand beside the wheel. "First, you step up to our Winner's Circle, here, and give the thing a spin. What the little arrow ends up pointing to is *it*, the field you're going to sample. Seeing as you haven't got the foggiest idea of what you *want* to do, or what's involved in any of them — right? — it shouldn't matter in the slightest where the arrow lands. Correct?"

And Herbie nodded. That was true. For sure. He could sample any kind of work, he guessed. Why not? Of course he'd never thought of Crime, a life of crime (organized or not) as being one of his alternatives. He'd always had a tendency to blush, or giggle, if his mother asked who put the ice tray back with just one cube in it. But he knew there was a lot of major money to be made in shady deals, "white-collar crime," and other kids from real good families were doing it without their mothers asking them about it. He decided he would keep an open mind on Crime. Chances were, he'd never have to deal with it, other than as a victim. There were seven other "choices," after all.

"*Then*," she said, "we take you to the tower, where you step into our vehicle and get transported, almost

44

magically, into the time and place where your job identity awaits you. There and then you try it out, and after you have done so, you return for your debriefing." Herbie blinked. "If the two of us agree that wasn't *it*, for you, we make a new appointment and you try again."

She sat back in her chair and smiled at him some more. "Any further questions?" she inquired.

"What kind of *vehicle* is that?" said Herb. "I'm not sure I've ever heard of — "

"No, probably you haven't," she said, interrupting. "It's called an Upwardlimobile. You'll see. And better still, *experience*. It's really on the cutting edge of space-slash-time vocational technology."

"I'll bet," said Herb enthusiastically. And then he had another thought. "But maybe, if you have a phone, I ought to call my mom. I told her I'd be back by suppertime."

"No sweat," said Ses deBarque. "You will be. A week in any of the places you might go lasts only fifty-seven seconds, here. We use a time compressor; it's a handy little thing. I wish that there was something half as good for hips and thighs."

Herb nodded and stood up. "Well, in that case I believe I *am* all set," he said. He went and spun the wheel.

Around and 'round it went. And when it stopped, it stopped, of course, on Crime — Organized or not.

"Zoo-eee," said Ses, excitedly, "you sure don't kid around! Gonna be real ba-ad right off the bat." She sobered up a little. "That's our very widest, *wildest* category, as I'm sure you've figured out already. You *could* end up on Wall Street, or in the halls of government — or in a long pink Cadillac with half a dozen rental properties named Misty. Only the Dispatcher knows, and it's not telling yet. But soon. . . ."

She started pushing buttons on a console on her desk. It reminded Herb of the automatic teller machine down at the bank.

"Come on, come on . . ." she said. She drummed her fingertips, impatiently. " 'Somewhere, over the rainbow . . .' " she sang, softly.

"Ah, here we are," she said at last, as a small plastic rectangle, no bigger than a credit card, appeared from out of the console's side. She glanced at it, and nodded and stood up.

"Let's go," she (simply) said.

She led him through three doors and down two halls, and so into the tower. To Herb's considerable surprise, the Upwardlimobile looked like a Ford or Chevy van, perhaps an '86, in tan. He'd been expecting something more along the lines of *Challenger*, *Apollo*, one of those. He was, in fact, relieved.

There was a slot between the windshield and the driver's door, and Ses inserted the small plastic card in that, before she slid the side door open.

Inside, it was exactly like a van, with breakfast nook and sofa bed and compact kitchenette. There was a calendar that had a color photo of Old Faithful on it. Behind the two big bucket seats up front, there was a heavy suede-look curtain, which Herb's hostess now pulled closed.

"So — I guess it's time for you to buckle up," she told the boy. "And we'll begin the countdown." She gestured toward the couch inside the van.

Herb clambered in, and sat.

"I guess they'll be expecting me, and all," he said.

46

"You bet they will," she said. "You'll see. All set, now, Mr. Argonaut?"

Herb had gotten his seat belt on and buckled tight. He smiled at her misspeaking "astronaut," like that. He was nervous, but not scared, he thought. It seemed to him he'd flown before, one time, when he was just a baby. He was pretty sure that he remembered landing. They had missed the runway, gone beyond it. But they'd landed safely, anyway.

"Roger, wilco," he told Ses deBarque, and flashed the thumbs-up sign.

"Five, four, three, two, one," she said, and slammed the door tight shut.

11
THE ISLE OF
WINCE 'N' WAILS

Herb was pretty impressed with the Upwardli-mobile's ride. "Smooth" was like an understatement; there wasn't any sense of motion whatsoever, and it didn't make a sound. Nor was there any pressure on his ears, or anywhere, while taking off or landing. And because there weren't any windows back where he was, Herbie couldn't see what he was going through, or over. Also, the time compressor made it hard for him to even guess how long the trip was lasting, and he never saw a driver, either.

If he hadn't gotten there, it might have seemed to Herb as if he hadn't gone at all.

The door slid open suddenly, and there he was. Because he wasn't into preconceptions, he wasn't that surprised at where. The Upwardlimobile had landed on a hillside, it appeared, and from his couch the boy was looking down upon a — what? — a *settlement* (he supposed you'd say) that someone had established on a rocky, treeless island mostly covered up by ice and snow. At least Herb *thought* it was an island; it had a sort of shipwrecked look about it.

The settlement consisted of some twenty Quonset huts and other different kinds of structures (that included one big gray affair that looked to be inflated), most of them connected to another one or two by covered passageways. Wind had piled the snow in whale-sized drifts in places; elsewhere it had swept the ground as bare as blubber, revealing quite a grand array of trash: metal drums, black plastic bags stuffed full and broken crates of many shapes and sizes, some with weathered lettering on them. Herb saw one that read: Designer Leather Telephones. Taken as a whole, this didn't look like all that great a place to practice criminal activities — except, of course, for littering.

A moment later, he had company. It was a fellow wearing pac boots and a parka with that wolf's fur trimming on the hood.

"Don't anybody *tell* me!" he cried out. He had a cultured and enthusiastic voice. "*You* are — You *must* be — Herbie Hertzman. With the pizza that we ordered, am I right?" He laughed and stomped across the van with hand outstretched. He didn't look much more than thirty — *forty*, anyway — and was about the most clean-shaven guy that Herb had ever seen.

"Uh — I'm Herbie," said the boy. "Without the pizza, though. Nobody told me anythi — "

"I'm not surprised," the man went on. "We *are* a *tad* beyond the outer limits of deliverance, up here."

49

He winked. "But, *grand* to see you, anyway." He sounded almost English, but not quite. "*Welcome* to the Isle of Wince 'n' Wails! I'm Greenfield Hill, proprietor, in charge of the igloonatics who call this godforsaken outpost home!"

Herb let the fellow wring his hand. Greenfield Hill used both of his to do so, holding onto Herb's and kind of cupping it between the two of his. Hill's hands were very warm and smooth; Herb thought his grip felt honest and sincere. He welcomed both the warmth *and* honesty. An icy, arctic wind had blown in through the open door and almost set his teeth to chattering. And feeling that you're being dealt with honestly by someone who you know to be a crook is warming in its own way, too.

"Chop-chop, let's hand up Herbie's mitts and parka, Trev. Good *man*." Hill spoke to someone still outside the door. "Just slip these on, my beamish boy. There you go. How's that? A perfect fit, *I'd* say. I bet I was a haberdasher, in some other incarnation. Now, how about we scat-tail out of here and rush to sample Wince 'n' Wails's brand of northern hospitality? A warming cup of cocoa, or some Gray old Earl will hit the spot, I'll bet."

"The Isle of Wince 'n' Wails?" said Herb. The windproof parka'd made a difference right away. Now that he was pretty sure he wasn't going to freeze to death, he thought he'd better get a few things straight. Was he where he belonged? For sure? He'd heard of people flying from Seattle to New York (for instance), who'd had their baggage go to, say, Karachi, Pakistan. Maybe, in this instance, *he* was like lost luggage.

"Well," said Greenfield Hill, "its *real* name isn't

that, of course. According to the gang at Rand McNally, this *most* unprepossessing piece of real estate is Prince of Wales Island, and a part of Canada, District of Franklin in the Northwest Territories, *well* above the Arctic Circle and *not* far from the North Magnetic Pole. By most of us, however, it's thought of as *the* jumping-off place in the world entire — and hence the Isle of Wince 'n' Wails. But at the same time it's just *perfect* for our purposes because it *is* — except for inside, where we do our work — so *totally* unbearable! Now what say you to a jump right on that noisy little Arctic feline there, and letting our young Trevor whisk us to a place of warmth?"

Herb hesitated, still. Although what Greenfield Hill had said suggested that this place was, like, a hideout of some sort, he still had doubts about the guy himself. Vic, of Vic and Vera, his own dad and Dr. Bismuthson, his high school principal, all looked more like criminals than Greenfield Hill.

"One thing," Herb started, rather haltingly, "perhaps a stupid question, but, well — to save some time, just don't get mad, all right? — the stuff that's going on down there," he nodded toward the settlement, "it *is* illegal, isn't it?"

"Oh, you can bet your . . . Abenaki knicky-knacky there, it is," said Greenfield Hill, pointing at Herb's tomahawk. "Could you imagine any *homo sapiens* who hadn't been *lobotomized* living in a place like this for *funzies?*"

With which he laughed, delightedly, and helped Herb out the door, with an aren't-we-all-buds-together arm around his shoulders.

* * *

"The Mounties think we're just a bunch of silly science types — geologists and weather-weirds," Greenfield Hill was saying over dinner, hours later.

When they'd gotten to the settlement, they'd had a cup of cocoa in a room with a door that had Lounge on it. There were some other men and women there, but none of them was dressed in a chalk-striped suit with extra shoulder pads, or pointed, narrow shoes. But seeing how they greeted Greenfield Hill, Herb became convinced he was the *capo*, Boss, whatever — never mind his good-guy preppy look. After cocoa, Herb was shown his room and given lots of time to get "cleaned up" for dinner. No word had yet been said about what anyone was doing there.

"In fact," G. Hill was saying now, after sipping from the glass of light white wine that Herb had said "no, thank you" to, "there's only one RCMP, a Mountie corporal — I think his name is Truscott or McKenzie, a sweet young *Scottish* sort of person — for this *immensity* of space, about the size of our Alaska." He shook his head and laughed. "He told us he'd swing by again in fourteen-fifteen years, he didn't know for sure. That's about how long it takes him to go once around his beat, traveling by *kayak* and on *snowshoes*. Thrice around and they retire him, I guess. With a citation from Her Majesty and a clock set in a walrus tusk."

The three of them were sitting at the table in the living-dining area of Hill's apartment: Herb and Hill himself and Trevor Rhinelander the 4th, the "Trev" who'd handed in the parka and the mittens, and who'd been the driver of that snowmobile, an Arctic Cat. He seemed, to Herb, to be another pleasant person, lean and dark, but with a friendly, flashing smile, much closer to his age than Hill's. It had been Trev, in fact, who'd cooked the dinner; Herbie'd found that out from Hill, who seemed extremely proud of him for having done so. Hill had whispered to the boy when Trev was in the kitchen, saying it was very "now" of Trev to pick up gourmet cooking, to really get to know his sauces.

While he was eating, Herb tried to think of questions that his father might come up with in this situation, the sorts of questions he would ask another man about his business, when he didn't have a clue *about* that business, even what it was.

"So," he said, at last, filling an infrequent silence, "it sounds like this'd be a great location for your kind of . . . operation." The other two both nodded, vaguely, but they kept on eating, didn't speak. Herb tried another tack. "So, how long have you-all been . . . operating, here?"

"I wondered that myself, when *I* first came," said Trevor. "And I was quite surprised to learn they started up right after World War II. Which means — let's see" — he looked at Hill — "forty-five full years?" Hill nodded. "With but a single change in management, and that was just two years ago."

"True, true," said Greenfield Hill. "Our founder's heir, who was the president by then, he got a sudden urge one springlike Friday morning. To get into something else, I guess. An hour later, he was gone." He snapped his fingers. "Poof! Like that!"

"That was my second year up here," said Trev. "And thanks to him" — he bobbed his head at Hill — "we never missed a beat."

"*Well*," said Hill, "we had our programs going, and a product to . . . produce. Nature — as you

53

know, Herb — just *abhors* a vacuum. I stepped in, picked up the reins, and here we all are now. Happy as a flock of larks." He smiled, and so did Trevor.

"Exaltation," Trevor said.

"What?" said Hill.

"Exaltation," Trevor said, again. "An *exaltation* of larks. That's another way of saying lots of larks. If not preferred, at least accepted."

"*Is* it, now?" Greenfield Hill seemed thrilled to get that news. "That's just *delightful*, Trev! And good for you for *knowing* that. I'm proud of you, I really am."

Trevor dropped his eyes in modest pleasure. Herb wondered what the story was with Hill and Trevor. He didn't care what larks were called. He decided he would have to switch to very pointed questions.

"You know," he said, "I'm really in the dark about . . . well, what you're *doing* here. What the 'programs' are, and what the 'product' is — all that. And what a guy like *me* could do, what *role* I'd play in . . . everything."

Herb hadn't planned on saying "role," but when he did, he was extremely glad he had. He definitely preferred to think he'd just be *playing* "criminal" on Wince 'n' Wails, walking through a *part*, like in a play. Greenfield Hill and Trevor Whatshisname were nice enough, but he just didn't see himself as one of them, their type. "Robert Cohn was once middleweight boxing champion of Princeton," went flashing through his mind. Those were the first words in *The Sun Also Rises*, he knew, a book by Ernest Hemingway.

Hill stood up, but not to answer Herb, to go for seconds. The food was on the sideboards. It consisted of what Herbie would have said were fish chunks and long onions in a thick white sauce that tasted slightly licorice-y, along with rice that had some kinds of nuts in it, and a salad that was only funny-looking lettuce leaves, no cukes or peppers or tomatoes. Herb gathered that this food was like what people ate in France; Hill and Trevor had French names for all of it. He'd seen a movie that was all in French, one time, and the girl in it was shown completely naked in one scene. Going by the way she looked, Herb guessed French food was good for people.

"Basically," said Hill, returning to his seat, "the thing we want for you to do is be yourself, over-qualified as you might be for that . . . responsibility. As for our little operation here. . . ." He took a bite of food, and chewed, and swallowed.

"What we're *up to* is what certain nasty tongues would probably describe as *smuggling*," Hill said, and sighed. "We don't, because it ain't — exactly. We see the work we're doing as a *service*. To our *products*, on the one hand, and our *country*, on the other."

Greenfield Hill then wiped both corners of his mouth. "Show Herbie how we manage, Trev, all right?" he said. "I can barely wait to see that look of utter aghastonishment, as it, like, spreads across his pure but honest countenance."

"Check," said Trevor, springing to his feet. "Just let me bring the world to him." And he strode into the living room and grabbed the big round globe from off the walnut desk. He put it on the table in between his place and Herb's.

"Everything begins down here," he said, "in Acapulco, *May-he-co*." He got his finger on the spot, on the Pacific coast of Mexico.

"We take our raw material from there and set off 'round the world on Route One Hundred," Trevor said, and he started to run his finger south, straight down the globe, down to Antarctica and (after picking up the globe and turning it) then up the other side.

"A.k.a. the one hundredth meridian of longitude," confided Greenfield Hill. "We just like to *call* it Route One Hundred." And he gave a cozy little chuckle.

"We *pause* in Bangkok, Thailand, here, a while," said Trev, "and then resume our journey up, right through Siberia, above the Northern Pole, and down the other side to end up here on Wince 'n' Wails, still smackeroo on Route One Hundred." His finger'd settled on a tiny island, well above the Arctic Circle.

"Where we unload," said Greenfield Hill, "and *process* for a while. In time, our products end up in the States, of course."

"The land of opportunity," and Trevor smiled, "for us."

"I *see*," said Herb, and so he did, but all too well, alas. What he saw was plain disaster, thanks to Alexander Rex and Sesame deBarque, drug lord and lady.

Beyond a doubt, he thought, the product was cocaine, the lady that became a tiger, Doctor White. Like everyone his age, Herb had an attitude concerning drugs, already. It was the same one that he'd had toward bullies, back in grade school: He both feared and hated them. Like bullies, drugs might kill him, he believed, even if they didn't mean to.

That's not to say Herb wasn't *curious*; indeed he was. He wondered how drugs made you feel — exactly how, the different ones. He knew the words and phrases for the feelings. People talked of them, sometimes, compared to how sex felt, or how they made sex feel. Herb had had some limited experience with sex, with what you might call "starter sex." He loved the way *that* felt. But the thing with sex was this: it was built in to everyone, and harmless, even maybe good for you, and with you all the time. You had to have, were *meant* to have, sex feelings. Drugs, however, were made up of chemicals you had to *get* and *take*, knowing they could hurt your precious body, and your mind. It seemed to Herb that people who took drugs were trusting, like, to *luck* — hoping they would not be hurt too bad. He absolutely wasn't going to do that; he would just stay curious. It wasn't fair to T.K., to ask her to protect him from himself. So it was quite unthinkable that he'd be part of getting drugs to other people, helping them to do what he believed they shouldn't. What he wouldn't do himself.

Even if he had a minor, temporary "role," that wasn't any good. There was a principle involved. The boy stood up. It was right to stand on principle. Then, if you had to run for it, you wouldn't have to take the time to get up, first.

"I'm sorry," Herbie said. "But I won't have anything to do with drugs."

He knew exactly where the door was, and that Hill's parka hung there on a rack beside it. Getting to the van might be a problem, and starting it and driving it.

57

"Drugs?" said Greenfield Hill, brows drawn together.

"Drugs?" said Trevor Rhinelander the 4th, eyebrows up, as in amazement.

"Yes," said Herbie Hertzman. "Drugs. Cocaine. That's the 'product,' isn't it? The 'raw material'?"

The other two cracked up. They looked at one another and they both said *"Drugs?"* again, but in entirely different tones. And then they started to guffaw. They laughed and laughed and pounded on the tabletop, and laughed some more, and said the magic word again, which made them laugh, if anything, much harder.

And when they'd finally finished laughing and had wiped their eyes and hiccuped, Greenfield Hill looked up at Herb and spoke.

"No, dear heart," he said, "the 'product' isn't drugs, far from it. Although we've *had* a dope or two come through, from time to time." He looked at Trev, and for a moment there, Herbie was afraid they might crack up again. But this time they controlled themselves, and Greenfield Hill continued.

"Our standards are at least as high as yours, concerning drugs," he said to Herb, "and possibly a good deal higher. Drugs are not our 'product.' But to give you an example of what is. . . ."

Hill started smiling once again, and then he pointed at the person sitting next to him, at Trevor Rhinelander the 4th.

"Well," said Greenfield Hill, "*he* is."

12
THE ERSTWHILE
JOSÉ BLOW

"What?" said Herb. He sat back down — collapsed, more like it.

"Mm-hmm," said Greenfield Hill. "Four years ago, our Trevor was some little José Blow, or might as well have been. A barefoot, brown-eyed *bumpkinito*, feeding chickens near Chihuahua. *But*" — he held a finger up — "he was our type: *intelligente*, ambishoso, not afraid of work. And thus, darn close to four years later, he's a man transformed, a product of the *most* intensive education ever offered anywhere, to anyone, at anytime. He is, as far as any eye can see, a perfect . . . need I say it? Rhymes with common word for baby dog? And next spring he'll have kennel space at Shearson Lehman Hutton."

He beamed at Trevor who beamed back at him and nodded, modestly.

59

"Each and every spring thereafter," Hill continued, "a quarter of his gross shall fly on home to roost with us. In a year or two that won't be chicken feed, my friend, but he will go on paying, gladly, for good reason. Paying his tuition in installments, you could say, and buying some insurance, and delighted to be doing so. Am I correct, young Trev?"

"*Por supuesto,*" said the erstwhile José Blow, now grinning broadly at his mentor. Herb knew that meant "of course," of course.

13
STUDENT TEACHING

Two days later (time-compressed) Herb was standing in his "classroom," waiting for his "students" to arrive. He was extremely nervous, naturally enough, although the room that he was in was nothing like the ones that he'd inhabited before, in "school." There was a sofa and a love seat and a wooden bench; there were some poofy cushions on the floor and three upholstered chairs; there were assorted tables, end and side and coffee, one of them with leather on it, one with a brass tray on top. An oval mirror and three paintings graced the walls: one super-realistic still life of a hot dog and an orange drink, so detailed you could see the wiener and the tulip glass both sweat — also a beachscape showing bathers, in Brazil, perhaps, going by their brief and cheeky outfits, and another that was just a vase of quite familiar yellow flowers.

"This classroom looks more like a classy living room," Herb said out loud, just making sure his nerves had not deprived him of his voice.

He walked across the room and looked at his reflection in the oval mirror.

"The teacher of this class resembles some dumb ditzy dweeb," he told himself. "I *hate* him."

He went and peered out one of the wide windows, which was triple-glazed, at least.

"Nine A.M. up here could pass for nine at night," he said.

Herb sat down on the bench and ran his palms along his thighs again. He told himself it was *all right* that he was nervous in this role: The Teacher. He decided he felt more like an impala. All your life you've feared and hated lions, and all at once you're meant to *be* a lion. You go and get a drink and look down at the water hole, at your reflection. What you see is an impala.

Could he possibly be popular (he asked himself), convince his students he was "one of them"? The trouble was, he wasn't one of them, not even close. They were going to be a bunch of Mexicans, ten people from another culture altogether who, he understood, would range in age from under seventeen to twenty-seven.

And probably the ones his age would all have mustaches.

Greenfield Hill had told him that there wouldn't be a language gap. Like all the other students there on Wince 'n' Wails, these (he said) would speak American, "and maybe even *English*." And *without* an accent you could put your finger on.

"Incredibly enough, they all *arrive* in that condition, thanks to our dear founder's great discovery," he said. "And their four months in Bangkok, speaking only Thai — or, as I prefer to call it, Siamese."

"What?" said Herb. "You teach them Siamese *before* you teach them English?"

"Yes, exactly," Hill explained. "You see, the Siamese sets off a 'gross linguistical reaction' (as the founder said). When you put Siamese on top of Spanish, you completely 'cleanse the palate' (as that dear man would also say). The learner's slate is left as clean, phonetically, as any newborn babe's. Of course there *is* one *caveat*: too much Siamese and they get stuck in sing-song city. Four months of it is pretty nearly perfect. And at that point we can start to sock the English to 'em."

"Wait," said Herb. "Just so I'm sure I understand. . . . You're telling me that Siamese and Spanish are such different languages they more or less, like, *cancel one another out?*"

"Precisely," Hill agreed. "It reminds one of the process where you add some *chlorine*, which of course is poisonous, to *sewerage*, another poison. And you end up with a harmless glass of water."

"Yes," said Herb, "but doesn't — "

"The water may not taste that great," said Hill, "because it isn't truly natural. The same with these folks' English, in a way. It's kind of . . . *blah*, sometimes. Perhaps a little *yucky*, even. That's something you'll be working on."

"You mean," said Herb, still trying to get this straight, "that once they reach this state of 'speaking-

63

readiness' that you've described, they *then* can pick up *English* on the trip between, like, Bangkok and the island, here?"

"Absolootle," Greenfield Hill replied. "We've found a journey through Siberia is just a *fabulous* accelerant to learning."

"How so?" asked Herb, the innocent impala.

"Well, just imagine," Hill confided. "Suppose that *you* were one of them, and someone said to you — your *teacher* said to you: 'Now, look here, kids. Everybody who *correctly* reads, out loud, the first ten paragraphs of the article "Why You Can't Laugh At Cher Anymore" in the Feb 88 issue of *Premiere* magazine (we use a lot of cultural material) will *certainly* be on a dogsled when we start from this location on Steppe One, tomorrow afternoon. The rest, the ones who make *mistakes*, will just stay here and do the best they can without, like, tents or food.' I mean, would *you* get words like 'Meryl Streep' — and even 'Chastity Bono' — down pat, or what?"

"I see," said Herbie, nodding thoughtfully. "Whoever wants a plate of musk ox stew say 'triskaidekaphobia.' Pronouncing it correctly, please." That was, of course, a very lucky word, for him.

"Say *what*?" said Greenfield Hill.

"Triskaidekaphobia," said Herb. "Fear of the number thirteen." He decided not to mention T.K.

"Oooh," cried Hill. "I *love* it! That's *fantastic*, Herb!" For a moment, there, the boy felt positively Mexican.

Herb's class came tromping in the room at 9:08 A.M., exactly. They were accompanied by Trev, who said he'd come along to "do the honors," introduce the group to its new teacher.

Herb was amazed. They didn't look like cartoon Mexicans at all, any more than Trevor did. None of them had on sombreros or huaraches, none of them flopped down against a wall and promptly fell asleep. Four of them wore sunglasses, but two of those had shoved them up onto the tops of their heads, and all of them had colorful elastic neck straps on the things. They all were dressed informally, but with a certain flair, the kind that spoke of uniformly carefree affluence. In other words, they looked as if they'd *shopped* in a Banana Republic, but not as if they'd *lived* in one.

One girl, in addition to her stylish, narrow cotton canvas pants and leather ranch boots, had on a dark green Dartmouth (in white letters) sweatshirt. Herb rocked back on his heels. Unless he missed his guess — was very much mistaken — *that* girl's name was — *might have been* — well, Tyree Toledano.

Trevor Rhinelander the 4th was doing the honors by then. He explained that Herbie Hertzman, seventeen, was now a high school senior, and that he'd spent his entire life being "a typical American kid." At that, a murmur of respectful awe swept through the room. One slightly older male was already evolved enough to say "fantastic." The fellow had on broken-in blue jeans by St. Laurent, a bright red Loft Wool sweater (L. L. Bean), and a bright blue baseball cap from Eddie Bauer. There was something funny written on the front of it; it said, *Mikey likes it*.

Herbie Hertzman, Trevor said, was going to tell them all about himself: his family, his school, his bedtimes, his taste in food and drink and television shows, the games and sports he'd played while growing up, the things boys did with other U.S. boys (and then with U.S. girls), the contents of his room, his pockets, his desk drawers, his bathroom cabinet, his *dreams*.

"He's going to give you folks the works," said Trev. "From soup to nuts, from ticktacktoe to tofu. Is that the pure unvarnished, double-H?" he turned and said to Herb.

Herb nodded. He noticed Trevor's easygoing, totally informal, casually idiomatic way of speaking had set off still more sounds of adulation. Clearly, all the members of this younger class could look at Trev and see the sort of person that they planned to also be. And, too, potentially as someone who, at some still unknown point in future time, they might just do a deal with. Trev was now, and always would be, an *"hermano"* — part of what they knew to be a network of "designer Mexicans" (as Hill referred to them behind their backs, from time to time) scattered all across the states, dug into power slots of one sort or another.

"You'd be surprised, I'll bet — I'm talking *real* surprised," Greenfield Hill had said to Herbie, day before, "at the number of . . . let's just say 'prominent Americans' who are, in fact, our products. Who are 'drybacks,' as I sometimes call them." Chuckling.

"What?" said Herb. "You mean that there are people that I've *heard of*, people who . . . well, people like my father just assume are real Americans, who aren't?"

66

"Ooh, yes indeedy," said Hill, with a mischievous expression on his smooth, pink face. That day he had a yacht club necktie on, and he was looking droll as any davit, sharper than a marlinspike.

"Of the thirteen major presidential hopefuls, back in early '88," he said, "seven Democrats and six Republicans in all, no less than four were once on Wince 'n' Wails. Of the CEOs of the Fortune 500 companies, some forty-six, just under ten percent, are ours. Real estate developers? We've got a dozen of the biggest in the country! Major auto dealers? More than you can shake an old transmission at. A third of the network news anchors. Nobelists: just one, and that was just a fluke; there isn't that much dough in prizes. Two of our people *did* win the Publishers Clearing House biggie, but that's because that fellow — what's his name? he's always on TV — he's one of us."

"Good grief," said Herbie. "And I suppose you're going to tell me half the guys who make a million bucks or more a year from playing baseball are *also* products of this program."

"Oh, heavens, *no*," said Hill. "*Baseball* is a game of *skill*. You have to *play* it, pitch the ball, or hit it. Baseball calls for some specific *talents*. Fernando is a Mexican, of course — Fernando Valenzuela, *you* know — but, hell, the guy was great. He *earned* the money that he made. That's like a different ball game altogether. *Terribly* old-fashioned." And he laughed.

"I see," said Herbie, thinking what Hill said made lots of sense. There was skill and talent, on the one hand. You either had them, or you worked real hard to get them. You *needed* them for certain kinds of jobs. Or you had to know a lot to do those jobs.

67

But, it seemed, there also were a bunch of other jobs, which almost anyone could do, and even be successful at, provided that they had a lot of nerve, looked good and had connections, and were lucky.

Herb thought about the fields a person could be real successful in and also be a . . . well, *dumb jerk*. Politics, it seemed, was surely one. And all those businesses in which a person's job was pretty much to "put together deals," and make (Herb had to gulp) a lot of money.

But was that necessarily so bad, he asked himself? Take what was going on at Wince 'n' Wails. Was this so terrible, the act of helping Mexicans to be productive citizens? Rich instead of poor? After all, the boundary separating us and them is artificial, arbitrary, really. It could be anywhere, or nowhere. People cross it all the time, and most of them end up in sweatshops, or the lettuce fields. Isn't this a far, far better thing?

When looked at in a certain light, Greenfield Hill was nothing more or less than a *developer*. Of course, this scheme of his had an Orwellian dimension in that he, Big Brother, made these people all the same. But he also, at the same time, was creating jobs and giving talent and hard work a chance to show what they could do.

Of course (and to be sure) Hill also took a heaping handful of the fruits that they had labored for. In that respect, the deal on Wince 'n' Wails was borderline *Fal*wellian, Herb thought.

"Your class was *fabulous*," said Tyree Toledano. Except that during introductions at the start of it, she'd said her name, her U.S. name, was Hepzibah

Medallion, and for "nickname" on her college application she'd put "Zippy."

She'd lingered after class, after all the rest of them had gone.

"I thought that that was really interesting," she said, "the stuff you said about how guys your age, *our* age, all want to . . . 'make a touchdown,' is it? With their girlfriends?"

"That's 'score,' " said Herbie, trying not to blush. "The word I used was 'score.' Making a touchdown just applies to football — that's our kind of football — and to space landings, I guess. 'Score,' or 'making points,' can either be, like, in a game or with a girl."

"That's cool," said Zippy, and she wrinkled up her nose and grinned at him.

Herbie'd never seen a girl at such close range to match her. Zippy Medallion. He decided that she had a "pixie-panther" sort of face, and beautiful. She had a thick and shiny mop of jet-black hair, parted in the middle, dropping down in waves until it hit her shoulders; and then there were those fancy-flashing coal-brown onyx eyes. Her lips made Herbie think of cherry bombs; her teeth were straight and white as ice cream wagons. She also had the smoothest golden tan, the best complexion, that our boy had ever seen. And when she'd slouched back on a poofy cushion lying on the floor, and her Dartmouth deep green sweatshirt had, like, ridden up a ways and bared five inches of her belly, Herbie also saw that it was equally as golden-smooth and tan.

"But what I *still* don't get," she said, "is whether girls like me would want to 'score' ourselves — or even, like, 'get scored on.' Or is it that a person who is 'scored on' is a 'loser'?"

"It's kind of complicated," Herbie said, and that was true. The more so in that he really didn't know the answers to her questions. What *would* a girl like Zippy *really* want? From boys, in general. From him, specifically, Rob Lowe, or football captains, anywhere. All he really knew was what guys *said*, what he had heard. But he surely knew the answer to another question, one she hadn't asked, and it was, "Yes, guys lie."

"In my own case," Herbie said, improvising as he went along, but also trying very hard to tell the truth, "I'm the kind of guy who . . . well, let me put it this way: if *I* scored on a girl, I'd never *call* it that, or tell another guy I had, 'cause if I did — I mean, like *when* I do, of course — I'd have done it, *did* it, with a person that I really liked a *lot*, which means I'd think about her in a different way than if I'd just set out to try and *score* on someone — anyone." He was almost out of breath when he had finished saying that.

"But when I get to *Dartmouth* . . ." Zippy said, softly but with great concern, "you know I'm going to *Dartmouth*, right? When I get *there*, I'm just afraid I won't know how to tell the guys like you from all the other ones."

"Well, up there at *Dartmouth*, the first thing that you've got to do," said Herb with great conviction, "is probably not believe a word of what they tell you. The guys up there will all be really smart — like thirteen hundred on the SATs and up. And a lot of them are big fans of . . . well, of guys like Oliver North and Elliott Abrams, if you've ever heard of them. That means they'll *say* — they'll tell you — that they'd never do it with a girl unless they really liked her. And they'll *say* they care about a woman's reputation and her feelings. Unlike all the *other* guys, they'll say, in 'this fraternity' — or club, or class, or dorm, whatever. But the chances are that they'll be what they call 'misstating,' half the time."

"Mmm," said Zippy, thoughtfully. "But let's suppose I meet a guy I *want* to score on . . ." And she looked at Herb and took a step, and then a glide, in his direction, smiling with her coal-brown eyes. ". . . someone tall, and with beautiful blue eyes, I bet."

She was standing right in front of him, by then.

"In fact," she said, "let's say that this is *not* a Dartmouth College situation, even, . . ."

And with that she took her sweatshirt by its bottom hem and pulled it up and over her head and arms, and tossed it on the floor.

Then, smiling up at Herb, she shook her mop of wavy hair, to settle it. When she did that, other parts of her shook slightly, too.

"Great goddess," Herbie said, and meant it from the bottom of his heart as he, responding quite reflexively, and following the program in his genes (and jeans), reached out for her. He hadn't for a moment thought — expected — this would happen, especially on this remote and frozen wasteland. He'd come to check out Crime — Organized or not, as a career. Now this other option had . . . arisen. And it seemed like something he would like to *do*.

"OH, NO! OH, NO! OH, NO! OH, NO!" said Greenfield Hill, as he came striding into the room.

He sounded and he looked extremely cross. He scooped up Zippy's sweatshirt, when he got to it, and handed it to her.

"You put this on at once," he scolded. "You're meant to be in C-15, and doing Nautilus this hour. Though on the *face* of things" — he smirked, clean-shavenly — "you have *some* muscle groups that don't need much along the lines of . . . more development." He shook his head, perhaps in awe and admiration, Herbie thought.

"But you have a lot of things to learn, young woman," he went on, "about . . . oh, making *proper* use of assets, just for instance. Luckily you've got some time to learn them in, before you get to college."

Zippy'd slipped her sweatshirt on while he was saying that, and with a guilty look, a half-apologetic smile for Herb, she sidled out the door.

"In your case, though," Hill said to Herb, when she was gone, and in a fury, Herb could tell, "there isn't *any* time left on the clock. You are through, *kaput*, and *finis*, boy; you're history. So get off my geography, before I totally forget myself."

"But," said Herb, "I didn't know . . . I didn't do, like, anything except . . . you see, she was — "

But then he broke it off, bit down on all the self-absolving sentences that jumped into his mind. He *wasn't* going to put the blame on her, and say that she'd come on to him. Even though he didn't know her — never would, it looked like, now — he wouldn't do that to her, make her out to be what other guys referred to as "some pig" or "that old slut." What he'd felt she was was, basically, a simple country girl, direct and truthful, warm and friendly.

Probably intelligent. Discriminating. Sensitive.

Hill was pacing all around the room by then, extremely agitated still, still shaking his blond, perfect haircut back and forth, and wringing his clean hands.

"We simply can't permit a member of the staff to be not only *stupid*, but a bad example, also," he was saying. "Even temporary staff. Overt behavior, like yours, can cancel out a month of drill, of classroom work, of memorizing theory. It's just *disgusting*. All the rest of us are trying to act a certain way, preach one solid set of standards, *practice* what we preach — and then I run spang into this . . . this *outrage*." Hill stopped and glared at Herb.

"Isn't it a *fact*," he asked him, "that if this whole curriculum were summed up in a single word, that word would be *Deceive?*"

Herb nodded, not exactly getting it, but keeping silent, anyway. He *had* seen, sure enough, that all the Mexicans were being taught deception, everywhere. Even on the tennis courts, inside the gray inflated bubble, they learned to say 'Just out,' and shake their heads, as if they were sincerely sorry. When opponents' shots were on the line, of course.

"We're not a bunch of straightlaced puritans up here," insisted Hill. "You won't hear me or any of my full-time staff suggest there's anything that's wrong with *screwing* people. In fact, day-in, day-out, techniques for doing just exactly that are what we teach. But if you do it right out in the open, where anybody in the whole wide world might come along and see exactly what you're doing . . . why, then you're screwing *up!* You've got to *sneak, pretend, be devious, lock doors, look innocent,* goddamn it! We

73

want our people to succeed in life, you stupid little
. . . *Hertzman*, you!"

With that, he started to make shooing motions,
flicking out the shiny, pink-nailed, *clean*-nailed fingers of both hands.

"Go on. Go on with you," he said. "You just get
out of here. I'll be in touch with Ses deBarque on
this. I'm *very* disappointed. You can leave the clothes
you borrowed in your room, and Trev will take you
to your . . . *van*." His voice was drippy with disgust.

"And don't forget your tomahawk," he yelled at
Herb's retreating back.

14
TEMPTATION

Herb's return trip — *dep* Wince 'n' Wails some time or other, *arr* Castles in the Air whenever — was every bit as quick and quiet as the one that got him to the Arctic to begin with. It maybe even seemed a little quicker, given how time tends to drag when you are going somewhere new, and feeling nervous, having peanut butterflies.

Sesame de Barque was in the tower, still, to greet him. That wasn't too surprising. If a week was time-compressed into a space of fifty-seven seconds, he had run through an entire criminal career in something under twenty-five, he thought.

"Well, here I am again," said Herb, managing a laugh, "ha-ha," as the van's door slid open. Ses had used the time that she had had alone to take one knee pad off, and as Herbie's Reeboks hit the floor, her other one did, too.

"That sure was *interesting*," he said. He knew that he was feeling awkward, having trouble picking out a tone to take. He really hadn't had sufficient time to cop a final attitude toward Crime — Organized or not.

His first reaction to the "work" of Greenfield Hill and Co. was homonymic (he believed), combining as it did both *awe*: amazement at the scope and ingenuity embodied in the scheme, and "*Aw*" ("they aren't doing anybody any harm"). No question that the field *did* seem to offer opportunities for someone like himself (without experience, or skills, or any special training) to both make a lot of money and succeed in one of the . . . professions: teaching.

Yes, he thought, he'd done a pretty darn good job of teaching that one class. They'd taken notes; he'd gotten laughs. No one had gone to sleep, or thrown wet garbage at a fellow student, or said out loud that "this class sucks." Maybe doing what he'd done was *technically* a crime — conspiracy or something — but still he had to think he'd scored real well, *professionally*.

However, on the other hand, he'd found it hard, apparently, to meet a certain set of standards, as defined, or anyway implied, by Greenfield Hill. The way he'd dealt with Zippy had been . . . unacceptable. He hadn't lied to her, or tried to sneak a furtive fondle well before she had invited one; he hadn't (just for instance) made a date to meet her underneath the stage at midnight, which would have been a major violation of the rules. And when he'd had the chance to put the blame on her for what had happened (and so save his own sequoia), he had held his tongue.

76

What that little . . . episode with Zippy caused was, like, a switch. Before, he'd been a young man trying out a job in Crime — Organized or not, a teaching job, as it turned out. After, though — and on the basis of that one so-called mistake — he was a has-been: judged, convicted and expelled. *His* crime had been *not* being sleazy, being chivalrous, in fact.

So, how (he wondered) was he meant to feel about this "failure"?

Meanwhile, Ses deBarque was looking at him. Analytically, he thought. Or, possibly, askance.

Was it possible, he had to ask himself, that she, somehow, knew everything about his trip, already? Knew all the details of that final incident? Knew who'd said what, *done* what, to (with/for) whom, to what effect? Blush City, if she did. He decided that he'd better tell her most of it himself, and right away. Sort of get his version on the books.

"I guess I'm not too, too surprised," she said, when he had finished. "As types, you and Mr. Greenfield Hill are not exactly rolls and butter." And she laughed.

Herb rubbed his nose and smiled at that one. "Well, I thought he seemed to have a real nice personality," he said. "But he didn't seem too tolerant of different life-styles. Different from his own, I mean."

"Well, *that's* a fact," said Ses. "He didn't used to be that way, but every year it seems as if he's gotten worse. More greedy. *And* unprincipled. As poor old Mason Furbish, Junior, probably found out."

"Mason Furbish, Junior?" Herbie asked.

"Yes," she said, "poor, rotund little dude. He

could make the finest garlic salad dressing in the world, I think. His father was the phoni-linguistical genius who discovered how the sounds of Siamese react with those of Spanish. That's the honest truth. You'll hear some people say it was a total accident that happened due to overcrowding in a Bangkok jail, one time, but I know otherwise. And then what happened was that Mason, Senior, realized that his discovery was meaningless, unless there was a use for it. So it was he who came up with the scam — who made the very first designer Mexicans up there on Prince of Wales. He ran the operation there for years and years."

"Huh," said Herb. "And Mason, Junior . . . ?"

"As you'd suppose, inherited," she said. "And ran it quite successfully, himself. Right up until the iceberg race, that is."

"The *iceberg* race?" asked Herb. "You don't mean *iceberg* race."

"Yup," she said, "sure do. It's something that the Eskimos and Inuits and them have done up there for centuries, in summer, when the ice breaks up. Two guys each choose an iceberg, big huge ones with peaks and ridges, you know what I mean. Each guy has a paddle and a push-pole, and a lot of freeze-dried food or blubber, I suppose. It's hard to get the 'bergs to go real fast, and they don't turn too easily, but once you're under way, those babies sometimes give you quite a ride. The idea of the race is just to see how far you get before you run aground, or melt, or winter comes."

"Mmm," said Herb. "That doesn't sound particularly exciting."

"Ordinarily it's not," she said. "But this one had

its moment, in a way. You see, the 'berg that Mason, Junior, got had other passengers aboard. A family of polar bears. How they got there is uncertain, but some think that Greenfield might have chummed them onto it the day before, using lemon sole and brook trout amandine, if I know him."

"Wo!" said Herbie, pretty shocked already.

"Right," said Ses, "and, well, the race got started on a Thursday night, I think it was — remember, it's as bright as day at night up there, in summertime — and either then or early Friday morning Mason, Junior, left the firm, real suddenly. I doubt he ever knew what hit him." She shook her head and smiled a crooked smile.

"He probably went bustling around a crag, or scarp, or cube of ice," she said, "going 'round to paddle on the other side, and bingo! Down the hatch he went. I'm sure those bears just loved the guy, poor little tenderloin." She changed her voice to speak the way she thought a bear would sound. " 'Fine full-bodied fellow, that — robust, and with a pleasant garlic aftertaste.' " She laughed, but bitterly. "The rule of fang and claw, I guess you call it."

"And Greenfield Hill took over," Herbie finished for her. He was remembering how Hill had said the founder's heir, who was the president by then, had gotten into "something else" — how on one specific day it just was "poof!" and he was gone.

"Brrr." Herb made the shiver sound. Gotten into "something else" indeed — the belly of a bear! "I'm just as glad I didn't . . . well, *work out*, up there."

By that time they were strolling down the corridor that led back to the castle proper.

"What's your pleasure now?" she asked. "Care to take another spin? It's early, yet."

"No, I don't believe I will," said Herb. "I'd sort of like to head on home and just space out a while before my Uncle Babbo gets there. He's got some thoughts about my future that my mom thinks might be pretty tempting. You just never know."

"That's true," she said, and bobbed her broad-brimmed hat, emphatically.

"Uh," Herb found his feet had sort of stopped, right there in the corridor. "Could I, like, ask you something? It's on account of what you just now told me."

"Sure," said Sesame deBarque. She stopped, too, and faced him, friendly-looking as the dickens. "Anything. At any time."

"Well," he watched his right-foot Reebok step right on the other's toe, for no good reason, "how come you'd even *send* a person — such as me — up to a place like Wince 'n' Wails? To work for someone who's a murderer."

"Because it's there?" she said, and then, "Of course that's not the answer; it isn't only there, it's everywhere. I guess the first part of the answer is: It wasn't my idea. That category's there 'cause people want it, though sometimes they'd rather call it by another name. 'Marketplacing,' or 'Intelligent Manipulation of the Status Quo.' The road to hell is paved with small deceptions, Herb. And Greenfield Hill? A lot of folks would say . . . he's only human, after all. Ambitious. And he *does* fill needs. Everybody makes mistakes. Possibly the bear-thing was a little joke gone tragically awry." She didn't look at him when she was saying that, the last part. "Or just damn bad luck."

"I guess I didn't have to go," said Herb.

She didn't answer him. Instead, she put a hand out, held him by the arm a moment.

"All I hope is that you *do* come back, and try again," she said. "And that you don't regret the process."

They started walking down the corridor again. He thought that over, nodded to himself. Every nowhere that you got to was, in one sense, somewhere that you hadn't been before, somewhere that you maybe learned you didn't want to go to again. Getting lost is also finding out that's not the way to go. Maybe he'd get into fortune cookies.

"I guess I might be back," he said.

And she said, "Okey-doke. Like, anytime." And going on her tiptoes, she then kissed him. Herb felt approved of, close to her, and wondered why.

15
UNCLE BABBO

"Let's take a little drive," his uncle, Babbo Orgalescu, said to Herb when they had finished dinner,
Chicken (have you guessed?) Paprika. "I got something that I want to show you. *Plus*" — he winked
at Herb — "you'll get to park your buns on super-
soft Moroccan leather getting there, and go riding
in a mighty mean machine."

Herb had seen the car from his bedroom window,
when Babbo'd pulled it into the little driveway, right
beside his house. He wasn't sure exactly what it was,
what kind of car, that is. But you couldn't miss its
reason for existence. On both sides of its long, white
hood there were three words, in black block letters,
big ones: YOUR MANE MAN. On the backside,
right across the trunk, was: HONK IF YOU LOVE
HAIRSPRAY.

Herb didn't have to call a friend to learn that *Your*

Mane Man® was one of the (if not *the*) most popular complete home hairstyling systems in America. During dinner, though, he'd learned that Uncle Babbo, nowadays, was way, way up there in the company. As Regional Administrator (Sales), he was one of four; he reported *only* to the Sales Director, who was just a door away from Mr. Big, himself, the CEO.

Babbo Orgalescu had a gorgeous head of hair: thick and glossily inviting, wildly and excitingly adventurous, but at the same time never out of his control. When he first started out at *YMM* selling store to store, he used to ask the beauty products buyer to go wild, to do a total number on his hair, dishevel it in every way she could.

"Make me look the way I would if I'da spent ten hours in the sack," he'd say, and then he'd wink and add, "with, like, a real close friend." The buyer often was a prospect in more ways than one.

Well, nine times out of ten she'd take the challenge, and she'd do a muss-job on his head that made him look as if they'd left him staked out in the barnyard, back in Kansas, at tornado time. But all that Babbo'd do, when she was done, was smile and raise one pointer-finger and one eyebrow, and then give his head the slightest little . . . toss. Like that, just . . . *toss*. And — *schvipp!* — a hundred thousand hairs or so would first leap up, and then dive back into their rightful places in such perfect order that you'd swear they'd got the word from someone like the Chinese People's Army's calisthenics leader.

Babbo's hair was beautiful, but also *trained* — make no mistake about it.

* * *

"There's only two things in the world that hold my interest, nowadays," Babbo said to Herb, as they pulled out of the little driveway. "Other than the way I look, of course." He laughed and turned his head to look at Herb, made sure that he was laughing, too.

"Chicks," he said, "and buckarooties. Do you follow me?"

Herb believed he did. "Buckarooties," he was pretty sure, meant "money." So he said, "Sure," and nodded. In a way, this sounded promising.

"*Right*," said Babbo. "So. Now let me ask you this. Are you the same as me, in this regard? Or, wait — instead, let's put it this way — I'll make the question slightly broader by rephrasing it." He laughed again. "Are broads and bread, like, two of *your main interests*, too?" This time, he turned and winked at Herb.

"You see," he said, "I know a smart young guy, such as yourself, is apt to have a lot of interests, still. That's only natural. *My* world, however, it has shrunk a little, interest-wise — which happens, as a man gets older. Like, take, for instance, cars. I used to be fanatical about my cars. *Fanatical.* Tell you the truth, I used to *love* the cars I had. But nowadays, although I still insist, as you can see, on having decent-looking wheels that handle good et cetera, et cetera, cars are not like something that I put a lot of time and effort into, anymore. In other words, *they didn't hold my interest* in the way that chicks and dough have done. You follow me? So, tell me, Herbie, anyway. *Are* chicks and bread, like, two of *your* main interests, too?"

"Well, I guess they *are*," said Herb. He thought

84

that sounded cool and "with it," two qualities that he was pretty sure his uncle would be looking for, would want to find, in him. He also thought he spoke the truth. He guessed that "chicks" and "bread" *were* two of his main interests. Weren't they the same as "love" and "money"?

"Okay," said Babbo, sounding pleased. They were heading out of town, already on the outskirts, whizzing past the car lots and the fast-food places and the outlet stores, past the drop-in plastic surgeons' clinics, like *McSvelte*. Herb wondered where they might be going to. Straight ahead were, mostly, just the hills.

"Okay," his Uncle Babbo said again. His voice got serious and thoughtful, his tone the one Herb's teachers were disposed to use when they were setting out to show the class some stuff they thought was difficult to follow. And important. Reflexively, Herb straightened up and seemed to pay attention.

"Suppose I told you," Babbo said, "I know a way for you to get — I mean *have access to* — a huge supply, a *mothuh* lode" — he snickered — "of the both of them?" He sat back in the driver's seat and seemed to push against the steering wheel. He looked as if he might be holding something in; he also looked as if he might be pushing something out.

"Well, I guess I'd say 'That sure is interesting,'" said Herb. He rolled his window down and paused. He thought that maybe sounded *too* cool, almost flat. He tried to flesh it out a little, warm it up. "I suppose I'd say 'What is it?'"

That wasn't much of an improvement, Herbie thought. Why *was* he being so laid back? Wasn't this, perhaps, the knock of opportunity? Wasn't it a fact that "*who* you know" was *everything*, when you were looking for a job, something to do? Why *couldn't* Uncle Babbo be the genie from the lamp? He *could* be. Shouldn't he start drooling?

"Hubba-hubba," Herbie added.

The car was climbing now, gaining elevation in the hills outside of town. Uncle Babbo started shooting glances to his left, as they kept climbing. It also seemed to Herb that they were slowing down.

"The *way*," said Uncle B, "involves a job that's more than just a job. Because the way involves . . ." He swung the car sharp left, going all the way across the road and into this small Scenic Lookout on the other side.

". . . a *territory*," Babbo said. He shut the engine off and killed his headlights.

Below them was — what else? — the valley, miles and miles and miles of it, every bit as far as you could see. More or less straight down from where they were, there were the lights of town: streetlights, house lights, stoplights; these had a certain symmetry and order to them. Away from town the lights were much more random, widely spaced, most of them along the major highways, but also many others here and there, around the countryside. In the northern distance you could see the City Airport, lighted up, and the City, too, beyond it. The City sort of *glowed* out there, crouching in the distance, letting off its rays.

"You see that, Herbie?" Babbo said. "You *see* all that?" He lifted up his hand and moved it in an arc from left to right, horizon to horizon, and then back again, but lower down this time.

Herb followed Babbo's hand. He saw it, and the

view behind it. He'd seen both things a lot of times before.

"All of it, everything you see, is yours — or will be yours — if you say 'Yes' to me," said Uncle Babbo.

"What?" said Herb, instead — although he had a pretty good idea of what was going on. His mother had been right. Babbo's thoughts about his future were *extremely* tempting. *He* could have, like, all of that, for nothing?

"This area we're looking at is called a 'territory,' " Babbo said. "*You* can be the 'Mane Man' in that territory, Herb. You know how come I know that, Herb? I know *that*, and more, because I am in charge of much, much more than that. It's mine to offer, yours to take. All you have to do is just say 'Yes' to me." And Babbo struck the steering wheel a good one with his fist. "Yes! And yes! And *yes!*" he said.

Herbie said, "To what, exactly?" He could feel himself becoming nervous. That was quite a string of 'yeses' Babbo'd just reeled off.

"Why, to the work," his Uncle Babbo said. His tone of voice was one of mild surprise, as if to say: Who wouldn't know *that*? "To all *Your Mane Man*'s products: to our shampoos and our conditioners, and to our styling sprays and gels and holds and spritzers. To *Your Mane Man*'s dryers, scalp conditioners and brushes, combs (both hot and cold) and curlers. To what hair *means*, to all the *fun* it is. To waking up and thinking hair, the first thing in the morning. To treating your own hair with reverence, to working with it, letting it be all that it can be, to making sacrifices for it."

"Sacrifices for it?" Herbie said. A friend of his

named Luther Bates had tried out for the football team, and he'd told Herbie he was prepared to "make the necessary sacrifices." Herb hadn't really known what Luther meant — he didn't think that he was talking sandwiches and shakes — but he hadn't liked the sound of it. Hair, however . . . hair would be a less demanding god than football, wouldn't it? Or would it?

"Of course," his Uncle Babbo said. He turned his upper body all the way around, so he was facing Herb. He tucked a leg up on the leather seat.

"Any person who succeeds at this — I mean *succeeds*," said Babbo, "has to regard the care of hair as fundamental. Hair is, after all, a gift of nature and a part of one's creation. I'm asking you to make a deep commitment to the care of hair. Not nine to five, five days a week, and then forget about it, might as well be bald. Even when you aren't talking hair, or working with a product or a customer, you are still a witness, right? You understand what I've been telling you? This isn't something that you only *do*; I like to feel it's something that you *are*." He stopped and took a deep, deep breath.

"It isn't walking on the beach without a hat on," he explained. "It isn't walking on the beach *with* a hat on, either — supposing that the hat is any one of all the kinds that *stifle* hair, don't let it breathe, enjoy itself. It also isn't swimming in salt water at the beach, except when you can rinse with fresh, like, right away. It isn't letting someone *touch* your hair who's just been reading, say, the Sunday *New York Times*, or eating with nomadic desert tribes, or making model airplanes. It isn't staying in a room where there are onions cooking, or people smoking

88

anything that's thicker than a pencil, or women named Delilah. It's letting it grow out, *your* hair grow out, to where it makes a statement, Herb. And it's putting one of these on, every night," and Babbo leered, "for . . . *business's* sake, you know?"

He'd reached into his pocket, found his wallet, reached inside of *it*, and tossed what he took out of it right onto Herbie's lap.

"You really shouldn't keep these in your wallet," he told Herb. "They say it isn't good for them at all. But what the hell."

Herb looked down at the little packet. Yes, it *was* a hairnet — black, one-size-fits-all.

"Get outa here," said Herb, agreeably, before he'd even had a chance to think about it.

"Hey?" said Babbo. He gave his head a little shake, then tilted it and struck himself above one ear with just the heel, like, of his open hand, as if he'd gotten water in that ear. "Wazzat?"

For just an instant there, Herbie thought that what he'd heard was *qué?* and that his Uncle Babbo was a dryback, not his mother's brother after all. But then he knew that wasn't right, that he had seen too many pictures that his mother had of them both growing up, first over in Romania and then right here. Even at the age of eight and twelve and seventeen, Babbo had had memorable hair.

"I just can't do it, Uncle Babbo," Herbie said. "Call it immaturity, stupidity, whatever. But I just can't do it."

Of course he didn't think that it was any of those things.

"But what about the *chicks?*" his uncle said. "The *bread?* The schools of eager lovelies, skinny-dipping in a huge, unchlorinated pool of dough?" He slouched back in his bucket seat. His head shook back and forth again, as he threw question after question, not at Herb, but up into the empty evening air.

"What kind of guy is this, I'm talking to?" he said. "What kind of relative of mine, with hot ambition throbbing in, *engorging*, all his veins? What kind of son of apple pie, and amber waves of grain?" He stopped and shook himself, then turned to Herb, again. "Wait, wait. We aren't blood-related, right? Is *that* it, huh — is *that* it? My sister found you on her doorstep, or maybe on an airport runway, in a ladies' room."

"Whatever," Herbie said. He didn't feel related, not to Babbo, not to *Your Mane Man*. He didn't want to talk about it, either.

Babbo started up the car. He looked like someone in a state of shock.

"It seems to me that I remember Lena being pregnant, though," he muttered, talking mostly to himself, it seemed. "Or was that Anna, or Maria? Look," he said to Herb, "suppose I leave it open for a while? I don't need a yes or no *today*."

"I just said 'no,' " said Herbie. And he leaned back in the seat and closed his eyes.

Monday, he'd try Castles in the Air again, he thought.

16
HOMETOWN, USA

Herb found his second trip to Castles in the Air was about half the hassle and twice the fun that his first one had been. Instead of *groping* around the northwest part of town, *hoping* to bump into a street called Sunset Strip, he was able to stride confidently along in the proper direction until he got to it. And, rather than encountering unpleasant creatures such as Private Buford "Buddy" Road along the way, and having to exchange sharp jabs with some pretty nasty pickets near his destination, he was whisked along the Strip and up the Castles driveway in a panel truck that stopped and offered him a ride.

The truck was driven by a friendly-looking, paint-bespattered man, and had *Pigments of Your Imagination* written on the sides of it. Inside, behind the seats, there were a lot of different cans of paint, and brushes, jars of turpentine and drop cloths.

"Seven-eleven?" said the man, as soon as Herb had clambered in the door and told him where on Sunset Strip he hoped to get to. "So it's Castles in the Air that you'll be visiting, I guess."

"Exactly right," said Herb. "And looking forward to it. Do you know the place, yourself? Or Ms. deBarque, by any chance?"

"Ses?" the painter said. "Hell, yes. I've done a lot of work for her. And I'm heading up to Castles now, to do some more — so you're in luck. She wants the lady-in-waiting's room done over in a beige, I think. Or, was that the ladies' room beside the wading pool, and she was in a rage when she called up?" He made a clucking sound and scratched his head.

"But maybe it's the waiting room for pages to the ladies in the car pool," he went on, and gave a small, self-deprecating chuckle. "Hell, I can't remember. Wants *something* painted, anyway. And I'm a painter, so I'll see to it. I'm pretty sure my name's John Jaspers, anyway. And what might your name be?"

"Well," said Herb, infected by the man's good humor, "it *might* be Peter Falconer, I guess. But if it was, the chances are I wouldn't be here, and I'd know exactly where I'm going, what I'm going to do and where the snows of yesteryear are now. In fact, I'm Herbie Hertzman."

"It's a pleasure," said John Jaspers, dealing out a hand for Herb to shake. "If you're a friend of Ses deBarque, I want you for a friend of mine. And if you haven't met her yet, you've got a treat in store for you."

Herb nodded and admitted that he knew and liked the lady very much, and so the atmosphere inside

92

the truck was one of warmth and cordiality, as it pulled up to Castles in the Air. And there, outside, was Ses deBarque herself, wearing pale pink pedal pushers and a black Hawaiian shirt, while gamely pitching horseshoes on the lawn.

"Hey, John Jaspers, good to see you," she cried out, speaking to the truck, the way one's apt to do, before she'd even seen its occupants.

"You've come to do the baby's spool bed in the weight room, I assume," she added. "In that nice, light sage we talked about, correct?"

The painter climbed down from the truck and tapped his temple, wisely — as if to say he'd known that all along. Meanwhile, Ses deBarque caught sight of Herb.

"And look who else you brought along," she said. "Welcome back to Castles, Herb. I'll be with you in no time at all. Just watch my smoke, you'll see."

Herb nodded cheerfully and thought about the way that Don DeLillo's novel *End Zone* started. ("Taft Robinson was the first black student to be enrolled at Logos College in west Texas. They got him for his speed.") John Jaspers picked out all the painting gear that he would need from back inside his truck. And Sesame deBarque resumed her game.

She had two horseshoes left, a gold one and a silver, both gleaming brightly in the sunshine, and in spite of what she'd said, she didn't rush her throws. She first got set, then concentrated fiercely on her target, this black metal stake, no thicker than a crowbar, driven deep into the ground. At last, now squinting, with her tongue between her teeth, she threw — first one and then the other shoe.

Each of the two throws she made, however, was

completely different from the other — that's in every way except for outcome. The shoes spun crazily, in two peculiar arcs, tumbling and twisting. They looked, to Herb, like two "wild heaves." But at the end, both shoes had wrapped themselves around the stake, and she had made two ringers. Two more ringers, Herb could see.

"Wow!" said Herb as she approached him, dusting off her palms. "Two on top of two!"

"Yeah," she said. "Just luck, I guess. But all the bending over *must* be good for me." She laughed. "And how was Uncle Babbo?"

"Good," said Herb. "Pretty much the same as usual. He had a proposition for me, but I didn't take it. Maybe I was foolish, *I* don't know."

"Mmm," she answered, noncommittally. They started strolling toward the castle's door. Ses dug out a bag of salted peanuts from her pocket, and she poured them each a heaping handful. As they got onto the drawbridge, Herb saw that there was someone swimming in the moat, really motoring along, way down and to his right, and almost out of sight. He couldn't tell what kind of someone, just that he or she could really handle swimming on a curve.

"There's someone swimming in the moat," said Herb. "Someone really *good*."

She glanced in the direction he was looking, at the disappearing swimmer.

"Yeah," she said, "it's probably the maid. She's got good form, all right. But don't start thinking that she's perfect. She won't do windows on a bet, or polish armor, either." She opened up the huge main castle door.

94

"So, now you think you'd like to take another spin," she said.

"Yes," he said. "I really would."

"Well," she said, "you've got a lovely afternoon for it."

Riding in the Upwardlimobile was more pleasant and less stressful, Herbie thought, now that both the van itself and the whole . . . process were a bit familiar. He also was amazed — intrigued — by what he'd spun: Public Service, Including Government. He had to wonder if there maybe was a reason that he'd gotten it. Was T.K. *with* him or *against* him on this deal? First he'd gotten Crime — Organized or not, and *that* had not been right for him at all. But while he was involved with it, back there on Wince 'n' Wails, he'd come to some conclusions, one concerning *politics*. That *it* was a career a real *dumb jerk* could prosper in. So, what does he spin next? Public Service, Including Government — or politics, in other words, you *could* say. Was this going to be a different kind of test? If he *liked* what happened next, would he have found out something he was *glad* to know? Herb touched the child-sized wristwatch that he'd shoved into his pocket as he left his room that morning, the first timepiece he'd ever gotten, his old "TicK-TocK."

When the 'mobile settled to a stop this time, the door did not fly open and a blond guy jump right in. In fact, for just about a count of ten there was no action whatsoever. Then the door *eased* open, real informally. And when he rose and looked on out, he saw that he was in . . . a parking lot.

Well. Herb thought that over, and he had to smile. The van had had the sense to come down in a parking lot, this time; it had landed in its native habitat! And when Herb stepped outside and looked around, he saw that he was also not on hostile, unfamiliar ground, like permafrost. It seemed that he was in a town about the size and shape of his hometown, with more or less the same degree of homeliness. There beside him was a building that could only be a nice, brick, ugly City Hall.

He stretched and strolled a short way from the van to look around. Running left to right, in front of him, was — hey, what else? — a Main Street, which of course was wide and had on it, beside a bunch of stores, the post office and library. Prospect Street crossed Main Street, looking left, while Church Street crossed it on his right. Both Church and Prospect looked like Main, except they might have been a little narrower, and Church Street had some steeples on it. Almost all the buildings in the town were more or less four stories high.

Herb next checked out the stores. Shops could tell you quite a lot about a town; their names, the different storefront styles and what they sold were all significant. He thought this town seemed sort of average. He saw Bull's China Shop, Take a Gander Opticals, One Great Danish Bakery. There was a Kitty Hall, which he assumed to be a pet shop, and a Bear's Din that appeared to be a record store. On the corner was a drive-in feed store. Its sign, at first glance, looked familiar. It had a likeness of a white-haired gent on it, with mustache and goatee, a string tie 'round his neck. But underneath it said that this was Kernel Jimmy Leghorn's, "Cracked Corn You

Can Care About." Herb made a shrewd deduction: If there was a feed store in the heart of town, the chances were he wasn't in New Jersey.

At just about the moment after he thought that, Herb had another thought, more like a feeling, actually. He felt as if he might be being . . . well, *observed*. He looked around and, sure enough, behind him was a man, a small but speculative man, who looked at Herb with narrowed eyes, and one arm crossed, his sharp chin in his hand.

When he saw Herb looking back at him, he gave a kind of start and trotted in the boy's direction, saying, "Hertzman? Herbie Hertzman, is it?"

"Yo," said Herb. "I'm Herbie. In the fellow flesh."

"Danville Pine," the small man said, and offered Herb a slender hand held backside up, the way a dog would, or a noblewoman. "I'm the M.O.S., the Mayor's Official Spokesman. Welcome, welcome, welcome. That's one for her and one for me and one for all the rest of good ol' Hometown, USA."

Herb liked the sound of all of that, but still he didn't rush to judgment on the man. Greenfield Hill had come across as Mr. Cordiality, at first. Danville Pine, by contrast, seemed more *shrewd* than anything: curious, and sharp and maybe even slightly devious. He looked to be a man who'd find a way to get things done. With his copper-colored hair and mustache (both neatly parted in the middle), and his slight and narrow-shouldered build, he probably could slip quite nicely through a door, just before it closed, or any sort of loophole. He was dressed in clean white shirtsleeves on this pleasant, sunny day, but he also wore a bright red bow tie and a

97

sporty vest, a tattersall. Herb guessed his age to be
. . . oh, forty-eight.

"*Her?*" said Herb, hoping to show sharpness of
his own. "The mayor's a woman, here?"

"Well," said Danville Pine, "the mayor's a *female*,
sure enough. But not a woman, no. I guess you don't
take *Time* or *Newsweek*, do you? 'Cause if you did,
you'd know that she's a chicken. The elected mayor
of all us folks in Hometown is a **Big Red Chicken**."

"Wo!" said Herb. "Time *out!*" He took a blink or
two, digesting that. "That's pretty darn unusual, I'd
say. Or are there lots of, like, . . . *elected fowl*, out
here?" Wherever "here" was, it seemed to Herb that
it was really out there.

"Not so far as *Time* and *Newsweek* know, I guess,"
said Danville Pine. "Years ago, I read about a La-
brador retriever winning an election out in Idaho, I
think it was. But I'm pretty sure that this one is
the only full-fledged chicken to succeed in politics.
Stand-up comedy, of course, would be a different
story."

"But," Herbie had to ask, "what happened with
the other candidates? I mean, were there, like, any
people in the race? Or not?"

"Oh, sure there were," said Pine. "Both the major
parties put up people, same as always. The Big Red
Chicken was an independent, like you'd think. Part
of it was that the folks around this area were looking
for a change. They were tired of the same old two-
faced candidates, the fat cats and corrupt machines.
They felt that with the Big Red Chicken, what they
saw would be exactly what they'd get."

"I see," said Herb. "And you're the Mayor's Official Spokesman. You must have lots of, well, *re-*

sponsibility — being spokesman for a Big Red Chicken." Herb made sure he didn't smile. He felt that it was possible his leg was being pulled. Given Mr. Pine's appearance, that *certainly* was possible. But yet, Kentucky Fried Chicken had been moved — or driven — out of town, and there was cracked corn in its place. He decided just to play along, and try to get a handle on the situation, be prepared, be cool. More so than he'd been on Wince 'n' Wails, for all that it was way above the Arctic Circle.

"Well, the thing is this," said Danville Pine. "I understand her perfectly. That helps. Few people can. But me, I understand the things she says in chicken talk, and then I say them to the people — but in English, naturally. They, of course, are looking just to hear the things they *want* to hear. That's the way that people are. They have their needs or interests in their minds and not much more. Other than the things that they're against, of course. If they think a politician's *for* those needs or interests, and *against* that other crap, then they're going to be for her. The Big Red Chicken understands that pretty good, I'd say." He chuckled.

"You mean," said Herb, "that everything the chicken said in her campaign, and everything that she says now, as mayor, is clucked to you, a sentence or a paragraph at a time, and then you say it to the people?"

"*Exactly*," Danville Pine replied. "What we do in public is just like all those speeches at the airport on TV. Soon as Gorbachev gets off the plane, they take him to the microphones, him and some short guy with glasses, right? He goes: '*Najdee sposseeyay dubnoyet . . .*' and then he pauses and the short guy says:

99

'People of my favorite country in the whole wide world . . .' We do just like that."

"Boy," said Herb. "It sounds as if you've got a real hard job. On top of all the time you've got to spend with her, it also seems fantastically *complex*. Like, our Spanish teacher told us that a lot of jokes in Spanish can't even be put in English, word for word. She said they aren't even funny, that way."

"Right," said Pine, "The same thing's true of chicken jokes. I'll throw in a line sometimes that isn't hardly like the one that she just said. But if it gets a laugh, she doesn't mind."

"Wow," said Herb. "The two of you must have a great relationship. *She* may be the mayor, but hey, without your willingness to do the job you do for her, the Big Red Chicken would be nowhere, nothing."

"You catch on quick," said Danville Pine. "So let's go meet Her Honor."

The Big Red Chicken was, for sure, imposing poultry, Herbie thought. When Danville Pine ushered him into her office, she was pacing up and down her desk muttering to herself and, from time to time, pecking at the different piles of paper that surrounded her. He guessed her feathered weight to be a hefty ten–twelve pounds, her height at least a foot from claw to comb; her color was a lustrous reddish-brown. She sure was Big, all right.

Clearly, Herbie thought, this was a working bird who liked to stay on top of things. A sign, inscribed THE CLUCK STOPS HERE was the only frivolous, or personal — unbusinesslike — appurtenance on her entire desk.

100

As soon as she caught sight of Danville Pine, she stopped her pacing, faced the man, and started in to squawk and cluck. This chicken is a rapper, Herbie thought, for sure.

The Mayor's Official Spokesman gave an almost simultaneous translation, this time.

"She says she's really glad to see you, and she hopes you had a pleasant trip," said Danville Pine. "She has nothing but respect and, more than that, affection for Ms. Sesame deBarque and her entire family and all her friends, and she only wishes they could get together much more often. She hopes that you'll enjoy, and profit from, your stay with us in Hometown, and that the plan that she's drawn up for you — a five-year plan you can accomplish in a week, heh-heh — will prove to meet your every need. Said plan, as presently envisioned, calls for you to spend a little time in each and every main department here in City Hall, starting with the Office of Assessment and continuing right through to the Zoning Board. She feels that this will give you some real basis for a judgment as to whether what she sometimes calls 'this Public Service bullbleep,' is the ideal field for you, or not."

As the Mayor's Official Spokesman said all that, Herb looked back and forth, from man to chicken. He'd never needed an interpreter before, and so he didn't know, for sure, how many nods and smiles to give to *him*, beside the ones he felt he *owed* the Chicken. One peculiar thing, it seemed to him, was that the mayor's expression — the anger in her eyes, the sharp emphatic gestures with her beak — didn't really match the words that Pine was saying. And right there at the end, when he'd employed that

101

. . . barnyard epithet, she'd let out a sound that seemed to him to be a squawk of outrage.

"And now," said Pine, concluding, "she says she'd like for me to run and fetch the Chief Assessor, so's she can introduce you. For obvious reasons," he said to Herb in a different tone of voice, "her office, here, don't have a phone."

"Hey, fine," said Herb. "I'll just wait here till you get back." He produced another round of nods and smiles. "That sounds *terrific*," he assured the mayor, and he sat down in a chair, prepared to go on looking affable and grateful for as long as they were left alone together.

But, no sooner had the Mayor's Official Spokesman left the room, than Her Honor started acting very weird, it seemed to Herb. She seemed to be a chicken in a frenzy. She didn't *say* a word; instead she shut her beak and used it to seek out, from underneath a pile of records and reports, an ink pad. This, she first flipped open and then, much to Herb's surprise, she started to *dance up and down* on it. After that, she jumped upon a sheet of plain white paper, seemed to think a moment, and then began to run across it, taking quick and careful steps, the way a ballerina might. When she'd finished doing that, she pushed the paper *off* the desk, in Herb's direction. It fluttered to the floor, of course. Between them.

Herb looked at it. He looked at her. She was staring at the paper, and she bobbed her head at it and clucked. Then she bobbed her head at *him*.

"You want for me to pick the paper up?" Herb asked the Big Red Chicken, feeling something of a fool. He'd had a dog who understood some words like "out" and "dinner" and "cryonics," but he'd never posed a question to a chicken.

She nodded, and her eyes were locked on his, and very bright.

He picked it up. There was a line of chicken scratchings on the page. He leaned to put it back on her desk.

The Big Red Chicken had a minor fit. She shook her head; she also shook her neck, her wings, her breast, her thighs, her drumsticks. It's fair to say she shook all over. After that, she danced a bit, jumped up and down. For her closing number, she then jabbed her beak in Herb's direction — one time, two times, three times, four.

"You want for me to keep this?" Herbie asked her, holding up the sheet of paper.

The Big Red Chicken nodded.

"Well, I will," said Herb. "I'll keep it."

The Chicken nodded, and then stretched her neck, like, "And . . . ."

"And something else," said Herb. "But what?"

The Chicken's head went left to right, a little herky-jerkily. She stopped and stared at Herb. When he did nothing, she went left to right, again.

"You want that I should *read* it?" Herbie asked, sounding maybe just a bit incredulous.

The Chicken nodded.

Herb went along with it. He was, as has been said, a trained good sport. He focused on the paper. The "writing" on it looked like chicken scratchings — naturally. But that reminded him of something. All through school, his teachers had described *his* penmanship in just that way. "This paper looks like chicken scratchings!" they'd exclaim, holding up some work of his for public ridicule.

103

And so, he looked down at the Big Red Chicken's paper once again, and . . . read it!

Her claws had surely not produced a perfect Palmer method script, but it was *legible*, all right, to him. *This isn't all that bad*, he thought.

What it said was: "Thairs a rotten fox in this heer henhouse. Help!"

No sooner had he finished reading that, than Herb heard someone at the door. He just had time to tuck the paper in his pocket, flash a thumb's-up at the Chicken, and lean toward the desk and whisper "I'll come back tonight." The Chicken gave him one quick final nod, and Herb sat back and crossed his legs, and got real busy with a hangnail.

"Well, well, well," said Danville Pine as he came in. With him was a tall and very skinny man who looked as if he might be smelling quite a bad potato.

"This," said Mr. Pine, "is Mr. Bon Ballou, our Chief Assessor. Bon, our young friend Herbie Hertzman."

"Hoy," said Mr. Bon Ballou to Herb. He looked the young man over carefully, no doubt including any hangnails.

"It don't appear to me that you'd be worth much in a tug-of-war," was his assessment.

"Heh-heh," said Danville Pine. "Now what the mayor was hoping, Bon . . ."

Danville Pine, thought Herb, looking at the crafty little man again, but in a different light. Of course! *He's* the fox "in this heer henhouse." Say the name a little differently and Danville Pine becomes . . . well, *Damn Vulpine!*

As Herb politely listened to the Mayor's Official Spokes . . . *fox*, he also checked the Chicken from the corner of his eye. She seemed a lot less agitated. She'd closed the ink pad noiselessly, and slid it out of sight, again. Then she opened a report and seemed to settle down to read it. She looked, to Herb, like one relieved, and even hopeful, fowl. She looked the way a prisoner might look who'd gotten word that her appeal was being heard.

17
SCRATCHING
UNDERNEATH
THE SURFACE

It didn't take young Herbie all that long to convince the Mayor's Official Spokesman that he'd rather spend his nights in the Upwardlimobile there in the City Hall parking lot than in the AKC-approved and color-cabled Sleeping Dog Motel, which was way the hell and gone out on the edge of town. For one thing, Danville Pine could not care less about our hero's comfort. For another, he was sure that, seeing as he owned the place, he could collect and also pocket one fat refund on the motel room (which Castles in the Air had paid for in advance), and then proceed to rent the room again to someone else. Double his profit, double the fun, was pretty much the way he looked at it. And for a third thing, this meant that chances were he'd never have to see the kid past 5 P.M. Pine often hung around the motel lounge at night, playing strip Parcheesi and a little chamber music with the guys and gals who'd holed up there (for this or that immoral purpose) and who'd told their wives and husbands they were out of town. As Danville Pine had planned when he had built, and named, the place, the Sleeping Dog attracted lots of liars.

In any case, by being in the van at night, Herb got exactly what he wanted most: a place to stay right close to City Hall, from which he could . . . *invade* it, after hours. "Public Service," it appeared to him, now included doing all he could for this deserving Big Red Chicken.

His task was made a good bit easier, initially, by Hometown's easygoing hometown way of doing things. No one locked his door, or hers, at night in Hometown and so, therefore, it followed that no one locked the City Hall. Herb waited until after 2 A.M. to creep out of the van, assuming he might have to break a window to gain entrance to the place, but first he did just *test* a door, almost as a might-aswell. It swung right open, gladly, though, and so he slipped inside it fast and skittered up the stairs and to Her Honor's door.

That one didn't yield so easily. The Big Red Chicken was what Hometown seldom had in its small jail, a prisoner.

Her office wasn't maximum security, however. Let's face it, when the person that you're holding is a chicken, you don't need a lot of fancy locks and dead bolts. In fact, all Herbie had to do was lift the little hook out of its eye, and go on in.

A lamp was lit inside the Big Red Chicken's office,

and when her eyes snapped open and she saw that it was Herb, she started in to cluck, at once, but in a soft, enthusiastic tone of voice.

The boy decided this was not the time for small talk and amenities. He walked right to the desk and got the ink pad, flipped it open. Then he found a pile of plain white paper, put a few sheets in a clipboard that was there and set that down before the mayor.

"So, what's the story, here?" he said.

The Big Red Chicken hopped up on the ink pad right away, and in another minute she was writing, just as fast as her two feet could carry her. As she finished every page, Herb would pick it up and read it and then stuff it in his pocket. Her tale was really quite a simple one — the age-old tale of Trust Betrayed.

When Danville Pine had put her up for mayor, she'd gone along with the idea, quite willingly. Things were not exactly copacetic in the coop where she'd been perched. Although she was a top producer, she was getting only chicken feed, by way of a reward; there was an awful lot of wrangling about who got to peck ahead of whom; and sisters had a way of "disappearing" just before a yellow van with the mysterious license plate, FPRDU, was seen near the barnyard. Finally the rooster she'd been living with was an impossible chauvinist, loud-mouthed, self-important and (she told the boy) "if yoo want to no the trooth, a louzy lay." She'd taught herself to write (if not to spell too well) to combat henhouse boredom, and although in her early weeks in office she'd tried to send Pine memos, he had clearly felt that they were only "chikken skratch-ingz."

"So, Danville Pine is not aware that you can write, or even *understand* the spoken word?" asked Herbie, rather grandly.

"I dont beleve so," scratched the Chicken.

She then went on to "say" that she'd believed, at first, that Danville Pine was an authentic Hometown hero, interested in good, but not intrusive, government, an end to machine politics, and the restoration of such traditional values as honesty, integrity and father-knows-best. She was pretty sure, she said, that Pine had had a phone call from the President, telling him he was "hiz kind uv guy."

Shortly after that, she'd come to see that her Official Spokesman was a crook. It hadn't been that difficult.

"Becauze he thot — he *noo* — that I wuz just 'a chikken,' " wrote the Big Red Chicken, "he didden make the slitest effurt to, like, cuvver up wot he wuz dooing. He did hiz dirde deels rite in this offis, rite in frunt uv me, and hede put the munni that he got — the bribez, paola, kikbaks or wotever — rite into my offis safe, thair." She flapped a wing in the direction of this huge cast-iron vault that took up one whole corner of her office.

"In that safe," she wrote, "is all the evidents wede need to hang him hier than a . . . *wethervane*." She paused to cluck, morosely. "If we cood only get to it." She shook her head. "To think that wunce upon a time, a meer too weeks ago, I had the combi-nashun."

"What?" said Herb, although he'd read her perfectly. "You *had* the combination to the safe? Why don't you have it now? Or, wait, just *tell* me what it is, and I will . . . do the honors." He made some twirling motions with his fingers, trying to be a little sensitive in bringing up this thing that Man, not because of any great intelligence or virtue of his own, could do, and Fowl could not. Herb was very conscious of the fact that Man could not lay eggs.

"O, I dont *no* it," wrote the Chicken, "and he got it bak. Tho not befor I led him kwite the mary chace. Dyuring wich I also rote it down — that iz to say I coppied it."

"You *did*?" said Herbie, all excited once again. "That's *great*! So all I have to do is get the copy — right? — and. . . ."

But the Chicken wasn't listening. She was writing, fast and furious. She had another tale to tell, a tale of courage and adventure, of one bird's ability to improvise and to show the kind of grace under pressure that is the hallmark of a . . . well, as Herbie read, he found out for the first time in his life what it really meant to be a *chicken*.

"The furst thing that yoove got to realize," wrote the Chicken, perhaps to justify — explain — her lack of recollection, "iz that a big olefashun safe haz lotz of numberz in its combinashun. *Ate*, to be eggzact. Danville Pine himself, he haz to keep them ritten on this little pece of paper in a pokket uv hiz vest. Well, this one day, he came in heer in sumthing of a rush. Yoojalee, he makez reel shoor heze clozed the dor tite so I cant get out — az yoo no, I cant do nobs — but this one day, I notissed that it didn latch. So, when he took hiz little paper out, and started opunning the safe, I saw my chantz and took it. . . ."

What the Chicken did, apparently, was to, like, launch herself from off the desk in one great flapping, falling swoop, and seize the little piece of paper out of Pine's left hand. Then, with the paper firmly in her beak, she nudged the door enough so she could flutter through it to the hall and *up* the stairs.

Almost before she'd thought what she was doing, the Big Red Chicken had gone up two flights of stairs and out the fire door the janitor had left propped open for the breeze. She was on the roof!

"I gess wot happend wuz," she wrote to Herb, "that misster smarty chaste me *down* the stairz, at furst, insted of up. So, for a wile, I had a reel good leed on him."

While she had this lead, the Chicken sped across the roof of City Hall and flutter-flew across the wall between it and the roof next door. She said that she was hoping for another open door that she could use to head back down again and make it to the street. Her plan, from there, would be to run down to the corner, to the feed store, hide herself in some old farmer's truck, and disappear into *his* flock of chickens for a while, until she'd hatched a plan. The only trouble was, she didn't find an open door on that roof, or the next one, or the next. By then, the Mayor's Official Spokesman had found out his quarry'd never gone downstairs at all, so he, along with half a dozen henchmen, had reversed his field and run upstairs, and reached the top of City Hall and seen the fleeing fowl four roofs away.

The fifth roof that the Chicken reached was dif-

111

ferent than the others, though. That roof was . . . occupied. There was a young and comely woman on it, lying on a beach towel, getting rays. She appeared to be asleep. Beside her, was the book that she'd been reading and the thick, absorbent terry bathrobe that she must have doffed before she'd stretched out on her stomach. When the girl had taken off that robe (the Chicken told our boy), there wasn't any more undressing left for her to do. Except for her white terry mules, the woman was completely naked.

"Of corse, at that point I wuz in a total *panik*," wrote the Big Red Chicken. "Not becauze Ide cum upon a female in the nood, but rather over seeing all those raskels cumming after me, and me with no way to get off those roofs. We chikkens, az yoo may *not* no, doo not sirvive for storey fallz too offen, enny mor than peepul doo." The Chicken paused and shook her head, as if in painful recollection.

"Ime shoor yoove herd that reel dizgusting fowlist fraze that peepul uze sumtimez," she wrote. " 'Running around like a chikken with its hed cut off'? Well, thatz probablee the way I woodve looked to enny fowlists in the area. All I cood think, the moment that I landed on that roof, was that Ide better make a coppy of that combinashun — kwik, befor they got me, got *it*, bak again."

So what she did, the Chicken made completely clear to Herb (in spite of her misspellings) was to run and lay the combination down where she could read the thing, and then to quickly scratch a copy with her dancing feet, using . . . well, the first smooth surface that had "cawt her I." After which, she picked the combination up again and kept on

112

going, over to another rooftop, and another, and a third — at which point Pine and Co. caught up with her and grabbed her, and snatched the little paper from her beak.

"Wow," said Herbie, much impressed again, or still — whatever. "You made a copy and they didn't even know it. I'll bet you scratched those numbers in the roofing tar up there. It'd get a little soft on days like we've been having, right?"

"Why, no," the Chicken wrote. "Thay mite have seen it in the roofing tar, and rubbed it out."

"Well, then, where else . . . ?" asked Herb, completely mystified again, or still — as usual.

"Why, on that gurlz behind," the Chicken wrote. "I noo shede get it covered up and outa thair, befor thoze men arrived. And so I put for numbers on her left bun, and the uthers on her rite wun."

"Good *grief*," said Herb, amazed, amused — and acting scandalized — by what he'd heard. "You carved eight numbers into some poor person's . . . *butt?*"

" 'Carved,' " the Chicken wrote, a little testily, "wood be a huje eggzagerashun. 'Litelee scratched' wood be the wurdz Ide yooze. And if yood seen the butt in kwesschun, I dout yood say 'poor person,' eether."

The Chicken then went on to say that just as she had thought, the girl, awakened by the *gentle* scratching on her rear, had sat right up and seen the people coming (and the Chicken going, I'd presume), put her bathrobe on and grabbed her book and towel, and gotten off that roof, posthaste.

When he had finished reading all of that, Herb took a step or two directly backwards, so he could

113

sink down in the chair he'd occupied the day before. He felt he needed just a minute, there, to get this whole amazing story settled in his mind. And then to think about exactly what it *meant*, what action(s) it suggested should be taken by one very junior Public Servant by the name of Hertzman, H.

The thoughts that soon flashed through his brain began to take the form of questions:

—Was the Big Red Chicken now in any danger from the foxy Mr. Pine?

—Did she really not remember any of the numbers she had written on that girl's behind?

—If, indeed, she didn't . . . well, who *was* the girl? and where?

—And would that combination still be where she'd put it, two weeks later?

—And, finally, would the finding and the reading of the combination be the sort of thing that one would call a "Public Service"?

Not really having answers to a single one of those, Herbie stood back up again and put them to the Chicken.

The Chicken said that, first of all, she didn't feel that she was now in any danger. Not *yet*, that is to say. She was sure there wasn't any way — because of all the walls between the roofs — that Pine had seen her put the combination on the girl. And, don't forget — she said — Pine didn't even know that she could write. Her best guess was that Pine had not yet stashed away inside the safe enough illegal bucks to set himself up comfortably for life. She figured once he *had*, that she'd be instant barbecue (she shuddered). But, for the moment, no, she said, she didn't feel she had to fly the coop.

Also, no, "alass," she *hadn't* memorized the combination; she'd just been too shook up. She *thought* that she remembered 8, 19 and 46, but all the other numbers had completely left her mind — and even those *could* be her father's mother's birthday. She said that even at the best of times, numbers and arithmetic were not her "fortays."

But *names*, she told the boy, were quite a different matter. She'd always had a "nak" for names, she wrote. She could, she wrote, still give him everybody's name in her homeflock, the one that she'd grown up in ("Combhed," "Wattleface," "Gizzardbreth," "Geekbeek" were the ones she rattled off before he stopped her). And just before she'd scratched the combination on the girl's rear end, she'd glanced down at the book the girl had earlier been reading, which was right beside her elbow, on the towel. The girl, apparently, had marked her place in it with an old credit card. The Chicken saw her name, as it was printed on the card, and thought it every bit as elegant as her behind had been: Felicity Tantamount. "Gawjus," she opined.

The Chicken then went on to say she didn't *know* if Herb could read the combination still, or not — but that she *assumed* he would be able to. That, of course, was when Herb learned that she expected him to try.

"The gurl was nice and tan all over, if yoo follo me," she wrote, "so even if the scratches are all heeled, thaird still be liter-cullerd . . . *marx* back thair, Ide thnk."

And then the Chicken looked at Herb and wrote a final line, which she then also underlined.

"*Yoor my only hope*," she put down on the page,

and looked again in Herbie's eyes. Quite unexpectedly, the start of Roth's *Goodbye, Columbus* popped into his mind. ("The first time I saw Brenda she asked me to hold her glasses.")

He'd never seen such trust, and also desperation, in a chicken's face, before. In *her* mind, anyway, his finding this young woman, this Felicity, and getting her to let him have the combination would be . . . well, a Public Service of the very highest order. He decided that he'd give the thing a whirl, he really would; maybe he'd be lucky. And even if the combination wasn't there, or wasn't *visible*, at least he would have . . . tried.

Herb smiled and nodded at the bird. "Okay, I'll start to look for her today," he said.

Looking some pounds heavier — he'd stuffed about a ream of paper in his pockets — Herb left the Chicken's office just at daybreak. If he'd been out there at the Sleeping Dog, he might have heard a rooster crow.

18
KITTY HALL

When Herb's alarm clock shocked him out of sleep a scant three hours later, he just lay there in his bunk a while. In his present sleep-deprived condition, our young man felt anything but "up" for Public Service.

He thought about the day ahead of him. He was to spend it in the company of Mr. Bon Ballou, Hometown's Chief Assessor, in (or maybe out of) the Office of Assessment. The idea was for him to "learn the ropes," as he assumed they used to say on whaling ships, or in a Hanging for Beginners class — what ropes you pulled to get which things to happen.

In other words, he realized rather dully, today he'd spend some hours doing just the sort of stuff he'd *hoped* to do in Hometown. He'd be doing research, you could say, on future possibilities. Wasn't that his central purpose, being there? The only trouble was, it sounded pretty deadly, given how he felt, just then.

That other whole involvement with the Big Red Chicken's crisis was a side-light, only — a kind of a *parenthesis*, or a digression. His English teacher, Ms. Katrina Pell, had urged him to avoid parentheses; she said they were annoying to "the reader." He wondered how Ms. Pell would feel if she found out he was knee-deep in one that had the earmarks of a major scandal — a scandal that would come to light *only* when and if he read eight numbers off the bare, allegedly attractive, *derrière* of one Felicity Tantamount. He thought she'd be annoyed. (Most likely.)

Herb pulled himself together and got up. He'd be a sport and take a bite of this assessment world and see how it went down. Furthermore, he'd keep an open mind, at first, and see what it was full of by, say, 5 P.M. that afternoon.

At 4 P.M. he had his answer and it was "not too much." That was the hour Mr. Bon Ballou had called it "one fine d - a - y," saying that he had to meet with Mr. Danville Pine, in order to discuss some "classy-fied" material. Up until then, they had mostly driven here and there, both inside Hometown's city limits and outside them in what Mr. Bon Ballou referred to as "the Greater Hometown area."

What they did was look at property that Mr. Bon Ballou would first assess and then heap heavy scorn on. Herb learned that the average ranch house in the near vicinity "wasn't worth the chowder to fill a cup," while the old Victorians near the center of town mostly "weren't worth a mart in a maelstrom." Nor would Mr. Bon Ballou give you "a slug's tickle" for some renovated capes they saw; he felt the condos going up just on the edge of town were "worth about as much as an iguana in a cuddle contest."

At first, Herb found it impossible to figure out how Mr. Bon Ballou arrived at all the dollar values that he placed on different homes. At one point in the afternoon, the Chief Assessor turned to him and said, "As you can see, this work's part art, part science, part pure quasi-mystical experience." He pronounced that "q" word "kwayzee."

Herb saw none of that, but he decided not to press the point. By late afternoon, however, he *had* observed that Mr. Bon Ballou would often take whatever price the property just sold for, and then add or subtract another number that he'd get from anywhere — the one from off the license plate of the next Cadillac they passed, for instance — and that'd be the new official value, the assessment of the place. As far as Herb could tell, the only reason that they *looked* at any properties at all was so that Mr. Bon Ballou could criticize the way the occupants kept house.

But, no matter. By the time that it was 4 P.M., the assessing day was over, and an exhausted and befuddled Herb was pretty sure that this was not his future line of work. He went back to the van and lay down on his bunk. The big parenthesis was next; he hoped to get a plan of action clearly in his mind.

First, of course, he had to find the building that the girl, Felicity, resided in, the one that she'd been sunning on, two weeks before. That shouldn't be too hard; the Chicken had been sure it was the fifth one down from City Hall. Next, he'd find the door that led to the apartments on the upper floors (he knew there'd be a store below); he'd learn which one she lived in from the nametag on her mailbox. When he rang her doorbell, and she answered it, he wouldn't be that far from what they called (Herb smiled at his ironic wit) "the bottom line."

Just what he'd *say* to her was something of a problem. "Hello. Would you please turn around and drop your pants?" did not sound either "him" or promising. He thought that maybe he'd just wing it, be spontaneous. He'd always heard that it was good to be spontaneous.

The next thing that Herb didn't know, he'd fallen fast asleep.

When he woke up it was near dark inside the van, and he was hungry. He heard a clock chime someplace up on Church Street; it was eight o'clock.

Drat! he thought. He hoped he hadn't missed Felicity. She could have taken out, and gotten home, then eaten in, and gone right out again. Gone to the movies with a girlfriend. Gone to a class in Tae Kwon Do, or Homestyle Cooking. That last reminded Herb that he was really, *really* hungry. Time compression was confusing. He wondered how his body's cells were taking this. Were they aging faster than they should have been? Could he be *losing* time from the future he was trying to make? Would it be worth it? What did "it" mean, in that sentence? How about the other "it"?

Herb knew he wasn't making sense. He stood up, groggily, and splashed some water on his face. Two minutes later, he was standing in a fast-food place called Pig Out. Apparently they specialized in pork to go. A sign said they had hot dogs, ribs, ham sandwiches and sausage rolls and bacon buns, as well as pig's feet and pig's knuckles, even snouts on special order. "We carry everything except the squeal," the sign concluded — rather tastelessly, Herb thought. And so our youthful epicure selected hot dogs (three of them and "all the way") and two large cups of chocolate milk and went back to the van to gobble down his supper.

With that accomplished, Herbie hit the streets again. The time had come to make his move, to "go for it." He felt a pounding and a queasiness inside his chest: excitement, yes, but something more — a touch of heartburn, surely. Covering a burp, he turned the corner just past City Hall and started counting buildings. One, two, three, four, five. And there he was.

The building was the one that all along he'd thought contained a pet shop, Kitty Hall. Before, when he'd first come to town, he'd seen its sign from down the block; it was the kind that stuck out from the building and projected out above the sidewalk. But, now that he was there, in front of it, the place did not look pet-shoppy at all. There wasn't any big glass window, just for instance, behind which you could watch a bunch of cunning little puppies being totally adorable on shredded newspapers. There wasn't any window, *period*. Instead, there was a big, opaque front door, a heavy-looking wooden one, with long, black, metal hinges. In the center of the door was just this painting of a sleek black cat that

121

stretched and arched its back, and had an odd expression on its face. Wise, but still distinctly playful. It almost looked as if the cat were smiling — or it could be singing — showing just the pink tip of its tongue. *Doink.*

Herb stood and stared at it. He wished he'd had some coffee with his supper. He wasn't feeling sharp or on the ball, at all. He'd come this far expecting he would see a pet shop window with its door beside it, and then another door that opened onto stairs that led up to apartments. He wasn't seeing that, at all.

He looked above the one big door in front of him. It *did* appear there were apartments on the second floor, and on the third and fourth, as well. He could see that there were lights in lots of windows. But how did anyone get up to them? He guessed this *had to* be the door.

He tried the handle of it, pushed, but nothing happened. The door was tightly locked. He looked around. The fourth and sixth buildings down from City Hall had the kinds of doors on them that he'd expected the fifth would have, so Herb went into both of them and checked the nametags on the mailboxes. The only one remotely like the one he sought was "Pete Lamonica."

"*Great,*" he said, out loud. He was feeling really tired and a little sick. And stupid. Also, angry, in a way. He didn't know what at, exactly.

He decided he would go across the street and see if he could see inside the rooms upstairs. He'd stand in a doorway and observe the building. When people — like, *detectives* — did that in the movies, something always happened.

As it turned out, he couldn't see inside the rooms

at all. They all had shades or curtains, which were drawn. For all he knew, those rooms were full of catnip mice, or tattooed ladies. They could be full of people watching boring slides of someone's trip to Yellowstone. They *could* contain a lunatic named — let's see — *Mordecai*, holding lots of hostages, including Frank Sinatra. Or possibly Felicity was there, in one of them.

"*Wonderful*," he muttered to himself, this time.

But then a movement caught his eye from up the block, across the way.

"Hark," our young man whispered. And, "A *stranger*."

The "stranger" was a man, and he was *sauntering* along. He had his hands thrust deep inside the pockets of his pants, and he was whistling. Herb didn't think he'd *ever* seen a person look as casual as this guy did. The song that he was whistling was "Start Me Up," composed by Messrs. Jagger, M., and Richards, K., a song that, to Herb's mind, was not the least bit casual.

"Naturally I'm trained to notice little contradictions of that sort," our private eye informed himself, to pass the time.

As the man was just about to pass the door of Kitty Hall, he bent, as if to tie his shoe. But as he did so, Herb was pretty sure he saw the man look quickly up and down the block. Seeing only (possibly) a boy detective pressed into the shadow of a doorway on the other side, the man arose and faced the door of Kitty Hall. He knocked: three shorts, a pause, one short, another pause, a long-two shorts-a long. The door swung quickly open and he disappeared inside.

123

"Gol-*lee*," the boy exclaimed. It seemed that Kitty Hall was not, for sure, a pet shop — not, at least, as those two words are understood by normal people. It *seemed* that it was what he'd known — and feared — it might be, the moment he had seen that painting on the door.

"But let's not jump to a conclusion," our young Mister Fairness told himself. "This is America, and every storefront is presumed completely innocent, until it's proven guilty." He tried to think of other things that Kitty Hall might be, other than a pet shop and a . . . *that*.

It *could* (he thought) be, like, a *veterinary hospital*, perhaps. That would account for evening hours, wouldn't it? Conceivably the man he'd seen was there to visit his sick spaniel, or to hold the paw of, say, a convalescent coon cat.

Or, *possibly*, the guy had come to practice the *piccolo*, for instance, on the darkened stage way in the back of this *recital* hall. Hadn't he first thought the kitty in the painting on the door was (maybe) *singing*? There were lots of different kinds of Kittys. Kitty Carlisle Hart, for one example. And *Carnegie* Hall.

In fact — Herb's eyes grew large when he came up with this one — *this* "Kitty Hall" could *also* simply be a woman's name, the way that *Annie* Hall was. A woman's name that had to do with fashion and design! The way "Liz Claiborne" did, or "Norma Kamali," or "Coco Chanel." The cat could (merely) be her *logo*! Yes (Herb thought), he'd heard that some boutiques had special evening shows where gorgeous models showed off all the latest and most daring clothes from Paris, Venice, Tokyo, et cetera to wealthy and sophisticated buyers. Such buyers would be *casual* and cool, and they would come by invitation only, and they'd have to knock to gain admittance. The clothes would probably have first been shown in Paris, Venice, Tokyo, et cetera, and after they'd been seen in Hometown, they'd go on to San Francisco and New York, to Minneapolis. Felicity could be a model, easily, he guessed. The reason she'd been sunning naked on the roof was so she wouldn't show a tan line anywhere, when she was wearing daring, latest-fashion clothes. And of course she'd have to have — as the BRC had said she did — a *most* outstanding figure.

Herb crossed the street, as casually as possible. He knocked on the big door of Kitty Hall, using the same tempo that the other "buyer" had.

The door came open fast. A fellow in a butler's uniform looked out at him. The boy was glad the man was dressed that way. If he had had a bathrobe on, or shorts, Herbie would have thought he was a boxer.

"Well? You coming in or not?" the butler said, when Herbie simply stood there, staring at him.

"I'm looking for Felicity . . . uh, Tantamount," he finally said, and stepped inside. The butler quickly shut the door behind him.

"I ain't the lost and found," the butler said. "Tell it to the lady at the desk. Betcha she can fix you up, all right." He'd jerked his thumb behind him, down the entrance hall. Then he opened up what could have been a closet door and disappeared behind it.

Herb took a breath and looked around. One thing was absolutely clear: He was not in any Pets-R-Us, smelling an exotic blend of wildlife odors, hearing yelps and birdsong, chattering and hisses. Nor were there any of the sorts of sounds that you'd expect from music studios or concert halls: no rattles from a drum machine, no synthesizer's whine.

No, he was standing in a stylish, gracious entry-way — a *foyer*, if you please. It was a place that looked a lot like many he had seen, in passing, on TV, on *ETV* to be exact, on shows that had a lot too many episodes for him. Close at hand, there was a bentwood coatrack, just beyond it an umbrella stand. On the other side there was a table, like a sideboard, with a dish of mints on it, and flanked by straight-backed chairs, upholstered in a deep red velvet.

A little farther down the hall, and facing him, quite near the foot of curving stairs, there was a little desk, an *escritoire*, behind which sat a woman, old enough to be — but not — his mother. She had on a long, full, flowing, silken high-necked gown. Way up on the left side of her bosom there was pinned an orange plastic card that read: "Hi, pilgrim, and *bon soir*! I'm Madame Marguerite, Marquise de Marinade."

"Good even-ing, *m'sieur*," she said to Herb, and smiled.

"Good evening," our young man replied, politely. Having taken Spanish, he'd never met a madame in his life. Up ahead, beyond the woman, in a sort of formal drawing room, the boy could see some younger females, dressed in evening clothes. Though Herb was not well qualified to make such judgments, it appeared to him that some of them were dressed for evenings in the home, like, in their own . . . *boudoirs*, was it? while others wore the sorts

126

of gowns you'd see at nightclubs, or the theater, or at a dinner party at the Hefners', or in a James Bond movie. In other words, in every case Herb thought those younger women looked sophisticated, stylish . . . *daring*.

Although he knew darn well he shouldn't, Herbie gawked. Face it, this was not a scene he'd ever been exposed to in his life, so far. Nor was it one he'd been prepared for by the ambiance of Hometown. It didn't really go with feed stores in the heart of town, and restaurants named Pig Out and a mayor who was a Big Red Chicken.

But while he gawked, he also had to face the fact that he was *scared*. Being on this spot, the spot that he was on right there, right then, was scary. Sure, he understood — if just a little vaguely — what sorts of things went on in places of this sort. But knowing what goes on somewhere is not the same as going on yourself. He knew what happened in a play-off game in Boston Garden, but still he wouldn't want to play in one. Not that very day, at least. Later on? Perhaps.

"Felicity?" Herb tried his magic words again. "Felicity . . . uh, *Tantamount*?" He arched both brows this time, at the Marquise. Unfortunately, he looked to be in pain, instead of merely curious. "She's here?"

"But, yes," the woman said. "Ub gorse," her next words sounded like.

"Well, may I see her, please?" said Herb, feeling that politeness knew no social borders.

"Oh, absolyou," the woman said. Reaching down, she slid the most discreet small drawer imaginable just slightly open. "Wi' zat be cash or charge?" She said the last three words completely undemandingly, but also most distinctly.

"Cash or charge," repeated Herb, as if deciding.

"*Oui*," the woman said. "Mamzelle's retainer is one hundred dollars." She said *those* last three words, "wan hondraid dough-lars," but there was no mistaking that she meant $100.

"Retainer?" Herb was stalling, now. "One hundred dollars?"

Back in junior high, the boy had known some kids whose parents made them go to orthodontists, and who (therefore) had to *wear* retainers, yukky plastic things with wires on them that they stuck inside their mouths at night. What these retainers did was help to straighten teeth. But he was pretty sure he wasn't being asked to buy a thing like that right now, a sort of kinky souvenir of Madame What'sherface's place. The "retainer" that Madame was speaking of was like a fee for services, he knew. But even if he wanted to employ the girl, he didn't have a hundred bucks.

"Well," the boy said slowly, "well, I mean, if I could *see* her for a minute, and find out — "

He cut it off, himself. Amazingly, he'd gotten through to the Marquise. She was nodding at him now, and smiling, once again.

"Ub gorse," she said, once more. "You weesh to *see* her first. Can be arrange." She gaily punched some buttons on her fancy telephone. "Felici-*tee*? Can you come down *un moment*, dear? A gentleman would like to *see* you. Yes. *Mare-see*." She put the phone back down and said to Herb, "She come. You see. You won' be disappointment."

128

Herb smiled and stepped back from the desk to wait, leaning up against the newel post at the foot of the staircase. This possibly was working out, he thought. For sure, it was a fact that he was getting closer. He was going to see the girl, perform that public service — and that was the whole point, the thing that *had* to happen. If he was going to do his *job*.

A minute later, he heard footsteps, coming down. And so he turned his head to say hello to this Felicity, at last.

Luckily for him, he wasn't chewing gum.

Technically, perhaps, Felicity was "dressed." She did have on a little lacy wraparound, belted at the waist, but it was shorter than the shortest mini Herb had ever seen, and *totally* transparent. Herb confirmed, at once, she didn't have a tan line, anywhere. And it's fair to say that although he experienced a whole *thesaurus* of emotions, "disappointment" wasn't one of them.

You see, our Herb had never seen a real, in-person, female's hypogastric region — all of it — in his entire life, before. The place he swam at in the summertime was not, let's face it, Sweden.

So *this*, he thought, is Tyree Toledano, in the total flesh.

"Oh, hi," he said, when he was able to. He tried to say it just as if she wore a down-filled parka over a floor-length Amish woman's housedress. By then, he'd wrenched his eyes away from *terra incognita* and was staring at a point right in between, and just above, her lovely, long-lashed, hazel eyes.

"Okay?" she said — to him, Herb thought. She was asking *him* if she was, like, *Okay?* She had a pleasant, cultivated voice. It made him think of words like "Williams College," "music lessons," "drama club" — and from his own real life, "Forget it." She moved her eyes from Herb to the Marquise.

"All set?" she asked the woman. Then, she sounded like the same girl, still, but clerking down at Grenville's Pharmacy — working at a summer job, perhaps.

"No, no, not yet, my dear," the Marquise said. "The young m'sieur has not yet pa — "

"Oh, well, the thing *is*, Miss Felicity," the boy began, talking without thinking, without *breathing*, actually. His ears were ringing and his eyes were watering, his nose was running, but his mouth was dry as ashes. "All I need is just five minutes of your time," he babbled *sotto voce*. "Or even less, a *lot* less, really. If there was someplace we could *go* and — "

"Sure," she told him, sticking to that same agreeable tone, "I understand. I really do. Truthfully — it might be only fifteen *seconds*, mightn't it? But all the same, you see, you have to pa — "

"But I don't *have* a hundred dollars." Herb's whisper sounded desperate, even to himself. "And I promise you, I won't do anything but *look*. I've got to see if . . . well, if — "

But he had to break it off, again. This clearly wasn't working. The girl had sighed, and shook her head and started up the stairs. Herb could plainly see the Chicken's . . . notepads; they *were* beautiful. But not, of course, what had been written on them. Not in *that* light, anyway, or through the little mist of lace she wore.

"I'm sorry, really," floated back to him.

The next thing Herbie knew, the butler had him

130

by the elbow and had moved him out the door and to the sidewalk, where he left him, once again.

Herb, perhaps reflexively, looked up and down the street, and then turned left, toward City Hall. He started humming something, "Can't Buy Me Love," by Messrs. Lennon and McCartney. He didn't even know that, so confused — and warm — was he.

It was hard for him to get his feelings straight — again. Back there on Wince 'n' Wails, he'd reached for Zippy, sure he had, when she'd whipped off her shirt like that. He hadn't known — expected — she would do it, and his reaching out for her had been a reflex, you could say; he'd *wanted* her. *Naturally* he had. And vice versa, so it seemed. And she *had* started it. If Greenfield Hill had not come in the room, they would have crossed each other's stop lines and each other's goal lines, too. If it wasn't for that murderer, he would have *scored*! Which would have been all right, he thought. It had to happen sometime.

But seeing as it hadn't happened *then*, he had these worries and confusions *now*. It almost seemed like it was just his luck to keep on finding gorgeous and exciting girls on these excursions out of Castles in the Air. Zippy had been simply uninhibited but, well, with this Felicity . . . scoring was her *business*, you could say. Could a person make the argument that he was *meant* to do it on some trip or other, such as this one? That *that* might be a part of his good fortune?

But trip or no trip (Herbie told himself) he still, presumably, could exercise free will. What he did would always be his choice; he didn't have to "do," like, anything (except, perhaps, eventually, some "something" with himself). So let's suppose, on some occasion at some place he could not presently imagine, Felicity was willing. If not for love, perhaps, at least, for money. What would he do then?

He simply didn't know. The turmoil in his mind, which seemed to have to do with what "love" meant to him, somehow, just wouldn't go away. There were some things — Am I really just another Dartmouth guy? — that he could not get straight.

The trouble in *this* situation — as compared to what had happened there on Wince 'n' Wails — was that he had the time to think about it, first. Or so Herb told himself, right then.

19
NUMBERS GAME

Herb walked straight back to the van, seeing almost no one on the sidewalks and few cars in the streets. That figured. Hometown was a real dull place; it always had been, always is, and always will be. They roll the sidewalks up real early, there in Hometown.

Lots of kids maintain they just can't wait till they're adults so they can bug on out of there and live someplace where something happens, sometimes — where there's something, like, to *do*. A few of them go on and do that, too. But adults, as a rule, speak well of Hometown. Its nowhere-ness and nothingness appeal to them; they call it quiet, peaceful, homey and affordable. So, if you're going to get out of Hometown and live somewhere else, the best time to do it is after you've stopped being a kid, but before you get to be an adult. You have to move real fast.

It was still too early to go to the mayor's office, Herb thought. Plus, he didn't much look forward to telling her he hadn't got the combination. Or that there was a . . . what? *bordello*, right there in the heart of town. He was sure the Big Red Chicken didn't know that fact already; she would have a fit. Or would she? Who was he to say where chickens stood on sex, free enterprise, or feminism? Herb decided that perhaps a little sleep would make him both a better bearer of bad tidings and, in general, a smarter, more resourceful public servant.

He sat down on his bunk and reset his alarm clock. His stomach rumbled, and he realized he was hungry. Not for hot dogs "all the way" awash in chocolate milk, however. What he thought would really hit the spot would be a plate of mom's home cooking, of Paprika Chi- . . . uh, whoops! A nice plate of *linguine*, but with tomato sauce, not clams.

Herb shook his head, and then got up and went outside and walked back to an Arco station, where he had some Hometown-type excitement getting cheese-and-peanut butter crackers out of a machine. He put his money in the proper slots, and — bingo! — the machine delivered. Talk about a grand old time! He walked back, munching, to the van again.

The alarm was set for 2 A.M. already, so the boy lay down and soon was fast asleep and, later, dreaming. In his dream he was back in the great hall at Castles in the Air, but Ses deBarque was nowhere to be seen. Instead, Felicity was standing by the

134

wheel, dressed as she had been when he last saw her. She spun the thing, and when it stopped, the arrow pointed right at . . . *her*!

"All right!" This dream of a Felicity said that to Herb. "You're just a hundred dollar bill away from heaven."

"But how about good government?" the dream-state Herb inquired.

"When winter comes, can spring be far behind?" she asked.

Of course, he didn't have that kind of money (even in his dreams), and he wasn't sure he understood the saying, so he awakened, sweating in frustration, very close to tears. It was a quarter after one, so he got up and brushed his teeth and tried to get his act together. He knew he wanted to get something from the girl, all right. Was it more than just the combination to that office safe? Now that he had *seen* her in that . . . habitat.

This "Public Service" deal was turning out to be a lot like "Crime—Organized or not," he realized. Or, at any rate, it had that side to it. There were people in the field who had an eye and both their hands out for big bucks. And who would break the law to get them, gladly. Break both the law and anyone who showed up in their way — a boy, for instance.

He had to wonder how his values were surviving this experience. Were *love* and *money* still the things he wanted most in life? Or would he settle for a night with someone like Felicity, a decent meal, and, maybe, peace and quiet? For *benefits*, in other words.

Herb walked across the parking lot, into City Hall, and up the stairs, heading for Her Honor's office. Right now, he thought, he didn't seem to have a choice.

The mayor was snoozing when he stepped into her office, but as soon as she woke up and saw that it was Herb, she started clucking loudly in excitement, just as he had feared she would. And of course she next flipped open and jumped on the ink pad, too, wild to fire off some loaded rockets in the form of Good News-seeking questions.

The boy held up his hand. He figured he could save her tread-wear.

"I didn't get the combination," he admitted. And so learned, to his regret, exactly what the word "crestfallen" meant.

"But I found the girl, all right," he said. "The fifth place down is Kitty Hall. I'd thought it was a pet shop, but it's not — not even close. It's a . . . well, a house of ill repute."

The Big Red Chicken looked, first, puzzled, then aghast. Before he'd finished, she was writing, madly; there was no way that he could have stopped her, short of chickicide.

Herb once again read every page as it rolled out from underneath her feet. It seemed the Chicken was *extremely* pleased that there was not a *second* pet shop, here in Hometown. She had, in fact, this *thing* against the one she knew about already, a place called Katz's Meows and Bow-wows, which was down on Prospect Street. Apparently this Mr. Katz had chicknapped half a dozen youngsters from the Big Red Chicken's former coop one Easter season, years before, and had even dyed them different colors in his shop before he sold them off to families with children, there in town.

"Sum peepul still indulj in stuff like that, u no," she told the boy. "They dont think uv it as slaveree, uv corse."

And then she wrote, "So whatz a howse of ill repewt?"

As Herb explained how it, too, tended to promote a sort of slavery (which he described, but not in great detail), the Chicken's eyes grew round with horror, once again. Soon she started stamping back and forth, from one side of her desk back to the other. Herb didn't think he'd ever seen a more disgusted fowl.

"Boy," she finally stopped and wrote, "peepul ar scrood up, u no that? How can u treet each uther so uncaringlee?"

But she wasn't letting moral outrage blind her to her central purpose.

"Wot yule hav to do — thatz if ur game to take anuther shot at this — iz try the roof. *If* that dorz still opun, mabee u can get down to the gurlz room after ourz — when sheze finished . . . wurk," she wrote.

Herb thought that over. He supposed he *could* do that. House of ill repute or no, this was Hometown, still. People wouldn't keep late hours, even in the bawdy business, probably. But still, no matter when he saw the girl, or which door he came in by, there was still this central problem he had. He was lacking any *leverage*, any means of gaining her cooperation. To put it bluntly, any money. Like, $100.

He said as much, succinctly, to the bird.

She scratched her head and thought it over. Then she rummaged in the mess atop her desk until she found a nice clean piece of Town of Hometown stationery. Taking lots of time and care, she wrote on it the following:

IOU $100
Town of Hometown
Big Red Chikken, Mare

Of course! Herb could have kicked himself for . . . well, not having been the first to think of such a Neat Idea. Never in his life, again, would he call someone "birdbrain." He did, however, feel that given this Felicity's well-educated style, it might be worth the risk of hurting mayoral feelings to request a rewrite of this little document with all the words spelled right.

No problem. The Chicken wasn't in the least offended, just amused.

"U say u spel Mare 'Mayor'?" she wrote. "Thatz dum. But not ur fallt Ime shoor," she finished, gracefully, and started on the copy.

Before the clocks struck three, young Herb was climbing over rooftops, like a burglar in Paris.

When the boy arrived on rooftop number five, he tried the door he found on it with mixed emotions, truth to tell. Having it be locked could save him quite a lot of trouble and excitement and confusion. Or at least postpone them for a while. Sometimes it was easier if you *couldn't* do anything with yourself (he thought), if you could put the blame on circumstances that were clearly out of your control. ("All doors were closed to me . . ." et cetera.) Then, in that case, you could simply lie, or wallow, where

138

you were, safely in a rut (you'd *never* call Self-Pity). He tried the door; of course it opened, easily.

Herb crept down a flight of narrow stairs and found they ended in a lighted corridor with doors on either side of it. It was the sort of hall you find in cheap small-town hotels, or older dorms in less demanding colleges. He listened, left and right, and to his great delight and real relief, he heard no sounds of any sort, from anywhere. He began to reconnoiter and discovered all the rooms had names: "Annabelle," "Babette," "Cherie," "Dolores," "Eloise," "Felicity," he read. And went no further up the hall, or alphabet.

He turned the knob and slipped into "Felicity."

Like the mayor herself, his quarry kept a nightlight on, and by its gentle glow our boy could see a shape like hers beneath a sheet, but turned toward the wall. He looked around the room. In style, it was Victorian, with heavy wooden furniture, mahogany perhaps, and velvet drapes, and prints and paintings on the walls. Tacked above the bed, however, was an Amherst banner with a college playbill pinned to it; apparently Felicity had once been in *A Doll's House* (too). And, yes, there was a mandolin, leaning up against her dressing table.

While Herb had still been up there on the rooftops, he'd thought about what method he might use to wake the girl — assuming that she'd be asleep — but not alarm her. The Big Red Chicken's Hometown IOU would surely be a help, or a necessity, at some point in the conversation they would have, but maybe there was something better he could flash at her, at first. It seemed to him the first few seconds would be critical; if she were to scream, he might

139

be sunk — *deep*-sunk, and possibly for good. What he had to do was *somehow* find a way to let her know, *at once*, that he was harmless. Weird, perhaps, and needy, but quite harmless.

He tiptoed to the bed. First, he took the bellpull that was hanging by the head of it and got it hooked onto the Amherst banner so that she couldn't reach it easily. Her having gone to Amherst was a plus, in light of what he'd planned. Then, he put a hand down on her sheeted shoulder and began to shake it, very gently. And, as he saw her coming to, he whispered this:

"Felicity! Felicity! Could you help me with my *Hampshire* application, do you think?"

Her eyes snapped open, and perhaps in horror, but not in fear at least, or even loathing. More like horror mixed with pity — condescension, maybe.

Herb kept on with his whispering. "Please. I only want to talk to you. It's a matter of life and death, I promise you. I'm just a kid; I'm absolutely harmless."

The girl looked puzzled, now, also just a bit annoyed.

"Look," she said. "It isn't *really* a matter of life and death; it only *seems* that way, right now. There are a *lot* of first-class colleges out there, some of which aren't even *in* New England. And as far as Hampshire is concerned. . . ."

It took Herb another few minutes to explain to the groggy girl that there was something other than his college application on his mind. He sketched the story in the sort of big bold strokes he favored: a Simple, Honest mayor held Captive and against her will by Crooked Underlings; the records of Corruption locked inside an office Safe; the need to get the Combination to that safe so Righteousness could Triumph over Evil.

"Hmmph," Felicity replied, when she had heard all that. "All well and good. But where do *I* fit in?"

"Well," said Herb, "do you remember — sure you do — about two weeks ago? A little incident when you were lying on the roof and, well, a chicken came and . . . ?"

"You're damn well tootin' I remember!" flared the girl. Her hand moved, underneath the covers. "Talk about fowl play! I got your 'little incident,' all right. I still get *flashbacks* from it! How d'you think *you'd* like to be just lying on your roof, asleep, and have a chicken come along and *sink* her nails into your . . . body? I'm a vegetarian, myself, but still — if I'd had a knife right then, believe me, I'd have cut that chicken into serving pieces *long* before you said '*Bon appetit*, my little *cacciatore*.' "

It took a lot of "I don't blame you"s and a bunch of "That sounds really, really *awful*"s before Herb got the girl calmed down again and listening to reason — and the facts, the full facts of the case.

This time he went into detail: how the Chicken was the honest, simple mayor that he'd been speaking of, and that what Felicity had gone through on the roof was not the mindless piece of pure brutality it might have seemed to be. That, in fact, the scratch marks she had "suffered" were, he was quite sure, eight numbers, and the combination to that office safe.

When Felicity had heard all that, she looked reflective, and she didn't answer right away. She moved her hand again, back out from underneath

141

the covers, and she nibbled on its thumbnail.

"I never even knew there *was* a mayor of Hometown," she began — and then went on to say that she and all the other girls in Kitty Hall were prisoners in there, forced to do the "jobs" they did by threats against their persons and their reputations, both.

Herb didn't know exactly what she meant by that — the "reputations" part — but he kept right on talking anyway, and when he said that perhaps when Danville Pine, the mayor's . . . well, puppeteer and chief tormenter, got his well-deserved comeuppance, maybe lots of things in Hometown would be changed, it turned out that he'd used the magic words.

"Danville Pine!" the girl exclaimed. "Why, he's the lowlife scum who owns this place! *He's* the one who . . ." And away she went.

Her story was an ugly one and all too commonplace, I fear. Danville Pine had somehow laid his rotten paws upon some photographs "a roommate took in college — silly things," and had (of course) threatened to send copies to Felicity's mother, aunts and fiancé, if she didn't . . . you can just *imagine*. What she realized *now* was that those pictures, in all likelihood, were sitting *in* the safe that Herbie and the Big Red Chicken hoped to open with the combination she'd been sitting *on* the last two weeks.

In another minute they had cut a deal: Herb could look for numbers on her bottom, here and now, but if he found them, *she* would get to go with him and be there when the safe was opened, to regain her "property," and so her freedom and respectability.

One moment, Herb was shaking the hand on the

142

end of the bare arm Felicity had slid out of its hiding place beneath the sheet, and they both were saying "It's a deal," and the next moment she was out of bed and turning every light on in the room — all the lights that possibly might help him see what he was looking for.

And that illumination — all those watts or lumens or what have you — also helped him see that all the rest of her, just then, was just as bare as that one arm had been.

"There!" Felicity exclaimed. "How's that?" She'd just rigged up her desk lamp so that, turned around, it threw a beam of special brightness and intensity directly on the bed.

Herb looked from girl to bed to girl again. If this be Public Service, make the most of it, he told himself. It seemed a pity that this job was going to end — that he couldn't just do *this*, this sort of thing, as a career, forever.

The more he got accustomed to . . . well, looking at the girl, the more he loved to do it — the more he was attracted by, and dazzled by, excited by, the sight of her. Herb wished he *knew* her better, wished that they were friends. Then, perhaps, he wouldn't feel so weird about the feelings he was feeling. If only he could tell her that he *loved* her. . . .

"Great," he said, out loud, at last. And she flopped down, face forward, on the bed.

"Oh, I've got a magnifying glass," she said. "It's on the dresser, there, I think." She wiggled her butt a bit as she said that, perhaps in her impatience and anxiety, he thought. He wondered if he might pretend that he was having trouble finding it — the magnifying glass, that is.

Of course he didn't, though. He got the glass and went to work. In the beginning, it appeared that he was going to get the combination easily. The first four numbers, on the left cheek of her round behind, were clear to what is called "the naked eye": 8, 46, 19, 15. But the others, on the other side, were nowhere near as easy.

The boy leaned forward, framed the well-healed scratch marks with his hands. 38 — that was the first one. The panicked Chicken had been scribbling by then, for sure. 23 — that was the second one, no doubt about it, but he'd had to take a hand away and use the glass.

The last two were the hardest. The Chicken must have been, like, slipping off the girl's smooth rump, by then. Herb was kneeling on the bed, his eyes just inches from the . . . information. 4, he thought, and . . . 12. He traced the last two numbers with a finger. He was sure of them; he had it! 8, 46, 19, 15, 38, 23, 4, 12.

And, just as many great explorers all through history supposedly knelt down and kissed the ground they'd landed on, so did our boy (spontaneously and joyfully) bend forward just a little farther and . . . yes, *kiss* this great discovery of his!

"Hey!" the girl cried out. "What's going on back there?" She lifted up her head and turned a bit around to try to see. "Did you get, like, what you need?"

It was then that Herb remembered what he had in his back pocket: the mayoral IOU. He closed his eyes a moment, thinking, contemplating; when he opened them again, she was still there, this gorgeous naked girl, and lying on a bed. He fished the paper out and thrust it toward her face.

Felicity looked puzzled, looked at it, and then at Herb.

"Well — how about it?" croaked the boy, his voice not equal to the question, its momentousness.

"Yeah, how *about* that?" said the girl, either misunderstanding it, and him, or not; he'd never know.

She bounded off the bed. "So. You got it, right?" she said.

"I guess," said Herbie with a sigh, in heat — and some confusion.

It didn't take her long to dress. She put on a rugby shirt, some baggy yellow pants, a lime-green unconstructed jacket with the sleeves turned up and sandals.

This was a *really* odd relationship they had, Herb thought. He'd realized that up till then, he'd never seen her with her clothes on. He thought about the way *Green Mansions* started. ("Now that we are cool, he said . . .")

20
GRAND OPENING

When Herbie had unhooked the Big Red Chicken's office door, he motioned to the girl, Felicity, to go on in ahead of him. Her Honor was awake this time, so naturally she focused on the girl at once, and then her bright round eyes went darting back and forth from girl to boy and back again, alight with eager curiosity.

"We *got* it!" Herb exclaimed, excitedly, before the bird exploded, or could even ink a claw. Then, remembering his manners, "Miss Felicity Tantamount, I'd like to introduce you to our mayor, the Big Red Chicken."

"Your Honor, it's my pleasure," said the girl — sincerely, Herbie thought. She made a little half a curtsy, instead of holding out her hand. A nice touch, that, Herb thought. Like, *sensitive*.

The Chicken nodded cordially, and then she

146

started scribbling away. When she had finished, and the boy had picked the paper up, the Chicken jerked her head toward the girl, as if to say, "For *her*. Just hand it over."

Herb caught a glimpse of what she'd written, anyway.

"Ime *reely* sorry that I had to uze ur epidurmus for a postit pad," she'd written, showing sensitivity, herself. "Buhleve me, it wuz nuthing pursonul."

"Please, think nothing of it," Felicity replied. "From what I understand, you did us both a favor." And she chuckled in a natural, and friendly and unvengeful way, Herb thought. The fact that she could read the Chicken's writing but did not get rude about the spelling showed the boy two other pluses, too.

Herb then explained exactly why Felicity was there: how Danville Pine had cruelly bent her to his will, and how she hoped to find her property inside the safe, along with all the other evidence of Pine's misdeeds.

While he was laying all that out, Felicity just stood there with her head down, and her hands deep-buried in her jacket pockets, the picture (thought the boy) of both humiliation and . . . a certain high resolve to, well, go on from there to future, finer things.

"Wel, letz get to it," wrote the Chicken, with a head-swing toward the safe.

Herb hadn't written down the numbers, back in Kitty Hall. He felt that they were deeply etched in both his long- and short-term memories. Years from now, he thought, he'd see them still: 8, 46, 19, 15; then 38, and 23, 4, and 12. And even if he didn't see all eight of them, he'd surely recollect the fundamental features they'd been written on. Just as you remember, say, the shape of, well, the Eiffel Tower or your favorite baseball glove, long after you've forgotten what the writing on it may have said.

He rubbed his fingers on his shirtfront, took the dial and twirled it once, for practice. Then he fed the combination into it, slowly, carefully; he was glad to put this aspect of his high school education into useful, real-life practice.

The huge doors opened on his first attempt. That almost made him think that darned old safe had not been locked at all. As big and heavy as it was, it might have been a Hometown native, and so have had a lifelong, deep-dyed prejudice against all you-know-what-ed doors.

"Boy!" said Herb, when he beheld the quasi-mess inside the safe. "It's a good thing Mr. Bon Ballou's not here."

Most of the shelves were stuffed with money, stacks and stacks of the stuff, piled this way and that, with different colored rubber bands around them; they were sorted by denominations, yes, but these were not in any order. Fifties lay on top of twos (yes, twos!), on top of twenties, fives and singles. Herb took out a big fat wad of fifties; tucked inside its rubber band there was a note: "Hot digs! A new Ford Ranger, here!" Clearly, crook or no, this Mr. Danville Pine had kept his Hometown tastes intact.

On the topmost shelf there were some three-ring binders of the kind that younger children sometimes take to school, with cutouts of a lot of Disney char-

148

acters glued onto them. These were labeled on their spines, as follows: *Protection $, Vice, including Rock & Roll, Narcotics/Vending Machines,* and *Trash, other than Manure.* And next to the notebooks was a folding file that had the label *Letters, Photographs and Useful, Silly Things — Plus other spreadable Manure.*

The girl looked over at the Chicken and then gestured at the file.

"May I?" she inquired. And the Chicken nodded her assent. Herb shifted slightly in the girl's direction, and he craned his neck a little.

"Hmm," she mused. She was looking at a letter. "Whoa!" She blushed and turned a scrap of parchment over, fast. "I *see,*" she nodded at another item in the file.

When she got to the first photograph, she bit her lip and folded it real fast; she did the same with both the next one and the next, and that was all of them. Herb saw enough to know that they were hardly Mother's Day material. The person in the photos with Felicity was possibly another roommate or, if not, a real close friend, as well as something of an acrobat. The folded photos went into her inside jacket pocket.

Herbie had expected that the girl would just relax and look delighted, then. He'd imagined that a clubby little scene, quite possibly, would follow, one in which the two of them — the ones who happened to have hands — would organize the evidence against the foxy Mr. Pine, while Her Honor clucked around and listened to the juicy bits they passed along to her, while writing memos that were full of witty, wise suggestions. Once everything was organized and counted, packed in cardboard boxes that they'd get from somewhere, they would carry down the evidence and lock it in his van.

After that, the three of them would head out to the homey Hometown Diner on the edge of town. There, they'd have a huge and satisfying breakfast that included lots of homefries, and a plate of steaming cornbread for the mayor. Then, stuffed and satisfied, they'd drive the contents of the safe down to the Hometown county sheriff's office and accept his heartfelt and astounded gratitude for about the best-done exposé of governmental crime since Whatsitsface and Whatchacallit.

From that point on, things (meaning, Herb's imaginings) were somewhat vaguer. *Probably*, they'd drop the Big Red Chicken off somewhere, and then the two of them would . . . maybe take a little trip? Like, to the *shore*, or somewhere? Someplace, *any-*place, that everybody knew was fun, relaxing, with a lot of privacy. Herb imagined them beside the hotel/motel registration desk. "Mr. and Mrs. Herbert *Hansen*" he'd put down in the register, in case his mother ever stopped there — just dash it off, as if it were a thing he'd done a thousand times. Hopefully they wouldn't bump into a former . . . client of Felicity's. "Dream on," Herb told himself.

". . . hate to do this to you two," the girl was saying when he left the world of fantasy and came back to the present moment, *now*.

Herb stared; he gaped. Felicity had used the gun before; he could just *tell*. She didn't seem afraid of it at all; it didn't look too long or heavy for her hand. She must have had it in her jacket pocket, all that time.

150

Now she shrugged, almost apologetically, Herb thought.

" *'Carpe diem'* — seize the day," she said, "as our old friend, the poet Horace, said. 'A woman's time of opportunity is short. . . .' That's from the *Lysistrata*. But, either way, this here is dirty money, and I'm a-gonna take it with me. Here's how I excuse myself: It isn't Danville Pine's, nor is it yours, or Hometown's. Maybe, someday, *some* of it would find its way back to a rightful owner, but a lot of it doesn't even *have* a rightful owner. *Some* of it is really mine, in fact. Money that I earned for Pine, the hard way." She made a little gesture with the gun.

"What I'm saying is," she said, "this money is a springboard to a brand-new life for me, a long, long way from here. And so it's going with me, almost all of it. And you two aren't going to stop it."

Herb didn't get a lot of pleasure from the next half hour. Some, a little bit, but not a lot. First, she made him pack the money, most of it — she left one wad of fives and one of singles — into plastic liners of the sort you put in wastebaskets. While he did that, she composed a note that said *about* how many dollars had been in the safe when they had opened it, and also said that she, "Miss X," had "liberated" almost all of it. That was so, she said, the cops and IRS would know how much that "rotted Pine" had stolen and extorted and evaded paying taxes on, she'd bet.

Then, she made Herb cut a length of cord from off the office blinds. She used that, swiftly and convincingly, to tie his hands behind his back, *and* to the handle of the massive safe's main door.

151

"Those notebooks and the file, together with my note, are evidence enough to put that swine away for good, and then some," said the girl. "And, having firsthand knowledge of her . . . well, *dexterity*, I'm sure Her Honor will be able to untie those knots I made before the janitors — or Pine — come in. I'm really sorry, both of you; I know you'll be all right."

She looked over at the mayor. "I never had a Chicken for a friend, before," she said. "If I can get a ballot — absentee — I'll vote for you for reelection, that's a promise. Assuming that you want to run again, of course. I kinda hope you do."

And then she came right up to Herb, where he stood cinched against the safe.

"I don't even know your name," she said. "But if you tell me what it is, I'll write to Hampshire for you. I'd like to tell them you're a hero, *and* a gentleman."

"Herbie Hansen — *Hertzman*," Herbie muttered. He didn't even know if he'd apply to Hampshire, but he didn't see how it could hurt to be a hero in a file in the Admissions Office there.

She made a note of what he'd said, and put a hand on Herbie's cheek, then leaned and kissed him on the mouth, letting all her attributes press up against his body for a moment. It was, he thought, a meaningful occasion, in a way.

"*Ciao*, now," were her final words to them, and she was out the door, the plastic bags in hand. They heard the little hook drop into place.

21
BUMMERS

"I can't get *over* Kitty Hall!" said Ses deBarque. She shook with glee, as usual, and smelled, perhaps, of frangipani, which might have been the flower on her black Hawaiian shirt. "I mean, I've been around forever, but I've never heard of any cat house with a *sign*, before. Not on any *Church* Street, in a *Home*town, anyway." She fluffed her dark blonde curls above one ear, and seemed to think about her last remark. "Nevada, *maybe*," she appended, "but Nevada can't be blamed for being different. They're always testing nuclear devices there."

"I just didn't want to think about it," Herbie said. He shook his head and laughed, remembering. "Having it be what it was just seemed like such a bummer." He and Ses had talked about "the Hometown caper," as he'd dared, just once, to call it in his mind — but not out loud, of course. He'd given her a lot more details, this time. And he'd shown her the small silver-plated loving cup with *Hometown Hero* on it that the Chicken had presented to him, once the sheriff planted Pine inside the local lockup.

The two of them were sitting on the second floor of Castles in the Air, in Ses's living quarters. When Herb had gotten back from Hometown, and she had asked him if he'd like to come on up, "for figs and flummery," he'd been delighted to accept. The figs turned out to all be members of the Newton tribe; he didn't know if "flummery" was what they washed them down with. If so, it was a fairly nice cold drink that tasted sort of like cream soda, only flat.

Herb had never been on Castles's second floor before, and he'd been knocked darn close to sockless by the room that they were sitting in — her living room, he guessed it was.

The space was huge and circular, the ceiling very high; what they were in, in fact, appeared to be a canvas *tent*, suspended from the castle's ceiling. In shape, it would have been a half a sphere, or slightly more, except that it had walls that came straight down, the last eight feet. But the most amazing thing about it was: The inside of the tent was *painted*, not just in a single color, like off-white, but as if it were a scene, and you were looking out at *landscapes*, *vistas* and *horizons*, topped by an enormous bright blue dome of sky, with just a few white, puffy clouds.

The overall effect was very much like sitting on a lovely mountaintop; all around were these delightful views, views of other mountains, rolling hills and valleys full of groves, with rushing rivers running through them and, on one side in the distance, dark unfathomed ocean with, he thought, some islands

154

in it. They were sitting in the center of the room, where nice, low furniture was grouped for conversation, relaxation and enjoying sweet, refreshing drinks with cookies (Herb was thinking), and the views. It had also crossed his mind that Ses deBarque was much — *way* — farther out than any of his parents' friends, and that John Jaspers, if he'd done this paint job, simply had to be a modern master.

"You know what else I still don't want to think about?" Herb said.

"Maybe." Sesame sat back and smiled, her head just slightly tilted to one side.

"There's *two* things," Herbie said, and smiled himself. Mysteriously, he hoped. More or less above it all.

He'd noticed something in the last half hour. He was more relaxed, right then, with Ses deBarque, than he had ever been with any woman, maybe any *person*, other than his mom. When he was ten-eleven, right in there, he'd been bosom-roughhouse-buddies with one Harvey Parker, Junior, better known as "Porksome." That was different, though. It seemed to him that he could really *talk* to Ses, that he could tell her *anything*.

"Maybe I'll tell you one of them," said Herb.

"Only if you want to," she replied.

"Well," he said, "remember when Felicity pulled out the gun and said that she was going to take the money?"

"Yup." She nodded.

"I don't think I would've stopped her if I could've," Herbie said. "That's the kind of person that I am."

"Oh?" said Sesame.

"Uh-huh," said Herb. "It really sucks, but that's the truth. People never hesitate to do minor damage to school property when I'm around. You know what else they do? They over-claim insurance when their cars get broken into, and they tell me all about it."

"Hmm," said Sesame. "How come?"

"Because they know I'll say it isn't any of my business," Herbie said. "Like I said — that's the kind of person that I am. *I'll* say they aren't really hurting anybody. And of course they know I want all of them to like me. Which, of course, they don't."

"But now you realize all that really *bothers* you," she said. "That stuff."

"Right," said Herb. "*I* bother me. And you know who'd never go along with stuff like that? Who never would have, ever?"

"No, who?" said Sesame. Possibly she did, and possibly she didn't, Herbie thought.

"The Big Red Chicken," said the boy. "Need I say more?"

"She's a plucky one, all right," said Ses.

Herb looked at her suspiciously, but Ses deBarque just stared straight back at him, the picture of a wide-eyed, friendly innocent. When he didn't go on talking, she took a big deep breath, and sighed.

"No man is an island, eh?" she said. "Not even Simon and Garfunkel." The boy looked puzzled, so she said, "Just kidding."

Herbie nodded. "Sometimes I wish I *was* an island," he opined. "Islands never have to worry. Islands have girls crawling all over them. They don't have to think about . . . well, *anything*."

"Let me guess, like — what?" said Ses, and she

156

was smiling. "Let me guess the *second* thing that you don't want to think about."

"Feel free," said Herbie. "Be my guest." He wondered if she would. He didn't think she would. Or, actually, he thought she maybe *could*, but wouldn't.

"You don't want to think about what *didn't* happen with Felicity," she said. "Correct?" She let out one of her most juicy chortles yet. "How you *didn't* end up at the luxurious Elysian Fields Motel on the virtually uninhibited Ecstatic Isles with her. How you *didn't*, as they used to say, get your ashes hauled."

She paused and looked at him; he kept his face as straight as possible.

"Come on. Provide a one-word answer, please," she said. "Is the teacher right or wrong?"

Herb had to laugh. Laugh and nod and sort of gurgle "*Right*." She had said it, after all, not him; *he* didn't have to be embarrassed. But were they going to talk about it? Apparently they were.

". . . don't get, then," she was saying, "is why you didn't go for Uncle Babbo's deal. He was promising that kind of stuff, galore."

Herb tried to think. Had he gone into all of that with Sesame, everything that Babbo'd said? He guessed he must have.

"That was different, though," he said. "The girls that Babbo meant, they were into surfaces, like *hair*. Chances are, they wouldn't even get to know me, first." He was staring at the floor between his feet.

"Well, it doesn't seem to me," said Ses, "that either Zippy or Felicity were what I'd call 'old friends.' "

Herbie made a small, despairing gesture with his hand. "I know, I know," he said. "But both of them

at least had, like, a little reason to look up to me —
for who I *was*, I mean. Before, with girls, it's been
as if I didn't . . . well, *you* know, *exist*."

The boy looked up at Sesame, again.

"Maybe this is crazy," he continued, "but what I
keep thinking is that once I've *done* it, and I know
about that kind of thing, then maybe I can just relax,
have a normal life, like other guys. Have *girlfriends*
that I do it with, the way that everybody else does.
Now, I seem like such a total *doofus*, usually. . . ."

Sesame deBarque stood up and did a kind of little
dance, all by herself — dipping, swirling, pirouet-
ting, just around a quarter of the room, singing softly
to herself. When she stopped, she was behind Herb's
chair; she touched him on the shoulder.

"I think I understand the way you feel," she said.
"But let this wise old woman tell you something,
possibly important. The danger of your plan is that
you end up thinking *doing* it is most of what there
is *to* do, with girls. That was the Big Red Chicken's
barnyard boyfriend's problem, of course. I've known
a lot of guys like that, down through the ages; I even
married one or two of them, you want to know the
truth." She sighed, and then she laughed. "Luckily
for me, they died," she said. "Of course."

"Have you had kids, yourself?" asked Herb, looking for a minor change of subject. He wasn't in the
least surprised to hear that Ses had been a widow,
more than once. Somehow, she *looked* as if she'd had
a lot of husbands.

She roared with laughter at his question, who
knows why.

"Hell, yes," she said, "a ton of 'em. And every
one a treasure. I'm the only mother in the history

of the world who's never had to worry. That's the junior member of the clan, right there — destiny's tot, herself." She pointed at a photo on the table, next to her old seat.

Herb had noticed it, before. It was a photo of a girl about his age. She looked a lot like Ses, take away a lot of confidence and much experience, especially around the mouth and eyes. Of course Herb liked her . . . general appearance (as he put it to himself).

"Does she live at Castles, here?" he asked, offhandedly.

"Sometimes," said Ses. "She travels quite a lot. E.T., I call her, sometimes. Her father is, or was, a Spaniard of some sort." She didn't sound as if this was a subject she would welcome further questions on.

Herb nodded. "Oh, I see," he muttered. He didn't know what else to say, at that point.

Ses did, though. She was the type who always would, he thought.

"Well — how ya feeling now, about another spin?" she asked. And winked.

"Oh, I really want to take one," Herbie said. "But maybe not right now, if that's all right. I'd like to more or less digest this one another day or two. But how about on Thursday? Would that be possible? Another spin on Thursday?"

"I don't see why not," said Sesame. "You can come right after school?" He nodded. "Perfect."

When he stood up, she slipped a hand under his arm again, and held it as they strolled toward the door.

"You know," she said to him, "I think I'm going

to send that Sandy Rex a five-pound box of truffles."
She nodded to herself. "That little cutie."

When Herbie got back to his house, on that late
afternoon, he found that preparations for a cookout
were in progress. He knew his father had, as usual,
begun the process with a small wood fire in his rustic
fieldstone grill, and had added charcoal later. The
coals were close to cooking-ready when the boy arrived, and steaks were on a platter, close at hand.
Ben Hertzman liked to say he was a "purist," when
it came to outdoor cooking. He only used old-
fashioned hardwood charcoal, no briquets, and
wouldn't touch those liquid firestarters. "I may eat
a peck of dirt before I die," he'd say, "but no one's
gonna make me wash it down with distillations of
petroleum. You tell me you can't taste the stuff in
food, and I'll tell *you* you need to get your buds
examined."

"Hey!" he called to Herb that day, when he
caught sight of him. "Come say hello to Mr. Gardenside. I promised him a piece of beef so tender,
tasty and delicious that he'll think he's at Four Sea-
sons — or Five Spices, anyway. Ira, this is my son
Herbert. Herbie, tell him what the relatives all say
about my steaks."

"Hello, sir," Herbie said to the legendary Mr.
Ira Gardenside, who was eighty-seven and his father's boss. He knew that this was some occasion.
Mr. Gardenside had never been to Herbie's parents' house before, but he *had* been to the White
House — fourteen times, spread out through nine
administrations.

"Dad's steaks are famous from here to Wissa-

160

hickon," Herbie said. "He's a legend in his own time. Indisputably the best."

"I like that in a man," said Mr. Gardenside, dapper in a double-breasted blazer and white flannels, an ascot at his neck. He was absentmindedly (or not, perhaps) pouring bourbon whiskey in a squatty glass that also had three ice cubes in it. When the glass was almost full, he stopped and said, "Oh-oh," and put the bottle down.

Herb already knew, thanks to his father, that when Mr. Gardenside was *his* age, he'd held down six jobs at once. He was a newsboy and a milkman in the morning, driving his own horse-drawn cart at 5 A.M. In the afternoon, he mowed a bunch of lawns, or raked some leaves, or shoveled walks — *while* exercising different people's dogs. And in the evening he both baby-sat *and* tutored either French or long division. Now, he was president of his own company, a director of eight others and, the year before, had played the lead in *Fiddler on the Roof* and goalie on a local water polo team. There were rumors that he planned to run for Congress; Herbie's father thought that was a neat idea.

"So, young man, I understand you're in your senior year in high school. Good for you," said Mr. Ira Gardenside. He filled his mouth with bourbon and said, "Ahh!"

"Thank you very much, sir," Herbie said.

"You have a game plan, yet?" asked Mr. Gardenside. "I'd say you're at about the most exciting time of life there is. All those possibilities in front of you, for you to pick and choose from. Real estate, investment banking, mergers, acquisitions, energy — there's untold fortunes still, just waiting to be

161

made." He did a little further whistle-wetting.

"Yes," said Herb. "It's an exciting time, all right."

"So — what direction is your thinking running in?" asked Mr. Gardenside. "What plans and schemes, what dreams, are yours, young man? Oh, how I'd love to be in *your* shoes, at this point in history." Pause. Ingestion of libation. "Ahh!"

"Well," said Herb, feeling for the first time in his life that he had something he could say, in answer to that question, "I'm toying with the possibility of public service."

"Public service?" The old man's eyes were clear; his speech, however, might have been a little slurred. "That wouldn't be too bad, I guess. But let me make a small suggestion to you, something that you maybe wouldn't think of, otherwise. You want to know what I would go for, supposin' I was in your shoes, right now? The best idea that I could give you, free of charge? C'mere."

He pulled Herb two-three steps aways from where Ben Hertzman stood, long fork in hand. The boy looked back and saw his father beaming; they'd watched a movie called *The Graduate* together.

"I'm only going to say this once," whispered Mr. Gardenside, a merry twinkle in his eyes, now. He licked his lips and Herb could see that he was concentrating very hard, making sure he got what he was going to say exactly right. Then, with a rush of bourbon breath, he whispered once again, and quite distinctly: "*Mixed nude synchronized swimming.*"

After which, he suddenly sat down — ker-plunk! — the victim of a *massive* heart attack, from which he died, in seconds. Bummer.

When the hubbub occasioned by the phone calls

162

and the ambulance and having to take the steaks off and then, later, adding a lot more charcoal before putting them back on again had subsided, his father asked the boy what Mr. Gardenside's last words had been.

Herbie looked at him, all blue-eyed innocence.

"He said that I should follow, like, my *bliss*," he said.

"Whatever *that* may mean," his father said, sounding, Herbie thought, quite disappointed.

22
THURSDAY

The Thursday Herbie headed back to Castles in the Air had started pretty well, as Thursdays go. The shock of Mr. Gardenside's "untimely coronary accident" (as Herbie's mother chose to call it) had worn off by then, and all three Hertzmans had resumed their (so-called) normal lives.

Herb's father'd moved into a different office with a much, much better view, and original artwork on the walls instead of photographs of factories and beavers. His mother'd finally bought the breakfast food that had, in laboratory tests, improved the hang-time of a group of adolescent male orangutans. And Herb himself had stopped blaming himself for *not* blaming himself for being in some way responsible for "I.G." 's death.

In school that day, Herb had handled seven tricky academic fungoes flawlessly, and helped a girl whose name he didn't know retrieve a Nerf ball from atop a row of lockers.

"Wow, you're really *tall*," she'd said to him, and smiled in such a way he had to wonder if she meant much more than that.

Later on, when he had barely started on the walk to Castles, he'd come upon two grade-school kids about the age of nine or ten, both busy writing on the sidewalk with some sticks of orange chalk. Just as Herbie reached them, they finished writing this:

Pee on Omalley

"Hey! Be nice, you guys!" he said to them. Much to his surprise, they dropped their writing tools and ran.

Herb picked up the orange chalk and looked again at what they'd written. With the help of crossings-out and carets, he made their message read:

Pee in the O'Malley

and continued on his way.

At the four-way stop where Sunset Strip and Ginseng Lane collide and cross each other, though, Herb found some items he was sure had not been there before. First of all, there was a large white Cadillac, sitting on a patch of public lawn. And leaning up against its shiny side was an instruction: TAKE A CHANCE — $5! Next to *that* there was a round white metal table with a striped umbrella, open, sticking out of it. Behind the table sat a red-faced man. He wore a wide-brimmed planter's hat, a red bandanna knotted 'round his neck, dark trousers and a light gray frock coat.

"How you doin', sonny?" he asked Herb. And, "Isn't she a beauty, now?"

"I suppose," said Herb. He laid an honest stare right on the car. "Though frankly, for myself, I'd rather have a compact. They're a lot more fuel-efficient, plus I think I'd look a little foolish dressed like *this*" — he gestured at his jeans and western shirt and leather vest — "driving in a car like *that*."

"Please-please-please-*please*," the red-faced man replied, holding up a palm. "Let's not be dull, all right? You win the car, you *sell* the car. You take the money and you get yourself a decent suit of clothes, and any sort of *compact* car you want, some fancy luggage and a pinky ring. Of course if you feel foolish *then*, riding in your little Yugo or whatever, don't blame me." He laughed, but not unpleasantly.

"So, take a chance, why don't you, sport?" he said. "I've only got one left. Later on today, we'll have the drawing and — hey, hey! — *you* could be a *winnah*!" The man appeared delighted by that prospect.

Herb didn't really mind it, either, but he still was cautious.

"How many chances are there?" he inquired. "Five bucks would darn near clean my wallet out, right now. So, what's the odds against my winning?"

The red-faced man said, "Well, uh, not *too* bad at all. I mean, really pretty good, in fact, as these things go. Or maybe even better." His face had gotten slightly redder.

"I believe," said Herbie quietly, "you *have to* say. I'm pretty sure that there's a law about that. It was put in to protect the consumer from his own irrational hopefulness — or that's my understanding, anyway."

"All right, all right, I'll tell you," said the red-faced man. "If you buy this last remaining chance, you only have one chance in three of winning. I've sold two other chances to four other parties — one to me, myself, and I. So, chances are you *wouldn't* win. The *odds* are that you wouldn't. *Probably* the other buyer or myself will win."

"What?" said Herb. "You're telling me you're going to raffle off this twenty-thirty-thousand dollar car by selling just *three* tickets? You're going to risk that car for fifteen dollars?"

"Hell, why shouldn't I?" the man replied. "Possibly I'll win the raffle, which'll mean I get to keep the car *and* all the money that I got from you (if you decide to play), and from my other customer. And even if I don't, I've got no great affection for this car. I've never had the time to learn to drive, and once you've sat down in the back of one block-long white Cadallic, you've pretty much sat down in all of 'em."

"You mean, you actually don't *want* this car?" said Herb. "Then why not sell it, like you said?" He gave a little chuckle. "You could get yourself some jeans, a nice new pair of running shoes, and possibly a business of your own — a little candy store, or something."

"*Please.*" The red-faced man held up his hand again. "I used to own a candy store. And then eight *hundred* candy stores, in fact. I made a fortune selling candy. Then I made another more enormous fortune selling candy *stores*. Now I'm into something new: acting like a damned old fool — or so my children say. Tomorrow I may give someone a year's supply of Christmas trees, or build some natives-only, low-cost housing in Vermont, or Northern California, so that local people can afford to go on living there." He shook his head. "Now, please, go on and take a chance. Think how good I'll feel if I can put a total-stranger kid behind the wheel of his first car."

"Well, if you're going to put it *that* way," Herbie said. "And anyway, Mother's Day is — what? — next month? I'll bet my mom would be surprised to get a Cadillac instead of candy."

He gave the red-faced man five singles.

"The drawing ought to be in maybe half an hour," said the man. "Just tell me where you'll be, and if you win, you'll find this baby parked out front, with all the necessary papers in the glove compartment."

Herb explained that he'd be at Castles in the Air for probably at least an hour, but he also gave the man his home address, in case of any foul-ups. In turn, the red-faced man made Herbie take his card, on which he'd written: "Rec'd, from Herbert Hertzman, Esq., 5 simoleons for 1 great chance in the Big Caddy raffle."

His name was printed on the card, but he also signed the thing, quite clearly, with a flourish: *Francis Farmer.*

* * *

168

When Herb arrived at Castles in the Air, Sesame deBarque was out on the front lawn again, but sitting on a folding stool, this time, before an easel, with a palette in her hand. From the way that she was facing, Herb assumed that she was painting Castles's portrait, and that proved to be the case.

"Boy, that's really *great*," he said, when he was close enough to see what she had done. "I didn't know you were an artist!"

In fact, the picture that she'd made looked mighty like a masterpiece, to him. Not only had she gotten all the shapes and colors right, but also she had managed to reflect the *spirit* of the place, its enigmatic joyfulness (as Herbie thought of it). Clearly, she was almost finished with the painting. There was only one small section left to do, just where the driveway curves up to the drawbridge, right outside the big front door.

"Yes," she said. "It came out pretty well." She cocked her head and looked at what she'd done some more, and smiled. She had a black beret on, worn at quite a jaunty angle, and a yellow smock that didn't have a single dab of paint on it.

"Maybe it's beginner's luck," she added. "Thing is, I saw this hat and smock right in the window of an art store, and I had to have 'em. Don't I look great? I got this other junk to go along with them." She gestured at the easel and her paint box and the palette. "And I thought, well, what the heck." She'd gotten up, by then. "But, anyway, let's go," she said. "I got some peanut brittle on the same excursion, and I'm looking forward to your spin."

"Hey, wait," said Herb. "Why don't you go ahead

and finish, first? I'm not in all that big a hurry."

"No, no," she said. "I've got some time right now. Fact is, that I *can't* finish, yet. I want to get the car in there, and it hasn't been delivered."

"Car?" said Herb, suspiciously. "What car?"

"It's a humongous, big, white Cadillac," she said. "You saw it coming over, right? The raffle car?"

"Sure I saw it," Herbie said. "*I* bought the other chance. But you're already sure you won?"

"Not *sure*," said Ses deBarque. "Especially not now. But, yeah, I had a feeling, like you get, sometimes. What I figured was, that Upwardlimobile of mine has got an awful lot of spatiotemporal miles on it. I thought I'd kind of like to let it end its days as just a normal car, going on real roads, getting into gridlock, taking trips to concerts, rubbing fenders with some other vans. Then, I could modify the Caddy, turn it into 'mobile II." She shrugged. "But now, with you a player — well, I just don't know. Maybe I won't win it, after all. Maybe you will — or the geezer. I guess we'll have to wait and see."

"Well, I don't really *want* it," Herbie quickly said. "I'd love it if the Upwardlimobile could just take it easy and enjoy itself. So, maybe if *I* win the Cadillac, I'll give the thing to *you*!" That thought made Herb excited. "You've been so great to me, and anyway, my mom's already got this real nice Pontiac."

"All right, all *right* already." Ses laughed and dropped a hand down on his shoulder. "Leave us not forget what we are here for, right? I've got a wheel in there that needs a spin, real bad. That's more important than some silly status symbol, right?"

They crossed the drawbridge and went into the

castle. The peanut brittle, in a bowl, was right there in the hall; they both had some, Herb quite a handful. He also looked around. He listened, hoping that he'd hear some rock and roll, or something.

But there weren't any sorts of sounds.

"Um," he said, and "Well." He shrugged. "Just wondering. Your daughter home from school? I was thinking . . . I've been taking up a lot of time — *your* time — when she might want to talk to you, or something. So, I was thinking, maybe if I just said 'Hi,' and told her that I didn't mea — "

"Oh," Ses cut him off, "*she* doesn't mind. You kidding? She likes it when there's something different going on, a little action. Like your trips and all. She eats all that stuff up."

"So — I shouldn't try to talk to her?" said Herb, pausing by the door to the great hall. If this daughter was enjoying hearing all about his trips, his "action," he wasn't sure that meeting her would be a good idea at all. Probably, she'd bust out laughing at the sight of him.

"Maybe not right now," said Ses, but not as if the whole idea was hopeless.

They reached the wheel, the Winner's Circle. Herbie put his hand on it, and looked at all the different categories. It struck him that they *all* were *interesting* — even Crime — Organized or not, which he had learned he didn't want to do. He had a thought (a flash, an inkling) that he could work in any one of those careers, *or any other one.* And that what he was *really* trying to find was which jobs would be *fun* for him, the only Herbie Hertzman in the universe, a guy that he was still discovering, and possibly (new thought!) *creating.*

Herb gave that wheel a healthy spin.

It came up Health Care. Fascinating.

Ses deBarque agreed, apparently. "Now there's *another* doozie," she opined. She started pushing buttons on her console.

Herb wondered if this meant he'd be involved, somehow, with AIDS, which he had heard described as Public Health Care Problem Number One. Getting AIDS would be about the biggest bummer he could think of. But so would *having* AIDS, he thought. People who had AIDS were people like himself, he thought, but more unlucky. That was the only way to think about it. It really was that simple.

"Hmm," said Sesame, looking at the little card that the machine provided her. "This should be a *very* interesting turn."

Herb felt he shouldn't ask for information at this point — for any sort of preview. What was going to happen, would; better just to let events unfold. Health, both good and bad, was everywhere (like Crime, he guessed). He might go anywhere and have to do with anyone, even Tyree Toledano, if there truly was a person by that name. So be it. They started walking toward the tower, he and Ses.

"There's something that I want to ask you," Herbie said. "Not about this spin. It's more of a general question."

"So, ask away," said Ses. "Liberty Hall, and all that rot."

"Well, I've been wondering," said Herb. "How many trips do clients take? Like, on the average."

"I really couldn't say," she said. "I don't pay attention to that kind of stuff. You know what I mean:

172

like scores, and medians, and averages. That's all a lot of bush-wa. Everybody's different, thank the Lord, so why compare so much? And everybody's got a magic number: One. That's the one they get it on. You see?"

"Um," said Herb. He laughed. Get it? Get *what*? He thought he *maybe* got it, but he wasn't sure.

He climbed into the pleasantly familiar van. It had a certain fragrance he would miss, when he stopped taking trips (he thought). When he was sure he'd gotten it.

23
"SHALIMAR SLOAN,"
SHE SAID . . .

When the Upwardlimobile had settled to a stop, Herb stretched and yawned and looked expectantly across the van, waiting for the door to open, or *be* opened, either one. It didn't and it wasn't; time dragged by. He sat and fidgeted for at least a half an hour. It was like when he was eight, and waiting for his mother to get off the phone and take him to the pool, or — who knows! — *Disneyland*, or *Europe*. At last he couldn't sit there any longer. There were discoveries just waiting to be made, he thought, falling trees that needed him to hear them, unseen blossoms that might never bloom without him.

He raised himself up off the seat and, crouching, took the steps that brought him to the sliding door. Then, after a last small hesitation, he reached out and opened it.

Of course it was a different setting, not the tundra

174

or a parking lot. They, the 'bile and he (he'd right away jumped out of it), were in a pleasant, yet exotic, courtyard, parked on one side of a flagstone walk that went around the space. Neatly tended flower beds were in the center of the court, bordering a statue; they also ran along outside the walk, between it and the building that surrounded everything. On one end of the courtyard was an arch that seemed to open on a street; at the other end, a big, red, wooden door gave access to the building. Straight overhead, the sky was very blue.

From an open window on the second floor there came a rhythmic drumbeat and the sound of something being chanted, not in English or in Spanish, not for fun. And, from time to time, as if to serve as punctuation, or to keep the chanters mellow, there was a gong sound.

Shuffling along the walk in front of him were half a dozen very senior individuals, all men. They all were dressed alike, in dark red robes and sandals, and they muttered to themselves — a little whiningly, Herb thought — while moving in the same direction, clockwise. Herb was pretty sure that these were monks, or priests, or devotees, who had their minds on higher things. None of them had any hair to speak of, and their concentrated calm suggested to the boy that stuff like sex was not a big concern of theirs. They were living in a zone that Herb was not familiar with, in terms of personal experience.

From time to time, one of the old men would stop and face the statue in the middle of the court, and bow, and whine a little louder. The statue kept on sitting; it was of a man — clean-shaven, empty-eyed and poker-faced, bare-chested. It could have been

175

Lee Iacocca, younger, without glasses, add a funny hat, but Herb was pretty sure it wasn't. Given the religious atmosphere, the chances are the statue was a Buddha. It paid the same attention to the boy as everybody else did.

Adaptable as ever and anxious to fit in — and also to leave the courtyard — Herb stepped out into a gap between two monks. Under his breath and just a bit complainingly, he spoke the first twelve words of Bellow's novel, *Herzog* ("If I am out of my mind, it's all right with me . . ."), while he shuffled at the speed of traffic till he reached the open arch that led out to the street. Then, with a small, respectful nod, he exited the courtyard. He was in the open, on the street.

Herb looked around, but *all* around, not totally surprised, considering the sorts of things he'd seen and heard inside, but totally agape, impressed. He was standing in a town, or possibly a tiny city, built on a small, treeless knoll on a large treeless plain, surrounded by the highest mountains he (or *anyone*, he'd bet) had ever seen.

"Chomolungma, Kangchenjunga, Nanda Devi." Herbie rummaged through the mental knapsack where he kept his Himalayan word supply. *When in Rome . . .* and all that jazz. He felt like President Kennedy at the Berlin Wall. "Levi Strauss," he added, knowing those two words were understood, and spoken, everywhere.

He decided that the street he was on was Market Street. On either side of it were shops and stalls; some vendors had their goods laid out on blankets on the ground. Herb checked his pockets, found a dollar thirty-five, American; he figured that made him a browser, only. And so, hands clasped behind his back, he started strolling down the middle of the street, hoping that his face reflected any three of these: ease, good humor, admiration, only modest means, a total lack of chauvinism. All in one neat package called "experienced adventurer."

At once he saw he was a great deal taller than the local people all around him, but that didn't seem to matter much, to anyone. No one gawked at him, or tried to sell him goods or services, or relatives. A lot of men and women, both, wore running shoes, not always in their size, or in real great condition; by and large, they smiled and laughed a lot, particularly the ones who hung around the stalls where cups of something could be bought and drunk. Herb smiled at everything they had for sale, and said "Real nice!" a lot of times. He looked at bolts of different-colored cloth, woolen socks and woven belts, straw placemats and badminton sets, felt shoulder bags and wooden bowls and backscratchers, beads of many different sizes, and some silver jewelry that certainly included nose rings, going by the noses of some women that he saw.

When he'd gone the length of Market Street, he turned onto another, wider thoroughfare. Here, clearly, were the local tourist traps, the shops and businesses that catered to whatever foreigners might be in town for any arcane purposes. Many of the buildings here had signs on them in English, such as Bank and Barber, but the grandest of them was The Great Couloir Hotel, which Herbie thought was almost equal to the monastery, size-wise. Next to it was the Because It's There Cafe and Restaurant, while right across the street there was a clothing store (Darjeeling Traders) and an Abida's Fitness Center — Running Shoes and Croissants Fresh Hot Daily Ice Cream.

Herb headed for Abida's, fingering his change, like worry beads.

Three local youngsters, boys who looked to be no more than ten, were right outside it, eating gooey-covered ice cream out of paper cups with plastic spoons. As Herb approached, he noticed they were staring at his Reeboks in the way — adoringly — that kids back home would stare at, say, their parents' credit cards.

"Man, you American?" squeaked one of them.

"Sure am," said Herb. Then, diplomatically, "You speak great English."

"Be cool," the second boy chimed in. "Peace, love, good vibes, nonviolent change."

"Oh, wow," said Herb, adaptably.

"You know our teacher?" said the third boy. "Mister Dhubi-dhubi-dhu?"

"We all good deadheads, man," said number one.

"That's great," said Herb, who'd never figured out what deadheads *did*. Once again, he touched the money in his pocket. He wondered if he possibly might change the subject.

"So, here's a question for you," he continued. "How much might a sundae be up here — in dollars *or* piasters?"

The three boys looked at one another. They conferred among themselves, speaking very fast and mostly not in English. Herb was pretty sure he caught a "sundae" jammed in there, along with "might," and (he was pretty sure) "piaster." Finally, they all nodded; general agreement had been reached.

"Nixon fulla blooey," the third boy said to him, and smiled delightedly.

Herb nodded vaguely, muttered, "Thanks." He could go along with that, all right, but thought he'd be a little cautious when it came to speaking out on politics. After all, he didn't even know the *name* — not to mention the alignment — of the country he was in. Clutching his small bunch of money, still, he started toward Abida's door.

Before he reached it, it flew open. Someone came rushing out, but stopped in front of him, as if he were a traffic light. It took him just a moment to be sure; she was a girl. She was wearing an eclectic outfit if he'd ever seen one, and she held a large vanilla cone.

Her lower half was purely western, starting from New Balance running shoes and working up to baggy painters' pants. Above the waist, most of her was covered by a sort of tablecloth she'd draped around her head and shoulders and which hung down to that waist, where it got belted. This was a shorter version of the robe that all the local men and women wore, except that theirs just started at their shoulders. Perhaps to hold this shawl of hers around her head, the girl had on a well-worn cowboy hat, jammed over it, and her eyes hid out behind a pair of glacier glasses, real dark gray ones.

For all of that, she looked, to Herb, in some small, unspecific way, familiar. Apparently that went both ways.

"Herbie Hertzman," was the way she greeted him.

"Yes," he said, not totally surprised.

"Shalimar Sloan," she said, and changed the cone from one hand to the other. Then she wiped the empty one on her right thigh and offered it to him. They shook.

"I'm pleased to meet you," Herbie said. Her name set zero bells a-ringing.

"We've still got quite a trip ahead of us," she said. "Our final destination's way up there." She pointed toward the set of mountains to the right. "And time is of the essence, as they say. We'd better get ourselves in gear and hit the yak-track."

Herb was looking where she'd pointed. He couldn't tell, of course, just where on "way up there" she meant. It looked as if they'd have to first go down a ways, and then back up, and then repeat that sort of thing again, another time or two. In other words, they faced not just a "walk," or even, as she'd said, a "trip"; it seemed to him that she was talking "major expedition."

"Why?" he said. "Why *are* we going way up there? And what's the rush?"

She pressed her pointer finger to her temple, wiggled that same thumb a time or two. "Idiot," she told him, speaking of and to herself, he was quite certain. "How *could* he know?" And then to him, "I'm sorry."

She touched him on the forearm. It was a little, gentle, pacifying touch that more than did the job. Herb smiled and nodded: Hey, okay. She took a couple real quick hits on her vanilla cone. He thought that she had one terrific-looking tongue. A woman's eyes might be the windows of her soul,

Herb thought, but her tongue was like the maitre d' of her entire restaurant.

"We're going there to meet a man," she said. "A teacher and a scientist of sorts — some say a saint, but that's debatable. He's weird, all right. He runs an ashram way up there that has a modern lab in it, and if our information's right, he's made a major scientific breakthrough. Something on the order of a cancer cure, or possibly an AIDS vaccine; we're not exactly sure, except we know it's big and that we want it."

She tilted her head to one side and took a big, long slurp around the top rim of the cone, to keep the thing from dripping.

" 'We'?" said Herb. "You don't mean you and I."

"Well, yes," she said. "I *hope* you want it, too. You're into Health Care, right?" He nodded. "But lots of other people, too. We're acting on behalf of . . . well, of certain agencies that'd like to see this stuff — whatever it may be — become available to everybody everywhere who needs it. Without regard to who or where or what they can afford."

"That sounds terrific," Herbie said. It seemed to him that maybe Ses had punched him in a winner, this time. "And you want to hurry up and get this stuff, so's the people that we're acting for can start alleviating untold amounts of human misery as soon as possible!"

"Well, that, too," she said. "But there's a second reason we should ditch the dawdles — two of them in fact. We're pretty sure there are a pair of other expeditions, either in the area or soon to be. One of them is Japanese, the other is American. Both of

181

them are representing huge consortiums, major corporations who would hope to share enormous profits from this product. If our information's right, they're both prepared to lay at least a billion on the table — cash, small bills, no plastic." She licked across the summit of the cone, from one side to the other.

"While we," said Herb, "will offer . . ."

"Nothing," said the girl. "Or nothing in the way of that which men call cold and hard. Our appeal will be to Baba's . . . reputation. To his better side — his saintliness, his spirit of fair play, his love of all mankind." She grinned. "Although we may remind him of Pearl Harbor and the IRS."

Herb wrinkled up his brow, not wholly sure that he was following.

The girl bit off a chunk of ice cream, and then sucked on it a bit, before she swallowed. Then she took a last, long lick across the slightly flattened top of it and held the cone toward Herb.

"You want the rest of this?" she said to him.

Herb felt his heart race in his chest. He knew that that was silly — kids often share an ice-cream cone with other kids — but there you are.

"Sure," he said. And, "Thanks a lot." He took the cone from her, and right away he ran his tongue from one side to the other of it; then he gave the thing a quarter-turn and took a second lick covering, that way, the whole entire surface of the ice cream. It was, to him, a little ceremonial that made the two of them (don't laugh) . . . saliva brothers.

She nodded, either noticing or not. If he only could have seen her eyes, he might have known.

"Baba Malomar is an American," she said. "His real name's Sidney Drexel Arthur. Like most Americans, he's very dual about the Japanese. Much as he admires them, and *loves* his four-wheel-drive Toyota truck and his whatever stereo — including CD player, probably — and VCR, he also fears them. Not the *stuff*, you understand, the people, some of them. He doesn't really *trust* them; they're, like, too much of a threat. Not to bomb another naval base, perhaps, but possibly to buy . . . Montana. And the IRS is why he came here in the first place. *He* called it a small, correctable misunderstanding. *They* were thinking more in terms of ten-to-twenty and a million dollar fine. Negotiations still continue, I believe."

"Yes," said Herb. "I see. And you are also hoping we can get there first and make the opposition more or less . . . superfluous."

"Exactly," said the girl. He wondered if he should bring up the van. In a moment he decided not to. If he'd been *meant* to get to this guy Malomar's in the Upwardlimobile, he'd have gone direct, he figured. And, too, he'd no idea how they could start the thing, or steer it. Plus, if this girl had been expecting him — as she so clearly had — she also knew both Ses deBarque and how her clients traveled. So, it had to be that he was meant to just shut up and take this monster trek with her — the two of them alone for countless miles and days, he reckoned — and go through whatever *that* entailed.

Herb began to nibble bits of cone and ice cream, going 'round and 'round. Let it be, he thought.

24
YAK TRACK

The first part of the trip to Baba Malomar's turned out to be a mingling of pain and pleasure such as Herb could not remember having known before, at least not since his birth, about which there is still uncertainty.

To begin with, Shalimar Sloan had made all of the arrangements, using what for money he had no idea. It must have added up to quite a bundle. She'd bought them packs and freeze-dried food and one-man tents, as well as extra clothes and boots and sundries, all at the *Giant Warehouse Sale* going on behind Abida's Fitness Center — Running Shoes and Croissants Fresh Hot Daily Ice Cream at Abida's Super-Discount Barn — Prescriptions Travel Agency. At that same location, she had also gotten places for the two of them in a trading caravan led by someone by the name of Pookie Woodchuck, going by the way Herb heard it, anyway.

"This is definitely a break for us," she told the boy as they confirmed their reservations just before the caravan pushed off. "I've asked around, and everybody says that Pookie is the best — for speed and safety, both. He isn't into booze or drugs, and he even doesn't mind Americans; he says that they're a lot like yaks: you're going to get some good ones and some bad ones. So, if it's true that we're ahead of those two other groups right now — as I believe we are — there oughta be no catching us. The air-strip here's the closest one to Baba's by three hundred miles, and Pookie's yaks move right along on trails and — um — *terrain* no other vehicle would last an hour on."

She'd said that he could call her "Shali," if he wanted to. She'd also said she hoped he didn't have flat feet or hate to walk on "sort of — well — uneven ground."

They left just after dawn: fifteen loaded yaks, two assistant trainers, the indomitable Pookie Wood-chuck, and the "honored guests," Shali and himself. As such, they had the right, or privilege, to walk beside a yak and hang onto its coat, a horn, or even — in an emergency — its tail, for balance on the sort of — well — uneven rocky stretches, which were almost all of them. The yaks seemed not to notice much of anything. They could have passed for '60s oxen, being long-haired types whose mien suggested they had done a lot of downs that day, and possibly for days before. They just went along, bearing Herb's and Shali's luggage in addition to their loads of woven belts and nose rings and the

185

other sorts of goods that the owner of Abida's Import-Export — Spices Concrete Intimate Necessities believed that people in the valley would go crazy for.

Before their trek began, Herb would have said he was in "not that bad" condition, physically — meaning that he wasn't overweight, could run upstairs at home without distress, and that if looked at naked, in a certain kind of light, he had some muscle definition, here and there. But after about a third of the first day of this expedition, "pathetic" was the only word that came into his mind about himself as, say, a specimen of manhood (*genus* Young American). While everybody else trudged manfully and girlfully and yakfully along, their faces showing minimal discomfort (to his eyes), it seemed to him he panted like a St. Bernard in the Bahamas, conscious every step of both the altitude and of the message that his legs and feet were sending him: "Why us?"

But still, if djinn or fairy godmother, the chairman of the State Lottery Commission, or Mrs. Quigley (who, if you recall, once read the stars for our First Lady) had come to him and told him that he really didn't have to do this anymore, that all good things would happen in his life in any case, he still would certainly have kept on going. Indeed, Shalimar Sloan *did* say something of that sort to him, in camp, the first night out, minus guarantees, of course. Clearly she'd observed his sufferings.

"Look," she said, in that direct, unornamented way she generally expressed herself, "why don't you do yourself a favor and head back to town, tomorrow. Get a nice room at The Great Couloir and just hang out till I get back. It's not your fault you're not acclimatized, or used to the terrain. And it isn't as if you have some particular *skill* we'll need to help us get ahold of what it is that Baba has, up there."

"Tell me about it," Herbie said, more in deep regret than bitterness. Bitterness was not his kind of thing — not bitterness, self-pity or anchovies on a pizza.

"Well, you're not a trained negotiator," Shali said, willing, it appeared, to do so. "I don't believe that you're a hypnotist, either, and you're not like Albert Schweitzer or Mother Teresa — someone he'd be, well, *embarrassed* to turn down. In fact, those last few miles you looked like someone in an extra-strength Excedrin ad, or ready for the fifteen-day disabled list."

Herb stared at her. This clearly wasn't any ordinary girl, the kind that he'd grown used to, back in high school. He hadn't thought she'd answer his rhetorical request at all, but she had done so, not just calmly, but in a tone of voice that didn't seem at all insulting. It had been the tone of voice you'd use to tell a friend the ball scores, or a recipe.

"You're right, of course," said Herbie, mildly. "But in a way, that's why I'm going. Or why I'm not *not* going, anyway."

That seemed to puzzle her. When they'd made camp, she'd taken off her shawl and shades for the first time, and he'd found out she had blue eyes, about the same electric blue as his, and light brown hair with just a glow of reddish light in it. She still kept on her cowboy hat, but tilted back, and Herbie thought that she was gorgeous — her entire, open, friendly face, not just her tongue. But, looking in

187

her eyes, he saw that she was puzzled, too. He'd seen that same look in his own blue irises enough, while looking in a mirror.

"Why you're not *not* going," she repeated, slowly. Then, with a little head shake, she appeared to change the subject. "Can't you finish this? There's just about two bites, is all."

She was offering him the pot that they'd been eating out of; Herbie took it. Their dinner had been freeze-dried Tuna Something, to which she'd added curry powder, and then had heated on their little Coleman stove. And though they had a lot of plastic plates and extra spoons, she hadn't gotten any of them out. Instead, they'd simply eaten from the pot, taking alternating mouthfuls, using just the one big spoon. Herb had been reminded of the way they'd shared her ice cream cone, except that this was even better.

So, now he scraped the pot and ate the last two mouthfuls, saying "Yum." The dinner *had* been good, and using the one spoon had been an *extra* reason he'd decided he was going to make this trip, and not turn back, regardless. He'd come to that decision earlier, while walking right beside — and talking to — a yak, that afternoon. Now he said the same things to the girl, repeated them.

"If I quit now, and wait for work I'm good at, or that isn't hard for me," he'd told the shaggy beast, "I might have quite a wait."

The yak had just accepted that, in stoic silence; it *was* doing something it was good at, fair to say. The girl, however, nodded her agreement, and affirmed it.

188

"Sure, that's absolutely true," she said. "Except for a few odd prodigies, no kid is good at *anything* that matters much in life. Getting A's in subjects, or being all-state soccer, doesn't guarantee you squat."

"Also, I don't think that having to be great at everything you do is quite the *point*," he said.

"Um," she answered, neutrally. From the yak he'd gotten some digestive sounds.

"Everything I do with any point to it will probably be hard for me," he said. "But that's okay. I think that's the way it is for everyone."

"Almost everyone," she said. The yak had audibly chewed cud, or maybe something from between its teeth.

"I guess I also think that if I didn't go, this time, I maybe never would," he said. "Go anywhere, for any halfway decent reason."

The yak, for reasons of its own, had chosen just that moment to relieve itself. The girl was much more positive.

"You know," she said, "it sounds as if you've really thought this out. I never did. I just *do* whatever it might be." She shrugged, perhaps apologetically. "And it works out, somehow."

"You're one of those," said Herb. "One of those fine feathered few."

"A-yup," she said, and grinned.

He couldn't get too mad at her. Her kind of honesty was so completely uncontaminated. She just said whatever she thought and let it lay there, didn't try to stand on it, so she'd seem taller.

"Well, let me ask you this," he said. "Is what we're

189

doing now" — he made a rolling gesture with one hand, signifying *everything* — "like, just a *cinch*, for you?"

"Hell, no," she said. "Of course it's not. I'm going to be a tortured mass of aches and pains tomorrow morning, same as you. It's just that I think about it differently, the whole *idea* of hardness."

"I get it," Herbie smiled. "You're a . . . whatchacallit? — *masochist*."

"Uh-*unh*," she said. "It isn't that." She stood up and stretched. "Hardness is to things I want to do as eggshells are to eggs. I don't even *think* about the shells when I eat eggs. They're just a part of something that I love, so I don't sweat 'em." And she grinned again and turned to rummage in her pack, came up with toilet articles in hand.

"But now I've gotta get some sleep," she said. "Those yaks, they look like early risers. I'll go a little ways upstream to do my teeth and stuff."

Pookie, his assistants and the yaks had bivouacked downstream from them, their choice. Herb hadn't heard them talking for a while, and he supposed they were asleep, already. He watched his fellow honored guest until she disappeared around some boulders. She wasn't headed for a scented bathroom in a nice warm house, but for some other rocks, "a little ways upstream." Apparently she just was "doing it," as usual.

Later on, when they were both in their respective sleeping bags in their respective tents, their heads perhaps ten feet apart, he heard her whisper, "Herbie?"

"Yes?" he whispered, too.

190

"I would have hated it, if you'd gone back," she said.

"Me, too," he said. "I'm really happy to be going on. With you." The last two words were said a lot more softly, less distinctly, muffled by the pounding in his chest. There was silence for about a minute.

"I'm not as brave and philosophical as how I sounded." She spoke very softly, too. "I should be, but I'm not. But even if I was, I'd still want you to take this trip." A minor pause. "With me." And then, "Good night."

"Good night," said Herb. He tried to tell himself he shouldn't make too much of it, this conversation.

Before he fell asleep, he tried to classify what he was feeling, when it came to Shali. So, what things were there that he *didn't* like, about her looks or personality? As a rule, that was an easy one for him to answer. Most real girls were much too *this*, or really short on *that*. But, that night, the question didn't seem to hold his interest.

25
GETTING BALMED

Herb woke up hearing noises from downstream. Pookie and his men were clattering around, and talking to each other in their mother tongue. Herbie, only half awake, a little bit disoriented, semi-panicked. He thought they sounded like three guys who'd had their showers and their second cups of coffee, and were just about to leave the house. At any moment, he might hear a yak start up, he thought. So hurriedly and thoughtlessly, he reached around his shoulder for the zipper on his sleeping bag.

"UMfff," was more or less the sound he made, his quickly muffled groan. It seemed as if the muscles in his back had been replaced by Sheetrock, over-night — Sheetrock with a lot of *wires* in it, through which currents bearing *pain* could pass — and did, and did, and did.

Slowly, slowly, Herb began to semi-crawl and semi-wriggle — to creep out of his envelope of down.

"Ta-ra-ra-boom-de-yay," said quite a cheerful voice from real close by. "This should be *quite* a day. For those of us who seek enlightenment through suffering, that is." She laughed, perhaps not all *that* heartily.

Shalimar was sitting on the ground, fully dressed as usual, her left leg stretched straight out in front of her, her right leg bent and pulled around to one side, sort of in a hurdling position. As he watched, she slowly reached way forward with both hands, until she touched her pointed toe. Then she bent her hat brim to her knee.

"Egad," said Herbie. "How did you do that?"

"Easy," Shali said. "First, I took a sauna at my health club, followed by a deep massage. Then I kept on trying for about ten minutes. It took me all of five to get my clothes on, bubba."

Her saying "clothes" reminded Herb that he was much too close to naked to be comfortable — with her. He'd gone to bed in just his underpants, an older pair of boxer shorts; at the moment they had left him pretty well exposed, all things considered. He quickly grabbed at what he'd taken off the night before and, making sudden jerky movements (nicely synchronized with sounds like OOh-ah-ooh), he managed to put on his sweatshirt, jeans and running shoes, and socks. Then he limped a little ways upstream for just a minute.

"Perhaps you'd like to try some stretches?" Shali said when he came back. "I know a bunch of different ones. Here, for instance, is my favorite. . . ."

193

She showed him one after another. In between each demonstration (followed by Herb's repetition), they put together and prepared a pan of scrambled powdered eggs, which they then ate with local bread, chapatis and big mugs of sweetened tea.

Although nobody said to anybody else how glad she was to be with him while packing up, the two of them worked well together. Or so it seemed to Herbie, anyway.

The first mile out there on the track passed painfully, but uneventfully. Herb would have said it was a mile, in any case — say, twenty minutes worth of walking. But then he heard some bursts of laughter, *foreign-sounding* laughter, coming from behind him. Naturally he had to look around and check it out.

Mistake.

What he saw was one of Pookie Woodchuck's helpers, Pema, doing an exaggerated — *much* exaggerated — imitation of the way *he*, Herbie, walked. This little limp that he'd been using.

It never had occurred to him he might look *funny*. Actually, he'd sort of hoped the thing would be *respected*, as a flare-up of an old, old football injury, or conceivably a war wound. He tried to walk more normally.

Pookie Woodchuck, though, had caught him looking.

" 'Avin' us a spot of pain this mornin', guv?" he called out in a cheerful tone of voice. So far as Herb could tell, he was the only English-speaking yaksman. He surely was the only one with real long hair and granny glasses, who spoke English like a native of, say, Liverpool.

194

" 'Fraid so," said Herb, good-sportingly, adding on a rueful head shake. "A touch of Osgood-Schlatter's. It kicks up from time to time," he added, pulling out the name of a disease some neighbor's kid had said he had, when he was in his early teens. Herb thought it sounded serious.

"But I won't slow us down," he said. "Don't worry; I'll keep up. I *promise* you."

He smiled and shifted gears into a faster hobble. He'd just remembered different tribes had different ways of dealing with the aged, or infirm, or wounded — the ones who couldn't keep up with the rest. Who knew what customs Pookie and his gang observed? He wouldn't want to find himself dropped into some crevasse with, say, a can of deviled ham, a book of poems by Robert Browning and a yo-yo.

"Coo," said Pookie, "where's the bloody rush? Our customers ain't goin' nowheres, that's for sure."

This Pema guy, a grizzled little man who sported J.C. Penney running shoes and a Denver Broncos woolen cap, then had to get his two cents in, speaking to his boss in that strange language Herbie only knew to be not-English and not-Spanish.

" 'E says our customers is nowheres now, already," Pookie said, and everybody laughed, including Herb and Shali just a beat behind the others. Pema's eyes went back and forth between them, sopping up approval like the curtain-raising act at Mr. Laff's. Herb wished he'd pull the woolen cap a little lower on his head; half of his right ear was missing.

By that time, everyone, including yaks, was standing still.

"Pookie," Shali said. She walked toward him,

whipping off her Ray-Bans, looking blue-eyed up into his grannies. "You know, it *would* be great if, just today, we possibly could take some extra rest stops? Like, maybe every hour, even? My legs and back are really killing me, and that'd make a big, big difference. Then, tomorrow — or the next day, certainly — I know that I'd be fine. I realize that it'd be, like, an *enormous* favor. . . ."

Herbie watched the yaksman melt. He was sure that all through history girls from everywhere had gotten guys to answer "Sure!" "You got it!" and "My pleasure, babe!" by using tones of voice like that.

Pookie grinned at her.

"Don't even think about it, ducks," he said. "And 'ere" — he reached inside a yak pack — "every time we stop, the two of you can rub on some of this. . . ."

He gave the girl a wide-mouthed jar, its top draped over with Saran Wrap held on by a bright red rubber band. She took it, looking much the way that cancer patients look when someone's handed them their chiropractor's name and number.

In fact, the stops that Pookie ordered came at more like every *half* an hour. At the first one, Shali pushed the jar at Herb.

"You try it first," she said. "I want to see if it grows hair, or anything." She smiled. "Want me to come and rub it in for you?"

Herb was pretty sure she wasn't serious.

"No. No, thanks," he said. He looked around. "I guess I'll just slide over there. . . ." There were — there *always* were — large rocks not far away.

Shali shrugged and off he went. The stuff was slick and warming, with a pleasant piney odor.

196

When he came back and handed her the jar, he said, "It's nice." She nodded, headed for the place he'd gone to. Pema, pantomiming rubbing motions, made as if to follow her. Pookie grabbed him, and the guys all laughed, including Herbie, nervously.

The salve turned out to be not merely good, but unbelievable, miraculous. Herb had always thought that Eastern medicine was mostly getting punctured here and there by needles, and drinking different herbal potions with an empty mind. This stuff made him think again. By early afternoon, he and the girl were telling Pookie that they didn't have to stop that often. By evening, they were just a little stiff, about the way you get from walking in a mall all afternoon. Moved by more than *heart*felt gratitude, Herbie promised Pookie quite a splendid gift, his Reeboks, just as soon as his new boots were broken in.

If Baba Malomar possessed a health care product better than this salve, it really must be something, Herbie thought.

26
YAKSMEN

For the next six days the caravan moved right
along, running like a roller coaster, up and down,
from ridges into valleys and back up again. Every
day, the boy and girl felt more like yaksmen, less
like supercargo, tourists. By the third day, they were
pitching campsites right beside the men, tasting one
another's food and sharing one another's cultures.
("Take out the papers and the trash, or you don't
get no spending cash . . ." sang Pookie and his boys,
before too long, ". . . Yakety-yak. Don't talk back."
"Regard as one this life, the next life, and the one
between . . ." recited Herb and Shali.) On the morning of the fifth day, early-rising Pema stuck a lizard
into one of Herbie's boots.

Herb didn't know exactly what to make of their
relationship — not the one with Pema, his with
Shali. Sometimes the two of them would share a pot

and spoon, and sometimes not; that seemed a good deal less significant, as time went by. They talked a lot, both walking on the trail and with the heads of their two tents pitched close together, lying down at night. Mostly they just stuck to everyday occurrences, like weather, food and washing socks, or the birds and views they saw, the personalities of different yaks, and how much hot sauce was about enough. She still did not repeat that line about how glad she was to have him with her, although from time to time she'd say or do some little thing that made him think she might be.

The most surprising and direct remark she made along those lines was what she said the sixth day of their journey, on a sunny morning. Herb had dared to put on hiking shorts, instead of trousers, and he'd even taken off his shirt.

"I *like* looking at a guy who has your kind of body," she had told him. "The long and lanky type."

Herbie'd blushed and almost said, "Me, too," instead of what he meant, which was that he liked looking at *her* kind of body, too, or would if he were ever given such an opportunity.

So far, he hadn't been, for sure. She always changed her clothes some place where she was out of sight, and perhaps to show respect for local customs, perhaps for other reasons of her own, she kept herself as covered up as all the native women Herb had seen in town. But still, from just the indications that he'd had, the generalities of size and shape that even *spacesuits* can't entirely hide, he was sure she had a lovely body. *Of course* he hadn't dared to say a thing like that, not yet.

In fact, he hadn't dared to say or do . . . well,

anything. Not any of the things like telling her he liked her, holding hands, or kissing — all the stuff that he was sure that almost anybody else would certainly have tried to do, by then. He'd told himself that was because he didn't want to maybe *ruin* it, the real nice way that everything was going.

At least he got some confirmation of the fact that he did not *repulse* her. She *touched* him all the time. Not on any of the *zones*, of course, and not . . . carressingly, exactly. But it *was* true her fingers *lingered* on his shoulder, arm, or neck, sometimes, or on his knee if they were sitting down. He'd made up his mind that he was going to start to touch her, too, offhandedly, but not until they'd left the caravan, and it was just the two of them. Then, in case she slapped his face, or stabbed him in the gut with some jeweled dagger she kept hidden in her sleeve, he wouldn't have to hear old Pema giggle at him.

That day, the day that it'd be the two of them, drew closer all the time. Soon, they'd reach the sacred river in the final valley, the place where Pookie and the boys would stop, unload and set up shop.

"Yop, they're wot you might call pilgrims, like," said Pookie Woodchuck, leaning back against a rock and slurping at his after-dinner drink, yak butter tea. "Blokes come up by the thousands, all year long. As soon as ten goes 'ome, 'ere comes another twenty."

"It is a *very* sacred river," Shali said, in tones of great respect, "from what I understand."

The five of them had finished eating and were sitting in a group around the little fire that they'd

200

made, yawning and digesting in the twilight.

"Bloody right it is — top five," said Pookie. "Some'd say top *two*. This 'ere's the virgin river: sacred, pure and undefiled. No boats allowed on 'er, no bridges over 'er. You want to 'ear 'ow sacred? Bloody river's so damn sacred, 'er ain't even got a *name*!"

"Wo!" said Herb. "That's just about as sacred as you get, *I'd* say. Even Eric Clapton — "

"An' there's more," said Pookie, talking right on through the interruption, in the way old friends are apt to do. " 'Er be so sacred, *they* don't even put 'er on their maps! Lots of foreigners come up to it an' think they must be bloody *lost*!"

Pema had some things to add to that. He spoke to Pookie, in their native tongue, but looked at Herb and Shali. It had become entirely clear he understood *all* spoken English, never mind what accent, perfectly. But though he'd learned the words to certain songs, he didn't seem to *speak* it.

" 'E says that you should know the river's on *our* maps," said Pookie, with a thumb-jerk at the half-eared man. "But bein' such respectful sods, we don't give it a real name, neither. No," he shook his head, "the Leh-ze River does *not* have a name." It seemed he'd finished speaking.

Pema shook his shoulder, looking cross. Then he made a gesture that, in any language, means "Go on."

" 'Leh'ze' meaning 'that which is too sacred to be named,' " said Pookie, and old Pema and the silent one, named Sendup, cackled merrily.

"So, when the pilgrims come, they stick around

and paddle in the sacred waters," Shali said. "And they also *shop* a lot?"

"Yop," said Pookie. "Some of 'em 'ang out for *weeks*, sometimes. Just dip and shop, and shop and dip — like that. Some learn 'ow to swim while they're about it. Try to catch themselves an eel or two."

"An *eel* or two?" said Herb. "To *eat*?"

"Bugger, no," said Pookie. "Catch 'em for the *slime* they're covered with. Them pilgrims, they scrape off the slime and put it in a jar; then they toss the bloody eel back in. Them eels are sacred, too, y'know."

"Gross," said Shali. "I hate eels."

"Not this lot, you don't," said Pookie. "Eel slime's part of wot you rubbed on you, before. Wot took your aches away? It's full of 'ealin' properties. Even *we* believe in eel slime, ducks."

"Well, eels or no eels, we have got to swim across that river, Herb and me," said Shali. "To get to where we're going." They'd never talked about their destination with the men before.

"You better plan to 'ead upstream, then," Pookie said. "Twenty miles, or better thirty. Get up where she's narrower, you know? 'Er's just too bloody wide, where we'll be 'ittin' 'er."

But Shali shook her head. "We don't have time," she said. "It's Baba Malomar's we're going to. You know his ashram, right? We've got to beat some other people there, get there just as soon as possible. *Up*stream would be *way* out of our way."

Pema had some more to say, at that point. He had a funny sort of *naughty-boy* expression on his face. That seemed peculiar, strange.

202

" 'E says Baba Malomar's too much," was Pookie's terse translation. "Of course, there's some believe's that 'e's a saint," he added, moments later.

Shalimar decided she would head for bed, on that.

"Let's hope they're right," she said, rising rapidly and taking off, with toothbrush.

27
COMPETITION

The next day, Pema went ahead alone. His assignment, Pookie said, was, first, to find a good location for their caravan to park, where they would set up their boutique. Its name would be Abida's Secret Sharpest Image, Pookie said. Then, having found some kids to work as counter help, Pema'd hustle back that evening and report.

When he did, he also brought back local news, one piece of which was passed along to Herb and Shali by his boss.

" 'Member wot I said about the river bein' left off all their maps?" said Pookie. He then laughed, self-satisfiedly, the way that prophets often do. "Well, yesterday, 'ere comes this bleedin' bunch of foreigners, five or six of 'em, all Japanese, an' drivin' supercharged Suzukis, four-wheel drives. An' when they see wot-all they got in front of 'em, an' not a

204

bridge or boat to cross it on, they like' to puke, from wot ol' Pema said. An' 'e said even if they *could* swim over 'er, they can't, 'cause one of 'em, 'e's got 'is wrist, like, chained to this big bloody steamer trunk. A thing the size of some young yak, wot Pema said, but not as smart by 'arf, I'll bet." He broke off into chuckles.

"So, looks as if *that* bunch is gonna 'ead upstream, all right," concluded Pookie, "goin' by wot Pema said."

Herb and Shali looked at one another. It seemed her information had been incorrect; the Japanese *had* been ahead of them. And now they'd soon be heading upstream — possibly they'd started up, already — where eventually they'd reach a place where they could ford the river in their vehicles. And then race on to Baba's.

Shali sighed, and licked her lips, then spoke.

"I can tell you what they've got there, in that trunk," she said, in an *extremely* offhand tone of voice. "Those Japanese."

"Wot's that?" said Pookie, sounding equally uninterested. The other yaksmen looked off into space, as if they had their minds on other matters altogether.

"A billion dollars cash, American," said Shali. "It's chained onto that fellow's wrist because it's his responsibility."

"That so?" said Pookie, and he yawned, enormously. Pema and the silent Sendup also yawned, and shook their heads, and looked like guys about to drop from tiredness.

"Well, time for nighty-night, I guess," said Pookie. "I'll just be checkin' on the yaks before I turn on in." He rose and started toward the tethered beasts, and both assistants followed.

Next morning, Pookie was the only yaksman present at the breakfast rock, and when the boy inquired where the others were, he said he'd told them they could go ahead and do a little early dipping in the sacred waters, if they wanted to.

"We, too, believe the river brings good fortune," he explained.

28
CROSSING

By mid-morning, Pookie's caravan had reached the sacred river on the valley floor, but the two assistant yaksmen still had not rejoined it.

"I guess you'll have to say good-bye for us," Shali told their boss. "We've got a couple of things to do before we make the crossing."

Pookie said he understood. He said that he could not *imagine* where those two " 'ad gotten to." But he also was a proud and happy man. Herb's Reeboks were a *little* narrow, but they basically felt great, and when it came to looks, they *really* did the job. When he had led his loaded yaks between the rows of pilgrims' tents, a lot of almond eyes had widened at the sight of them and words were softly spoken that their wearer found, if anything, *en*couraging. Pookie told the two that if by any chance they made it back to there before this "sales event" was over,

207

he'd offer them real savings on the trip back to their point of origin.

"We'll just pretend you bought a round-trip ticket to begin with," he told them with a wink. "Abida, he don't like it if I 'ave to come back empty."

And so, after a round of hugs, "God blesses" and "Good 'untings," the boy and girl turned left, while yaks and Pookie wheeled off to the right, all of them in hopes of happy days ahead. Neither group seemed bothered by the fact that each faced a fairly major (although very different) challenge: in the case of Herb and Shali, swimming this huge river; for Pookie, finding where the hell it was that Pema'd gotten him a parking space.

Herbie found the pilgrims' "city" to be a real eye-opener. There were people by the many hundreds, all of them in plain white outfits, living in their vari-colored tents, and either walking through the streets with shopping bags, or going down to linger in the waters and be cleansed of lust and greed, and anger, envy, covetousness — in other words the sins that go along with shopping.

Although the people living in the city were all transients, the place seemed very orderly and organized, to Herb. Larger stores, such as the one that Pookie'd soon set up, were grouped in mini-malls, while smaller quik-stops, launderettes and franchised eateries (McCurry's) were scattered here and there and everywhere, throughout the different neighborhoods. You got the feeling that there weren't lots of drugs for sale, but Shali found and bought a bunch of blow-up beach balls: bright idea.

"Boats aren't kosher," she remarked to Herb, "and

so I don't imagine rubber rafts are, either. But I'll bet you we can tie a few of these together, and then float our packs across on them, as pretty as you please. I just hate hiking in wet undies."

"My biggest worry," Herbie said, "is floating *me* across. I mean, this kid can *swim*, all right, but not like here to Pago Pago."

She stared at him a moment, somewhat blankly, Herbie thought. As if it never had occurred to her he wasn't Tarzan.

"Well, I'm a *real* good swimmer," she said, finally. "So, if you have to, any time, you can hitch a ride from me a while — just grab onto the raft and let me pull you. I know you'll be all right. All you have to do is have the proper attitude. You do have that, now, don't you?"

"*Absolutely*," Herbie said, with great conviction, nodding. The river looked as if it would be nice and warm, and it was just as smooth as glass — in all ways very like himself, he thought, ha-ha. And besides, before he drowned, he'd get to see his girlfriend in a swimsuit, certainly a major goal in every young man's life. That was "girlfriend" with a ha-ha *also* after it, of course.

Once she'd had a chance to analyze — assess — the river's current, gentle as it was, Shali knew that it'd be impossible to swim, like, straight across the thing; they *would* get carried sideways, some. And so she figured they should start at least two miles above the city, maybe three. That way, they ought to come ashore a little ways downstream from it.

Herb believed it was a good thing that they had to do it that way. By going upstream they would get away from where the pilgrims congregated; they wouldn't call attention to themselves, or to their raft — in case some people thought it was improper. The pilgrims only swam where they had easy access to the river, where the banks were low to non-existent, and there were a lot of nice, wide beaches. That's the way it was beside the city, and below it, downstream. There, too, the river bottom slanted very slightly out for probably a hundred yards or more, and so they had a lot of room for standing, chatting in the water, and for taking swimming lessons. As Pookie'd said, there were a bunch of different swim schools there, a lot of competition for the doggy-paddle dollar.

But by the time you'd walked upstream a mile — there was a dusty road that paralleled the river — the topography had changed. Your feet were well above the water level, and the river's banks were steep and overgrown with brush. There were some narrow beaches at the bases of these mini-cliffs, but when you waded out from them, the river's bottom dropped off sharply. Herb and Shali spotted one such beach a good ways from the city that looked perfect for their purposes; they slid and scrambled down to it. Partway there, they heard a car come down the little narrow road — fast, and therefore recklessly. Shali thought it sounded like a super-charged Suzuki, four-wheel drive, but being driven in a way no Japanese would ever drive it. "Aston-Martin. That'd be James Bond," said Herb. And Shali smiled.

Once on the beach, they first took out, and then blew up, the dozen beach balls that they'd bought; they both got spots before their eyes before they'd finished doing that. And then they stuffed the balls, in groups of three, into these big mesh laundry bags they'd also found for sale. When they tied the bags together, there it was: a colorful and useful raft. Herb christened it *Con T.K.*, showing off his knowledge of both Spanish and mythology, drawing from the girl a look he didn't choose to analyze. Now all they had to do was put what they had on — or most of it — inside their packs and load them on the raft. Then: Swimmers Take Your Marks, Get Set and Go.

They started to undress. Herb couldn't help but notice Shali hadn't pulled a swimsuit from her pack, although she had dug something out of it. That was a length of sturdy cotton rope. He didn't think that it would be in character for her to tie him up, when he'd undressed, and torture him or something. And so he guessed it was a towrope for the raft.

Ahem. Herb dawdled. He decided he'd undress one article behind (or after) her. That way, when she was taking off her socks, he'd be on his boots, still. He'd know exactly when to stop, and when — how far — to go. He'd go as far as she did, and no farther.

Shali was a fast undresser. Before Herb's conscious mind had dealt with anything beyond that fact, she'd both whipped off and stowed away her cowboy hat, and shawl, and long-sleeved shirt, and painter's pants, and boots and socks. That meant she still had on an undersized (it seemed to him) green cotton camisole and matching underpants. Only those; that's all. Not much, quite little, hardly anything.

Because he'd stuck with fierce determination to his plan, Herb was in the act of rolling up his blue

211

jeans at that moment, standing there in just his T-shirt and plaid boxer shorts. He took his eyes off her to open up the zippered pocket in his pack, the one he planned to stow the jeans in. And as he did so, Shali spoke to him.

"There," he heard her say. "They say it's good to have the absolute bare minimum of drag, on swims as long as this one."

Herb froze; he didn't think he moved a muscle for a minute. He was pretty sure he knew what he was going to see, in general, when he turned back in her direction. Yes. Oh, yes. He'd heard kids, swimmers in his school, telling one another how many hundredths of a second they could "save" by buying such-and-such a swimsuit, which had much less "drag." Oh, yes. But no swimsuit could provide "the absolute bare minimum of drag." What Shali meant was something altogether different, he was pretty sure.

He almost didn't want to look, but also knew he would-would-would, regardless of the consequences. He pivoted and stared.

Oh, yes. For sure. It was just as he had guessed, known, hoped and dreaded. Shali'd taken off her camisole and underpants and made them disappear inside her luggage, somewhere. She'd also put her pack onto the floating raft. That meant Herb had to watch her bend and pick up that soft cotton rope and tie one end of it around her waist, the other to the raft. And then look straight at him and smile.

If anything (he thought) she looked more naked with the rope on than without it; don't ask him why. But, either way, she was . . . oh, yes: big-shouldered, pink and honey, but still sleek as any

212

otter, with that swimmer's build and swimmer's ease (he just assumed) with having it exposed. Her body parts were not exactly like Felicity's, he didn't think, but they all held his interest to the same degree. She was waiting for him, standing there, her arms just hanging at her sides, her weight more on her left leg than her right, that small smile on her lips.

But *he* was in a fix. He lacked her . . . social confidence (you *could* say). Or maybe her experience. That probably was it. She'd been in situations of this sort before. She could remember times and places it made sense to strip right down and tie a cotton rope around her waist to drag a raft and possibly a boy across the widest river in the world. Times and places where a boy had looked at her the way she was right then.

She could probably remember all that happening before, but he could not. He had no experience and, worse than that, no confidence. What he did have was a mind awash in negativity. What was the worst thing that could happen? He imagined it right then. Shali taking one long look at him, and laughing.

So, desperately, he seized his pack, a nerdy (he was certain) smile on his own face and, holding it in front of him, he took the three short steps that got him to the raft. That solved exactly nothing. He couldn't simply stand there, playing Statues.

"Hey, it's okay," said Shali, suddenly. "It really is. Come on."

So, Herbie put the pack down, mumbling "God help me." Herkily and jerkily, he pulled his T-shirt up and off his head, and then with equal haste but also carefulness, maneuvered those plaid boxers down and off his feet. Trying unsuccessfully to make

213

his mind a blank, he jammed both articles into the pocket of his pack and, very much avoiding looking anywhere but straight across the river, he then sprinted pell-mell into it. ("Eels, meet your master," was the line that galloped through his head, insanely, as he dove beneath the surface.) When he came up again, as far away from her as one held breath would take him, and looked back, he saw that she was also almost totally submerged. All her points of interest, other than her comely head, were hidden by the muddy water.

"You looked *great*," her shapely mouth informed him casually, offhandedly, as if she'd seen him (for the first time) in a bow tie. "Even greater than I'd guessed." And then she laughed, a pure enjoyment sound, without the smallest trace of mockery.

"You, too," said Herb, exhaling those two words in more than just relief — in exultation. He felt the same as when he'd seen his favorite band: U2 . And then he turned and started swimming toward the other side.

Before he'd gone a quarter of a mile, Herb had made a number of decisions, all pertaining to this feat he was attempting. One, he wasn't going to try to talk too much, while swimming. Two, he was mainly going to use the restful, but effective, breast stroke, even at the risk of looking wimpish. Three, he wasn't going to offer to help out and pull the raft, part-time. Four, he wasn't going to keep on looking at the other shore, and noticing how very far away it was.

He did, however, notice certain other things. The river's temperature was comfortable — warm

214

enough, but still not soupy. There *was* a current, but it didn't seem like any problem. Swimming naked — which, in fact, he'd never done before — was definitely the way to go. Shali *could* swim like a fish; most of the time she used a lazy crawl, and even with the raft to pull, she stayed right up with him, with ease.

They swam about ten feet apart. Herb felt safe, but not in any fear of bumping into her. He tried to stay relaxed and glide as far as possible with every kick. Stroke-kick-glide. He let his face go slightly underwater on the glide. He was more of a *torpedo* than a lumpy frog (he thought), cutting like an arrow through the water.

"How you doing?"

Herb was almost startled by her voice. He stopped his rhythmic stroking and looked over at the girl, made a little cranky by the interruption.

He discovered she'd rolled over on her back and now was lolling in the water, barely moving. Compared to him, she was extremely buoyant. Herb felt himself become less cranky, more a social being.

"Okay," he answered, treading water.

"Want a rest?" she asked. "A tow?"

"No, let's keep going," he replied. "I'm fine." More than ever, then, his mood was *do* it, *make* it, get it over with.

She nodded and rolled over and resumed her stroke. She had to work a little harder, right at first, to get the raft restarted. Herb got glimpses of the muscles in her shoulders, shiny when they broke the surface of the murky water. She really *was* a swimmer; her leg kick was an engine, pushing her along.

215

He took a peek ahead. They'd come a ways. He looked back where they'd come from. They sure had. They were really out there, now; there *was* no nearby shore — either way was just a huge expanse of water. Herb felt a little fear, a tiny panic bouncing in his chest. For the first time, it seemed very *deep*, the river.

He asked himself how he was feeling — honestly. The answer was: Okay. He really was okay; he hadn't tightened up or anything. He got back in his rhythm: stroke-kick-glide. He was pretty sure that he was going to make it, sure he was. If he ever needed help, it was ten feet away, but he was pretty sure he wouldn't. He was going to make the crossing on his own.

He thought at least another half an hour passed before she stopped again. This time he was glad she had. He paddled over to the beach-ball raft, and got both elbows up on it. His body now admitted to his mind that this was much the longest swim they'd ever taken — by a factor of some five or ten, already, maybe even more. His legs were starting to feel heavy. They always had a tendency to sink, but now they didn't seem to want to kick the way they had before, with that same snap and drive. His lower back felt tired, too, and his shoulders, slightly, just a little. But he still could go. He saw that they were much, much closer to the other side than to where they'd started from. That was a boost. He bet they were three quarters there; he said that to the girl. He thought about how good he'd feel to reach the other side, to make it. This had really been hard work. Making it would be a real accomplishment.

"You're looking good," she told him. She, too,

was hanging on the raft, across from where he was. "You feel okay?"

"For sure," said Herb. He wanted to say something to encourage *her*. "A piece of cake. You want to do some eeling when we get there?"

She laughed at that.

"Sure," she said. "It won't be too long, now."

It took another thirty minutes, though. Herb found he couldn't glide the way he used to. His stroke got choppier, and he was panting. He didn't know whose fault it was, but Shali and the raft were always closer than they'd used to be. He couldn't keep himself from looking at the shore. It made him mad the way it stayed so far away. The current over here seemed stronger, so that for every body length he'd swim — like, *forward* — he seemed to drift one, to the side.

When they were, *finally*, forty-fifty feet from shore — which was another little beach, deserted, brown, with hardly any bank behind it — Herb saw the girl stop stroking. He thought she must be treading water, maybe checking out the depth. But then she gradually stood up! The water was no deeper than the middle of her thighs. They'd made it!

Herb stood up, too, of course. And promptly fell right down again. His legs had turned to stilts made out of cardboard tubes, with maybe melted butter in them. He knelt there in the water, feeling foolish, helpless, grateful, lucky, proud. Knowing he could not get up.

She waded toward him, moving very stiffly, smiling, picking at the rope around her waist. Herb saw how it had chafed her skin, and when she got the knot undone and took it off, she had this fat red line

217

around her middle, and a big red scrape mark on one side from where the knot had rubbed against her hip. Probably he also noticed she was naked, but it didn't register except as something that just happened to be so. It didn't have a thing to do with him. He didn't think about himself, in that regard, at all. Everything was kind of spacey, dreamy.

She helped him up and got his arm around her shoulders.

"This happens," she explained. "Don't worry. In a little while, they'll feel like legs again."

They staggered forward, onto the small beach, she still pulling on the towrope. When the raft was beached, and couldn't float away, she dropped the rope and kept on walking with the boy, up onto the riverbank to where there was a fat, round log, a major piece of driftwood. Herb sat down, and it was then he noticed he was naked, too. He didn't feel embarrassed or, like, anything except *of course* he was, so what.

He was very, very tired. He didn't think he'd felt this kind of tiredness, before. He didn't think he could get up, but that was fine; he didn't want to.

Herb watched the girl walk back along the riverside and get their packs, and then the raft, and set them all down near where he was sitting. That was fine with him.

"I guess I'll take the raft apart," she said.

He nodded, perfectly agreeable, watched her systematically reduce this useful vehicle, the *Con T.K.*, to one small pile of limp, striped rubber blobs and four mesh laundry bags. One of those she folded twice and put by Herbie's feet. Then, from out a little pocket in her pack, she pulled that jar of Pook-

218

ie's salve, the eel-slime stuff and, kneeling on the laundry bag, began to rub it on his legs. He watched her breasts move, as she did that.

"You're really something, you know that?" she said. "For someone not in training that was one enormous swim."

Herb could feel his legs begin to feel like legs again. But still, he didn't want to jump right up and test them. Actually, he felt much more like lying down than jumping up.

"I wasn't sure I'd ever walk again," he told her, looking at his palms. His finger ends were still quite shriveled, prune-ish.

"Tomorrow will be soon enough," she said. She turned her head to check the setting sun. "It must be seven, eight o'clock already. Morning, you'll be good as new." She tapped his knee. "So, there." She scrambled to her feet and turned back toward her pack, the jar still in her hand. She shifted weight from one leg to the other; Herbie watched her bottom move.

"Wait," he said. He didn't want her to begin some new activity before he'd told her something. They'd just accomplished this great feat together. She was proud of him. They both were naked. Tomorrow she would disappear again inside those layers of clothes. Opportunity, it seemed to him, had knocked *and* maybe even shouted out "Hey, Herb!" Would he ever be in love like this, back home? He'd never been before, except with Tyree Toledano.

"In my younger and more vulnerable years . . ." he thought, the seven words that were the start of *The Great Gatsby*.

"Come here," he said.

She bent and put the jar away, and then came back to where she'd been. "Where?" she said. "I *am* here, aren't I?"

"No," he said, "right *here.*" And he patted the big log that he was sitting on, and then leaned forward, scooping up the laundry bag and spreading it for her to sit on. That made her smile. She settled down beside him.

"Yes?" she said. "What is it, now?"

"Shali," Herbie said, and he was stuck. So what he did was take her by the shoulders and a moment later he was kissing her, with one hand coming off her shoulder, dropping down to touch, and then to cup, her breast, holding it like something precious and . . . *sensational.* His hand was doing that.

"Herb," she took her mouth away from his to say. "Oh, absolutely, Herb." And then she kissed him back, her fingers buried in his curly hair.

"*I love you,*" Herbie said, soon after that. He took his hand away. It seemed to him that touching her had let the words out, made it possible for him to say the thing that he'd decided that he *had to* say to her right then. The thing that made it perfectly okay for him to want the rest to happen, now. He was sure that this must be the time for it, that he'd be able to, in just a little while. For sure. It wouldn't be too long; it never had been.

"I know," she said. "You sort of do." She laughed. "And me, I sort of do you, too. I have for quite a while. In fact, before we started with the caravan, I went and got some . . . intimate necessities, you know? From old Abida's warehouse? Blush if you believe you know the kind I mean."

220

Herb blushed. This wasn't any kid stuff they were talking, now.

"Well, I did, too," he said. He felt responsible, mature. "I've got a . . . intimate necessity myself. Right over in my pack."

"What?" she said. "Just one? I feel insulted." But he could tell her outrage was a fake.

"I only *had* a dollar thirty-five," he said, sticking with the total honesty.

"Boy," she said. She touched the top of Herbie's nose, with just the tip of her left forefinger. "You *are* a schemer, aren't you? And pretty *confident*, I'd say. Here you'd barely met me, hardly knew a thing about me. Never seen me in your life, before." She paused. "Or had you?" Now she had one hand on his shoulder, the other on his knee.

"No, of course not," Herbie said. What kind of question was that, anyway? Of course he'd never seen her. She wasn't any Tyree Toledano. And she had never seen him, either. Which meant that when she bought what *she* had bought, back at Abida's, *her* set (collection? carton? *ton*?) of intimate necessities, she must have wanted not so much himself, specifically, but more just anyone who was a boy, a man. He'd heard guys talk about such girls, at school; he'd *never* heard guys talk about what wasn't happening.

"And you didn't know *me*, either," Herbie said, feeling sort of swept along. "And that makes you a schemer, too, but worse than me because you planned to do it *lots*, regardless." He hardly knew what he was saying.

"Uh-uh," she said. "Or, well, I *am* a schemer,

221

maybe, but I had my reasons. It's not the way you think, at all." She'd brought her hand up to his cheek, and then she kissed his mouth again, but not with heavy emphasis, he didn't think.

"I don't understand," said Herb. "How is it?" He was feeling funny, hurt. He didn't know what by, exactly. There was something wrong, he knew that much. He noticed then that she was looking pretty beat. She'd done that long swim, too, and she had had the raft to pull, as well. But she had got him into this. Well, hadn't she?

"I can't tell you now," she said. "I can't tell you anything. It's a sort of promise that I made. Besides, I'm awful tired now. I really am about to drop." She got up on her feet.

"I can tell you this much, though," she said. "It's you, specifically — you, Herb — I'm loving, time compressed, right now. I promise you. Let's not make love unless you totally believe that. And unless you really still believe you love me, too."

Herb sat there nodding, looking at the ground. The pace of all these speeches, and events, and non-events, had been too much for him. He was afraid that if he spoke right then, he'd start to cry, which was absurd. When he lifted up his eyes, he saw that she was laying out their sleeping bags. She hadn't put on any clothes, still.

"Come on, you," she said to Herb, holding out a hand as she approached him. "It's time for beddy-bye."

Herb might have been asleep before his feet had made it to the bottom of that sleeping bag.

* * *

222

When Herb woke up, the sun was well up in the sky, already. He heard some birdsong and some splashing sounds, and he turned over in his sleeping bag to look. Amazingly that didn't hurt at all.

Unbelievably (thought Herb) Shali had been *swimming*: hair of fifty thousand dogs. She'd just picked up a towel, and she was walking toward him from the beach, fluffing out her auburn hair. She still had that red mark around her waist. He didn't have to think to know he loved her more than anyone had ever loved a woman since the dawn of history. Oh, yes.

"I want to tell you," he called out, "I *totally* believe you and I *absolutely* love you, not just *still*, but more, and. . . ."

He'd got the bag unzipped and started crawling toward his pack, trying to remember if there was *another* thing he had to say, and where he'd put. . . .

But she was trotting toward him, grinning.

"Look, look, look," she said. "Beside your pillow. It can't have been the *tooth* fairy . . ." And — bingo — she was kneeling on his sleeping bag with him, their arms around each other in the friendly morning sunshine.

"Oh, Herbiferous," she said.

And thus did Herbie Hertzman, if indeed there ever was a person by that name, come to have (by great good luck) a taste of what he always *thought* he needed most in life, in order to be happy.

29
FAR-OUT ENCOUNTER
OF SOME KIND

In the next few days, some words of Ses de-
Barque's kept sneaking up inside of Herbie's head
and saying "Boo!" Each time, he jumped a little.
The way you do when you remember that you're
going to the dentist's pretty soon, a week from Friday, say. Just before he'd started on this trip, she'd
said, quite enigmatically, he thought, "Everybody's
got a magic number: one. That's the one you get it
on. You see?"

At first bite, he had thought that "it" was something cosmic, like "the point" — the whole darn
story of the way it is. But almost right away he
doubted such an explanation. Ses deBarque was
down to earth, a steak and baked potatoes sort of
person. Maybe "it" was, like, a *job*, the thing you
end up doing with yourself.

But then, beginning on that morning by the sacred

river, and continuing for three more days, he wondered if "it" simply was what guys meant when they asked each other if they'd gotten any lately — namely, sex. Sex sure seemed magical to him.

Herb, typically, did *not* feel he was what you'd call a *natural* at sex, in terms of being *great* at it, the second he came flopping on the field. But what he *did* feel was this worshipful commitment, not just to the act, but her — to Shali, *aka* his "partner" — that allowed him to be *there* for her, with her, and so *enthusiastially* that she would have to laugh, and also gasp, for joy.

Herb knew the setting helped. It didn't rain; there wasn't any smog, or corporation odors. The scenery was beautiful, and there weren't any other actors anywhere around who might pop up and scream, "If you don't stop and get some clothes on by the time I count to ten. . . ."

On top of that Shali was as much involved as he in not just *making* love, but also in discovering and shaping it, permitting it, and using it in ways that had to do not only with their bodies but also with their spirits, their whole attitudes. Herb knew he'd never had such friendly feelings toward another person as he felt toward her — this big, broad-shouldered, easygoing girl. Except for what she wouldn't tell him, she allowed him total access to her being, to her here-and-now. Both of them were so darn glad to see each other, every morning, that the past and future, both, seemed more or less irrelevant.

But on the day before the day they started up the massive snowcapped ridge that was the last high barrier between the two of them and Baba Malo-

225

mar's, Herb wondered if perhaps the "it" that Ses had talked about was not sex, after all. Feeling older, more mature and philosophical, he wondered — *mused* — if maybe "it" was that man's highest goals and aspirations, such as perfect love, could never be attained except in fleeting moments, little "nows." And that only other sorts of things, like baseball cards and money, could be worked for, saved and kept.

The thing that put those rather cynical and sad ideas in Herbie's mind was realizing he and Shali — perfect lovers, the ideal — would not, no matter what, go on and on. Once this Health Care business finished, so would they be finished. He'd go back to Castles in the Air, and she'd return to either central casting or his own imagination — or *wherever* — and hang out there with chicks like Zippy and Felicity, and older hens such as the Big Red Chicken.

Herb wondered if the *basis* for the love that he and Shali had for one another *now* was that the two of them, at both the conscious and unconscious levels, knew that what was going on between them was ephemeral, unreal. They could love each other unreservedly, holding nothing back, and saving nothing for a rainy day. They didn't have to cling, or worry that the other one would change — or start to make demands, or find somebody else, or die or take up the trombone. Not just because there wasn't *time*, but for another — maybe better? — reason: that it wouldn't really matter if they did. Everything would soon be over, anyway.

When Herbie thought all that, he also thought: But if what happens doesn't matter, how can there be love like this at all?

226

And then he thought: Being in love — if this be really love — is making me peculiar.

And then he thought: The only thing that I want now is something I can't have — just like before — which is for Health Care to go on and on forever, and to hell with baseball cards and money. Is that the way it always is: You can't *ever* get what you want?

When he looked at Shali, hiking happily along in front of him, he felt himself get furious. How can she be so carefree, so oblivious?

Shali stopped and turned around. She had an ice ax in one hand.

"You're walking funny," she informed him. "What's the matter?"

"Walking funny? You can *hear* me walking funny? How?" said Herb. He knew he wasn't going to tell her what the matter was — that nothing really mattered, which included how he walked or didn't walk. He *loved* her, after all. Why make her sad or grouchy? There wasn't anything that anyone could do about the situation.

"Just funny," Shali said. "What is it?"

"I was thinking that I didn't want to die," said Herb.

"Oh, that," she said, and turned around and started hiking toward the ridge, again.

Herb thought he heard the whistle first. Quite possibly, the sound of it was in his head a while, while he just clomped along, thinking of a lot of things, including Shali's butt. He remembered Malcolm Lowry's start for *Under the Volcano*: "Two mountain chains traverse the republic roughly from north to south. . . ."

227

When he recognized the whistle, he also had to realize, *admit*, it was a special kind of whistle, blowing in a special kind of way. It sounded like the kind of whistle British bobbies use, rather than the kind that Coach blew at P.E., and it was going "beeep, beeep, beeep," then "bip-bip-bip."

"Hey, listen," Herbie said, just as Shali stopped and raised one pointer-finger in the air.

They were almost at the snowfield on the ridge. Except that it was clear to Herb the snow in front of them had not just gently fallen there, direct from up above, the heavens. Instead, it looked as if it had come avalanching down from higher up the mountain, possibly the day before, bringing tons of rock along with quite a weight of ice with it, white and wet and grainy-looking — cold. Basically it was a mass of snow and ice and rocks, all jumbled up together, a heap of stuff that anyone would rather walk around, if possible, than climb up on. But it was also where the whistling was coming from.

"It's . . . sure it is, a signal — an SOS," said Shali. "Coming from up there, somewhere." She gestured at the mess in front of them. "Come on."

"*Weird*," said Herb, and followed her. They started climbing up the jumbled snow and rock and ice. Shali, leading, scrambled up on hands and knees, going very carefully, and trying not to make a sound. At last she peered down on the other side of one big heap of frozen rubble, and when she had, she turned and looked at Herb, her blue eyes big as willowware.

"It's not a *person*," she informed him in a whisper. "It's a *yeti*! It's trapped under a monstro pile of junk."

Herb stared right back at her. Of course he knew

about the yeti — the "Abominable Snowman" to the English-speaking world. Pookie Woodchuck and his men all claimed they'd seen a lot of them; they talked as if the things were just as common on the routes they traveled as are groundhogs by a parkway in Connecticut. They said (as Herb had heard before) the yeti was a hairy biped, built like a power forward in the NBA, but taller, shy and basically benign, good folks if sometimes just a little mischievous and scary. But Herbie also knew that people with his color eyes were meant to call the yeti stories "folk-lore," with a little, condescending laugh. He went quickly up the slope and lay there on his belly next to Shali.

Yup, no doubt about it (Herbie thought); it was a yeti, sure enough, hairy, huge and lying on its stomach and its side, with one leg and one arm pinned underneath a ton or two of rocks and ice and snow.

"Now what?" breathed the girl, in her companion's ear. "There may be others in the area. You think *we* ought to try to help this one?"

"Of course," said Herb. He didn't have to think. What this trip was all about was Health Care, after all. To him, the figure lying in the snow was no abomination. It was a living thing, pinned beneath some rocks and stuff; its Health was very much in need of Care.

"EXCUSE me," Herbie said, or rather called, down toward the captive yeti.

The thing stopped blowing on its whistle.

"EXCUSE me," Herbie called again. "I don't suppose that you, by any chance, speak English?"

"*Horace?*" said the yeti. His voice was slightly

229

muffled, but the word came loud and clear. The yeti couldn't turn his head toward the boy and girl.

"Horace, you damn Lapsang-lapper, you." The yeti parodied Herb's voice and style of speaking. "I don't suppose that *you*, *by any chance*, would like to kiss my foot." And he chuckled and continued in his normal voice. "Or failing that, to get your ass down here and cut me loose? Tell you one thing: I *am* getting cold. And I b'lieve I've got a little fracture of the astrogalus, maybe."

Herb and Shali looked at one another. The yeti didn't just speak English; he spoke it like a black American who'd gone to Cornell Med.

"Hor-*ass*!" came the yeti's voice again, but now with just a little sharpness in it. "I've been like this for four-five hours, buddy, and I'm getting to the edge of sick of it!"

"Uh — we're not Horace," Herbie called. "Sorry about that. We're just two people on their way to Baba Malomar's. But you — you really are a yeti?"

"Well — yes," the yeti said. "Although, of course, the very nature of reality ought to be defined, before we talk about who's really who, or what — or almost anything else, I guess."

Herb looked at Shali, eyebrows up. She nodded. And so they swung their feet around and slid down to the place where the yeti was.

Up close, the yeti was a pretty scary sight. From head to toe, he had a coat of thick and silky-looking hair, about as long as, say, a collie dog's. His, however, was a mix of black and gray and pure white hairs, which made him, overall, look gray. His deep-set eyes were black and fierce; facially, he looked to be a cross between Benito Mussolini and a mandrill,

230

or some other large baboon. He had a powerful and well-proportioned body, with enormous calloused hands and feet.

"Hi," said Herb, when they'd hunkered down beside the yeti. "I'm Herb and this is Shali. I've got about a million questions that I'd like to ask you. But I guess we ought to try to get those boulders off you, first."

The yeti heaved a sigh; it sounded like a mix of resignation and regret.

"Yes," he said. His voice had gotten much more formal, talking to this pair of youthful strangers. "I'm Doctor Arthur Bradford Cushing. I hope you'll call me 'Cushy,' though; everybody does. But what I'm thinking is that you two youngsters sure as hell would get two hernias apiece before you got those rocks on me to move. I'm afraid you're going to have to do a little — what did Hawkeye call it? — 'meatball surgery'? Go in some place above my captive elbow here, and cut around a bit. You've got a knife with you, I trust?"

"Sure," said Shali. "But . . . well, I can't believe you want us to perform a — *you* know — *amputation* on you!"

Arthur Bradford "Cushy" Cushing chuckled. He seemed to be relaxing, once again.

"Good gracious gravy, *no*," he said. "I don't want you stickin' *me* with any ol' Swiss army! *I* happen to be five foot nine, when standing on my tippy-toes, and five — or make that *ten* — times better looking than my alter ego, here. I also happen to be mostly African and part American, by heritage, with not a drop of Himalayan blood — not that that's important in the least. No, everything you're looking

231

at right now is *costume*. The real me is underneath. And the master zipper that you have to use to get to me starts out, as luck would have it, on the *yeti's* wrist, the one that's trapped. Which means you'll have to cut into his arm to get to it. Hate to ruin a good suit, but that's the way it goes. Seems as if it's me or it . . . did he say *'Sherry'*?"

"Shali," Shali said. "It's short for Shalimar."

"Of course," said Cushy. "Well, then . . . *shall* you, Shali?"

She looked at Herb. He shrugged why not.

"Why not?" she said.

The total job took pretty near an hour. The yeti's "skin" was more or less the thickness of an asphalt shingle, but a lot more pliable and maybe fifty times as tough. Underneath the skin (in addition to the little doctor) there were lots of lightweight rods and cables, even little motors that the person in the suit could use to help him walk, bound, jump, go "ooga-booga" at a tourist or a yak train, or whatever.

Once they had the zipper working, things went right along. Dr. A. B. Cushing was a short black man with horn-rimmed, tinted glasses, and a light gray sweatsuit on. On the front of it, it said: "I'm a Living Legend." Beside not being tall, he also wasn't fat or young; Herb's guesses were 145 and sixty, but physically in real good shape. Unfortunately, though, a rock had landed not just on the yeti's leg, but on the doctor's ankle, too, and once they had it free, and he had checked it out, he said that he was certain it was broken.

Herb and Shali helped him into extra clothes of

theirs and, following instructions, rigged a sort of chair-sling they could use to semi-carry him between them.

"Luckily for you good young Samaritans — as well as for myself," said Cushy, "we aren't very far from base. When we get close to where we enter it, we'll have to pause so I can blindfold you. And I'm afraid I must insist you spend at least the night."

With that he then produced, from underneath the waistband of his sweatpants a lethal-looking little automatic, not unlike the one that Herb had seen in Hometown, when Felicity had pointed hers at him.

Herb never has remembered clearly much of all that happened in the next . . . oh, eighteen hours. They forced the two of them to take this pill before they left the place, and it made almost everything unclear and him unsure of what was even semi-clear. The stuff he thought he *did* remember was so totally farfetched — impossible — that Herbie knew that telling it to anyone would mean he'd end up on the inside of a cuckoo's nest with walls so high he never could fly over them, they'd see to that. Here are half a dozen items from his sample case of memories:

1. The "yeti" base was carved into a mountainside, and it was a cross between the Xanadu Plaza, Trump Tower and the Hall of the Mountain King.

2. The "yetis" themselves were members of a very secret, very old, society. They were men and women of all different nationalities, most of them with *most* advanced degrees from *very* well-regarded universities. Many of them had made *enormous* sums

233

of money and/or *major* scientific breakthroughs, before they joined the group; some of them were just great-looking.

3. But all of them had given up on "society" and "civilization" as those words are presently understood.

4. And so, they therefore spent their lives in peace and harmony, playing jokes — or this one joke — on all the rest of humankind.

5. In addition to the "yeti" base, there were some other similarly grand and hidden centers of these people's operations, scattered here and there around the globe. People at those other bases did their stuff as Sasquatch, as the Loch Ness Monster, Champ, and other local legends, and in the drivers' seats of flying saucers.

6. "Visitors," like Herb and Shali, are "treated and released" (if friendly), "absorbed into the group" (if suitable and willing), or "other."

In any case, the next thing Herbie knew for sure, he and Shali were walking *down* a ridge, its snow-capped top behind them, heading for a peaceful-looking valley. This valley, with a small but lovely river flowing through it, was also home to Baba Malomar's palatial ashram, surrounded by lush fields and meadows, orchards and, yes, vineyards, heavy with ripe fruit.

"Can you *believe* that place?" Herb said to her, meaning where they'd spent the night, he thought, meaning all they'd seen and heard including grateful Cushy's parting present to them: "I'm a Living Legend" T-shirts.

"What place?" said Shali.

* * *

234

For the rest of the way to Malomar's Herb kept turning over in his mind this question: Would he have liked to stay and be a "yeti," if they'd asked him to?

There were a lot of things he liked about the life, the whole idea. For sure. You got to hang around with people who were really smart, in comfortable surroundings, and your every need was taken care of. Also, in your "work" you got to put one over on . . . well, pretty much the world's entire population. That'd sure be something new for him, Herb thought.

The one big trouble Herbie saw with going into yeti-ing was that he wondered whether fooling everyone was quite the sort of high that kept a person happy for a lifetime. Was it enough to give up *Hoping* for, for instance. Or Tyree Toledano? Or Herbie Hertzman, really, for that matter?

30
AT BABA MALOMAR'S

"Shali. Herb. I'm going to tell it like it is, all right?" said Baba Malomar. "Being an American, like both yourselves I guess, I'm not the kind of guy that's comfortable with anything that smacks of caste, or class. I'm not into having servants, even. To me, all people are the same — co-equals. Yah.

"*But*," he added, and he held one finger up, "let's not try to kid each other. What we've got here is an ashram — that's an *eastern* institution — not a spa or a resort. And on an ashram you are going to have a *spiritual* leader, which on this one is myself. And *devotees* — that's everybody else, excluding guests, of course. However, that don't mean there isn't lots of *synthesis* on these fine, fertile acres. In this *eastern* setting I insist on certain *western* principles and styles and attitudes, such as — " He broke off suddenly to say, "Hi, sweetie!"

"Hullo, beloved teacher," said this particular co-equal. Herb had been watching her approach for quite a while. She was wearing steel-toed boots and a light blue silky tank top, skin-tight cutoff denim shorts, a pair of heavy work gloves and a knotted kerchief 'round her slender neck. She was pushing a sturdy wheelbarrow piled high with roofing tiles, and only puffing just a little; her skin was nicely tanned and slick with sweat. Like all the rest of them that Herb had seen since they had started on their guided tour, this devotee was in her twenties, probably, and blonde, and in fantastic shape. Baba was the only guy he'd seen, so far.

They'd been walking three abreast and arm in arm along a wide stone walk, with Baba in the middle. Not being into expectations, Herb had not flipped out when he'd first seen the guy. As far as Herbie was concerned, there wasn't any reason why the guru shouldn't be the shortest of the three of them, and look a little like a beaver, being bucktoothed, chubby and cherubic, in a chocolate-colored robe down to his feet, on which there were a pair of soft Italian leather driving shoes — slip-ons, orange-tan. And it was perfectly all right with Herb that Baba had pink cheeks, no beard at all, and friendly light brown eyes that certainly did not *appear* to see into the deepest secret spots in either his or Shali's soul.

Overall, in fact, he couldn't pass as being physically the same as *any* of the girls they'd seen; physically he looked co-equal to a dish of chocolate pudding, or a couch potato at the age of thirty-five. Herb, who'd never been there, thought he sounded like he came from Philadelphia.

But everywhere the stone walk went — and it

went everywhere around the grounds, Herb thought — it cut through, passed beside, or went around about the lushest, richest vegetation, and the best-kept-up facilities the boy had ever seen.

"The soil throughout this total and entire valley," Baba stated, "is a hundred and ten percent all-natural alluvial, the finest, purest dirt available, I don't care how much you paid an acre. Sink a shaft straight down for fifty feet, and it's the same. I'm talking decomposed organic matter, never under cultivation, containing no impurities, such as your rocks, your sand, your clay. Shali. Herb. This stuff is total *mother*, kid you not. It's so darn fertile . . . Herbie, if you spat your gum out *there*" — he pointed to a garden plot beside the walk — "and stepped on it, in twenty years I bet you'd have a rubber tree to tap."

Herb nodded, smiling, just in case the guy was kidding him. He wouldn't know a rubber tree if one bounced off his head, but he absolutely *did* know lawns and flowers, vegetables and shrubs and bushes, fruit trees, grape vines, and shade trees, tennis courts, a roofed but open-sided gym containing Nautilus equipment, a croquet lawn, an archery range and a riding ring. And he could see, had seen, all of those while on this tour, all of them (just like the girls who worked or played on them) in prime time, class A, number one condition. He was sure he'd never seen so many healthy blades of grass, or such shiny perfect leaves on every tree, or fruit so succulent, blooms so aromatic, tennis courts so straightly lined, or vegetables so ready to be picked they almost cried out "Eat me," as you passed. And speaking of the girls . . .

" . . . devotees all happen to be female at the moment, yah." Baba Malomar was answering a question put to him by Shali. "And, let's see . . . all of them *are* blonde now, aren't they? But that's okay. I test a lot of products from my little lab on them, and so it's better and more scientific, too, to have one kind of subject, only. Hey!" He gave a little laugh. "You can think of them as my white mice, or rabbits, similar in age, sex, body type, IQ, reaction times and friendliness, and sense of humor. You know, I did my first recruiting on a beach near San Bardoo, and there wasn't what you'd call a lot of choice. In fact, when I included 'boredom' as a must-have for admission, the group I ended up with was darn close to self-selected. Of the first eighteen that I approached — pretty much at random — fifteen qualified and later came."

"You mean, a lot of girls like *these*," said Herb, gesturing the way Magellan must have done, a lot, when he got home, "agreed to journey way out here with you, a guy they'd never seen before, before all this was even *here*?" That seemed to Herb to be so borderline miraculous that anyone who brought off such a coup deserved . . . well, sainthood at the very least. But not a billion dollars, necessarily, as well.

"Mmm, yah," said Baba Malomar. "I guess they did. They had your spirit of adventure, I suppose. Hey, sweetie," he broke off to say to someone in a maillot on a racing bike, her long bleached hair straight-streaming out behind. "And don't forget your magic of the Orient, as well as how a lot of them had been discouraged by their deans from taking any further shots at higher education. We also had a few unfortunate misunderstandings (I would

239

call them) over what I said to them about the highs I guaranteed they'd get off of pwolarky."

" 'Pwolarky'?" Shali said. " 'Pwolarky,' did you say? Is that — ahem — the stuff I mentioned wanting to discuss with you, when we first got here? The franchise-type material? The wherewithal to turn a cellar-dwelling Health Care situation into a pennant winner? In other words, *The Product*? If so, I think your name for it could use a little work, still."

Baba shook his head and smiled an enigmatic smile. They were getting close to what looked like a little awninged light refreshment stand, a sort of small gazebo. Herb had seen two others, earlier, spaced around the grounds. Behind the counter of each one, a devotee was apt to be involved with slicing juicy mangoes, which she would then proceed to squeeze (along with tangy citrus fruits) into a frosty glass container. Other, passing devotees would interrupt their work or workouts to flat-belly up and slake their thirsts, thereby (as Baba'd said) avoiding being hit by dehydration. There were also solid snacks available, Herb saw, and all of this completely free of charge, apparently. None of the women Herb had seen so far were carrying wallets; he could be quite sure of that.

"Treats time!" Baba sang out joyfully, when they had reached this latest stand. "Debi, sweetheart, here come three parched throats, I kid you not. And, look, my tongue is even swollen, too. So how about you pour us three nice tall ones, side by side and . . . let me see, I guess I'll have a Ding-Dong, too, all right? Herb? Shali? Say hello to Debikins. And how about a little something sweet? That's other

240

than herself, I mean. The Tastykakes are *very* nice, this year."

The boy and girl both passed on solid food, but they accepted drinks from Debi, an agreeable little devotee in fitted yellow, nearly legless, overalls, who told them that her name was spelled with just one b and e, and that she sure was pleased to meet them.

"Deb," said Baba Malomar, when he had swallowed half a glassful, "Shali, here, just asked about pwolarky. How about you do the honors? Tell her not just what it is, but how it makes you feel — as if they couldn't tell *that* just from seeing you."

"Sure, Baba-shoog," she said. "It'll be my pleasure." She turned and faced the visitors, then squared her shoulders, did a little left-right march in place, and cleared her throat.

"Pwolarky," she said, sounding thoughtful, serious, "is what I like to call a unifying system for a person's life. In it, Play and Work are one, as I shall shortly illustrate."

With that, she half turned to her right, and with a finger traced the letters P L A Y in the condensation on the juice container. Then she put a WO between the P and the L, and an RK between the A and the Y. And there it was for all to see: PWOLARKY.

"Play and Work are one," she said again. "All day and every day, we work at play and play at work. We *are* them, you could say, and they, the two of them, are us. We not only *work* at fixing up, and getting into shape, and making one another happy, but we also *play* at it! You see?" She paused, took one quick glance at Baba and relaxed. Reaching for a rag to wipe the counter with, she tacked on one last thought.

"The whole thing's just a gas," she said. "It really is."

"Isn't she a piece of *work?*" said Baba Malomar, delightedly.

The other two thanked Debi for the cool, delicious drinks *and* the enlightenment, and then the three of them continued on their tour.

"So, all of this," said Shali, with a sweep of her arm that included the ashram's half a dozen gracious wood-and-fieldstone buildings (plus the two under construction), as well as its gardens and its grounds, including the enormous swimming pool, "all this was done by devotees — by Debis past and present?"

"Absolouie," Baba said. "Every bit of it was done by good, old-fashioned girlpower. I can't prove this in a court of law, but — Shali, Herb — I honestly believe that given optimum conditions, blonde young women are the hardest workers in the world. I'd match our good friend Debi there against a Sherpa porter, kid you not. But notice" — finger up, again — "I said 'optimum conditions.' "

"Meaning what?" said Shali, sounding skeptical, to Herb. In his life already he'd observed that lots of girls with darker hair were not great fans of blondes.

"Background first," said Baba Malomar, agreeably. "I'm sure you know the saying 'a hard worker is a happy worker,' right? That line, of course, was doubtless coined by management, some branch of management, at least. Parents, teachers, employ-*ers* — they all repeat it gleefully and often. Hey, why shouldn't they? It sends a message, makes a statement, gives advice — and even happens to be partly true! The both of you know this, yourself: If *you* work really hard at something, you are apt to feel extremely happy — with yourself *and* with the job you've done."

"Ye-es, but," said Herb, remembering how working hard had gone for him, at least up till the time he'd gone to Castles in the Air, "the trouble is, sometimes it's hard to get yourself to work that hard. And so you're not a happy camper."

"Exactly!" said their host. "That's just exactly right. For me, that bromide's incomplete. The way it *ought* to read is this: 'A happy worker is a hard worker is a happy worker.' Follow me? Happy leads to hard, which leads to happy and to hard again, and so on to infinity." He beamed.

"Um," said Shali. "So, I guess the thing you've had to do is figure out some way to make the people here all happy, every day. Seems like quite a challenge, seeing as there's . . . twenty-five or thirty . . .?"

" . . . forty-three, just now," he said.

" . . . and only one of you. How *do* you try to do it?"

"I'd hafta say three ways," said Baba Malomar. "That's in addition to pwolarky." And he chuckled. "First, I don't have any favorites; I treat everyone the same, as best I can. And, believe me, I am happy doing that and I work hard at it."

The boy and girl both nodded. They believed him.

"Secondly," he said, "I do a lot of yakkin', to the congregation as a whole. Each day, every day, we have Transcendent Time, when Baba does his stuff. Face it, I'm the guru here, so it's expected of me. I even changed my name, right off, to help it work right. Sidney Drexel Arthur was okay for board-rooms and the clubs that I belonged to, stateside, but out here . . . ? Could you imagine someone called Sid Arthur being *anybody's* guru? I'm going to tell you something true: After — what? — five years of this, Baba Malomar feels more like me than Sidney Drexel Arthur ever did. Incredible, you say? It's true! Out here, I'm really finally total me. I've returned to my first love, which means that I'm a man of science on the one hand, and, I like to think, I *also* am a man with some attachments to a higher plane."

He nodded to himself and walked a ways in silence, maybe (Herbie thought) engaged in, like, a mini-meditation, knocking back some spiritual tall ones.

"And, finally, there's our weekly practice of — don't laugh — anointment," Baba said.

"*Anointment?*" Herb and Shali asked, almost together. But neither of them laughed. In fact, Herb felt his heart speed up, as if it had some inside dope concerning what was coming next.

"Yah," said Baba Malomar. "Once a week, I lay some unction on my devotees, right on their pretty heads. It's a compound of my own devising. Formally I call the stuff *Easelspirlimine*." He pronounced that "ee-zell-*spir*-li-mean," with the accent on the "spir."

"The girls believe it's hair conditioner," he said. "But my *pet* name for the stuff is 'Bummer Balm.' " He looked at Shali. "And, Shali — yes, of course it's what you've come here for. You and Herb, and Roni and Cecelia."

"And what, exactly, does it *do?*" asked Herb, a little breathlessly.

"Conscientiously applied, one time a week," said Baba Malomar, "it takes away all feelings of unhappiness."

"*Roni and Cecelia?*" Shali asked.

"Yah," said Baba. "They're the reps Amalgamated Pharmaceuticals sent down. They parachuted in last night. It's really quite bizarre, an almost unbelievable coincidence. Physically, they look a lot like devotees. The difference is, they have a cashier's check for more or less a billion dollars, after taxes and all penalties Internal Revenue assessed me for." He grinned and shook his head. "And also they're unhappy."

Neither Roni nor Cecelia *seemed* unhappy — not to Herb, at lunch, at any rate. Roni was the shorter of the two. She had a punky look about her: bleached streak in her short blonde crewcut, with a guess-what-I-got fishnet T above black Spandex running tights. Cecelia's honey-colored hair was cut in bangs and fell in waves well past her shoulders. She had as deep a tan as Herb had ever seen, and he was sure she'd been maintaining it that morning. For lunch, she wore a wraparound short skirt and what the boy assumed must be the top of her bikini. In any case, it left an awful lot of breast exposed. There were just the five of them at Baba's table, the guru and his guests. And, naturally, the conversation centered on this Bummer Balm.

"As far as I've been able to establish, this is tricky stuff," their host was saying to the other four. "It activates the neuropeptides in the brain. Almost at

245

once, within say half an hour of its application, symptoms of unhappiness begin to disappear, or lose their place in Subject's scheme of things. Stupendous? Absolutely. The only thing I can compare it to is what those jokers at Johns Hopkins and at UVA are working on for colds, the common cold. The idea *there* is that you give the person what is called a 'bradykinin antagonist' — weird name, huh? — a drug that keeps your body from producing kinins, which are one of its reactions to the virus of a cold. If kinins aren't there to dilate blood vessels and send out icky messages of pain, discomfort and the like, Subject may still *have* a cold, but she escapes the *symptoms*, what your people" — Baba looked at Roni and Cecelia — "like to call 'colds' miseries.' Likewise, and in this case, a person using Bummer Balm may be unhappy, still — and almost surely is, in my opinion — but with her neuropeptides acting out, she has no noticeable symptoms. She doesn't *feel* unhappy, and (I guarantee) she doesn't *act* unhappy."

Herb could scarcely believe his ears. He felt a sense of awe. This unimposing little man, this Sidney Drexel Arthur, seemed to him to be a new Pasteur, or Curie, the 1990s Jonas Salk.

"Far-freakin'-*out!*" said punky little Roni. She was definitely excited; you could tell. "What you're describing is like *heaven*. Can you imagine *anyone* not wanting it?"

"When you say a subject doesn't *act* unhappy," asked the ever-careful Shali, "what exactly do you mean by that? You mean she doesn't mope around, or cry a lot? Or is there other evidence?"

Baba Malomar refilled his large wooden eating

bowl with Rice-a-Roni (East meets West again, thought Herb), and smiled.

"A ton," he said. "You've seen the girls yourself. They have no neurotic symptoms of unhappiness, none whatever, zip-o. The longer time you hung around the more you'd be convinced of that. None of them is overweight — that's obvious — or listless, take my word for it. They never nag (about my eating habits, say); they never are unfaithful. None of them is into drugs or alcohol or cigarettes. And on top of all of that, I'm satisfied there aren't any harmful side effects — and it also seems to work on everyone."

"Everyone who's female, white and under thirty," Shalimar reminded him.

"Well, yah," he said. "But given all we know about the human brain, I'm confident the stuff'd work the same on Herb, here, or myself. Or Greta Scacchi, were she willing and available. Or Tina Turner, Chairman Mao, or Mr. Rafsanjani." And the guru laughed and winked across the table at Cecelia.

She thrust both fists up in the air and yawned and stretched. Baba didn't seem to mind.

"Jet lag," she explained. "This girl needs her nap. But Sidney" — she put elbows on the table and leaned out in Malomar's direction — "let's not beat around the bush. What you've said is good enough for us. We are very ready, Roni and myself; we have a proposition that, we're very, very sure, you'll totally get off on. With all due respect, we're confident that these kids here" — she flicked a glance toward Herb and Shali — "can't come up with anything that even *touches* all that we'll be putting on the table."

247

"Well, gollybucks, who knows?" said Baba, almost bouncing in his chair with cheerfulness. "Everybody gets an equal chance on this man's ashram! What I was thinking was: Maybe I could get together with the Shali-Herb proposal later on this afternoon — assuming that they're ready — after naps. And then the three of us" — his finger pointed to himself, and Cecelia and Roni — "might just have *our* huddle sometime after dinner. How's that sound?"

"Delicious!" said Cecelia.

"Para-freakin'-*dise*-ical!" groaned Roni.

"Sure. Okay," said Herb and Shali.

31
PROPOSITIONS

Nap time, Herb and Shali soon found out, was a regular and much beloved component of the ashram's daily schedule. *Everybody* napped, and not just sitting on a chair, reclining on a chaise, or lying in a hammock, say, with clothes on. No, at this man's ashram you took off your clothes and got in *bed*, and lolled around on nice cool sheets. And either slept or not, depending on the usual alternatives.

Herb and Shali didn't. There was too much to discuss.

"I don't know," said Shali. She'd propped her pillow on its end against the wall, and she was sitting up in bed and leaning back against it, one knee up, the other leg extended.

"I don't know," she said, again. "I'm very dual about this stuff, aren't you? Face it, Easelspirlimine is not what you could call a *cure* for anything; it's

more along the lines of Tylenol, or Advil, one of
those. It doesn't touch the *causes* of unhappiness at
all. In fact, it lets you go on being miserable and
never feel you ought to lift a finger. To *do* something,
you know?"

"Well, yeah," said Herb, "but it would help a
person function better, though, like Baba said." He
was lying on his stomach with his head on one extended arm, toward the foot of their big bed.

"Oh, sure," she said. "No doubt about it. I don't
doubt that all the devotees *do* function great." She
made a face, not all that sweet a one, Herb thought.

"Well, that's something, anyway," he said. "I
mean, supposing someone's really bummed, had,
like, a clinical depression, never mind what from.
Wouldn't it be great if Bummer Balm could let that
person lead a normal life? Not have to hit their head
against the wall, or be strapped down, or something?" He touched her foot, wrapped his hand
around it, rubbed his thumb along the underside of
it, from underneath the instep to the heel. Herb
couldn't yet believe how much he liked . . . her feet,
for instance. Just because they were a part of *her*.

"Oh, sure," she said. "Oh, absolutely — mmm."
Herb thought she might be speaking to his hand as
much as answering the questions that he'd raised.
"That'd be *fantastic* — and you're right. It ought to
be available to them, the real bad cases. The part
that worries me is other ways it could get used, like,
1984-ishly. 'Cause Roni's also right, I bet; almost
everyone'd *think* they wanted it. Let some Big
Brother start to give it out, and he could keep the
people in his country in some kind of docile, mellow

250

state . . . forever. They'd even work like demons, just the way the women here do. Perfect little Nazis."

"*Nazis?*" Herbie said, and he began to laugh. "You say that just because they're blonde — real blondes." He ran a fingernail straight down her sole. She pulled the foot away. "Which makes you envi — "

"Shut up, you," she said, in phony fury. She'd switched her body on the bed and got a palm across his mouth. "You keep on bringing up those blondes, and you'll need Bummer Balm yourself, a double shot of it. All I meant was — "

"Sure, I know," said Herbie, pushing off his gag. "And I agree with you. But still, if we don't get the rights to it, and other people do, that's much more apt to happen. I mean, their *business* is to do a lot of business."

"That's right," she said. "And I'm not saying that we ought to change our plans. All I was saying was that . . . well, this stuff is like an atom bomb. You want to be the only one to have it. But going up against a billion bucks *and* Roni and Cecelia . . ." She paused and pondered that a moment. "Maybe we can tie him down and tickle him until . . ."

"We thought perhaps we'd tie you down and tickle you until you gave us what we're after," Shali said. "But that seemed pretty crude, in light of all your hospitality."

They'd been there for a good three hours, chatting back and forth about . . . oh, everything, it seemed. The ashram and the devotees, Baba's past and pres-

251

ent life, all that he'd accomplished there, how great it was. The conversation couldn't have gone any better, Herbie didn't think.

Baba chuckled, liking Shali's thought. Maybe liking the idea of being tied and tickled, Herbie thought. Baba certainly was liking Shali, liking looking at her, absolutely, even though her hair was quite a few shades darker than acceptable.

Herb liked looking at her, too, of course — the more so given what she'd put on for this meeting, an outfit that he'd been amazed to see her pull from near the bottom of her backpack. Not only was it not like anything he'd seen her wear before, it also didn't even look as if it should have had to spend time in a *pack* at all, not ever. A Vuitton overnight bag, maybe, but a backpack, never.

What it was was a completely simple, plain, white tunic of a dress, short, made out of silky, sexy, *almost* see-through, wrinkle-free, synthetic stuff, and worn with just a bright green sash, and sandals. Herb could guarantee the "just"; he'd seen her slip it on, on top of only underpants.

"Don't worry," she had said to him, "this isn't going to be the free-peeks-for-the-fat-boys hour. I'm doing this for me — for how it makes me feel to dress this way; it's called 'creating atmosphere.' "

Oh, right. For sure (thought Herb). And he was thinking: hazy, hot and humid.

That really hadn't been the way it was, however. What happened was that Shali — feeling as she did — more or less became the one who ran their little meeting, smoothly steering them from topic A to topic B, and so on, finding out a ton of stuff about the way the ashram worked, establishing rapport with Baba Malomar. She and Herb found out, for instance, that the present group of devotees, and many of their families, were paying large amounts of money for the privilege of coming there, and that a slew of other girls had applications in, to come the moment Baba had an opening. The guru also told them much about the booming health food business they were doing there, shipping supplements and tonics (*Baba Bits* and *Baba Blend*, both made from products grown or found right in that lovely valley) to stores around the world.

It was pretty obvious to Herb that Baba Malomar was proud of all that he'd accomplished in this setting, and that he very much enjoyed the chance to tell the story to four fresh, enthusiastic ears. He also seemed to like to banter with the two of them about the future fate of Easelspirlimine. Like, whether they could get the secret out of him, as Shali'd said, by tickling.

"Oh, it's not so crude, that method," he maintained. "From what I've heard, some cultures do it, like, an *art* form, even. Seems that what they do — the girls — is fold up paper different ways, so as to look like birds and submachine guns, and tickle guys with *that*. All up and down their *spines*, I think it is. I don't know, of course, from personal experience. It's just a thing I heard."

The guru chuckled and reached down to grab the piece of crystal stemware he'd been hitting on. His guests had both declined his offer of martinis, so Baba drank alone.

"We'd rather stroke you with the facts," said Shali, touching Baba lightly on a brown-robed knee. Herb sensed that this was it, that she'd decided that

253

the time was ripe to hit him with their most compelling arguments, the heavy stuff.

"The truth," she said. "Reality, as it exists, right underneath our noses. It's pretty clear to me that, thanks to your initiative and acumen, you've got a life right here that's much more nearly perfect than the one you had before you came — and one that couldn't be improved by ten or *twenty* billion in the bank. You've got a waiting list of . . . what? How many did you say?"

"About two hundred," Baba said. And, yes, he licked his lips; his eyes glazed over, slightly. "That's counting just the ones who sent in a deposit, though. Inquiries and applications, I'd say . . . oh, another thousand."

"Two hundred comely but presently unhappy girls you know will give you almost every cent they have if they could come and work and play with you," said Shali. "Plus, your net from *Baba Bits* and *Baba Blend*, which, by your own admission, are in such demand that you've had record profits every year you've been in business."

"They *have* gone over great, I must admit," the guru mused. He nodded. The salesman in the guy kicked in real fast when he heard words like "net," "demand," and "profits." "But, hey, why shouldn't they? The stuff that we produce is now not merely natural/organic, but — thanks to Bummer Balm — it's also never touched or tainted by unhappy human hands at any stage of its production. Just *think* about that, Shali, Herb. No one else can match that guarantee. You can almost *taste* the happiness in Baba's products, guys."

"I'll bet you can," said Herb. "But, Baba, just

suppose some madman, like the guy they had down in Uganda, started using Bummer Balm — on everyone. Or even someone well intentioned but not extra bright, a politician with some bad advisors, say, who got to be the President, back home. Wait, let me put it this way. . . . How'd you like it if you *had to* use the stuff?"

Baba didn't have to think that over long.

"I'd totally despise it," he said, quickly. "Governmental interference with my *moods?* Forget it. Hmmm." He nodded his round head a time or two; the guy was clearly thinking that one over.

"I'm going to tell you honestly: You got a point there," he agreed, at last. "And it's a biggie. I'd *like* to take that check from Roni and Cecelia; a billion bucks would represent security. And I would have mobility, again — the right to go back to the ol' U.S. of A. and maybe run for public office, if I wanted to. Who knows how high a billion bucks might take a guy? I might like to see. But the thought that Bummer Balm might be imposed on some guy like myself . . . that's basically obnoxious and I kid you not. The thought does give me pause, Herb, Shali. Like you said, that 'some guy like myself' might even be, like, *me.* Conceivably."

"But, if you kept production *and the secret* in your hands," said Shali, jumping at his hesitation, improvising just like crazy, "you could continue with the life-style you enjoy so much right now, *forever* — and at no risk to yourself. And if, for reasons of your own, you sent the people that we represent a small supply each year, why, you'd be doing more for suffering humanity than any other Nobel laureate in history."

"Any *other* Nobelist?" said Baba. "You really think I'd be a . . . well, *contender* for the prize?"

Shali made a face, a gesture. Both of them said this: "*Of course* you would be, silly."

"Step aside, there, Schweitzer, Martin Luther King, Mahatma Gandhi, Florence Nightingale," Herb chimed in. "Say hello to Baba Malomar, *Time*'s Man of the Year, and probably the Decade. You doubtless saw his handsome face on *People* magazine, as well."

"Whereas if you *sell* the thing," said Shali, "you would lose control of it, and of your place in history. A box in *Fortune* or in *Business Week* would be about the best thing you could hope for."

She crossed her long, bare legs a final time, giving Baba still another chance to think their proposition over. After a count of ten, however, she stood up; the dress fell gently into place, perfectly unwrinkled, still.

"Well," the guru said, "you've scored some interesting thoughts, ideas, no doubt about it. You kids are sharp, and more than sharp; you're, like, *good people*. But, in fairness, I should listen to the other side, as well. Roni and Cecelia think that they can beat you; possibly they can. We know they've got a billion arguments to offer, but what else?" And Baba smiled. "I've got to give those girls a chance to show me everything they've got, just like I said I would. You know?"

"For sure," said Herb.

"I do believe I do," said Shali.

Herb and Shali took another walk around the grounds that night, instead of going to dinner. And it wasn't that they didn't like the ashram's food.

"I'm not sure that I could stand the sight of Roni and Cecilia warming Baba up," she said. "He'll have so many bosoms in his face, he'll think he's back in diapers, on the pediatrics floor."

"But how about our chances when they're through with him?" asked Herb. "I felt pretty good back there, when we were done. It seemed to me he took the stuff you said to heart. I mean it."

"Well, I think he did," she said. "The trouble is that Roni and Cecilia are — let's face it — specialists. Amalgamated Pharmaceuticals would get the best. The best of the *best* of the best. I'm sure the two of them are trained negotiators, Harvard MBAs, most likely. And that'd be on top of all their other skills. Chances are they'd be in line for two-three million dollars each, if they bring back a contract. Baba's heart could be outvoted *Shali, Herb*" — she said that just the way the guru would have — "by some other organ. Frankly, Herb, I fear the worst."

Herb spent some moments trying to guess — imagine — what-all Roni and Cecilia could/would do to Baba. He found he really couldn't. Maybe it was just as well, he thought. Herb wondered if, with sex, everybody thought that lots of other people knew and did a lot more stuff than they did, better. But he honestly could not imagine how there could be any *feelings* better than the best ones he was having now, with Shali. Did that make him unusual, or stupid, lucky, self-deluding, limited, or shy? (he asked himself). "We were in Big School when the Head came in," he thought. That was the way that Flaubert started *Madame Bovary*.

"If only," Herbie said, "if only we had something Roni and Cecelia wanted even more than that much money. Some fabulously rare and gorgeous jewelry, for instance. Or Eddie Murphy, maybe. Sly Stallone."

"Right," said Shali, drily. "Sure. Fat chance of our . . . hey, wait!"

She'd stopped dead in the middle of the fieldstone path. Her eyes were rolling, *sparkling*.

"Of course," she said. "Of course, of course, of course." And she was hopping up and down, both feet together, with her hands clasped tight in front of her, chest high.

"You got it!" she exclaimed, and grabbed Herb by both shoulders, hopping still.

"But what?" said Herbie. "Settle down, all right? What 'what' I got? Sly Stallone, you mean?"

The girl stopped jumping, anyway. "No, no, of course not, dope. It's something else we *know* that Roni and Cecelia want," she said. "*Must* want. Roni *said*, herself, remember? They're both — what? — *unhappy*! Baba, too."

"And so?" said Herb. "So what? I don't see how their being . . . normal helps us."

"Idiot," said Shali, "think. Suppose that we could find a way to get in Baba's bedroom. Late, late, late tonight. When Baba and the girls are totally exhausted. So fast asleep they wouldn't notice if the earth moved under them. *Again*, presumably."

"That wouldn't be too hard," said Herb. "The getting in his bedroom part. There aren't any locks on any doors in the entire ashram. That's something that I've noticed. You can walk straight into Baba's suite; anybody can. You're probably *encouraged* to —

your kind, that is. So what, though? What would we do then? Take pictures?"

"Hardly," Shali said. *"Then,* we'd . . ."

Though hardly what you'd call a rake, roué, or libertine, Herb had viewed X-rated movies in his life, two of them, in fact. There was a kid who went to school with him whose parents were collectors of the things. They didn't think their son knew that they had them, though, stacked right there behind his mother's sweaters, on a bedroom closet shelf. Their kid knew lots of things they didn't think he knew, including Herbie.

So, anyway, our Herbie, having seen those films, was somewhat prepped for what he saw in person when he entered Baba's bedroom, namely this erotic sprawl of naked flesh, both stretched and curled on Baba's super-king-sized mattress, overlapping lots of different ways.

He had to give the two girls credit — or their exercise instructors, anyway. Roni and Cecelia both looked great, from any angle. Each looked as if she was (or could be) hard *and* soft, round and flat, rough and smooth, wild and woolly, Hammacher and Schlemmer. Herb didn't choose to look at Baba all that much. Just enough to know he had no future in the porno movie industry.

All three of them were totally conked out. On the floor, beside the bed, there was a tall glass pitcher with a little near-clear liquid left in it. There were also empty, black-stemmed glasses, three, two of them tipped over. On the bedside table there was evidence that other ways had also been employed to alter local consciousness.

259

Herb and Shali tiptoed in, and kept on going, quickly, to the dresser; it had four drawers and it was made of blonde mahogany, of course. The graceful, widemouthed urn that both of them had noticed there before was still in place. This vessel had a silver chain, with nameplate, hung around its neck, the way decanters do, sometimes. But instead of saying "Scotch," or "Gin," this nameplate had another sort of mouthful on it: "Easelspirlimine."

Herb stared at it. And suddenly he felt like Henry Morton Stanley must have felt, when he laid eyes on Dr. Livingstone. Or Moses when the Red Sea parted. Or (getting closer to reality) as he had felt the moment that he understood the Big Red Chicken's scratchings. "Easelspirlimine" made *sense* to him; he bet he knew *exactly* what it was. He snuck a glance at Shali; she looked no different than before. He guessed her mind was altogether on their plan.

"I'll hold the urn," she whispered. "And you can be the one to slop it on." She picked up the container and approached the bed, looking at its bareskin cover.

"How much should I use?" asked Herb.

"He said it didn't take a lot," she said. "I'd recommend a good-sized dab, though; we wouldn't want to under-do. And try to rub it in, okay? It sounded like he really rubs it in, on devotees."

Herb put a dollop, first, on Roni's punky 'do, then another on Cecelia's part, behind her bangs. When he rubbed the ointment in, Roni seemed to half wake up. "You bad boy, you," she muttered, touching Malomar and changing her position, slightly. And she giggled. Super-tan Cecilia just accepted her anointment with a kind of queenly nonchalance. When Herb was done with her, his hand was still all covered with a thick layer of the gunk, and he wiped his greasy fingers dry on Baba's head. As he and Shali had it figured, Baba didn't matter, either way.

The first thing Herbie saw, when he and Shali hustled in the dining room at breakfast time, next day (with eyes and fingers crossed), was that the three were there already, fully clothed. That was good, for openers. The next thing that he saw — and this was truly excellent — was quite a little pile of torn-up pinkish paper, right beside Cecelia's plate. When he got close, he read *The Chase Manha-* inscribed upon the topmost scrap.

"Hey, 'morning, guys," said Roni to the two of them. She had a T-shirt on that day, all black except for one word "Masterpiece," in silver, on the front of it. "Guess what? It looks as if we *all* win, this time. Cece tore up the check, just now" — she gestured at the pile of pink — "so you can have the goo, for all we care. We're staying on with our new, all-time, favorite cookie. This Malomar, right here, feels like a million bucks to us." And she reached out to pinch the guru's cheek, and smile into his dark brown eyes.

Which Baba then proceeded to let drop, like Mr. Modesty, personified.

"What can I say?" he said to her, and to the other girl. "Welcome to the loving presence, Roni and Cecelia. And, hey, you weren't any slouches, either." The holy man then shook his head.

261

"I shoulda realized this might happen," he concluded.

When the meal was over, Baba asked the boy and girl to come with him. They went back to his suite, again. Someone had cleaned up, already — changed the sheets and made the bed and put the toys away. The place looked very nearly . . . monkish, Herbie thought, except for having such a huge expanse of bed in it.

"I got some things to tell you two," the guru said, when they had all sat down. "Amazing and surprising things, perhaps. Don't flip. For instance and get this: I do believe I'm going to give up booze and drugs and Ding-Dongs. When I first woke up this morning, I didn't have the slightest urge to reach for any one of them."

Herb looked at Shali; Shali looked at Herb. A single thought zoomed out of both their minds, collided in the empty space between them: Baba'd been affected by the Bummer Balm, and maybe it *did* matter. They would soon find out.

"But that's not all, there's more," he now was saying. "Shali. Herb. Guess what?" He gestured toward the dresser top, the place the urn of Easel-spirlimine had stood the night before. "There is no 'product' anymore. It's been taken off the shelf; it's unavailable. To you, to anyone. At any price, or no price."

"What?" said Shali, barely croaking out the words. "Unavailable? But why?"

"When I woke up this morning," Baba said, "I saw my situation in a truly different light. It was like a revelation, in a way. But also not. You see?"

He focused on the blankness of their looks. "I will try to make you understand."

"Please do," said Shali, staring at him in amazement, still.

"Revelations sometimes come from seemingly thin air," he said. "Like inspirations, genius-level thoughts, ideas, inventions, or creations. But they also sometimes come from people's mouths, but only if another person's ears can truly hear them."

Baba smiled at each of them in turn.

"Herb. Shali," he went on. "I'm speaking of *your* mouths, *my* ears. Yesterday, you laid a lot of wisdom on me — yes, the two of you. Some of it was mixed with nonsense, to be sure, but that's okay — nonsense has a way of getting into everything. Yesterday, however, I was not . . . in tune with wisdom, all that much. My ears were partly closed, my understanding limited. I heard, but did not see. You understand?"

Herb thought he might, and so he nodded. Shali sat there motionless.

"This morning, though, I understood, I saw," the guru said. "You had it right. I've got it made right here, the way things are right now. Fame and fortune?" Baba snapped his fingers. "Hey, who needs 'em?"

"The Nobel prize?" said Shali, hoarsely. "The *Time* and *People* covers?"

Baba smiled. "Yes, they're the nonsense part — you got it. Who needs that kind of crap? Not me. Those things are superficial trivialities, devoid of any lasting satisfaction. And you want to know the truth? I don't *deserve* them, even."

"Don't deserve them?" Herbie had to ask. "How

come?" Baba'd made a scientific breakthrough, after all; there was no denying that. Herb was pretty sure he'd seen some people on the *People* cover who'd done much, much less than that.

"My great discovery," the guru said, "my amazing scientific breakthrough — you want that I should tell you how I made it? Just by luck, my friends, pure luck."

Baba shifted in his seat, but not from nervousness; he was only getting comfy. He looked to be at peace with . . . well, the universe.

"Here's how it happened," he went on. "I was sitting in the lab one day with nothing whatsoever on my mind — a total blank, you know how it is, I'm sure." And Herbie nodded once again. "And then I started doodling, but not with pen and pencil on a sheet of paper, but with stuff I had around, just sitting on my workbench — chemicals et cetera. I'd grind up some of this and add a pinch of that or drops of something else. And then I'd maybe heat the glop I had until it changed consistency or color, or let off some interesting fumes. Well, one of these *experiments* (ha-ha) produced an end result that was both thick and rich, as well as quite good-looking." He beamed. "Like certain applicants we've had — hey, kidding!" And he shook his head and chuckled at his own good-naturedness.

"So," he then continued, "I just had it in a jar right on that counter top when a devotee named Brandi happened by and saw it. She must have thought it was a styling gel, because, before I knew it, she had put some on herself. And pretty soon she started acting strange — like, different — cheerful, happy, friendly, *eager*, even. I wondered

264

if it was the gunk that caused the change, so naturally I ran some tests on other girls. You know the rest; in two weeks' time, this place was just transformed — into a little slice of heaven, attitudinally. *I* soon figured out the scientific explanation — that whole neuropeptide bit — but that was all I did *on purpose*. The gunk itself was not the consequence of human genius. It was just a gift, like from the gods." And Baba smiled benignly, once again.

"That's an amazing story," Herbie said. "But there's one thing that I don't get. How come you're telling us all this?"

Baba shook his head. "I'm not exactly sure myself. It might be out of gratitude for how you've helped me, how you've made me see what's what. Or maybe it's because I feel a little sorry that you came so far for nothing. Or maybe it's because I'm hoping *one* of you will stay."

He stood up and offered Herb his hand.

"Herbie, thanks for coming," he said, pumping it. "You remember how to go, all right?"

Shali started talking right away, trying to talk the guru into giving her at least a little sample of the stuff and swearing that she'd never mention where she got it from. But Baba Malomar was adamant. The secret would stay where it was, he said. But wouldn't Shali — "hey, no fooling" — want to join it?

"Thanks but no thanks, Baba," she informed him with a smile. "Tempting as your offer is, I'm still with Herbie, here."

She took Herb's hand and squeezed it. Two hours later, they were on the trail.

32
PRESENTS OF MIND

After that, for umpteen days — which was how long it took to go from Baba Malomar's back to the monastery courtyard where the van was parked — Herb's mood swung back and forth as wantonly and wildly as a good aerobics class. Although he'd spent a lot of time in adolescence, he had never felt so certain *and* confused, so man *and* baby, so conforming *and* rebellious, so Siskel and so Ebert. Sometimes it even seemed he felt both miserable and great at once.

One trouble was that Herbie's mind kept leaping out of present time and landing in the future. It seemed as if he couldn't help that. And where, a week or so before, he'd pretty much accepted that his life with Shali, their relationship, was transitory, limited by circumstances he could not control, now he had a very different attitude. Within an hour of

266

the time they left the ashram, he had told the girl he *wasn't* going to leave; he was going to stay "behind" and stick around with her. The Upwardlimobile could do the same, or go back empty. That was all there was to that, so there.

Except she said at once he *had* to go, he didn't *have* that choice to make ". . . and please, let's not discuss it."

Her answer came so fast, her tone was so abrupt and so convincing that he blinked and didn't — that's "discuss it" — for a bunch of days. Then, casually, he mentioned that there wasn't any reason that he *should* go back to Castles in the Air. He was sure his *parents* wouldn't mind; lots of times they acted very much as if he wasn't there at all, he said. He was also pretty sure that Ses deBarque would be *delighted* if he stayed. Wasn't that what Castles in the Air was all about? To help someone like him find something meaningful to do? Well, what could be more meaningful, Herb asked the girl, than this? Working cheek by jowl with her on . . . *projects*, such as this one.

The two of them were in her sleeping bag when Herbie whispered that, and their clothes were scattered on the ground beside them, but his mind was so much on convincing her, he wasn't even touching her.

"The trouble is," she said, "you just can't understand. That isn't *your* fault, either. It isn't anybody's fault. It's part of life. No one knows what's best for them. They *think* they do, but they don't ever really know. And you know why? Because they're people."

"Well, you're a person, aren't you?" said Herb.

"I guess I am," said Shali. "What do you think?"

"I think if you're a person, too," said Herb, "then you don't know what's best, yourself. For you *or* me. So, how about: Whatever *you* do next, I'll do it with you, and we'll see what happens? *That* seems like a great idea, to me." And when she shook her head, "Why not? Just give me one good reason."

"*Because*," she said.

He said that wasn't any reason, and she knew it. And he gave her just a little pinch. He didn't want to get too serious. As long as things stayed light, he thought he had a chance. When he was trying to talk his mother into something, he would always try to keep it light. Any time she changed her tone of voice and got real serious, he knew that he was sunk.

"It may not be a reason," Shali said, "but that's the way it is. You *can't*. And no one's sorrier than me." She started crying, just a little. *That* was serious, for sure.

"When the time comes, please just *go*," she said, and wiped her eyes. "And if you love me, please don't talk about it anymore."

That was clear enough. Herb sat up straight, now half outside the sleeping bag. He had a strange sensation in his head.

"All right," he said. "I do, and so I won't. I *do* love you that much."

That was the only thing that he could think to say. His mind was out of arguments. "Alice was beginning to get very tired . . ." floated through his brain, the words that Lewis Carroll used to start those great adventures. *He* was going to go, not stay, and she would not, *could* not, go with him. And he'd never understand it.

"Love" had made him "Happy," just as he had thought it would, but he could not hold onto it, or her, the person who had made him love. What would happen to him now?

Well, at least (he thought) he had the secret of the balm, of Easelspirlimine. He hadn't even told her — Shali — what it was; only he and Baba knew. It could be the Golden Fleece that he'd bring back to Ses deBarque. It would be *something*, anyway. And she would be real proud of him, so proud that maybe she would fix it up so he could rendezvous with Shali on his next adventure! Maybe he would spin Space Exploration, and the two of them could take a trip to Neptune or Uranus — or, better, to a distant galaxy, somewhere. A trip like that *could* take forever, Herbie thought.

"I am a pawn of fate," he said out loud, dramatically. "I'm nothing but a minor piece on the big board game of life."

Shali looked at him, but didn't speak.

Or maybe I've *been* pawned, Herb thought, and am an item in a hockshop window, hanging next to a guitar. Whoever'd owned me formerly — my parents? Ses deBarque? — had gotten cash for me. Passersby along the sidewalks would glance up and see the items in the hockshop window. "Nice guitar," they'd say.

Herb couldn't tell what he was feeling. "Numb" seemed like a real good possibility. He remembered seeing baseball batters hit by pitches — on the arm, let's say — and seeing trainers run right out and spray some stuff directly on the spot the ball had hit. The announcer on TV would always say the spray would "freeze" the arm and kill the pain. The guy could keep on playing, even with the injury he had. Herb thought his thoughts were like that spray, all aimed directly at his heart.

A few days after that, Herb had a different kind of thought. Maybe it was triggered by that pawn-shop window fantasy, the thought of someone getting cash for him.

He realized he now had access to the other key to Happiness. Not just the Golden Fleece but (too) the goose that laid the golden egg. Even if he had no Love, back home, he still could have a ton of Money!

After he had showed the thing to Ses, he could *sell* the secret of the guru's Bummer Balm; he knew the way that Easelspirlimine was made! All he'd have to do was get in touch with . . . oh, Amalga-mated Pharmaceuticals, let's say. They'd give him millions for the formula. And they were good Amer-icans; they'd never sell the stuff to crazy zealots or ideologues. This (also) wasn't 1984. He'd be set up for life — and whoever *really* needed Easelspirlimine would get some, somehow, whether they could pay for it, or not. *Congress* would make sure of that. Or HEW, or HUD, or *someone* (other than himself).

When Herbie thought of that idea, he once again had something to look forward to. He'd never have to sweat that deal of "doing something with himself," and T.K. could have juicy "sTeaKs," for offerings. And he — he could get himself some *stuff*, the way that Pookie Woodchuck had, and Pema, too, and Sendup.

* * *

270

That was the first thing he and Shali noticed when the two of them rejoined the yak train for its journey home. The boys had made a *killing*. The evidence was right before their eyes.

The yaksmen all had Rolex watches now, three or four of them per wrist. Around their necks they wore what looked like double loops of tire chains, except that these glowed wickedly and wealthily as only eighteen-karat gold is apt to do. Sendup had swapped his tattered parka for a down-filled Chesterfield (the first that Herb had ever seen), and Pema'd had an artificial plastic ear-top (lined with Gore-tex) made. All the yaksmen sported brand-new expedition boots, $250 models from Asolo AFS, and in their inside pockets there were little black address books, stuffed with names and numbers. In those same pockets, Herbie spotted gilded edges, too — the kind that go on bonds, and stock certificates, and deeds of ownership, CDs.

The yaks, for their part, had acquired bright new horn guards that Herb thought — was pretty sure — were made of platinum; their shaggy hair appeared to have been trimmed and washed and styled, since he'd last seen them. No longer did they carry great, enormous loads; in fact, their only burden (which they took turns with) was a good-sized, well-made steamer trunk — of *Japanese* design, Herb thought. A cargo plane, with a PWA logo on its sides and tail, came overhead each afternoon and dropped, by parachute, hot dinners for the yaksmen and their honored guests, and bags of a nutritious Vitamalya Twenty-eight Grain Mix for every yak. Also, the next day's breakfast, and a VCR, a big-

271

screen Sony, and a microwave, along with half a dozen current films and batteries to run the whole caboodle on. They'd leave all those electrical conveniences beside the trail, next morning. At lunchtime, everybody dieted.

But, after three or four days with the yak train, Herb became aware that something bad was happening. In spite of all the movies and the *haute cuisine*, Shali wasn't looking happy. He asked her why; she told him it was nothing — and she seemed to pull herself together for a while. But then, next morning, he woke up to find her dressed and sitting on a rock, just staring into distant space.

Herb *hated* seeing that; he couldn't stand it. It hurt him much much more to see her sad than to be sad, himself. He knew he had to *do* something, to find a way to cheer her up before the closing credits started rolling on the screen: "Costumes by Abida," and "A Ses deBarque Production."

Because he was, if anything, American, his first idea was: Get her some great present. Something that would take her mind off . . . what he didn't want to think about himself. So, to that end he went and talked to Pookie, hoping that the guy might have the perfect gift in stock, left over.

"Gee, too bad I'm out of sterling silver nose rings," Pookie said, and scratched his head and thought some more. He finally had to say he really didn't think he had the kind of thing Herb wanted — unless he thought a "What Batman Doesn't, Katmandu" wall plaque fit the bill.

Herb said it didn't, quite, and thanked the guy and walked away to grind his teeth in desperation. He doubted that they'd (even) chance upon a dragon he could slay for her. Time was running out and there he was, his head as empty as his hands.

And both of them stayed empty, right up until the time they reached the monastery courtyard, and he and she, the two of them, were standing by the van.

Why he thought of it, and why he hadn't thought of it before, he never knew, but suddenly it came to him. *Of course.* He could give her something that he *knew* she really wanted.

So what if that meant giving up the second key to Happiness? He didn't hesitate. There'd be other ways, perhaps, for him to get some Money. Money comes and goes; Love never ends, not even at "Good-bye."

"Shali," Herbie said, "I've got a little something I've been saving for you. Look."

And on the van's big, dusty sliding door, he wrote two things, and neither one of them was "Wash" or "Me."

First, he wrote the words "eel slime," but oddly, just like this:

E ELS LIM E

And after that came "aspirin," this way:

AS PIR IN

dropping it into the spaces in the eel slime, so's to make the single word:

EASELSPIRLIMINE

"You see?" he said. "Isn't that pure Baba Malomar? A synthesis of East and West, a mixture of his old world and his new one? *And* a Baba-word, to boot — just like 'pwolarky'! He got the formula by luck; now you can have it, too. You can give it to

your 'people.' They can use it right — for *everyone*."
Herb couldn't say another word. All that was left
in him was sadness. Bawling like a baby, he reached
out and gave her one last hug, and turned and dove
into the van. She closed the sliding door for him.
But (he thought) at least his present worked. Before the door slammed shut, he saw that she was
smiling.

33
STILL MORE FAREWELLS

As usual, the trip did not take long. In fact, it lasted barely long enough for Herb to dry his eyes, subdue his sobs, and start to both appreciate and not appreciate at all, the fact that he had found and given up both Love and Money in this same adventure, back wherever he had been. He wondered what that meant, in terms of what significance it had — *would have* — in . . . well, his other life, his real one. Assuming that he had another life, of course; assuming anything at all was real.

Ses deBarque, as usual, was right there on the runway when he landed — the "runway" being, as before, the tower room at Castles in the Air.

"Well," she said, "that was a long-tailed Louie, eh?" She checked out that opinion on the pendant watch that hung around her neck. "Five minutes *plus.*" She whistled. "I was getting worried that you weren't coming back."

Herb gasped. "You mean that's possible?" he said.

She grinned, but she was serious. "Oh, sure. Sometimes, in certain cases," she replied. "But not for you, my dear. I'm much too sweet on you to leave you way out there" — she waved, a trifle vaguely — "somewhere. Let's go sit down — all right? — and have a nice cold drink. You look a little droopy."

Herb was glad to follow her back up to her apartment, to that same peculiar but delightful living room he'd visited before, the one that made you think that you were sitting on a mountaintop. He supposed his eyes were still a little red, but he was not that sad. What he mostly felt, by then, was numb. Again.

"There are some things I ought to tell you," Ses began, when they were seated, holding goblets of that most delicious drink she'd given him before. Its faint, sweet flavor was like nothing Herb had had in any other place. Although it didn't taste like them, it made Herb think of nectarines.

He nodded, thinking he could just accept whatever she would say. He wasn't worried. He seemed to have no expectations whatsoever. No yearnings, either, come to think of it.

"Aspirin mixed with eel slime, rubbed on people's heads, will not help anyone's unhappiness," she said. "Not here. Something worked up at the ashram, sure, but that was there and then, and this is here and now."

Herb took that in. His gift to Shali had been

worthless. He could have given her a set of woven placemats, or a backscratcher.

"Secondly, there is no Shali Sloan. Such a person does not now exist, was never born, and will not die, if you were wondering," said Ses deBarque.

"And neither was there any Zippy or Felicity, I bet," said Herb. "Nor will there be *whoever* on the next trip that I take. But that's all right."

"Two out of three ain't bad," said Ses. "Concerning Zippy and Felicity, you're quite correct. And absolutely, like you said, that *is* all right. But you're not taking any other trips. This was your last one, buddy-ro. In point of fact, I'm closing Castles in the Air and getting out of here. These shoes were made for walking, and I'm goin' home again."

She held her feet up off the ground. Herb saw that she had on a brand-new pair of walking shoes, a pair of Nikes, some design he'd never seen before.

"Air Olympuses," she said. "You know who Nike is?"

"Is that the way you say it?" Herbie asked. "I thought that you pronounced it 'Nee-kay.' I think she was a goddess, back in ancient Greece. Of victory, I'm pretty sure."

"Right on," said Ses, "but no, it's *Nie-key*, rhymes with Tie-key, take my word for it. And that reminds me, just in case you're wondering: I won the Cadillac, all right."

"I guess I'm not surprised," said Herb. And it was funny, but he wasn't. "Congratulations."

"Thanks," she said, "it wasn't hard; you never had a chance. I'm going to give the thing to Sandy Rex; you're more the compact type. I gave the van to my young daughter there, E.T." She gestured at the picture on the table. "The one you said you'd like to meet sometime, remember?"

"Sure," said Herb. He was looking at the picture. Although the girl looked quite a bit like Ses, she also looked (he now could see) a lot like Shali — and Felicity. And Zippy, too, in one or two respects.

"But Ses . . . ," he started, with his mind a momentary jumble of confusing facts, and anti-facts, and arty facts and speculations. "You're going to close this place and leave me on my own?" He stopped. "No, wait. That came out wrong. I *meant* to say: You're going to close this place and go on home? I really did."

"Yup." She nodded. "Yup. It's time."

"But what about *me*?" Herb asked. But he was smiling as he said it, teasing her.

"What *about* you?" she demanded.

"Well, I'm going to *miss* you," Herbie said. "A *lot*."

She grinned. "That's good," she said. "That means you'll think of me, from time to time, and we'll stay friends that way. And probably — who knows? — I'll pop on back and visit you — oh, now and then."

"I hope so," Herbie said. "If I'm not here, I might be up at Hampshire." And he winked.

The boy got to his feet, and so did she. They hugged and kissed each other on both cheeks, the European way.

"Good luck," she said, and looked into his eyes. "Good luck."

34
AND SO

The next thing Herbie knew, he found himself on Sunset Strip, meandering along. He *was* quite tired, but he felt he had a lot of time — and not to kill, to use. He decided that he'd try to hitch a ride, so he might get wherever he was going sooner. He turned around to see a van approaching, and he stretched his arm out to the side, his fingers in a fist, his thumb extended.

It stopped. The sliding door was shiny; he could see his own reflection in the thing. Ignoring it, he opened the *front* door and hopped right in, sat his butt in high-backed, bucket-seated comfort. That made him shotgun-wielder, navigator, maybe — and a step above the passenger he used to be, he thought.

The driver was a girl, the most attractive girl that Herb had ever seen. He smiled at her and she smiled back, right straight into his eyes, as if to send a message into them. "It was love at first sight" was how the writer Joseph Heller started off *Catch-22*, Herb knew. She wore a scent that seemed almost familiar, made him shake his head and sniff again. He thought this was a case of *déjà phew*.

They reached the end of Sunset Strip. Another road went left and right in front of them, a road that Herb had never seen before.

"Which way are you going?" she inquired.

"Well, I'm not exactly sure," he said.

"I think I've got a map in there." She pointed to the glove compartment.

Herb's hand went out, then stopped. Probably, he thought, next to the map in there, he'd find a small insurance ID card, and it would have her name on it. "Ekaterina Toledano" he might read. E.T. And he would have to face the fact he'd had it wrong for all those years, that it was not "Tyree" but "Teri" Toledano.

He looked at her, the driver; she was facing him and grinning. It didn't matter what her name was. He knew he didn't need the map. Chapter I of Vatsayana's *Kama Sutra* had this title, he had suddenly recalled: "Observations on the three Necessities for Happiness on Earth: Virtue, Riches and Pleasure . . ." Begin at the beginning, Herbie told himself.

"Take a right," he said.